PENGUIN BOOKS

THE PENGUIN BOOK OF GREAT LAW AND ORDER STORIES

John Mortimer is a playwright, novelist and former practising barrister. During the war he worked with the Crown Film Unit and published a number of novels before turning to the theatre with such plays as *The Dock Brief*, *The Wrong Side of the Park* and *A Voyage Round My Father*. He has written many film scripts and radio and television plays, including six plays on the life of Shakespeare, the Rumpole plays, which won him the British Academy Writer of the Year Award, and the adaptation of Evelyn Waugh's *Brideshead Revisited*. His translations of Feydeau have been performed at the National Theatre and are published in Penguin as *Three Boulevard Farces*.

Penguin publishes his collections of stories: *Rumpole of the Bailey*, *The Trials of Rumpole*, *Rumpole's Return*, *Rumpole for the Defence*, *Rumpole and the Golden Thread*, *Rumpole's Last Case*, *Rumpole and the Age of Miracles* and *Rumpole à la Carte*, as well as *The First Rumpole Omnibus* and *The Second Rumpole Omnibus*. Penguin also publishes two volumes of John Mortimer's plays, his acclaimed autobiography *Clinging to the Wreckage*, which won the Yorkshire Post Book of the Year Award, *In Character* and *Character Parts*, which contain interviews with some of the most famous men and women of our time, and his best-selling novels, *Charade*, *Like Men Betrayed*, *The Narrowing Stream*, *Paradise Postponed*, its sequel *Titmuss Regained* and *Summer's Lease*. *Paradise Postponed*, *Summer's Lease* and all the Rumpole books have been made into successful television series. John Mortimer lives with his wife and their two daughters in what was once his father's house in the Chilterns.

THE PENGUIN BOOK OF GREAT LAW & ORDER STORIES

EDITED AND INTRODUCED BY
JOHN MORTIMER

PENGUIN BOOKS

PENGUIN BOOKS

Published by the Penguin Group
Penguin Books Ltd, 27 Wrights Lane, London W8 5TZ, England
Penguin Books USA Inc., 375 Hudson Street, New York, New York 10014, USA
Penguin Books Australia Ltd, Ringwood, Victoria, Australia
Penguin Books Canada Ltd, 10 Alcorn Avenue, Toronto, Ontario, Canada M4V 3B2
Penguin Books (NZ) Ltd, 182–190 Wairau Road, Auckland 10, New Zealand

Penguin Books Ltd, Registered Offices: Harmondsworth, Middlesex, England

First published by Bellew 1990
Published in Penguin Books 1991
1 3 5 7 9 10 8 6 4 2

Printed in England by Clays Ltd, St Ives plc

This book is dedicated to The Howard League for Penal Reform. The League is an independent charity established in 1866. It accepts no government money and all the funds for its activities are donated by individuals, trusts and companies.

The Howard League campaigns for a fair and humane criminal justice and penal system. The charity holds conferences and seminars for the public and for people who work in prisons, with the police and the law. It publishes books and magazines and provides an information service to students and MPs. Special research projects into issues of the day are undertaken, and the Howard League maintains contact with offenders and the victims of crime.

The Howard League has a growing membership and list of subscribers. Full details about all its work can be had from:

The Howard League,
708 Holloway Road,
London N19 3NL

Tel: 071 281 7722

Acknowledgements

Grateful acknowledgement is made to the following for permission to reprint the material in this volume:

The Estate of Damon Runyon and Constable Publishers Ltd for the story 'The Snatching of Bookie Bob' from *More Than Somewhat, Runyon On Broadway.*

Ruth Rendell and The Peters Fraser & Dunlop Group Ltd for the story 'Ginger and the Kingsmarkham Circle'.

The Estate of Raymond Chandler and Hamish Hamilton Ltd for the story 'King in Yellow' from *The Simple Art of Murder.*

Patricia Highsmith and Diogenes Verlag for the story 'The Heroine'.

John Mortimer and The Peters Fraser & Dunlop Group Ltd for the story 'Rumpole and the Tap End' from *Rumpole and the Age of Miracles.*

H. R. F. Keating for the story 'Inspector Ghote and the Miracle Baby'.

Hamish Hamilton Ltd for the Secretariat of Georges Simenon for the story 'The Evidence of the Altar Boy'. Translation copyright © Jean Stewart 1977.

P. D. James for the story 'A Very Commonplace Murder'. Copyright © P. D. James 1967, reprinted by permission of Elaine Green Ltd.

CONTENTS

INTRODUCTION

In this book a number of writers of great fame and talent have been summoned to the aid of the Howard League for Penal Reform, and the living authors have most generously given their stories. In a way this is understandable because all writers depend, to a greater or lesser degree, on the criminal classes. If it weren't for their illegal industry all policemen, judges, the barristers down at the Old Bailey, a large number of solicitors and the editors of many Sunday newspapers would have to be put out to grass, and all authors of detective stories would be out of business. So think of these contributors as not only playing their part in making our country a fairer place to live in, but also as repaying a debt.

Crime writers, or mystery writers, are often treated absurdly in literary circles as second class citizens. They don't win the Booker Prize, or the Prix Goncourt, although certainly those mistresses of suspense, Ruth Rendell, Patricia Highsmith and P. D. James rank very high on the list of our most distinguished novelists. It's quite easy to write an unhappy novel about adultery in Islington, it's far harder and far more rewarding for the reader, to construct a story of suspense and mystery with a surprising and yet credible solution. Many of the greatest works of all time, including the *Orestaia*, *Hamlet* and *Bleak House*, have been crime stories. *Jane Eyre* has a mystery and *Orley Farm* is a classic tale of forgery. Even a novel like *Great Expectations*, perhaps one of the half-dozen most satisfying in our language, has a plot which misleads the reader and leaves him guessing until the end. Suspense and surprise, the essential tools of the art of fiction, are used with the most skill by crime writers. Life is a mystery which defies solution, and the only certainty we have is that in truth, and in the detective story, things are never quite what they seem.

In this uncertain world the detective is everybody's hero. He may be a comforting and sensible father figure, a man without pretensions or illusions like Inspectors Maigret and Wexford, he may be a chilly genius like Sherlock Holmes or an underpaid saint of the mean streets with an itching sense of justice like Raymond Chandler's private eyes. He may see the truth with the clear eyes of innocence and faith like Father Brown. Whoever he is, the fictional detective, like the artist, brings us comfort by finding order and reason in a chaotic universe.

In making this selection, my first requirement has been good writing, and I have tried to choose stories which throw some light on the human condition. I rejected the kind of detective story which merely manipulates events for the sake of confusing the reader, and is as detached from reality as a crossword puzzle. Such works provide, no doubt, a great deal of harmless pleasure, but the great subjects of sin and death are treated in them rather as though they were macramé or the art of flower arrangement. If our existence is mysterious it is also, in my view, comic and I have chosen for its comedy Damon Runyon's hilarious account of a kidnapping that went wrong. I also put in, as my contribution to the Howard League, one of Rumpole's more ludicrous encounters with the judiciary in 'The Tap End'.

No doubt Sir Arthur Conan Doyle would have supported the Howard League. He was a humane man who worked tirelessly for those he believed innocent and had a remarkable success in liberating Oscar Slater. Sherlock Holmes was also capable of acts of mercy to those wrongdoers he hunted so brilliantly. I could easily have filled the book with Sherlock Holmes stories, so strong and vivid is the writing and so irresistible are the plots and characters. They have always been my models in writing 'Rumpole' and on occasions I have stolen shamelessly from them. I chose 'The Copper Beeches' because the idea has always haunted me and has an echo in a novel of mine, *Summer's Lease*. I have owed a great deal to Sir Arthur since my childhood when my father, who had an almost total recall of these tales, first told them to me.

G. K. Chesterton's world is wonderfully lurid and the most ordinary suburban scenes become, in his prose, highly coloured landscapes with apocalyptic skies and radiant streets. Father Brown is not only a lovable innocent but he comes nearer than anyone else in fiction to applying Christian values to the sinful world of the crime story. Chesterton, and his detective, were also blessed with the God-given sanity of laughter. I like 'The Absence Of Mr Glass' particularly because it makes criminologists look so silly.

As I have said, Dickens was perhaps the greatest of all crime writers, and when he made friends with Wilkie Collins in his middle years the author of *The Woman In White* introduced him to a new and intoxicating world of women and detection. I have chosen examples of their less well known work: Wilkie Collins is represented by an ironic and funny piece about an intolerably self-satisfied policeman, and Dickens by an alarming story of murder which was first published in an American magazine, *The New York Ledger*. Dickens, a stalwart campaigner against the death penalty, would no doubt be delighted to come to the aid of the Howard League.

Ruth Rendell, more than any other writer I know, has an uncanny knack of getting inside the criminal mind, and she manages to make her most appalling characters understandable and human. How a particularly hardworking author living in an East Anglian village comes by such perceptions is another mystery, but her work has added a new and significant dimension to crime writing. In 'Ginger and the Kingsmarkham Chalk Circle' she has written a touching story about the contemporary world of policemen and minor criminals which she thoroughly understands. An equally human and welcome contribution is an investigation by H. R. F. Keating's admirable Indian sleuth, Inspector Ghote, into the mysteries of an apparently immaculate conception.

In the early years of this century Edith Thompson, unjustly sentenced to death for the murder of her husband by her lover, had her appeal dismissed. The court said, as I remember, that it was a 'very ordinary case', and this dismissive phrase has its echoes in the title P. D. James has chosen for her sad and strongly written account of a sad and haphazard murder. This story is far truer to the murder cases I was concerned with at the bar than the elaborately planned killings in the works of Agatha Christie. Patricia Highsmith's 'The Heroine' has been well described by Graham Greene as 'a study of apprehension'.

And there are other treats. Arnold Bennett, not known as a crime writer, nicely breaks the law of old Hollywood movies that all criminals should get their just deserts. One of the earliest detectives, Poe's Dupin, demonstrates the truth, graphically stated by Chesterton, that the best place to hide a corpse is in a graveyard. Baroness Orczy, who lit up my childhood with tales of the Scarlet Pimpernel, offers in 'The Woman in the Big Hat' what seems to be a classically well thought out murder mystery and in Lady Molly a rare and elegant female detective. Finally there is Simenon at his best, with writing which makes you feel the cold dawn in the streets, smell the coffee and new baked bread and long for a brandy on the zinc counter of the nearest steamy little bar.

I hope you enjoy all these stories. In enjoying them you will help their authors pay a little of their debt to those who get in trouble with the law. You may also help to improve a prison system which is at the moment not only a cause of much unnecessary suffering but something like a national disgrace.

The trouble is that most judges have never been to prison. They have no experience of being banged up with a couple of psychopaths and their own excrement for about twenty hours a day. They have been brought up, in their long-ago pupillage, to think of prison as the answer to all criminal problems. Prison is the easiest of all easy options and almost no judicial or political thought has gone into creative and sensible alternatives. So young people who offend are swept out of sight into custody so that they may be trained in crime and grow to swell the prison population of the future. Everyone knows that prison conditions today make it a cruel and unusual punishment, and yet bad judicial habits spread down to magistrates. Feckless people who have merely got into financial muddles and failed to keep up the payments on the television find themselves subjected to this thoughtless brutality.

About two hundred years ago John Howard, a man of considerable property and the High Sheriff of Bedford, found to his horror that hundreds of people were detained in prison in appalling conditions for no reason at all. In spite of his lifelong devotion to the cause of penal reform and the subsequent efforts of many men and women of goodwill, people are still in prison for quite inadequate reasons, and the conditions they are asked to endure are a disgrace to a so-called civilized country. There was a time when we had to admit, with shame, to imprisoning more people per head of the population than any other European country except Turkey. Now we have achieved the distinction of beating the grim record of the Turks and we are head of the European league.

If prisons are bad for the guilty, they are appalling for the innocent. Defendants on remand, who are awaiting trials at which they are often acquitted, are now kept in worse conditions than they were in the nineteenth century. Our national appetite for custodial sentences is matched by an enormous complacency at their appalling results. A succession of Home Office ministers have trotted out the same bland answers when faced with these problems. Large numbers of young people on remand commit suicide, they say, because they are worried about the crimes they have committed and not, of course, because the conditions in which they are incarcerated are other than idyllic. A high point of unconcern came when the then Home Secretary promised to build three hundred lavatories in one prison over *seven years*. All one can say is that those charged with building a luxury hotel could run them up in as many months. Now we have a new Home Secretary who has come out in favour of keeping more people in prison for longer. Such views can only be held in blind disregard of all the evidence.

The situation is now a desperate one. Our prison conditions are not only shameful but dangerous. The system is about to explode and prison, inflicted on the scale practised in this country, demonstrably does nothing to reduce the incidence of crime. A large proportion of people now in prison shouldn't be there; a small proportion should, perhaps, never be let out. In any case the punishment prescribed is the deprivation of liberty, not torture by overcrowding and the withdrawal of sanitation. We desperately need the Howard League, founded in memory of the eighteenth-century philanthropist, not only for penal reform but to think of sensible, practical and positive alternatives to prison and to persuade a lot of judges with one-track minds to think more imaginatively. Only when these aims have been achieved shall we be able to call ourselves entirely civilized.

So, in this book fictional criminals and detectives come to the rescue of real people suffering indignity and injustice, and of all of us who genuinely and sensibly want to reduce the incidence of crime. The cause is as good as some of the writing here and that is saying a good deal . . .

GREAT LAW & ORDER STORIES

THE SNATCHING OF BOOKIE BOB

Damon Runyon

Now it comes on the spring of 1931, after a long hard winter, and times are very tough indeed, what with the stock market going all to pieces, and banks busting right and left, and the law getting very nasty about this and that, and one thing and another, and many citizens of this town are compelled to do the best they can.

There is very little scratch anywhere and along Broadway many citizens are wearing their last year's clothes and have practically nothing to bet on the races or anything else, and it is a condition that will touch anybody's heart.

So I am not surprised to hear rumours that the snatching of certain parties is going on in spots, because while snatching is by no means a high-class business, and is even considered somewhat illegal, it is something to tide over the hard times.

Furthermore, I am not surprised to hear that this snatching is being done by a character by the name of Harry the Horse, who comes from Brooklyn, and who is a character who does not care much what sort of business he is in, and who is mobbed up with other characters from Brooklyn such as Spanish John and Little Isadore, who do not care what sort of business they are in, either.

In fact, Harry the Horse and Spanish John and Little Isadore are very hard characters in every respect, and there is considerable indignation expressed around and about when they move over from Brooklyn into Manhatten and start snatching, because the citizens of Manhattan feel that if there is any snatching done in their territory, they are entitled to do it themselves.

But Harry the Horse and Spanish John and Little Isadore pay no attention whatever to local sentiment and go on the snatch on a pretty fair scale, and by and by I am hearing rumours of some very nice scores. These scores are not extra large scores, to be sure, but they are enough to keep the wolf from the door, and in fact from three different doors, and before long Harry the Horse and Spanish John and Little Isadore are around the race-tracks betting on the horses, because if there is one thing they are all very fond of, it is betting on the horses.

Now many citizens have the wrong idea entirely of the snatching business. Many citizens think that all there is to snatching is to round up the party who is to be snatched and then just snatch him, putting him away somewhere until his family or friends dig up enough scratch to pay whatever price the snatchers are asking. Very few citizens understand that the snatching business must be well organized and very systematic.

In the first place, if you are going to do any snatching, you cannot snatch just anybody. You must know whom you are snatching, because naturally it is no good snatching somebody who does not have any scratch to settle with. And you cannot tell by the way a party looks or how he lives in this town if he has any scratch, because many a party who is around in automobiles, and wearing good clothes, and chucking quite a swell is nothing but the phonus bolonus and does not have any real scratch whatever.

So of course such a party is no good for snatching, and of course guys who are on the snatch cannot go around inquiring into bank accounts, or asking how much this and that party has in a safe-deposit vault, because such questions are apt to make citizens wonder why, and it is very dangerous to get citizens to wondering why about anything. So the only way guys who are on the snatch can find out about parties worth snatching is to make a connection with some guy who can put the finger on the right party.

The finger guy must know the party he fingers has plenty of ready scratch to begin with, and he must also know that this party is such a party as is not apt to make too much disturbance about being snatched, such as telling the gendarmes. The party may be a legitimate party, such as a business guy, but he will have reasons why he does not wish it to get out that he is snatched, and the finger must know these reasons. Maybe the party is not leading the right sort of life, such as running around with blondes when he has an ever-loving wife and seven children in Mamaroneck, but does not care to have his habits known, as is apt to happen if he is snatched, especially if he is snatched when he is with a blonde.

And sometimes the party is such a party as does not care to have matches run up and down the bottom of his feet, which often happens to parties who are snatched and who do not seem to wish to settle their bill promptly, because many parties are very ticklish on the bottom of the feet, especially if the matches are lit. On the other hand maybe the party is not a legitimate guy, such as a party who is running a crap game or a swell speakeasy, or who has some other dodge he does not care to have come out, and who also does not care about having his feet tickled.

Such a party is very good indeed for the snatching business, because he is pretty apt to settle without any argument. And after a party settles one snatching, it will be considered very unethical for anybody else to snatch him again very soon, so he is not likely to make any fuss about the matter. The finger guy gets a commission of twenty-five per cent of the settlement, and one and all are satisfied and much fresh scratch comes into circulation, which is very good for the merchants. And while the party who is snatched may know who snatches him, one thing he never knows is who puts the finger on him, this being considered a trade secret.

I am talking to Waldo Winchester, the newspaper scribe, one night and something about the snatching business comes up, and Waldo Winchester is trying to tell me that it is one of the oldest dodges in the world, only Waldo calls it kidnapping, which is a title that will be very repulsive to guys who are on the snatch nowadays. Waldo Winchester claims that hundreds of years ago guys are around snatching parties, male and female, and holding them for ransom, and furthermore Waldo

Winchester says they even snatch very little children and Waldo states that it is all a very, very wicked proposition.

Well, I can see where Waldo is right about it being wicked to snatch dolls and little children, but of course no guys who are on the snatch nowadays will ever think of such a thing, because who is going to settle for a doll in these times when you can scarcely even give them away? As for little children, they are apt to be a great nuisance, because their mammas are sure to go running around hollering bloody murder about them, and furthermore little children are very dangerous, indeed, what with being apt to break out with measles and mumps and one thing and another any minute and give it to everybody in the neighbourhood.

Well, anyway, knowing that Harry the Horse and Spanish John and Little Isadore are now on the snatch, I am by no means pleased to see them come along one Tuesday evening when I am standing at the corner of Fiftieth and Broadway, although of course I give them a very jolly hello, and say I hope and trust they are feeling nicely.

They stand there talking to me a few minutes, and I am very glad indeed that Johnny Brannigan, the strong-arm cop, does not happen along and see us, because it will give Johnny a very bad impression of me to see me in such company, even though I am not responsible for the company. But naturally I cannot haul off and walk away from this company at once, because Harry the Horse and Spanish John and Little Isadore may get the idea that I am playing the chill for them, and will feel hurt.

'Well,' I say to Harry the Horse, 'how are things going, Harry?'

'They are going no good,' Harry says. 'We do not beat a race in four days. In fact,' he says, 'we go overboard today. We are washed out. We owe every bookmaker at the track that will trust us, and now we are out trying to raise some scratch to pay off. A guy must pay his bookmaker no matter what.'

Well, of course this is very true, indeed, because if a guy does not pay his bookmaker it will lower his business standing quite some, as the bookmaker is sure to go around putting the blast on him, so I am pleased to hear Harry the Horse mention such honourable principles.

'By the way,' Harry says, 'do you know a guy by the name of Bookie Bob?'

Now I do not know Bookie Bob personally, but of course I know who Bookie Bob is, and so does everybody else in this town that ever goes to a race-track, because Bookie Bob is the biggest bookmaker around and about, and has plenty of scratch. Furthermore, it is the opinion of one and all that Bookie Bob will die with this scratch, because he is considered a very close guy with his scratch. In fact, Bookie Bob is considered closer than a dead heat.

He is a short fat guy with a bald head, and his head is always shaking a little from side to side, which some say is a touch of palsy, but which most citizens believe comes of Bookie Bob shaking his head 'No' to guys asking for credit in betting on the races. He has an ever-loving wife, who is a very quiet little old doll with grey hair and a very sad look in her eyes, but nobody can blame her for this when they figure that she lives with Bookie Bob for many years.

I often see Bookie Bob and his ever-loving wife eating in different joints along in the Forties, because they seem to have no home except an hotel, and many a time I hear Bookie Bob giving her a going-over about something or other, and generally it is about the price of something she orders to eat, so I judge Bookie Bob is as tough with his ever-loving wife about scratch as he is with everybody else. In fact, I hear him bawling her out one night because she has on a new hat which she says cost her six bucks, and Bookie Bob wishes to know if she is trying to ruin him with her extravagances.

But of course I am not criticizing Bookie Bob for squawking about the hat, because for all I know six bucks may be too much for a doll to pay for a hat, at that. And furthermore, maybe Bookie Bob has the right idea about keeping down his ever-loving wife's appetite, because I know many a guy in this town who is practically ruined by dolls eating too much on him.

'Well,' I say to Harry the Horse, 'if Bookie Bob is one of the bookmakers you owe, I am greatly surprised to see that you seem to have both eyes in your head, because I never before hear of Bookie Bob letting anybody owe him without giving him at least one of their eyes for security. In fact,' I say, 'Bookie Bob is such a guy as will not give you the right time if he has two watches.'

'No,' Harry the Horse says, 'we do not owe Bookie Bob. But,' he says, 'he will be owing us before long. We are going to put the snatch on Bookie Bob.'

Well, this is most disquieting news to me, not because I care if they snatch Bookie Bob or not, but because somebody may see me talking to them who will remember about it when Bookie Bob is snatched. But of course it will not be good policy for me to show Harry the Horse and Spanish John and Little Isadore that I am nervous, so I only speak as follows:

'Harry,' I say, 'every man knows his own business best, and I judge you know what you are doing. But,' I say, 'you are snatching a hard guy when you snatch Bookie Bob. A very hard guy, indeed. In fact,' I say, 'I hear the softest thing about him is his front teeth, so it may be very difficult for you to get him to settle after you snatch him.'

'No,' Harry the Horse says, 'we will have no trouble about it. Our finger gives us Bookie Bob's hole card, and it is a most surprising thing, indeed. But,' Harry the Horse says, 'you come upon many surprising things in human nature when you are on the snatch. Bookie Bob's hole card is his ever-loving wife's opinion of him.

'You see,' Harry the Horse says, 'Bookie Bob has been putting himself away with his ever-loving wife for years as a very important guy in this town, with much power and influence, although of course Bookie Bob knows very well he stands about as good as a broken leg. In fact,' Harry the Horse says, 'Bookie Bob figures that his ever-loving wife is the only one in the world who looks on him as a big guy, and he will sacrifice even his scratch, or anyway some of it, rather than let her know that guys have such little respect for him as to put the snatch on him. It is what you call psychology,' Harry the Horse says.

Well, this does not make good sense to me, and I am thinking to myself that the psychology that Harry the Horse really figures to work out nice on Bookie Bob is tickling his feet with matches, but I am not anxious to stand there arguing about it, and pretty soon I bid them all good evening, very polite, and take the wind, and I do not see Harry the Horse or Spanish John or Little Isadore again for a month.

In the meantime, I hear gossip here and there that Bookie Bob is missing for several days, and when he finally shows up again he gives it out that he is very sick during his absence, but I can put two and two together as well as anybody in this town and I figure that Bookie Bob is snatched by Harry the Horse and Spanish John and Little Isadore, and the chances are it costs him plenty.

So I am looking for Harry the Horse and Spanish John and Little Isadore to be around the race-track with plenty of scratch and betting them higher than a cat's back, but they never show up, and what is more I hear they leave Manhattan, and are back in Brooklyn working every day handling beer. Naturally this is very surprising to me, because the way things are running beer is a tough dodge just now, and there is very little profit in same, and I figure that with the scratch they must make off Bookie Bob, Harry the Horse and Spanish John and Little Isadore have a right to be taking things easy.

Now one night I am in Good Time Charley Bernstein's little speak in Forty-eighth Street, talking of this and that with Charley, when in comes Harry the Horse, looking very weary and by no means prosperous. Naturally I give him a large hello, and by and by we get to gabbing together and I ask him whatever becomes of the Bookie Bob matter, and Harry the Horse tells me as follows:

Yes [Harry the Horse says], we snatch Bookie Bob all right. In fact, we snatch him the very next night after we are talking to you, or on a Wednesday night. Our finger tells us Bookie Bob is going to a wake over in his old neighbourhood on Tenth Avenue, near Thirty-eighth Street, and this is where we pick him up.

He is leaving the place in his car along about midnight, and of course Bookie Bob is alone as he seldom lets anybody ride with him because of the wear and tear on his car cushions, and Little Isadore swings our flivver in front of him and makes him stop. Naturally Bookie Bob is greatly surprised when I poke my head into his car and tell him I wish the pleasure of his company for a short time, and at first he is inclined to argue the matter, saying I must make a mistake, but I put the old convincer on him by letting him peek down the snozzle of my John Roscoe.

We lock his car and throw the keys away, and then we take Bookie Bob in our car and go to a certain spot on Eighth Avenue where we have a nice little apartment all ready. When we get there I tell Bookie Bob that he can call up anybody he wishes and state that the snatch is on him and that it will require twenty-five G's, cash money, to take it off, but of course I also tell Bookie Bob that he is not to mention where he is or something may happen to him.

Well, I will say one thing for Bookie Bob, although everybody is always weighing in the sacks on him and saying he is no good – he takes it like a gentleman, and very calm and businesslike.

Furthermore, he does not seem alarmed, as many citizens are when they find themselves in such a situation. He recognizes the justice of our claim at once, saying as follows:

'I will telephone my partner, Sam Salt,' he says. 'He is the only one I can think of who is apt to have such a sum as twenty-five G's cash money. But,' he says, 'if you gentlemen will pardon the question, because this is a new experience to me, how do I know everything will be okay for me after you get the scratch?'

'Why,' I say to Bookie Bob, somewhat indignant, 'it is well known to one and all in this town that my word is my bond. There are two things I am bound to do,' I say, 'and one is to keep my word in such a situation as this, and the other is to pay anything I owe a bookmaker, no matter what, for these are obligations of honour with me.'

'Well,' Bookie Bob says, 'of course I do not know you gentlemen, and, in fact, I do not remember ever seeing any of you, although your face is somewhat familiar, but if you pay your bookmaker you are an honest guy, and one in a million. In fact,' Bookie Bob says, 'if I have all the scratch that is owing to me around this town, I will not be telephoning anybody for such a sum as twenty-five G's. I will have such a sum in my pants pocket for change.'

Now Bookie Bob calls a certain number and talks to somebody there but he does not get Sam Salt, and he seems much disappointed when he hangs up the receiver again.

'This is a very tough break for me,' he says. 'Sam Salt goes to Atlantic City an hour ago on very important business and will not be back until tomorrow evening, and they do not know where he is to stay in Atlantic City. And,' Bookie Bob says, 'I cannot think of anybody else to call up to get this scratch, especially anybody I will care to have know I am in this situation.'

'Why not call your ever-loving wife?' I say. 'Maybe she can dig up this kind of scratch.'

'Say,' Bookie Bob says, 'you do not suppose I am chump enough to give my ever-loving wife twenty-five G's, or even let her know where she can get her dukes on twenty-five G's belonging to me, do you? I give my ever-loving wife ten bucks per week for spending money,' Bookie Bob says, 'and this is enough scratch for any doll, especially when you figure I pay for her meals.'

Well, there seems to be nothing we can do except wait until Sam Salt gets back, but we let Bookie Bob call his ever-loving wife, as Bookie Bob says he does not wish to have her worrying about his absence, and tells her a big lie about having to go to Jersey City to sit up with a sick Brother Elk.

Well, it is now nearly four o'clock in the morning, so we put Bookie Bob in a room with Little Isadore to sleep, although, personally, I consider making a guy sleep with Little Isadore very cruel treatment, and Spanish John and I take turns keeping awake and watching out that Bookie Bob does not take the air on us before paying us off. To tell the truth, Little Isadore and Spanish John are somewhat disappointed that Bookie Bob agreed to settle so promptly, because they are looking forward to tickling his feet with great relish.

Now Bookie Bob turns out to be very good company when he wakes up the next morning, because he knows a lot of race-track stories and plenty of scandal, and he keeps us much interested at breakfast. He talks along with us as if he knows us all his life, and he seems very nonchalant indeed, but the chances are he will not be so nonchalant if I tell him about Spanish John's thought.

Well, about noon Spanish John goes out of the apartment and comes back with a racing sheet, because he knows Little Isadore and I will be wishing to know what is running in different spots although we do not have anything to bet on these races, or any way of betting on them, because we are overboard with every bookmaker we know.

Now Bookie Bob is also much interested in the matter of what is running, especially at Belmont, and he is bending over the table with me and Spanish John and Little Isadore, looking at the sheet, when Spanish John speaks as follows:

'My goodness,' Spanish John says, 'a spot such as this fifth race with Questionnaire at four to five is like finding money in the street. I only wish I have a few bobs to bet on him at such a price,' Spanish John says.

'Why,' Bookie Bob says, very polite, 'if you gentlemen wish to bet on these races I will gladly book to you. It is a good way to pass away the time while we are waiting for Sam Salt, unless you will rather play pinochle?'

'But,' I say, 'we have no scratch to play the races, at least not much.'

'Well,' Bookie Bob says, 'I will take your markers, because I hear what you say about always paying your bookmaker, and you put yourself away with me as an honest guy, and these other gentlemen also impress me as honest guys.'

Now what happens but we begin betting Bookie Bob on the different races, not only at Belmont, but at all the other tracks in the country, for Little Isadore and Spanish John and I are guys who like plenty of action when we start betting on the horses. We write out markers for whatever we wish to bet and hand them to Bookie Bob, and Bookie Bob sticks these markers in an inside pocket, and along in the late afternoon it looks as if he has a tumour on his chest.

We get the race results by 'phone off a poolroom downtown as fast as they come off, and also the prices, and it is a lot of fun, and Little Isadore and Spanish John and and I are all little pals together until all the races are over and Bookie Bob takes out the markers and starts counting himself up.

It comes out then that I owe Bookie Bob ten G's, and Spanish John owes him six G's, and Little Isadore owes him four G's, as Little Isadore beats him a couple of races out west.

Well, about this time, Bookie Bob manages to get Sam Salt on the 'phone, and explains to Sam that he is to go to a certain safe deposit box and get out twenty-five G's, and then wait until midnight and hire himself a taxicab and start riding around the block between Fifty-first and Fifty-second, from Eighth to Ninth Avenues, and to keep riding until somebody flags the cab and takes the scratch off him.

Naturally Sam Salt understands right away that the snatch is on Bookie Bob, and he agrees to do as he is told, but he says he cannot do it until the following night because he knows there is not twenty-five G's in the box, and he will have to get the difference at the track the next day. So there we are with another day in the apartment and Spanish John and Little Isadore and I are just as well pleased because Bookie Bob has us hooked and we naturally wish to wiggle off.

But the next day is worse than ever. In all the years I am playing the horses I never have such a tough day, and Spanish John and Little Isadore are just as bad. In fact, we are all going so bad that Bookie Bob seems to feel sorry for us and often lays us a couple of points above the track prices, but it does no good. At the end of the day, I am in a total of twenty G's, while Spanish John owes fifteen, and Little Isadore fifteen, a total of fifty G's among the three of us. But we are never any hands to hold post-mortems on bad days, so Little Isadore goes out to a delicatessen store and lugs in a lot of nice things to eat, and we have a fine dinner, and then we sit around with Bookie Bob telling stories, and even singing a few songs together until time to meet Sam Salt.

When it comes on midnight Spanish John goes out and lays for Sam, and gets a little valise off of Sam Salt. Then Spanish John comes back to the apartment and we open the valise and the twenty-five G's are there okay, and we cut this scratch three ways.

Then I tell Bookie Bob he is free to go on about his business, and good luck to him, at that, but Bookie Bob looks at me as if he is very much surprised, and hurt, and says to me like this:

'Well, gentlemen, thank you for your courtesy, but what about the scratch you owe me? What about these markers? Surely, gentlemen, you will pay your bookmaker?'

Well, of course we owe Bookie Bob these markers, all right, and of course a man must pay his bookmaker, no matter what, so I hand over my bit and Bookie Bob puts down something in a little note-book that he takes out of his kick.

Then Spanish John and Little Isadore hand over their dough, too, and Bookie Bob puts down something more in the little note-book.

'Now,' Bookie Bob says, 'I credit each of your accounts with these payments, but you gentlemen still owe me a matter of twenty-five G's over and above the twenty-five I credit you with, and I hope and trust you will make arrangements to settle this at once because,' he says, 'I do not care to extend such accommodations over any considerable period.'

'But,' I say, 'we do not have any more scratch after paying you the twenty-five G's on account.'

'Listen,' Bookie Bob says, dropping his voice down to a whisper, 'what about putting the snatch on my partner, Sam Salt, and I will wait over a couple of days with you and keep booking to you, and maybe you can pull yourselves out. But of course,' Bookie Bob whispers, 'I will be entitled to twenty-five per cent of the snatch for putting the finger on Sam for you.'

But Spanish John and Little Isadore are sick and tired of Bookie Bob and will not listen to staying in the apartment any longer, because they say he is a jinx to them and they cannot beat him in any manner, shape or form. Furthermore, I am personally anxious to get away because something Bookie Bob says reminds me of something.

It reminds me that besides the scratch we owe him, we forget to take out six G's two-fifty for the party who puts the finger on Bookie Bob for us, and this is a very serious matter indeed, because anybody will tell you that failing to pay a finger is considered a very dirty trick. Furthermore, if it gets around that you fail to pay a finger, nobody else will ever finger for you.

So [Harry the Horse says] we quit the snatching business because there is no use continuing while this obligation is outstanding against us, and we go back to Brooklyn to earn enough scratch to pay our just debts.

We are paying off Bookie Bob's IOU a little at a time, because we do not wish to ever have anybody say we welsh on a bookmaker, and furthermore we are paying off the six G's two-fifty commission we owe our finger.

And while it is tough going, I am glad to say our honest effort is doing somebody a little good, because I see Bookie Bob's ever-loving wife the other night all dressed up in new clothes and looking very happy, indeed.

And while a guy is telling me she is looking so happy because she gets a large legacy from an uncle who dies in Switzerland, and is now independent of Bookie Bob, I only hope and trust [Harry the Horse says] that it never gets out that our finger in this case is nobody but Bookie Bob's ever-loving wife.

GINGER AND THE KINGSMARKHAM CHALK CIRCLE

Ruth Rendell

THERE's a girl downstairs, sir,' said Polly Davies, 'and she says someone's taken her baby out of its pram.'

Chief Inspector Wexford had been contemplating a sheet of foolscap. On it, written by himself in the cause of crime prevention, was a politely worded request to the local authority, asking them to refrain from erecting scaffolding around their rented property a full nine months before building work was due to commence. Because of the scaffolding there had already been two burglaries and an assault on a young woman. He looked up from the paper, adjusted his thoughts and sighed.

'They will do it,' he said. 'Leave their babies about I mean. You'd never find them leaving their handbags outside shops.'

'It was outside her flat, sir, not a shop, and the thing is, whoever took the baby left another one in its place.'

Slowly Wexford got up. He came round the desk and looked narrowly at Polly.

'Constable Davies, you have to be pulling my leg.'

'No, sir, you know I wouldn't. She's a Mrs Bond and she says that when she went downstairs to fetch in her pram, her baby had gone and another one been put there.'

Wexford followed Polly down to the ground floor. In one of the interview rooms a girl was sitting at the bleak, rectangular, plastic-topped table, drinking tea and crying. She looked about nineteen. She had long straw-coloured hair and a small childish face, naive and innocent and frightened, and she was wearing blue denims and a tee-shirt with apples and oranges and cherries printed all over the front. From her appearance one would not have supposed her to be a mother. But also in the room was a baby. The baby, in short white frock and woolly coat and napkin and cotton socks, slept in the uneasy arms of Detective Constable Loring.

It had occurred to Wexford on the way down that women who have recently had babies are, or are said to be, prone to various kinds of mental disturbance, and his first thought was that Mrs Bond might only think or only be saying that this child was not hers.

'Now, Mrs Bond,' he began, 'this is a strange business. Do you feel like telling me about it?'

'I've told it all,' she said.

'Well, yes, but not to me. Why not start by telling me where you live and where your baby was?'

She gulped. She pushed the teacup away. 'Greenhill Court. We're on the fifth floor. We haven't got a balcony or anything. I have to go all the way down in the lift to put Karen out in her pram. She's got to have fresh air. And when she's there I can't watch her all the time. I can't even see her from my lounge on account of it looks out over the car park.'

'So you put her out in the pram this afternoon,' said Wexford. 'What time would that have been?'

'It was just on two. I put the pram on the grass with the cat net on it, and when I went to fetch it in at half-past four the cat net was still on it and the baby was asleep but it – it wasn't Karen!' She made little whimpering noises that exploded in a sob. 'It wasn't Karen, it was that baby he's holding!'

The baby woke up and also began to cry. Loring wrinkled up his nose and shifted his left hand from under its buttocks. His eyes appealed to Polly who nodded and left the room.

'So what did you do?' said Wexford.

'I didn't even go back upstairs. I got hold of the pram and I pushed it and I started to run and I ran all the way down here to you.'

He was touched by her childish faith. In real or imaginery trouble, at time of fear, she ran to those whom her sheltered small-town upbringing had taught her to trust, the kindly helmeted man in blue, the strong arm of the law. Not for her the grosser cynical image her city-bred contemporaries held of brutal and bribable policemen.

'Mrs Bond,' he said, and then, 'What's your first name?'

'Philippa. I'm called Pippa.'

'Then I'll call you that if you don't mind. Describe your baby to me, will you, Pippa? Is she dark or fair? How old is she?'

'She's two months old – well, nine weeks. She's got blue eyes, she's wearing a white frock.' The voice broke and trembled again. 'And she's got the most beautiful red-gold hair you've ever seen!'

Inevitably, Wexford's eyes went to the child in Loring's arms whom this description seemed perfectly to fit. He said gently to Pippa Bond, 'Now you're quite sure you aren't imagining all this? No one will be angry if you are, we shall understand. Perhaps you worried or felt a bit guilty about leaving Karen out of your sight for so long, and then when you came down you got a feeling she looked rather different from usual . . .'

A wail of indignation and misery cut across the rest of what he had to say. The girl began to cry with long tearing sobs. Polly Davies came back, carrying a small square hand towel from the women's lavatory. She took the baby from Loring, laid it on its back on the table and undid the big safety pin above its navel. Pippa Bond flinched away from the baby as if it were carrying a disease.

'I'm not imagining it,' she shouted at Wexford. 'I'm not! D'you think I wouldn't know my own baby? D'you think I wouldn't know my Karen from *that*?'

Polly had folded the towel cornerwise. She moved a little so that Wexford could see the baby's waving legs and bare crotch. 'Whoever this baby is, sir, it isn't Karen. Look for yourself – it's a boy.'

Trevor Bond was fetched from the Stowerton estate agent's

where he worked. He looked very little older than his wife. Pippa clung to him, crying and inarticulate, and over her bent head he cast despairing eyes at the policemen.

He had arrived in a car driven by a young woman he said was his sister-in-law, Pippa's sister, who also lived at Greenhill Court with her husband. She sat stiffly at the wheel, giving Pippa no more than a nod and what seemed like a shrug of exasperation when she came out of the police station with Trevor's arm round her. Susan Rains, her name was, and a quarter of an hour later it was she who was showing Loring and Sergeant Martin just where the pram had stood on the lawn between the block of flats and the main road from Kingsmarkham to Stowerton. While this thin red-haired girl castigated her sister's negligence and put forward her own theories as to where Karen might be, Dr Moss arrived with sedation for Pippa, though she had become calmer once she understood no one would expect her to have charge of the changeling boy.

His fate was removal to a Kingsmarkham Borough nursery for infants in the care of the local authority.

'Poor lamb,' said the children's officer Wexford spoke to. 'I expect Kay will be able to take him in Bystall Lane. There's no one to fetch him, though, they've got ten to bath and get to bed down there.'

Young Ginger, Wexford had begun to call him. He was a fine-looking baby with large eyes, strong pudgy features, and hair of a curious pale red, the colour of a new raw carrot. To Wexford's not inexperienced eye, he looked older than the missing Karen, nearer four months than two. His eyes were able to focus firmly, and now they focused on the chief inspector, a scrutiny which moved the baby to yell miserably. Young Ginger buried his face in Polly's boyish bosom, crying and searching for sustenance.

'You don't know what they're thinking, do you, sir?' Polly said. 'Just because we can't remember anything about when we were his age we sort of think babies don't feel much or notice things. But suppose what they feel is so awful they sort of block it off just so as they won't be able to remember? Suppose it's dreadful pain being separated from your mother and not being able to say and – Oh, I don't know, but does anyone think of these things, sir?'

'Well, psychiatrists do,' said Wexford, 'and philosophers, I expect, but not many ordinary people like us. You'll have to remember it when you have babies of your own. Now take him down to Bystall Lane, will you?'

A few minutes after she had gone Inspector Burden came in. He had heard the story downstairs but had not entirely believed it. It was the part about putting another baby in Karen's place that he couldn't believe, he told Wexford. He hadn't either, said Wexford, but it was true.

'You can't think of a reason why anyone would do such a thing,' said Burden. 'You can't think of a single reason why even a mentally disturbed person would do such a thing.'

'I suppose,' said Wexford, 'that by "you" you mean yourself or "one" because *I* can think of several reasons for doing it. First of all, you've got to take some degree of mental disturbance for granted here. Well-adjusted normal people don't steal other people's babies, let alone exchange them. It's going to be a woman. It's a woman who's done it because she wants to be rid of that particular child, yet she must have a child. Agreed?'

'Right,' said Burden. 'Why?'

'She has to show it to someone else,' Wexford said slowly, as if thinking aloud, 'someone who expects to see a baby nearer in age and appearance to Karen Bond than to young Ginger, or who expects a baby of Karen's sex. She may be a woman who has several sons and whose husband was away when the last one was born. She has told him he has a daughter, and to bear this out because she's afraid of him, she has to have a girl to produce for him. On the other hand, she may not be married. She may have told a boy friend or ex-boy friend the child is younger than it is in order to convince him of his paternity.'

'I'm glad you mentioned mental disturbance,' said Burden sarcastically.

'She may simply be exhausted by looking after a child who screams incessantly – young Ginger's got a good pair of lungs – so she exchanges him for a baby she believes won't scream. Or she may have been told that Ginger has some illness or even hereditary defect which frightened her so she wanted to be rid of him, but she still has to have a baby for her husband or mother or whoever to see.'

Burden seemed to be considering this inventiveness with reluctant admiration but not much conviction. He said, 'So what are we going to do about it?'

'I've taken everyone in the place off what they were doing and put them on to this. We're getting on to all the hospitals and GPs, the Registrar of births, and the post-natal and baby clinics. I think it has to be someone local, maybe even someone who knew the pram would be there because she'd seen it there before.'

'And seen the baby who was in it before?' asked Burden, quirking up an eyebrow.

'Not necessarily. A pram with a cat net over and whose occupant can't be seen implies a very young baby.' Wexford hesitated. 'This is a hell of a lot more worrying,' he said, 'than a run-of-the-mill baby-snatching.'

'Because Karen Bond's so young?' Burden hazarded.

'No, not that. Look, Mike, your typical baby-snatcher loves babies, she yearns for one of her own, and that's why she takes someone else's. But this one's *got* a baby of her own and one she dislikes enough to hand him over to a stranger. You can pretty well take it for granted the ordinary baby-snatcher will care for a child almost extravagantly well, but will this one? If she doesn't care for her own child, will she care for substitute? I say it's worrying because we can be certain this woman's taken Karen for a purpose, a use, and what happens when that use is over?'

The block of flats in which the Bonds lived was not one of those concerning whose vulnerability to break-ins Wexford had been drafting his letter, but a privately owned fire-storeyed building standing on what not long ago had been open green meadows. There were three such blocks, Greenhill, Fairlawn and Hillside Courts, interspersed with rows of weatherboarded town houses, and each block was separated from the main road to Stowerton only by a strip of lawn thirty feet deep. On this turf, a little way in from the narrow service road, Karen Bond's pram had stood.

Wexford and Burden talked to the porter who had charge of the three blocks. He had been cleaning a car in the car park at the relevant time and had noticed nothing. Wexford, going up in the Greenhill lift, commented to Burden that it was unfortunate children were forbidden to play on the lawns. They would have served as protection for Karen or at least as witnesses. There were a good many children on this new estate which was mainly occupied by young couples. Between two and four-thirty that afternoon the little ones had been cooped up in small rooms or out for walks with their mothers, the older ones at school.

Mrs Louise Pelham had fetched her son and her next-door neighbour's two sons from school, passing within a few feet of Karen's pram. That was at a quarter to four. She had glanced into the pram, as she always did, and now she said she remembered thinking Karen looked 'funny'. The baby in the pram had seemed to have a bigger face and redder hair than the one she had looked at when she passed on her way to the children's school half an hour before. Wexford felt that there was a real lead here, a pinpointing of the time of the substitution, until he learned that Susan Rains had been with Mrs Pelham before him and told her the whole story in detail.

Susan Rains and her sister Pippa had each been married at the age of eighteen, but Pippa at twenty already had a baby while Susan, seven years older, was childless. She was without a job too, it appeared, and at three years short of thirty was leading the life of a middle-aged houseproud gossip. She seemed very anxious to tell Wexford and Burden that, in her opinion, her sister was far too young to have a child, her brother-in-law too young to be a father, and that they were both too irresponsible to look after a baby. Pippa, she said, was always bringing Karen round for her to mind, and now Wexford, who had been wondering about the two folded napkins, the plastic spoon and bottle of concentrated orange juice on Mrs Rains's spotless kitchen counter, understood why they were there.

'Are you fond of babies, Mrs Rains?' Wexford asked, and got an almost frightening response.

Hard lines bit into Mrs Rains's face and her redhead's pale eyes flashed. 'I'd be an unnatural woman if I wasn't, wouldn't I? What else she might have said – a defence? An explanation? – was cut off by the arrival of a woman in her late forties whom she introduced in a mutter as her mother. It was left to Wexford to find out that this was Mrs Leighton who had left Pippa in a drugged sleep and Trevor trying to answer Sergeant Martin's second spate of questions.

Mrs Leighton was sprightly and not too concerned. 'Well, babies that get taken out of prams, they always turn up safe and sound, don't they?' Her hair was dyed to a more glorious red than her daughter's natural shade. She was on her way to babysit for her son and daughter-in-law who had a six-month-old son, and she had just looked in on Pippa to collect the one pound twenty she owed her for dry-cleaning. Imagine what she'd felt, the whole place full of policemen and Karen gone. She really thought Trevor or Susan might have phoned her, and now she was in two minds whether to go and babysit for Mark or not. 'But she's bound to turn up OK, isn't she?' she said to Wexford.

Wexford said they must hope so, and then he and Burden left the two women to argue between themselves as to which was the more important, keeping a promise to the son or commiserating with the daughter.

The world, or this small corner of it, suddenly seemed full of babies. From behind two doors on the ground floor came the whimpers and low peevish grizzlings of infants put unwillingly in their cots for the night. As they left by the glass double doors, they passed on the step an athletic-looking girl in sweater and denims with a very small baby clamped to her chest in a canvas baby carrier. The car park was filling as men returned home from work, some of them commuters from London, and among them, walking from a jaunty red sports car, a couple swinging between them a baby in a shallow rush basket. Wexford wondered just how many children under the age of two lived in those flats and small neat houses. Nearly as many as there were adults, he thought, and he stood aside to let pass a girl pushing twins in a wide push-chair.

There was very little more that he could do that night beyond embroiling himself in another discussion with Burden as to the reason why. Burden put forward several strange suggestions. Having previously declared that he couldn't think of a single motive, he now posited that the baby-snatcher was due to have her own baby immunized against whooping cough on the following day. She had read in the newspaper that this could cause brain damage but was too diffident to refuse the immunization, so planned to substitute someone else's baby for her own.

'The trouble with you unimaginative people,' said Wexford, 'is that when you do fantasize you really go crazy. She wants to protect her child from what's something like a one in a million chance of brain damage, but she doesn't mind entrusting him to the care of strangers who might do him far more harm.'

'But the point is she knew they wouldn't do him harm. She'd know that what's happened is exactly what must happen, that he'd be brought to us and then put in the care of the local authority.' Burden waited for some show of enthusiasm and when he didn't get it he went home. For three hours. At eleven that night he was destined to be called out again.

But not account of Karen Bond.

In normal circumstances Sergeant Willoughby, going off duty, wouldn't have given a second glance at the Ford Transit parked under some overhanging bushes at the foot of Ploughman's Lane. But the sergeant's head, like those of most members of the Mid-Sussex Constabulary, was full of thoughts of missing children. He saw the van as a possible caravan substitute, and his mind went vaguely back to old tales of infants stolen by gypsies. He parked his scooter and went over to investigate.

The young man sitting in the driving seat switched on the ignition, put the van into gear and moved off as fast as he could on a roar of the engine. There was no real danger of his hitting Sergeant Willoughby, nor did that seem to have been his intention, but he passed within a yard or so of him and swung down the lane towards the town.

The nearest phone was in the sergeant's own home in Queen Street, and he went quickly to it.

But the Ford Transit turned out to have had nothing to do with Karen Bond. It was the getaway car for two men who were taking advantage of the absence of a Kingsmarkham stockbroker and his wife to remove a safe from their home.

Ploughman's Lane was Kingsmarkham's millionaire's row, and Stephen Pollard's house, pretentiously named Baron's Keep, by no means the smallest or most modest house in it. It was a nineteen-thirties palace of red brick and leaded lattices and neo-Tudor twisty chimneys. All the windows on the ground floor had stout bars to them, but there were no bars on the french window which led from the largest of the rear bedrooms on to a spacious balcony. When Burden and Loring got there they found signs that two men had climbed up to this balcony, ignored the thief-proof locks on the french window, and cut the glass neatly out of its frame with a glass cutter.

Where the safe had been in the study on the ground floor was now a gaping cavity. This room was said to be a precise replica of some writing room or den or hidey-hole of Mary Queen of Scots in Holyrood Palace, and the safe had been concealed behind a sliding door in the linenfold panelling. The thieves had chipped it out of its niche with a cold chisel and removed it bodily. Burden thought it must have been immensely heavy, which explained the need for having the van nearby.

Although the weather was dry, a long wet spell had only just ended. Deeply indented footprints, one set of a size eight shoe, the other of a size twelve, had ground into the flowerbed under the balcony. These same prints crossed the rear lawn to where there was a gate in the tall wattle fence, and alongside them went parallel grooves about two inches apart.

'I reckon,' said Burden, 'they had a set of those wheels people have for pushing heavy luggage along. That's what they used. The sheer cheek of it!'

Loring shone his torch. 'They rested it down here, sir, in

front of the gate. Must have been a bit of a blow when they found their motor gone and they had to keep on wheeling.'

In vain they searched the lane, the ditches and the copse which bordered the lane on one side. They didn't find the safe and no fingerprints were found on the window ledges or in the study at Baron's Keep. The thieves had worn gloves.

'And Big Feet,' said Burden in the morning, 'should have worn snow shoes. There aren't going to be many villains about with great plates of meat like that.'

'I'd think of Lofty Peters first thing,' said Wexford, 'only he's inside.'

'Well, he's not actually. He came out last week. But we were round at his place, knocking him up at midnight and waking all the neighbours, and there was no doubt where he'd been all evening. He was blind drunk, smashed out of his mind. I reckon this lot came from London. Old Pollard's been shooting his mouth off around the City about his missus's diamonds and this is the outcome.'

'The van was nicked,' said Wexford. 'I've just had a call from the super at Myringham. They found it ditched on the edge of a wood with the licence plates missing.'

'What a lively time we are having,' said Burden, and he looked out of the window at the geraniums on the forecourt and the shops opening, striped awnings gradually being unfurled, shoppers' cars moving in, the July sun spreading a great sheet of light and warmth across the Pomfret Road – and a little figure walking through it in unseasonable black. 'My God,' he said, 'I don't believe it, not another one!'

Wexford got up and came over to the window. The small stout man in the black cassock was now on the forecourt, walking between the geranium tubs. In his arms was a bundle that was undoubtedly a baby. He was carrying the baby very confidently and securely as might be expected in one who so often performed the sacrament of baptism. Wexford watched him in silence, craning out to follow the priest's progress under the overhanging canopy and through the swing doors into the police station.

He said in a distant speculative voice, 'You don't suppose, do you, Mike, that this is the latest craze? I mean, we've had wife-swapping, are we going to have baby-swapping? Maybe it's something that bored young housewives are going to take up instead of going to evening classes or playing with their deep freezes.'

'Or maybe there's a maniac on the rampage who gets his kicks from changing them all round and confusing their mums.'

'Musical babes,' said Wexford. 'Come on, let's go down and see.' They descended to the foyer in the lift. 'Good morning, Father. And who might this be?'

The priest in charge of the Catholic church of Our Lady of Loretto was leaning against the long parabola-shaped counter behind which the station sergeant, Sergeant Camb, presided. The sleeping baby in his arms was swathed, indeed tightly cocooned,in a clean pale blue cellular blanket. Only its face, fragile yet healthy-looking, and one hand were exposed. Thick dark lashes rested on the rose-leaf skin, but otherwise the child was fair, eyebrow-less and with fine downy hair as bright as a new copper coin. Holding it with tender firmness, Father Glanville looked round from his conversation with the sergeant to give Wexford a mystified grin, while Polly Davies stroked the baby's tiny fingers with her own forefinger.

'Your guess is as good as mine, Mr Wexford. I went over to the church just before nine and when I came back this little one was on the front steps of the presbytery. My lady help, Mrs Bream, had come in by the back door and hadn't even noticed him.'

'You found him just like that?' said Wexford. 'Just wrapped in that blanket and lying on the doorstep.'

'No indeed. He was wrapped in this blanket inside a cardboard box. The cardboard box,' said Father Glanville, smiling, 'is of the kind one sees in grocery supermarkets. This particular one has printed on it: Smith's Ready Salted Crisps, Ten Family Packs.' He added rather anxiously, 'I'm afraid I haven't brought it with me.'

Wexford couldn't help laughing. 'Well, don't throw it away. It's very likely a vital piece of evidence.' He came closer to the child who slept on regardless of the talk and the four large alien presences. 'You brought it straight here?'

'I brought *him* straight here,' said Father Glanville with the faintest note of reproof in his voice. Wexford reflected that he ought to have known the priest would never refer to any human soul, however youthful, however unknown and unidentified, as 'it', and then he said:

'I suppose he is a he? Blue blankets don't necessarily denote maleness, do they?'

The three men, for some obscure reason known to none of them, turned their eyes simultaneously on Polly Davies. And she, somehow recognizing that to ascertain gender was her peculiar function, gently took the baby out of Father Glanville's arms, turned away and began unwrapping the blue blanket. The baby woke up and at once began a strenuous crying. Polly re-wrapped the blanket, set the child against her shoulder, her hand pressed against the four-inch wide back.

'This is a little girl, sir.' She put the baby's cheek against her own. 'Sir, don't you think it's Karen Bond? I'm sure it is, it must be.' Her voice had a catch in it. To her own evident horror, there were tears coming into her eyes. 'To think someone just dumped her, someone else's child, on a doorstep, in a cardboard box!'

'Well, the someone couldn't have left her in a better place, could she?' said Wexford with a grin at the priest. 'Come now, Constable Davies, this is no way for a liberated woman to go on. Let us pull ourselves together and go and phone Mrs Bond.'

Trevor and Pippa Bond arrived together, having again been brought to the police station in Susan Rains's car. The young husband was plainly terrified that the child would turn out not to be theirs, that their journey would prove to have been a cruel and vain awakening of hope, and for this reason he had tried to persuade his wife not to come. But she had come. Nothing could have kept her away, though she was fuddled and dazed still from Dr Moss's sedatives.

But once she saw the baby the muzziness left her and the glazed look went out of her eyes. She seized her in her arms, crushing her until Karen cried out and struggled with all her nine-week-old energy. Inscrutably, Susan Rains watched the little drama, watched her sister throw the blue blanket on to the floor, shuddering as she did so, watched the tears run down her cheeks on to the baby's head. Pippa began frenetically examining the white frock, the matinée jacket, the minute socks, as if hunting for visible germs.

'Why don't you burn the lot?' said Susan very coolly. 'Then you won't have to worry.'

Trevor Bond said quickly and awkwardly, 'Well, thanks very much, thanks a lot. I'll just see these girls of mine home and then I'll get off to the office. We've got a lot on our plates, always have this time of the year.'

'I'll take them back, Trev,' said Susan. 'You get off to work. And I'll phone Mother.'

'I'd let Dr Moss have a look at Karen if I were you,' said Wexford. 'She seems fine and I'm sure she is, but better be on the safe side.'

They went on their way. Susan Rains walked a little behind the others, already marked for her role as the eternal aunt. Wexford's thoughts went to her nephew, her brother Mark's child, though he didn't know why he should think of him just then, and then to young Ginger, that grass orphan, down in Bystall Lane. He picked up the blanket – young Ginger's blanket? – and examined it, coming to the conclusion at the end of a few minutes' scrutiny of its texture and its label, that it was made of pure wool, had been manufactured in Wales, was old but clean and had been mended in one corner by someone who was no tyro when it came to handling a darning needle. From its honeycombing he picked a quantity of hairs. Most of these were baby hair, very fine red-gold filaments that might (or then again might not) all have come from the same child's scalp, but among them were a few coarser longer hairs that were clearly from a woman's head. A red-headed woman. He was thinking about the two red-headed women he had encountered during the time Karen was missing, when there came a knock at the door.

Wexford called, 'Come in,' and Sergeant Willoughby first put his head round the door, then advanced a little sheepishly into the office. Behind him came Burden.

'The young chap I saw driving that van last night, sir,' said

Willoughby, 'I knew his face was familiar, I knew I'd seen him before. Anyway, I've remembered who he is. Tony Jasper, sir. I'm certain of it.'

'And am I supposed to know who Tony Jasper is?'

Burden said quickly, 'You know his brother. His brother's Paddy Jasper.'

'Paddy Jasper went up north.'

'That's what they said,' said Burden, 'and maybe he did, but his girl friend's back living round here. You know Leilie Somers, he's lived with her on and off for years, ever since she left Stowerton Secondary Modern when she was sixteen.'

'D'you know where she's living?'

'In one of those flats over the shops in Roland Road,' said Burden.

Roland Road was in Stowerton, running behind and parallel to the High Street. Wexford's driver took him and Burden along the High Street to reach it and, looking out of the window, Wexford saw Pippa Bond's mother walking along, shop-window-gazing and pushing a pram that was higher and grander than her daughter's and of a rich dark green colour. Its occupant was presumably her grandson. Mrs Leighton was also dressed in dark green and her dyed hair looked redder than ever.

The car turned left, then right into Roland Road. The row of shops, eight of them, was surmounted by a squat upper floor of aimlessly peaked roofs and, on its façade, a useless adornment of green-painted studs and beams. The block had been put up at approximately the same period as Baron's Keep, the time which Wexford called the Great Tudor Revival. He remarked to Burden that the whole face of urban and semi-rural Britain would have been changed immeasurably for the better if architects in the third and fourth decades of the century had revived the Georgian instead of the Elizabethan. Think of it, he said, long elegant sash windows instead of poky casements, columns instead of half-timbering and pediments instead of gables. Burden didn't answer him. He had given a push to the door between the newsagent's and the pet food shop, and it gave under his hand and swung inwards.

The passage was rather dark. At the foot of the stairs was a pram from which a young woman was lifting a baby. She turned round as the light fell on her and said:

'Oh, hallo, I was just coming back to shut that. Were you wanting something?'

Burden was inspired. He said, remembering Leilie Somer's character, guessing at her hopes and fears, 'We're looking for Mrs Jasper.'

The girl knew at once whom he meant. 'Leilie's door's the one on the right at the top of the stairs.' The baby on her hip, she parked the pram a little way down the passage, pulled and fastened the cover up over it.

'Do you know if her husband's at home?'

Her reply came guilelessly up to them as they mounted the steep stairs: 'Not unless he's come back. I heard him go out at just after eight this morning.'

At the top there was a door to the left and a door to the right. Burden knocked on the right one, and it was so rapidly opened that it was apparent Leilie Somers had been listening behind it. And she wanted them inside the flat just as fast. Her neighbour was steadily coming up the stairs and Leilie knew better than to let her hear the law introducing itself or see warrant cards flashed. She was a thin little person of twenty-eight or nine with a pinched face and hennaed hair. Throughout her whole youth she had been the mistress of a man who lived by robbery and occasionally by violent crime, and she had herself been in the dock. But she had never come to adopt, as other such women adopt, an attitude of insolence or truculence towards the police. She was always polite, she was always timid, and now as Wexford said, 'So you've moved back to your old stamping ground, Leilie,' she only nodded and smiled nervously and said yes, that was right, she'd moved back, managed to get this flat which was a piece of luck.

'And Paddy with you, I gather.'

'Sometimes,' she said. 'On and off. He's not what you'd call *living* here.'

'What would I call it then? Staying here for his holidays?' Leilie made no answer. The flat seemed to consist of a living room, a bedroom, a lavatory and a kitchen with covered bath in it. They went through to the living room. The furniture in it was ugly and cheap and old but it was very clean and the woodwork and walls were fresh white. The room had been re-decorated perhaps only the week before. There was still a lingering smell of paint. 'He was here last night,' said Wexford. 'He went out around eight this morning. When's he coming back?'

She would be rid of the man if she could be. Wexford had that impression now as he had received it from her once before, years before. Some bond she couldn't break bound her to Paddy Jasper, love or merely habit, but she would be relieved if external circumstances could sever it. Meanwhile, she would be unremittingly loyal.

'What did you want to see him for?'

Two can play at that game, thought Wexford, answering questions with another question. 'Where was he last evening?'

'He was here. He had a couple of pals in playing cards and for a beer.'

'I don't suppose,' said Burden, 'that one of these pals was by any chance his little brother Tony?'

Leilie looked at the rug on the floor, up at the ceiling, then out of the window so intently that it seemed there must be at least Concorde manifesting itself up in the sky if not a flying saucer.

'Come on, Leilie, you know Tony. That nice clean-living young Englishman who did two years for mugging an old lady up in the Smoke.'

She said very quietly, now staring down at her fingers, ''Course I know Tony. I reckon he was here too, I don't know, I was out at my job.' Her voice went up a bit and her chin went up. 'I've got an evening job down the Andromeda. Cloakroom attendant, eight till midnight.'

At sign of the times, was what Wexford called the Andromeda. It was Kingsmarkham's casino, a gambling club in a spruced-up Victorian house out on the Sewingbury Road. He was going to ask why an evening job, what had happened to her full-time work – for at the time of his last encounter with Leilie she had been a stylist at Mr Nicholas, the hairdresser's – when his eye fixed itself on an object which stood on one end of the mantelpiece. It was a baby's feeding bottle with dregs of milk still in it.

'I didn't know you had a baby, Leilie,' he said.

'He's in the bedroom,' she said, and as if to confirm her words there sounded through the wall a reedy wail which quickly gained in volume. She listened. As the cries grew shrill she smiled and the smile became a laugh, a burst of laughter. Then she bit her lip and said in her usual monotone, 'Paddy and them were here babysitting for me. They were here all evening.'

'I see,' said Wexford. He knew then beyond a doubt that Paddy Jasper had not been there, that his friends had not been there, but that on the other hand they, or some of them including Jasper and his brother, had been up in Ploughman's Lane robbing Baron's Keep. 'I see,' he said again. The baby went on crying, working itself up into a passion of rage or misery. 'Is Paddy the child's father?'

She came the nearest to rudeness she ever had. 'You've no right to ask me that, Mr Wexford. What's it to you?'

No, maybe he had no right, he thought. That ninety-nine out of a hundred policemen would have asked it was no reason why he should. 'It's nothing to me,' he said. 'I'm sorry, Leilie. You'd better go and see to him, hadn't you?'

But at that moment the crying stopped. Leilie Somers sighed. In the flat next door footsteps sounded and a door slammed. Wexford said, 'We'll be back,' and followed Leilie out into the passage. She went into the bedroom and shut herself in.

Burden let them out and closed the front door. 'That's her second child, you know,' he said as they went down the stairs. 'She had a kid by Jasper years ago.'

'Yes, I remember.' Wexford recalled Father Glanville's implied admonition and said carefully, 'Where is he or she now?'

'She's a baby batterer, is Leilie Somers. Didn't you know? No, you wouldn't. The case came up when you were ill and had all that time off.' Wexford didn't much like hearing his month's convalescence after a thrombosis described as 'all that time off' but he said nothing. 'I was amazed,' said Burden severely, 'to hear you apologizing to her as if she were a decent respectable sort of woman. She's a woman who's capable of giving a helpless baby a fractured skull and a broken arm. Those were her kid's injuries. And what did Leilie get? A suspended sentence, a recommendation for psychiatric treatment, all the nonsense.'

'What happened to the little boy?'

'He was adopted,' said Burden. 'He was quite a long time in hospital and then I heard that Leilie had agreed to have him adopted. Best thing for him.'

Wexford nodded. 'Strange, though,' he said. 'She always seems such a gentle meek creature. I can imagine her not knowing how to cope with a child or being a bit too easy-going or not noticing it was ill, say, but baby-battering – it seems so out of character.'

'You're always saying how inconsistent people are. You're always saying people are peculiar and you never can tell what they'll do next.'

'I suppose I am,' said Wexford.

He sent Loring to keep the Roland Road flat under observation, and then he and Burden went to lunch in the police station canteen. Polly Davies came up to Wexford while he was eating his dessert.

'I looked in at Bystall Lane, sir, and saw young Ginger. They said, did we think of making other arrangements for him or were they to keep him for a bit?'

'My God, they haven't had him twenty-four hours yet.'

'That's what I said, sir. Well, I sort of said that. I think they're short-staffed.'

'So are we,' said Wexford. 'Now then, I don't suppose anyone saw Karen Bond being put on that doorstep?'

'I'm afraid not, sir. No one I've spoken to, anyway, and no one's come forward. Mrs Bream who housekeeps for the priest, she says the cardboard box – the Smith's Crisps box, you know – was there when she came at nine only she didn't look at it. She thought it was something someone had left for the father and she was going to take it in once she'd got the kitchen cleared up and his bed made. Father Glanville says he went out at ten to nine and he's positive the box wasn't there then, so someone must have put it there in those ten minutes. It looks like someone who knows their habits, the father's and Mrs Bream's, doesn't it, sir?'

'One of his flock, d'you mean?'

'It could be. Why not?'

'If you're right,' said Wexford dryly, 'whoever it was is probably confessing it at this moment and Father Glanville will, of course, have to keep her identity locked in his bosom.'

He went off up to his office to await word from Loring. There, sitting at his desk, thinking, he remembered noticing in Susan Rains's flat, honoured on a little shelf fixed there for the purpose, a plaster statuette of the Virgin with lilies in her arms. The Leighton's were perhaps a Catholic family. He was on the point of deciding to go back to Greenhill Court for a further talk with Susan Rains when a phone call from Sergeant Camb announced the arrival of Stephen Pollard.

The stockbroker and his wife had been on holiday in Scotland and had driven all the way back, non-stop, all five hundred and forty miles, starting at six that morning. Wexford had met Pollard once before and remembered him as a choleric person. Now he was tired from the long drive but he still rampaged and shouted with as much misery as Pippa Bond had shown over the loss of her baby. The safe, it appeared, had contained a sapphire and platinum necklace and bracelet, four rings, three cameos and a diamond cross which Pollard said were worth thirty thousand pounds. No, of course no one knew he had a safe in which he kept valuables. Well, he supposed the cleaning woman did and the cleaning woman before her and all of the series of *au pair* girls, and maybe the builders who had painted the outside of the house, and the firm who had put up the bars.

'It's ludicrous,' said Burden when he had gone. 'All that carry-on when it's a dead cert his insurance company'll fork out. He might as well go straight back to Scotland. We're the people who've got the slog and we'll get stick if those villains aren't caught, while it won't make a scrap of difference to him one way or the other. And I'll tell you another thing that's ludicrous,' he said, warming to a resentful theme. 'The ratepayers of Sussex could have the expense of young Ginger's upbringing for eighteen years because his mother's too scared to come and claim him.'

'What shall I do about it? Hold a young wives' meeting and draw them a chalk circle?'

Burden looked bewildered.

'Haven't you ever heard of the Chinese chalk circle and Brecht's *Caucasian Chalk Circle*? You have to draw a circle in chalk on the ground and put the child in it, and of the mothers who claim him the one who can pull him out of the circle is his true mother and may have him.'

'That's all very well,' said Burden after a pause, 'but in this case, it's not mothers who want him, it's he who wants a mother. No one seems to want him.'

'Poor Ginger,' said Wexford, and then the phone rang. It was Loring on his radio to say Paddy Jasper had come into Roland Road and gone up the stairs to Leilie Somers's flat.

By the time Wexford and Burden got there Tony Jasper had arrived as well. The brothers were both tall, heavily built men but Tony's figure still had a youthfully athletic look about it while Paddy had the beginnings of a paunch. Tony's otherwise handsome appearance was ruined by a broken nose which had never been put right and through which he had difficulty in breathing. The repulsive and even sinister air he had was partly due to his always breathing through his mouth. Paddy and he were sitting facing each other at Leilie's living-room table. They were both smoking, the air in the room was thick with smoke, and Tony was dealing a pack of cards. Wexford thought the cards were the inspiration of the moment, hastily fetched out when they heard the knock at the downstairs door.

'Put the cards away, Tone,' said Paddy. 'It's rude to play when we've got company.' He was always polite in a thoroughly offensive way. 'Leilie here,' he said, 'has got something in her head about you wanting to know where I was last evening. Like what sort of time did you have in mind?'

Wexford told him. Paddy smiled. Somehow he managed to make it a paternal smile. He was stopping a few days with Leilie, he said, and his son. He hadn't seen much of his son since the child was born on account of having this good job up north but not a chance of accommodation for a woman and a kid, no way. So he'd come down for his holidays the previous Saturday and what does he hear but that Leilie's got this evening job up the Andromeda. Well, she'd taken Monday night off to be with him and done an exchange with another girl for Tuesday, but when it got to last night she couldn't very well skive off again so he said not to worry, he'd babysit, him and Tony here, and they'd have some of their old mates round. Johnny Farrow and Pip Monkton, for a beer and a hand of solo.

'Which is what we did, Mr Wexford.'

'Right,' said Tony.

'Leilie put Matthew in his cot and then the boys came round and she got us a bite to eat. She's a good girl is Leilie. She went off to work about half seven, didn't you, love? Then we did the dishes and had our game. Oh, and the lady next door came round to check up if four grown men could look after baby OK, very kind of her, I'm sure. And then at half eleven Pip went off home on account of his missus being the boss round his place, and at quarter past twelve Leilie came back. She got a lift so she was early. That's right, isn't it, love?'

Leilie nodded. 'Except you never did no dishes.'

Wexford kept looking at the man's huge feet which were no longer under the table but splayed out across the cheap bright bit of carpet. He wondered where the shoes were that had made those prints. Burnt, probably. The remains of the safe, once they had blown it open, might be in any pond or river in the Home Counties. Johnny Farrow was a notorious peterman or expert with explosives. He turned to Leilie and asked a question perhaps none of them had expected.

'Who usually looks after the baby when you're working?'

'Julie next door. That girl you were talking to when you came earlier. I used to take him to my mum, my mum lives up Charteris Road, it's not very far, but he started getting funny in the evenings, crying and screaming, and he got worse if I took him out and left him in a strange place.' Wexford wondered if she was giving him such a detailed answer to his question because she sometimes left the baby unattended and thought she might be breaking the law. He remembered the other boy, the one with the fractured skull and broken arm, and he hardened towards her. 'Then Mum had to go into hospital, anyway, she only came out yesterday. So Julie said to leave him here and she'd pop in every half hour, and she'd hear him anyway if he cried. You can hear a pin drop through these walls. And Julie never goes out on account of she's got a baby of her own. She's been very good has Julie because I reckon Matthew does cry most evenings, and you can't just leave them to cry, can you?'

'I'm glad to inform you, my dear,' said Paddy with outrageous pomposity, 'that my son did not utter a squeak last evening but was as good as gold,' and on the last word he looked hard at Wexford and stretched his lips into a huge humourless smile.

Julie Lang confirmed that Paddy Jasper, Tony Jasper, Pip Monkton and Johnny Farrow had all been in the flat next door when she called to check on the safety and comfort of Matthew at eight-thirty. She had a key to Leilie's flat but she hadn't used it, knowing Mr Jasper to be there. She wouldn't have dreamt of doing that because it was Mr Jasper's home really, wasn't it? So she had knocked at the door and Mr Jasper had let her in and not been very nice about it actually, and she had felt very awkward especially when he'd said, go in and see for yourself if I'm not to be trusted to look after my own child. He had opened the bedroom door and made her look and she had just glanced at the cot and seen Matthew was all right and sleeping.

'Well, I felt so bad about it,' said Julie Lang, 'that I said to him, perhaps he'd like the key back, and he said, yes, he'd been going to ask me for it as they wouldn't be needing my services any longer, thanks very much. He was quite rude really but I did feel bad about it.'

She had given Paddy Jasper the key. As far as she knew, the four men had remained in the flat with Matthew till Leilie got back at twelve-fifteen. By then, anyway, her husband had come home and they were both in bed asleep. No, she had heard no footsteps on the stairs, not even those of Pip Monkton going home at eleven-thirty. Of course she had had the television on so maybe she wouldn't have heard, but she was positive there hadn't been a sound out of Matthew.

Wexford and Burden went next to the home of Pip Monkton. Johnny Farrow's confirmation of the alibi would amount to very little, for he had a long criminal record for safebreaking, but Monkton had never been convicted of anything, had never even been charged with anything. He was an ex-publican, apparently perfectly respectable, and the only blot on his white innocent life was his known friendship with Farrow with whom he had been at school and whom he had supported and stuck to during Farrow's long prison sentences and periods of poverty-stricken idleness. If Monkton said that the four of them had been together all that evening babysitting in Leilie Somers's flat, Wexford knew he might as well throw up the sponge. The judge, the jury, the court, would believe Pip Monkton just as they would believe Julie Lang.

And Monkton did say it. Looking Wexford straight in the eye (so that the chief inspector knew he must be lying) he declared boldly that he and the Jaspers and Johnny had been in Roland Road, playing solo and drinking beer, until he left for home at half-past eleven. Wexford had him down to the police station and went on asking him about it, but he couldn't break him down. Monkton sounded as if he had learnt by heart what he had to say, and he went on saying it over and over again like a talking bird or a record on which the needle has got stuck.

When it got to six Wexford had himself driven to the Andromeda where the manager, who had an interest in keeping on the right side of the police, answered his questions very promptly. He got back to the station to find Burden and Polly discussing the one relevant piece of information Burden had succeeded in finding out about Monkton – that he had recently had an extension built on to his house. To cover the cost of this he had taken out a second mortgage, but the costs had come to three thousand pounds more than the builder's estimate.

'That'll be about what Monkton's getting for perjury,' said Burden. 'That'll be his share. Tony drove the van, Paddy and Johnny did the job while Monkton covers for them. I imagine they left Leilie's place around nine and got to Ploughman's Lane by a quarter past. They'll have got the safe out in an hour and got to the gate in the fence with it by ten-thirty, which was just about the time Willoughby spotted the van. Tony drove off, ditched the van in Myringham, came back to Stowerton on the last bus, the one that leaves Myringham at ten past eleven and which would have got him to Stowerton High Street by ten to twelve. God knows how the others got that safe back. My guess is that they didn't. They hid it in one of the meadows at the back of Ploughman's Lane and went back for it this morning – with Johnny Farrow's car. Then Johnny blew it. They used the wheels again and Johnny blew it somewhere up on the Downs.'

Wexford hadn't spoken for some minutes. Now he said, 'When Leilie Somers was charged with this baby-battering thing, did she plead guilty or not guilty?'

Rather surprised by the apparent irrelevance of this question, Burden said. 'Guilty. There wasn't much evidence offered apart from the doctor's. Leilie pleaded guilty and said something about being tired and strained and not being able to stand it when the baby cried. Damned disgraceful nonsense.'

'Yes, it was damned disgraceful nonsense,' said Wexford quietly, and then he said, 'The walls in those flats are very thin, aren't they? So thin that from one side you can hear a pin drop on the other.' He was silent and meditative for a moment. 'What was Leilie Somers's mother's maiden name?'

'*What?* said Burden. 'How on earth do you expect me to know a thing like that?'

'I just thought you might. I thought it might be an Irish name, you see. Because Leilie is probably short for Eileen, which is an Irish name. I expect she called herself Leilie when she was too young to pronounce her name properly.'

Burden said with an edge of impatience to his voice, 'Look, do I get to know what all this is leading up to?'

'Sure you do. The arrest of Paddy and Tony Jasper and Johnny Farrow. You can get down to Roland Road and see to it as soon as you like.'

'For God's sake, you know as well as I do we'll never make

it stick. We couldn't break Monkton and he'll alibi the lot of them.'

'That'll be OK,' said Wexford laconically. 'Trust me. Believe me, there is no alibi. And now, Polly, you and I will turn our attention to the matter of young Ginger and the Kingsmarkham Chalk Circle.'

Wexford left Polly sitting outside in the car. It was eight o'clock and still light. He rang the bell that had fetched Leilie down that afternoon, and when she didn't come he rang the other. Julie Lang appeared.

'She's upset. I've got her in with me having a cup of tea.'

'I'd like to see her, Mrs Lang, and I'll need to see her alone. I'll go and sit in my car for five minutes and then if she'll . . .'

Leilie Somers's voice from the top of the stairs cut off the end of his sentence. 'You can come up. I'm OK now.'

Wexford climbed the stairs towards her, Julie Lang following him. Leilie stood back to let him pass. She seemed smaller than ever, thinner, meeker, her hennaed hair showing a paler red at the roots, her face white and deeply sad. Julie Lang put her hand on her arm, squeezed it, and went off quickly into her own flat. Leilie put the key into the lock of her front door and opened the door and stood looking at the empty neat place, the passage, the open doors into the other rooms, now all made more melancholy by the encroaching twilight. Tears stood in her eyes and she turned her face so that Wexford should not see them fall.

'He's not worth it, Leilie,' said Wexford.

'I know *that*, I know what he's worth. But you won't get me being disloyal to him, Mr Wexford, I shan't say a word.'

'Let's go in and sit down.' He made his way to the table where it was lightest and sat down in the chair Tony Jasper had sat in. 'Where's the baby?'

'With my mum.'

'Rather much for someone who's just come out of hospital, isn't it?' Wexford looked at his watch. 'You're going to be late for work. What time is it you start? Eight-thirty?'

'Eight,' she said. 'I'm not going. I couldn't, not after what's happened to Paddy. Mr Wexford, you might as well go. I'm not going to say anything. If I was Paddy's wife you couldn't make me say anything, and I'm as good as his wife, I've been more to him than most wives'd have been.'

'I know that, Leilie,' said Wexford, 'I know all about that,' and his voice was so loaded with meaning that she stared at him with frightened eyes whose whites shone in the dusk. 'Leilie,' he said, 'when they drew the chalk circle and put the child in it the girl who had brought him up refused to pull him out because she knew she would hurt him. Rather than hurt him she preferred that someone else should have him.'

'I don't know what you're talking about,' she said.

'I think you do. It's not so different from Solomon's judgement of cutting the baby in half. The child's mother wouldn't have that happen, better let the other woman have him. You pleaded guilty in court to crimes against your first son you have never committed. It was Jasper who injured that child, and it was Jasper who got you to take the blame because he knew you would get a light sentence whereas he would get a heavy one. And afterwards you had the baby adopted – not because you didn't love him but because like the chalk circle woman you would rather lose him than have him hurt again. Isn't it true?'

She stared at him. Her head moved, a tiny affirmative bob. Wexford leaned across to the window and opened it. He waved his hand out of the window, withdrew it and closed the casement again. Leilie was crying, making no attempt to dry her tears.

'Were you brought up as a Catholic?' he said.

'I was baptized,' she said in a voice not much above a whisper. 'Mum's a Catholic. Her and Dad, they got married in Galway where Mum comes from, and Dad had to promise to bring the kids up Catholic.' A sob caught her throat. 'I haven't been to mass for years. Mr Wexford, please go away now and leave me alone. I just want to be left alone.'

He said, 'I'm sorry to hear you say that because I've got a visitor for you, and he'll certainly be staying the night.' He switched on lights, the living-room light, the light in the hall and one over the top of the door, and then he opened the door and Polly Davies walked in with young Ginger in her arms.

Leilie blinked at the light. She closed her eyes and lowered her head, and then she lifted it and opened her eyes and made a sort of bound for Polly, nearly knocking Wexford over. But she didn't snatch Ginger. She stood trembling, looking at Polly, her hands moving slowly forward until, with an extreme gentle tenderness, they closed over and caressed the baby's downy red-gold head.

'Matthew,' she said. 'Matthew.'

The baby lay in Leilie's lap. He had whimpered a little at first, but now he lay quiet and relaxed, gripping one of her fingers, and for the first time in their acquaintance Wexford saw him smile. It was a beautiful spontaneous smile of happiness at being home again with Mother.

'You're going to tell me all about it, aren't you, Leilie?' said Wexford.

She was transformed. He had never seen her so animated, so high-spirited. She was giggly with joy so that Matthew, sensing her mood, gurgled in response, and she hugged him again, calling him her lovely lovely sweetheart, her precious boy.

'Come on now, Leilie,' said Wexford, 'you've got him back without the least trouble to yourself which is more than you damn' well deserve. Now you can give an account of yourself.'

'I don't know where to start,' said Leilie, giggling.

'At the beginning, whenever that is.'

'Well, the beginning,' said Leilie, 'I reckon was when Patrick, my first boy, was adopted.' She had stopped laughing and a little of the old melancholy had come back into her face. 'That was four years ago. Paddy went off up north and after a bit he wrote and said would I join him, and I don't know why I said yes, I reckon I always do say yes to Paddy, and there didn't seem anything else, there didn't seem any future. It was all right with Paddy for a bit, and then a couple of years back he got this other girl. I sort of pretended I didn't know about it, I thought he'd get tired of her, but he didn't and I was lonely, I was so lonely. I didn't know a soul up there but Paddy, not like I could talk to, and he'd go away for weeks on end. I sort of took to going out with other fellas, anyone,

I didn't care, just for the company.' She paused, shifted Matthew on her knees. 'When I knew I was pregnant I told Paddy I wasn't having the baby up there, I was going home to Mum. But he said to stay and he wouldn't see the other girl, and I did stay till after Matthew was born, and then I knew he was carrying on again so I came back here and Mum got me this flat. I know what you're going to say, Mr Wexford!'

'I wasn't going to say a word.'

'You were thinking it. So what? It's true. I couldn't tell you who Matthew's father is, I don't know. It might be Paddy, it might be one of half a dozen.' Her expression had grown fierce. She almost glared at him. 'And I'm glad I don't know, I'm glad. It makes him more mine. I never went out with any other fella but Paddy till he drove me to it.'

'All right,' said Wexford, 'all right. So you lived here with Matthew and you had your job at the Andromeda and then Paddy wrote to say he was coming down, and on Saturday he did come. And you took Monday evening off work to be with him and exchanged your Tuesday turn with another girl – and so we come to Wednesday, yesterday.'

Leilie sighed. She didn't seen unhappy, only rueful. 'Paddy said he'd babysit. He said he'd asked Tony over and Johnny and a fella called Pip Monkton, and they'd be in all evening. I said he wasn't to bother, I could take Matthew next door into Julie's, and Paddy got mad at me and said Julie was an interfering bitch and didn't I trust him to look after his own child? Well, that was it, I didn't, I kept remembering what he'd done to Patrick, and that was because Patrick cried. Paddy used to go crazy when he cried, I used to think he'd kill him, and when I tried to stop him he nearly killed me. And, you see, Mr Wexford, Matthew'd got into this way of crying in the evenings. They said at the clinic some babies cry at night and some in the evenings and it's hard to know why, but they all grow out of it. I knew Matthew'd start screaming about eight and I thought, my God what'll Paddy do? He gets in a rage, he doesn't know what he's doing, and Tony wouldn't stop him, he's scared of him like they all are, Paddy's so big. Well, I got in a real state. Mum'd come out of hospital that morning, she'd had a major op, so I couldn't take him there and go back there myself and hide from Paddy, and I couldn't take him to work. I did once and they made a hell of a fuss. I just couldn't see any way out of it.

'Paddy went out about eleven. He never said where he was going and I didn't ask. Anyway, I went out too, carrying Matthew in the baby carrier, and I just walked about thinking. I reckon I must have walked miles, worrying about it and wondering what to do and imagining all sorts of things, you know how you do. I'd been feeding Matthew myself and I'm still giving him one feed a day, so I took him into a field and fed him under a hedge, and after that I walked a bit more.

'Well, I was coming back along the Stowerton Road. I knew I'd have to go home on account of Matthew was wet and he'd soon be hungry again, and then I saw this pram. I knew who it belonged to, I'd seen it there before and I'd seen this girl lift her baby out of it. I mean, I didn't know her name or anything but I'd talked to her once queueing for the check-out in the Tesco, and we'd got talking about our babies and she said hers never cried except sometimes for a feed in the night. She was such a good baby, they never got a peep out of her all day and evening. She was a big younger than Matthew but it was funny, they looked a bit alike and they'd got just the same colour hair.

'That was what gave me the idea, them having the same colour hair. I know I was mad, Mr Wexford, I know that now. I was crazy, but you don't know how scared of Paddy I was. I went over to that pram and I bent over it. I unhooked the cat net and took the other baby out and put Matthew in.'

Until now quite silent in her corner, Polly Davies gave a suppressed exclamation. Wexford drew in his breath, shaking his head.

'It's interesting,' he said, and his voice was frosty, 'how I supposed at first that whoever had taken Karen Bond wanted her and wished to be rid of her own child. Now it looks as if the reverse was true. It looks as if she didn't at all mind sacrificing Karen for her own child's safety.'

Leilie said passionately, 'That's not true!'

'No, perhaps it isn't, I believe you did have second thoughts. Go on.'

'I put Matthew in the pram. I knew he'd be all right, I knew no one'd hurt him, but it went to my heart when he started to cry.'

'Weren't you afraid someone would see you?' asked Polly.

'I wouldn't have cared if they had. Don't you see? I was past caring for any of that. If I'd been seen I wouldn't have had to go home, I'd have lost my job, but they wouldn't have taken Matthew from me, would they? No one saw me. Did you say her name was Karen? Well, I took Karen home and I fed her and bathed her. No one can say I didn't look after her like she was my own.'

'Except for delivering her into the hands of that ravening wolf, Paddy Jasper,' said Wexford unpleasantly.

She shivered a little but otherwise she took no notice. 'Paddy came in at six with Tony. The baby was in Matthew's cot by then. All you could see was its red hair like Matthew's. I remembered what that girl had said about her never crying in the evenings, and I thought, I prayed, don't cry tonight, don't cry because you're in a strange place.' Leilie lifted her head and began to speak more rapidly. 'I cooked egg and chips for the lot of them and I went out at half seven. I got back at a quarter past twelve and she was OK, she was fast asleep and she hadn't cried at all.'

Wexford said softly, 'Haven't you forgotten something, Leilie?'

Her eyes darted over him. He fancied she had grown a little paler. She picked up Matthew and held him closely against her. 'Well, the next day,' she said. 'Today. Paddy went off out early so I thought about getting the baby back. I thought of taking her to the priest. I knew about the priest, when he went out and when the lady cleaner came, I knew about it from Mum. So I got on the bus to Kingsmarkham and just by the bus stop's a shop where they'd put all their boxes out on the pavement for the dustmen. I took a box and put the baby in and left her on the doorstep of the priest's house. But I didn't know how I was going to get Matthew back, I thought I'd never get him back.

'And then you came. I said Matthew was in the bedroom and just then Julie's baby started crying and you thought it was Matthew. I couldn't help laughing, though I felt I was going to pieces, I was being torn apart. And that's all, that's everything, and now you can charge me with whatever it is I've done.'

'But you've forgotten something, Leilie.'

'I don't know what you mean,' she said.

'Of course you do. Why d'you think I had Paddy and Tony and Johhny Farrow arrested even though Pip Monkton had given them all a cast-iron alibi? How do you think I know Pip will break down and tell me that tale of his was all moonshine and tell me as well just where the contents of that safe are now? I had a little talk with the management of the Andromeda this afternoon, Leilie.'

She gave him a stony stare.

'You've got the sack, haven't you?' he said. 'Work out your notice till the end of next week or go now. They were bound to catch you out.'

'If you know all about it, Mr Wexford, why ask?'

'Because I want you to say yes.'

She whispered something to the baby, but the baby had fallen asleep.

'If you won't tell me, I shall tell you,' said Wexford, 'and if I get it wrong you can stop me. I'm going to tell you about those second thoughts you had, Leilie. You sent off to work like you said but you weren't easy in your mind. You kept thinking about that baby, that other baby, that good baby that never cried in the evenings. But maybe the reason she didn't cry was that she was usually in her own bed, safe and secure in her own home with her own mother, maybe it'd be different if she woke up to find herself in a strange place. So you started worrying. You ran around that glorified ladies' loo where you work, wiping the basins and filling the towel machines and taking your ten pence tips, but you were going off your head with worry about that other baby. You kept thinking of her crying and what that animal Paddy Jasper might do to her if she cried, punch her with his great fists perhaps or bash her head against the wall. And then you knew you hadn't done anything so clever after all in swapping Matthew for her, because you're a kind loving woman at heart, Leilie, though you're a fool, and you were as worried about her as you'd have been about him.'

'And you're a devil,' whispered Leilie, staring at him as if he had supernatural powers. 'How d'you know what I thought?'

'I just know,' said Wexford. 'I know what you thought and I know what you did. When it got to half-past nine you couldn't stand it any longer. You put on your coat and ran out to catch the nine-thirty-five bus and you were home, walking up those stairs, by five to ten. There were lights on in the flat. You let yourself in and went straight into the bedroom, and Karen was in there, safe and sound and fast asleep.'

Leilie smiled a little. A ghost of a smile of happy recollection crossed her face and was gone. 'I don't know how you know,' she said, 'but yes, she was OK and asleep, and oh God, the relief of it. I'd been picturing her lying there with blood on her and I don't know what.'

'So all you had to do then was explain to Paddy why you'd come home.'

'I told him I felt ill,' said Leilie carefully. 'I said I felt rotten and I'd got one of my migraines coming.'

'No, you didn't. He wasn't there.'

'What d'you mean, wasn't there? He was there! Him and Tony and Pip and Johnny, they were in here playing cards. I said to Paddy, I feel rotten, I had to come home. I'm going to have a lay-down, I said, and I went into the bedroom and laid down.'

'Leilie, when you came in the flat was empty. You know it was empty. You know Pip Monkton's lying and you know his story won't stand up for two seconds once you tell the truth that at *five to ten this flat was empty*. Listen to me, Leilie. Paddy will go away for quite a long time over this business. It'll be a chance for you and young Ginge -er, Matthew, to make a new life. You don't want him round you for ever, do you? Ruining your life, beating up your kids? Do you, Leilie?'

She lifted the baby in her arms. She walked the length of the room and half back again as if he were restless and needed soothing instead of peacefully asleep. In front of Wexford she stood still, looking at him, and he got to his feet.

'We'll come and fetch you in the morning, Leilie,' he said, 'and take you to the police station where I'll want you to make a statement. Maybe two statements. One about taking Karen and one about Paddy not being here when you came back last night.'

'I won't say a thing about that,' she said.

'It might be that we wouldn't proceed with any charge against you for taking Karen.'

'I don't care about that!'

He hated doing it. He knew he had to. 'A woman who knew what you knew about Paddy and who still exposed a child to him, someone else's child – how'll that sound in court, Leilie? When they know you're living with Paddy again? And when they hear your record?'

Her face had gone white and she clasped Matthew against her. 'They wouldn't take him away from me? They wouldn't make a what-d'you-call it?'

'A care order? They might.'

'Oh God, oh God. I promised myself I'd stick by Paddy all my life . . .'

'Romantic promises, Leilie, they haven't much to do with real life.' Wexford moved a little away from her. He went to the window. It was quite dark outside now. 'They told me at the Andromeda that you came back at half-past ten. You'd been away an hour and there had been complaints so they sacked you.'

She said feverishly, 'I did go back. I told Paddy I felt better, I . . .'

'All in the space of five minutes? Or ten at the most? You were quickly ill and well, Leilie. Shall I tell you why you went back, shall I tell you the only circumstances in which you'd have dared go back? You didn't want to lose your job but you were more afraid of what Paddy might do to the baby. If Paddy had been there the one thing you wouldn't have done is go back. Because he wasn't there you went back with a light heart. You believed he could only get in again when you were there to let him in. You didn't know then that he had a key, the key he had taken from Julie Lang.'

She spoke at last the word he had been waiting for. 'Yes.'

She nodded. 'Yes, it's true. If I'd known he had that key,' she said, and she shivered, 'I'd no more have gone and left that baby there than I'd have left it in the lion house at the zoo.'

'We'll be on our way,' he said. 'Come along, Constable Davies. See you in the morning, Leilie.'

Still holding Matthew, she came up to him just as he reached the door and laid a hand on his sleeve. 'I've been thinking about what you said, Mr Wexford,' she said, 'and I don't think I'd be able to pull anybody's baby, *any* baby, out of that circle.'

THE ADVENTURE OF THE COPPER BEECHES

Sir Arthur Conan Doyle

'To the man who loves art for its own sake,' remarked Sherlock Holmes, tossing aside the advertisement sheet of the *Daily Telegraph*, 'it is frequently in its least important and lowliest manifestations that the keenest pleasure is to be derived. It is pleasant to me to observe, Watson, that you have so far grasped this truth that in these little records of our cases which you have been good enough to draw up, and, I am bound to say, occasionally to embellish, you have given prominence not so much to the many *causes célèbres* and sensational trials in which I have figured but rather to those incidents which may have been trivial in themselves, but which have given room for those faculties of deduction and of logical synthesis which I have made my special province.'

'And yet,' said I, smiling, 'I cannot quite hold myself absolved from the charge of sensationalism which has been urged against my records.'

'You have erred, perhaps,' he observed, taking up a glowing cinder with the tongs and lighting with it the long cherry-wood pipe which was wont to replace his clay when he was in a disputatious rather than a meditative mood – 'you have erred perhaps in attempting to put colour and life into each of your statements instead of confining yourself to the task of placing upon record that severe reasoning from cause to effect which is really the only notable feature about the thing.'

'It seems to me that I have done you full justice in the matter,' I remarked with some coldness, for I was repelled by the egotism which I had more than once observed to be a strong factor in my friend's singular character.

'No, it is not selfishness or conceit,' said he, answering, as was his wont, my thoughts rather than my words. 'If I claim full justice for my art, it is because it is an impersonal thing – a thing beyond myself. Crime is common. Logic is rare. Therefore it is upon the logic rather than upon the crime that you should dwell. You have degraded what should have been a course of lectures into a series of tales.'

It was a cold morning of the early spring, and we sat after breakfast on either side of a cheery fire in the old room at Baker Street. A thick fog rolled down between the lines of dun-coloured houses, and the opposing windows loomed like dark, shapeless blurs through the heavy yellow wreaths. Our gas was lit and shone on the white cloth and glimmer of china and metal, for the table had not been cleared yet. Sherlock Holmes had been silent all the morning, dipping continuously into the advertisement columns of a succession of papers until at last, having apparently given up his search, he had emerged in no very sweet temper to lecture me upon my literary shortcomings.

'At the same time,' he remarked after a pause, during which he had sat puffing at his long pipe and gazing down into the fire, 'you can hardly be open to a charge of sensationalism, for out of these cases which you have been so kind as to interest yourself in, a fair proportion do not treat of crime, in its legal sense, at all. The small matter in which I endeavoured to help the King of Bohemia, the singular experience of Miss Mary Sutherland, the problem connected with the man with the twisted lip, and the incident of the noble bachelor, were all matters which are outside the pale of the law. But in avoiding the sensational, I fear that you may have bordered on the trivial.'

'The end may have been so,' I answered, 'but the methods I hold to have been novel and of interest.'

'Pshaw, my dear fellow, what do the public, the great unobservant public, who could hardly tell a weaver by his tooth or a compositor by his left thumb, care about the finer shades of analysis and deduction! But, indeed, if you are trivial, I cannot blame you, for the days of the great cases are past. Man, or at least criminal man, has lost all enterprise and originality. As to my own little practice, it seems to be degenerating into an agency for recovering lost lead pencils and giving advice to young ladies from boarding-schools. I think that I have touched bottom at last, however. This note I had this morning marks my zero-point, I fancy. Read it!' He tossed a crumpled letter across to me.

It was dated from Montague Place upon the preceding evening, and ran thus:

DEAR MR HOLMES:

I am very anxious to consult you as to whether I should or should not accept a situation which has been offered to me as governess. I shall call at half-past ten to-morrow if I do not inconvenience you.

Yours faithfully,
VIOLET HUNTER.

'Do you know the young lady?' I asked.

'Not I.'

'It is half-past ten now.'

'Yes, and I have no doubt that is her ring.'

'It may turn out to be of more interest than you think. You remember that the affair of the blue carbuncle, which appeared to be a mere whim at first, developed into a serious investigation. It may be so in this case, also.'

'Well, let us hope so. But our doubts will very soon be solved, for here, unless I am much mistaken, is the person in question.'

As he spoke the door opened and a young lady entered the room. She was plainly but neatly dressed, with a bright, quick face, freckled like a plover's egg, and with the brisk manner of a woman who has had her own way to make in the world.

'You will excuse my troubling you, I am sure,' said she, as my companion rose to greet her, 'but I have had a very strange experience, and as I have no parents or relations of any sort from whom I could ask advice, I thought that perhaps you would be kind enough to tell me what I should do.'

'Pray take a seat, Miss Hunter. I shall be happy to do anything that I can to serve you.'

I could see that Holmes was favourably impressed by the manner and speech of his new client. He looked her over in his searching fashion, and then composed himself, with his lids drooping and his finger-tips together, to listen to her story.

'I have been a governess for five years,' said she, 'in the family of Colonel Spence Munro, but two months ago the colonel received an appointment at Halifax, in Nova Scotia, and took his children over to America with him, so that I found myself without a situation. I advertised, and I answered advertisements, but without success. At last the little money which I had saved began to run short, and I was at my wit's end as to what I should do.

'There is a well-known agency for governesses in the West End called Westaway's, and there I used to call about once a week in order to see whether anything had turned up which might suit me. Westaway was the name of the founder of the business, but it is really managed by Miss Stoper. She sits in her own little office, and the ladies who are seeking employment wait in an anteroom, and are then shown in one by one, when she consults her ledgers and sees whether she has anything which would suit them.

'Well, when I called last week I was shown into the little office as usual, but I found that Miss Stoper was not alone. A prodigiously stout man with a very smiling face and a great heavy chin which rolled down in fold upon fold over his throat sat at her elbow with a pair of glasses on his nose, looking very earnestly at the ladies who entered. As I came in he gave quite a jump in his chair and turned quickly to Miss Stoper.

' "That will do," he said; "I could not ask for anything better. Capital! capital!" He seemed quite enthusiastic and rubbed his hands together in the most genial fashion. He was such a comfortable-looking man that it was quite a pleasure to look at him.

' "You are looking for a situation, miss?" he asked.

' "Yes, sir."

' "As governess?"

' "Yes, sir."

' "And what salary do you ask?"

' "I had £4 a month in my last place with Colonel Spence Munro."

"Oh, tut, tut! sweating – rank sweating!" he cried, throwing his fat hands out into the air like a man who is in a boiling passion. "How could anyone offer so pitiful a sum to a lady with such attractions and accomplishments?"

' "My accomplishments, sir, may be less than you imagine," said I. "A little French, a little German, music, and drawing–"

' "Tut, tut!" he cried. "This is all quite beside the question. The point is, have you or have you not the bearing and deportment of a lady? There it is in a nutshell. If you have not, you are not fitted for the rearing of a child who may some day play a considerable part in the history of the country. But if you have, why, then, how could any gentleman ask you to condescend to accept anything under the three figures? Your salary with me, madam, would commence at £100 a year."

'You may imagine, Mr Holmes, that to me, destitute as I was, such an offer seemed almost too good to be true. The gentleman, however, seeing perhaps the look of incredulity upon my face, opened a pocket-book and took out a note.

' "It is also my custom," said he, smiling in the most pleasant fashion until his eyes were just two little shining slits amid the white creases of his face, "to advance to my young ladies half their salary beforehand, so that they may meet any little expenses of their journey and their wardrobe."

'It seemed to me that I had never met so fascinating and so thoughtful a man. As I was already in debt to my tradesmen, the advance was a great convenience, and yet there was something unnatural about the whole transaction which made me wish to know a little more before I quite committed myself.

' "May I ask where you live, sir?" said I.

' "Hampshire. Charming rural place. The Copper Beeches, five miles on the far side of Winchester. It is the most lovely country, my dear young lady, and the dearest old country-house."

' "And my duties, sir? I should be glad to know what they would be."

' "One child – one dear little romper just six years old. Oh, if you could see him killing cockroaches with a slipper! Smack! smack! smack! Three gone before you could wink!" He leaned back in his chair and laughed his eyes into his head again.

'I was a little startled at the nature of the child's amusement, but the father's laughter made me think that perhaps he was joking.

' "My sole duties, then," I asked, "are to take charge of a single child?"

' "No, no, not the sole, not the sole, my dear young lady," he cried. "Your duty would be, as I am sure your good sense would suggest, to obey any little commands my wife might give, provided always that they were such commands as a lady might with propriety obey. You see no difficulty, heh?"

' "I should be happy to make myself useful."

' "Quite so. In dress now, for example. We are faddy people, you know – faddy but kind-hearted. If you were asked to wear any dress which we might give you, you would not object to our little whim. Heh?"

' "No," said I, considerably astonished at his words.

' "Or to sit here, or sit there, that would not be offensive to you?"

' "Oh, no."

' "Or to cut your hair quite short before you come to us?"

'I could hardly believe my ears. As you may observe, Mr Holmes, my hair is somewhat luxuriant, and of a rather peculiar tint of chestnut. It has been considered artistic. I could not dream of sacrificing it in this offhand fashion.

' "I am afraid that that is quite impossible," said I. He had been watching me eagerly out of his small eyes, and I could see a shadow pass over his face as I spoke.

' "I am afraid that it is quite essential," said he. "It is a little fancy of my wife's, and ladies' fancies, you know, madam, ladies' fancies must be consulted. And so you won't cut your hair?"

' "No, sir, I really could not," I answered firmly.

' "Ah, very well; then that quite settles the matter. It is a pity, because in other respects you would really have done very nicely. In that case, Miss Stoper, I had best inspect a few more of your young ladies."

'The manageress had sat all this while busy with her papers without a word to either of us, but she glanced at me now with so much annoyance upon her face that I could not help suspecting that she had lost a handsome commission through my refusal.

' "Do you desire your name to be kept upon the books?" she asked.

' "If you please, Miss Stoper."

' "Well, really, it seems rather useless, since you refuse the most excellent offers in this fashion," said she sharply. "You can hardly expect us to exert ourselves to find another such opening for you. Good-day to you, Miss Hunter." She struck a gong upon the table, and I was shown out by the page.

'Well, Mr Holmes, when I got back to my lodgings and found little enough in the cupboard, and two or three bills upon the table, I began to ask myself whether I had not done a very foolish thing. After all, if these people had strange fads and expected obedience on the most extraordinary matters, they were at least ready to pay for their eccentricity. Very few governesses in England are getting £100 a year. Besides, what use was my hair to me? Many people are improved by wearing it short, and perhaps I should be among the number. Next day I was inclined to think that I had made a mistake, and by the day after I was sure of it. I had almost overcome my pride so far as to go back to the agency and inquire whether the place was still open when I received this letter from the gentleman himself. I have it here, and I will read it to you:

'The Copper Beeches, near Winchester.

'Dear Miss Hunter:

'Miss Stoper has very kindly given me your address, and I write from here to ask you whether you have reconsidered your decision. My wife is very anxious that you should come, for she has been much attracted by my description of you. We are willing to give £30 a quarter, or £120 a year, so as to recompense you for any little inconvenience which our fads may cause you. They are not very exacting, after all. My wife is fond of a particular shade of electric blue, and would like you to wear such a dress indoors in the morning. You need not, however, go the the expense of purchasing one, as we have one belonging to my dear daughter

Alice (now in Philadelphia), which would, I should think, fit you very well. Then, as to sitting here or there, or amusing yourself in any manner indicated, that need cause you no inconvenience. As regards your hair, it is no doubt a pity, especially as I could not help remarking its beauty during our short interview, but I am afraid that I must remain firm upon this point, and I only hope that the increased salary may recompense you for the loss. Your duties, as far as the child is concerned, are very light. Now do try to come, and I shall meet you with the dog-cart at Winchester. Let me know your train.

'Yours faithfully,
'JEPHRO RUCASTLE.

'That is the letter which I have just received, Mr Holmes, and my mind is made up that I will accept it. I thought, however, that before taking the final step I should like to submit the whole matter to your consideration.'

'Well, Miss Hunter, if your mind is made up, that settles the question,' said Holmes, smiling.

'But you would not advise me to refuse?'

'I confess that it is not the situation which I should like to see a sister of mine apply for.'

'What is the meaning of it all, Mr Holmes?'

'Ah, I have no data. I cannot tell. Perhaps you have yourself formed some opinion?'

'Well, there seems to me to be only one possible solution. Mr Rucastle seemed to be a very kind, good-natured man. Is it not possible that his wife is a lunatic, that he desires to keep the matter quiet for fear she should be taken to an asylum, and that he humours her fancies in every way in order to prevent an outbreak?'

'That is a possible solution – in fact, as matters stand, it is the most probable one. But in any case it does not seem to be a nice household for a young lady.'

'But the money, Mr Holmes, the money!'

'Well, yes, of course the pay is good – too good. That is what makes me uneasy. Why should they give you £120 a year, when they could have their pick for £40? There must be some strong reason behind.'

'I thought that if I told you the circumstances you would

understand afterwards if I wanted your help. I should feel so much stronger if I felt that you were at the back of me.'

'Oh, you may carry that feeling away with you. I assure you that your little problem promises to be the most interesting which has come my way for some months. There is something distinctly novel about some of the features. If you should find yourself in doubt or in danger–'

'Danger! What danger do you foresee?'

Holmes shook his head gravely. 'It would cease to be a danger if we could define it,' said he. 'But at any time, day or night, a telegram would bring me down to your help.'

'That is enough.' She rose briskly from her chair with the anxiety all swept from her face. 'I shall go down to Hampshire quite easy in my mind now. I shall write to Mr Rucastle at once, sacrifice my poor hair tonight, and start for Winchester tomorrow.' With a few grateful words to Holmes she bade us both goodnight and bustled off upon her way.

'At least,' said I as we heard her quick, firm steps descending the stairs, 'she seems to be a young lady who is very well able to take care of herself.'

'And she would need to be,' said Holmes gravely. 'I am much mistaken if we do not hear from her before many days are past.'

It was not very long before my friend's prediction was fulfilled. A fortnight went by, during which I frequently found my thoughts turning in her direction and wondering what strange side-alley of human experience this lonely woman had strayed into. The unusual salary, the curious conditions, the light duties, all pointed to something abnormal, though whether a fad or a plot, or whether the man were a philanthropist or a villain, it was quite beyond my powers to determine. As to Holmes, I observed that he sat frequently for half an hour on end, with knitted brows and an abstracted air, but he swept the matter away with a wave of his hand when I mentioned it. 'Data! data! data!' he cried impatiently. 'I can't make bricks without clay.' And yet he would always wind up by muttering that no sister of his should ever have accepted such a situation.

The telegram which we eventually received came late one

night just as I was thinking of turning in and Holmes was settling down to one of those all-night chemical researches which he frequently indulged in, when I would leave him stooping over a retort and a test-tube at night and find him in the same position when I came down to breakfast in the morning. He opened the yellow envelope, and then, glancing at the message, threw it across to me.

'Just look up the trains in Bradshaw,' said he, and turned back to his chemical studies.

The summons was a brief and urgent one.

> Please be at the Black Swan Hotel at Winchester at midday tomorrow [it said]. Do come! I am at my wit's end.
>
> HUNTER.

'Will you come with me?' asked Holmes, glancing up.

'I should wish to.'

'Just look it up, then.'

'There is a train at half-past nine,' said I, glancing over my Bradshaw. 'It is due at Winchester at 11:30.'

'That will do very nicely. Then perhaps I had better postpone my analysis of the acetones, as we may need to be at our best in the morning.'

By eleven o'clock the next day we were well upon our way to the old English capital. Holmes had been buried in the morning papers all the way down, but after we had passed the Hampshire border he threw them down and began to admire the scenery. It was an ideal spring day, a light blue sky, flecked with little fleecy white clouds drifting across from west to east. The sun was shining very brightly, and yet there was an exhilarating nip in the air, which set an edge to a man's energy. All over the countryside, away to the rolling hills around Aldershot, the little red and grey roofs of the farm-steadings peeped out from amid the light green of the new foliage.

'Are they not fresh and beautiful?' I cried with all the enthusiasm of a man fresh from the fogs of Baker Street.

But Holmes shook his head gravely.

'Do you know, Watson,' said he, 'that it is one of the curses of a mind with a turn like mine that I must look at everything with reference to my own special subject. You look at these scattered houses, and you are impressed by their beauty. I look at them, and the only thought which comes to me is a feeling of their isolation and of the impunity with which crime may be committed there.'

'Good heavens!' I cried. 'Who would associate crime with these dear old homesteads?'

'They always fill me with a certain horror. It is my belief, Watson, founded upon my experience, that the lowest and vilest alleys in London do not present a more dreadful record of sin than does the smiling and beautiful countryside.'

'You horrify me!'

'But the reason is very obvious. The pressure of public opinion can do in the town what the law cannot accomplish. There is no lane so vile that the scream of a tortured child, or the thud of a drunkard's blow, does not beget sympathy and indignation among the neighbours, and then the whole machinery of justice is ever so close that a word of complaint can set it going, and there is but a step between the crime and the dock. But look at these lonely houses, each in its own fields, filled for the most part with poor ignorant folk who know little of the law. Think of the deeds of hellish cruelty, the hidden wickedness which may go on, year in, year out, in such places, and none the wiser. Had this lady who appeals to us for help gone to live in Winchester, I should never have had a fear for her. It is the five miles of country which makes the danger. Still, it is clear that she is not personally threatened.'

'No. If she can come to Winchester to meet us she can get away.'

'Quite so. She has her freedom.'

'What *can* be the matter, then? Can you suggest no explanation?'

'I have devised seven separate explanations, each of which would cover the facts as far as we know them. But which of these is correct can only be determined by the fresh information which we shall no doubt find waiting for us. Well, there is the tower of the cathedral, and we shall soon learn all that Miss Hunter has to tell.'

The Black Swan is an inn of repute in the High Street, at

no distance from the station, and there we found the young lady waiting for us. She had engaged a sitting-room, and our lunch awaited us upon the table.

'I am so delighted that you have come,' she said earnestly. 'It is so very kind of you both; but indeed I do not know what I should do. Your advice will be altogether invaluable to me.'

'Pray tell us what has happened to you.'

'I will do so, and I must be quick, for I have promised Mr Rucastle to be back before three. I got his leave to come into town this morning, though he little knew for what purpose.'

'Let us have everything in its due order.' Holmes thrust his long thin legs out towards the fire and composed himself to listen.

'In the first place, I may say that I have met, on the whole, with no actual ill-treatment from Mr and Mrs Rucastle. It is only fair to them to say that. But I cannot understand them, and I am not easy in my mind about them.'

'What can you not understand?'

'Their reasons for their conduct. But you shall have it all just as it occurred. When I came down, Mr Rucastle met me here and drove me in his dog-cart to the Copper Beeches. It is, as he said, beautifully situated, but it is not beautiful in itself, for it is a large square block of a house, whitewashed, but all stained and streaked with damp and bad weather. There are grounds round it, woods on three sides, and on the fourth a field which slopes down to the Southampton highroad, which curves past about a hundred yards from the front door. This ground in front belongs to the house, but the woods all round are part of Lord Southerton's preserves. A clump of copper beeches immediately in front of the hall door has given its name to the place.

'I was driven over by my employer, who was as amiable as ever, and was introduced by him that evening to his wife and the child. There was no truth, Mr Holmes, in the conjecture which seemed to us to be probable in your rooms at Baker Street. Mrs Rucastle is not mad. I found her to be a silent, pale-faced woman, much younger than her husband, not more than thirty, I should think, while he can hardly be less than forty-five. From their conversation I have gathered that they have been married about seven years, that he was a widower, and that his only child by the first wife was the daughter who has gone to Philadelphia. Mr Rucastle told me in private that the reason why she had left them was that she had an unreasoning aversion to her stepmother. As the daughter could not have been less than twenty, I can quite imagine that her position must have been uncomfortable with her father's young wife.

'Mrs Rucastle seemed to me to be colourless in mind as well as in feature. She impressed me neither favourably nor the reverse. She was a nonentity. It was easy to see that she was passionately devoted both to her husband and to her little son. Her light grey eyes wandered continually from one to the other, noting every little want and forestalling it if possible. He was kind to her also in his bluff, boisterous fashion, and on the whole they seemed to be a happy couple. And yet she had some secret sorrow, this woman. She would often be lost in deep thought, with the saddest look upon her face. More than once I have surprised her in tears. I have thought sometimes that it was the disposition of her child which weighed upon her mind, for I have never met so utterly spoiled and so ill-natured a little creature. He is small for his age, with a head which is quite disproportionately large. His whole life appears to be spent in an alternation between savage fits of passion and gloomy intervals of sulking. Giving pain to any creature weaker than himself seems to be his one idea of amusement, and he shows quite remarkable talent in planning the capture of mice, little birds, and insects. But I would rather not talk about the creature, Mr Holmes, and, indeed, he has little to do with my story.'

'I am glad of all details,' remarked my friend, 'whether they seem to you to be relevant or not.'

'I shall try not to miss anything of importance. The one unpleasant thing about the house, which struck me at once, was the appearance and conduct of the servants. There are only two, a man and his wife. Toller, for that is his name, is a rough, uncouth man, with grizzled hair and whiskers, and a perpetual smell of drink. Twice since I have been with them he has been quite drunk, and yet Mr Rucastle seemed to take no notice of it. His wife is a very tall and strong woman with a sour face, as silent as Mrs Rucastle and much less amiable. They are a most unpleasant couple, but fortunately I spend most of my time in the nursery and my own room, which are next to each other in one corner of the building.

'For two days after my arrival at the Copper Beeches my life was very quiet; on the third, Mrs Rucastle came down just after breakfast and whispered something to her husband.

' "Oh, yes," said he, turning to me, "we are very much obliged to you, Miss Hunter, for falling in with our whims so far as to cut your hair. I assure you that it has not detracted in the tiniest iota from your appearance. We shall now see how the electric-blue dress will become you. You will find it laid out upon the bed in your room, and if you would be so good as to put it on we should both be extremely obliged."

'The dress which I found waiting for me was of a peculiar shade of blue. It was of excellent material, a sort of beige, but it bore unmistakable signs of having been worn before. It could not have been a better fit if I had been measured for it. Both Mr and Mrs Rucastle expressed a delight at the look of it, which seemed quite exaggerated in its vehemence. They were waiting for me in the drawing-room, which is a very large room, stretching along the entire front of the house, with three long windows reaching down to the floor. A chair had been placed close to the central window, with its back turned towards it. In this I was asked to sit, and then Mr Rucastle, walking up and down on the other side of the room, began to tell me a series of the funniest stories that I have ever listened to. You cannot imagine how comical he was, and I laughed until I was quite weary. Mrs Rucastle, however, who has evidently no sense of humour, never so much as smiled, but sat with her hands in her lap, and a sad, anxious look upon her face. After an hour or so, Mr Rucastle suddenly remarked that it was time to commence the duties of the day, and that I might change my dress and go to little Edward in the nursery.

'Two days later this same performance was gone through under exactly similar circumstances. Again I changed my dress, again I sat in the window, and again I laughed very heartily at the funny stories of which my employer had an immense repertoire, and which he told inimitably. Then he handed me a yellow-backed novel, and moving my chair a little sideways, that my own shadow might not fall upon the page, he begged me to read aloud to him. I read for about ten minutes, beginning in the heart of a chapter, and then suddenly, in the middle of a sentence, he ordered me to cease and to change my dress.

'You can easily imagine, Mr Holmes, how curious I became as to what the meaning of this extraordinary performance could possibly be. They were always very careful, I observed, to turn my face away from the window, so that I became consumed with the desire to see what was going on behind my back. At first it seemed to be impossible, but I soon devised a means. My hand-mirror had been broken, so a happy thought seized me, and I concealed a piece of the glass in my handkerchief. On the next occasion, in the midst of my laughter, I put my handkerchief up to my eyes, and was able with a little management to see all that there was behind me. I confess that I was disappointed. There was nothing. At least that was my first impression. At the second glance, however, I perceived that there was a man standing in the Southampton Road, a small bearded man in a grey suit, who seemed to be looking in my direction. The road is an important highway, and there are usually people there. This man, however, was leaning against the railings which bordered our field and was looking earnestly up. I lowered my handkerchief and glanced at Mrs Rucastle to find her eyes fixed upon me with a most searching gaze. She said nothing, but I am convinced that she had divined that I had a mirror in my hand and had seen what was behind me. She rose at once.

' "Jephro," said she, "there is an impertinent fellow upon the road there who stares up at Miss Hunter."

' "No friend of yours, Miss Hunter?" he asked.

' "No, I know no one in these parts."

' "Dear me! How very impertinent! Kindly turn round and motion to him to go away."

' "Surely it would be better to take no notice."

' "No, no, we should have him loitering here always. Kindly turn round and wave him away like that."

'I did as I was told, and at the same instant Mrs Rucastle

drew down the blind. That was a week ago, and from that time I have not sat again in the window, nor have I worn the blue dress, nor seen the man in the road.'

'Pray continue,' said Holmes. 'Your narrative promises to be a most interesting one.'

'You will find it rather disconnected, I fear, and there may prove to be little relation between the different incidents of which I speak. On the very first day that I was at the Copper Beeches, Mr Rucastle took me to a small outhouse which stands near the kitchen door. As we approached it I heard the sharp rattling of a chain, and the sound as of a large animal moving about.

' "Look in here!" said Mr Rucastle, showing me a slit between two planks. "Is he not a beauty?"

'I looked through and was conscious of two glowing eyes, and of a vague figure huddled up in the darkness.

' "Don't be frightened," said my employer, laughing at the start which I had given. "It's only Carlo, my mastiff. I call him mine, but really old Toller, my groom, is the only man who can do anything with him. We feed him once a day, and not too much then, so that he is always as keen as mustard. Toller lets him loose every night, and God help the trespasser whom he lays his fangs upon. For goodness' sake don't you ever on any pretext set your foot over the threshold at night, for it's as much as your life is worth."

'The warning was no idle one, for two nights later I happened to look out of my bedroom window about two o'clock in the morning. It was a beautiful moonlight night, and the lawn in front of the house was silvered over and almost as bright as day. I was standing, rapt in the peaceful beauty of the scene, when I was aware that something was moving under the shadow of the copper beeches. As it emerged into the moonshine I saw what it was. It was a giant dog, as large as a calf, tawny tinted, with hanging jowl, black muzzle, and huge projecting bones. It walked slowly across the lawn and vanished into the shadow upon the other side. That dreadful sentinel sent a chill to my heart which I do not think that any burglar could have done.

'And now I have a very strange experience to tell you. I

had, as you know, cut off my hair in London, and I had placed it in a great coil at the bottom of my trunk. One evening, after the child was in bed, I began to amuse myself by examining the furniture of my room and by rearranging my own little things. There was an old chest of drawers in the room, the two upper ones empty and open, the lower one locked. I had filled the first two with my linen, and as I had still much to pack away I was naturally annoyed at not having the use of the third drawer. It struck me that it might have been fastened by a mere oversight, so I took out my bunch of keys and tried to open it. The very first key fitted to perfection, and I drew the drawer open. There was only one thing in it, but I am sure that you would never guess what it was. It was my coil of hair.

'I took it up and examined it. It was of the same peculiar tint, and the same thickness. But then the impossibility of the thing obtruded itself upon me. How *could* my hair have been locked in the drawer? With trembling hands I undid my trunk, turned out the contents, and drew from the bottom my own hair. I laid the two tresses together, and I assure you that they were identical. Was it not extraordinary? Puzzle as I would, I could make nothing at all of what it meant. I returned the strange hair to the drawer, and I said nothing of the matter to the Rucastles as I felt that I had put myself in the wrong by opening a drawer which they had locked.

'I am naturally observant, as you may have remarked, Mr Holmes, and I soon had a pretty good plan of the whole house in my head. There was one wing, however, which appeared not to be inhabited at all. A door which faced that which led into the quarters of the Tollers opened into this suite, but it was invariably locked. One day, however, as I ascended the stair, I met Mr Rucastle coming out through this door, his keys in his hand, and a look on his face which made him a very different person to the round, jovial man to whom I was accustomed. His cheeks were red, his brow was all crinkled with anger, and the veins stood out at his temples with passion. He locked the door and hurried past me without a word or a look.

'This aroused my curiosity; so when I went out for a walk

in the grounds with my charge, I strolled round to the side from which I could see the windows of this part of the house. There were four of them in a row, three of which were simply dirty, while the fourth was shuttered up. They were evidently all deserted. As I strolled up and down, glancing at them occasionally, Mr Rucastle came out to me, looking as merry and jovial as ever.

' "Ah!" said he, "you must not think me rude if I passed you without a word, my dear young lady. I was preoccupied with business matters."

'I assured him that I was not offended. "By the way," said I, "you seem to have quite a suite of spare rooms up there, and one of them has the shutters up."

'He looked surprised and, as it seemed to me, a little startled at my remark.

' "Photography is one of my hobbies," said he. "I have made my dark room up there. But, dear me! what an observant young lady we have come upon. Who would have believed it? Who would have ever believed it?" He spoke in a jesting tone, but there was no jest in his eyes as he looked at me. I read suspicion there and annoyance, but no jest.

'Well, Mr Holmes, from the moment that I understood that there was something about that suite of rooms which I was not to know, I was all on fire to go over them. It was not mere curiosity though I have my share of that. It was more a feeling of duty – a feeling that some good might come from my penetrating to this place. They talk of woman's instinct; perhaps it was woman's instinct which gave me that feeling. At any rate, it was there, and I was keenly on the lookout for any chance to pass the forbidden door.

'It was only yesterday that the chance came. I may tell you that, besides Mr Rucastle, both Toller and his wife find something to do in these deserted rooms, and I once saw him carrying a large black linen bag with him through the door. Recently he has been drinking hard, and yesterday evening he was very drunk; and when I came upstairs there was the key in the door. I have no doubt at all that he had left it there. Mr and Mrs Rucastle were both downstairs, and the child was with them, so that I had an admirable opportunity. I turned the key gently in the lock, opened the door, and slipped through.

'There was a little passage in front of me, unpapered and uncarpeted, which turned at a right angle at the farther end. Round this corner were three doors in a line, the first and third of which were open. They each led into an empty room, dusty and cheerless, with two windows in the one and one in the other, so thick with dirt that the evening light glimmered dimly through them. The centre door was closed, and across the outside of it had been fastened one of the broad bars of an iron bed, padlocked at one end to a ring in the wall, and fastened at the other with stout cord. The door itself was locked as well, and the key was not there. This barricaded door corresponded clearly with the shuttered window outside, and yet I could see by the glimmer from beneath it that the room was not in darkness. Evidently there was a skylight which let in light from above. As I stood in the passage gazing at the sinister door and wondering what secret it might veil, I suddenly heard the sound of steps within the room and saw a shadow pass backward and forward against the little slit of dim light which shone out from under the door. A mad, unreasoning terror rose up in me at the sight, Mr Holmes. My overstrung nerves failed me suddenly, and I turned and ran – ran as though some dreadful hand were behind me clutching at the skirt of my dress. I rushed down the passage, through the door, and straight into the arms of Mr Rucastle, who was waiting outside.

' "So," said he, smiling, "it was you, then. I thought that it must be when I saw the door open."

' "Oh, I am so frightened!" I panted.

' "My dear young lady! my dear young lady!" – you cannot think how caressing and soothing his manner was – "and what has frightened you, my dear young lady?"

'But his voice was just a little too coaxing. He overdid it. I was keenly on my guard against him.

' "I was foolish enough to go into the empty wing," I answered. "But it is so lonely and eerie in this dim light that I was frightened and ran out again. Oh, it is so dreadfully still in there!"

' "Only that?" said he, looking at me keenly.

' "Why, what did you think?" I asked.

' "Why do you think that I lock this door?"

' "I am sure that I do not know."

' "It is to keep people out who have no business there. Do you see?" He was still smiling in the most amiable manner.

' "I am sure if I had known–"

' "Well, then, you know now. And if you ever put your foot over that threshold again" – here in an instant the smile hardened into a grin of rage, and he glared down at me with the face of a demon – "I'll throw you to the mastiff."

'I was so terrified that I do not know what I did. I suppose that I must have rushed past him into my room. I remember nothing until I found myself lying on my bed trembling all over. Then I thought of you, Mr Holmes. I could not live there longer without some advice. I was frightened of the house, of the man, of the woman, of the servants, even of the child. They were all horrible to me. If I could only bring you down all would be well. Of course I might have fled from the house, but my curiosity was almost as strong as my fears. My mind was soon made up. I would send you a wire. I put on my hat and cloak, went down to the office, which is about half a mile from the house, and then returned, feeling very much easier. A horrible doubt came into my mind as I approached the door lest the dog might be loose, but I remembered that Toller had drunk himself into a state of insensibility that evening, and I knew that he was the only one in the household who had any influence with the savage creature, or who would venture to set him free. I slipped in in safety and lay awake half the night in my joy at the thought of seeing you. I had no difficulty in getting leave to come into Winchester this morning, but I must be back before three o'clock, for Mr and Mrs Rucastle are going on a visit, and will be away all the evening, so that I must look after the child. Now I have told you all my adventures, Mr Holmes, and I should be very glad if you could tell me what it all means, and, above all, what I should do.'

Holmes and I had listened spellbound to this extraordinary story. My friend rose now and paced up and down the room, his hands in his pockets, and an expression of the most profound gravity upon his face.

'Is Toller still drunk?' he asked.

'Yes. I heard his wife tell Mrs Rucastle that she could do nothing with him.'

'That is well. And the Rucastles go out tonight?'

'Yes.'

'Is there a cellar with a good strong lock?'

'Yes, the wine-cellar.'

'You seem to me to have acted all through this matter like a very brave and sensible girl, Miss Hunter. Do you think that you could perform one more feat? I should not ask it of you if I did not think you a quite exceptional woman.'

'I will try. What is it?'

'We shall be at the Copper Beeches by seven o'clock, my friend and I. The Rucastles will be gone by that time, and Toller will, we hope, be incapable. There only remains Mrs Toller, who might give the alarm. If you could send her into the cellar on some errand, and then turn the key upon her, you would facilitate matters immensely.'

'I will do it.'

'Excellent! We shall then look thoroughly into the affair. Of course there is only one feasible explanation. You have been brought there to personate someone, and the real person is imprisoned in this chamber. That is obvious. As to who this prisoner is, I have no doubt that it is the daughter, Miss Alice Rucastle, if I remember right, who was said to have gone to America. You were chosen, doubtless, as resembling her in height, figure, and the colour of your hair. Hers had been cut off, very possibly in some illness through which she has passed, and so, of course, yours had to be sacrificed also. By a curious chance you came upon her tresses. The man in the road was undoubtedly some friend of hers – possibly her fiancé – and no doubt, as you wore the girl's dress and were so like her, he was convinced from your laughter, whenever he saw you, and afterwards from your gesture, that Miss Rucastle was perfectly happy, and that she no longer desired his attentions. The dog is let loose at night to prevent him from endeavouring to communicate with her. So much is fairly clear. The most serious point in the case is the disposition of the child.'

'What on earth has that to do with it?' I ejaculated.

'My dear Watson, you as a medical man are continually gaining light as to the tendencies of a child by the study of the parents. Don't you see that the converse is equally valid. I have frequently gained my first real insight into the character of parents by studying their children. This child's disposition is abnormally cruel, merely for cruelty's sake, and whether he derives this from his smiling father, as I should suspect, or from his mother, it bodes evil for the poor girl who is in their power.'

'I am sure that you are right, Mr Holmes,' cried our client. 'A thousand things come back to me which make me certain that you have hit it. Oh, let us lose not an instant in bringing help to this poor creature.'

'We must be circumspect, for we are dealing with a very cunning man. We can do nothing until seven o'clock. At that hour we shall be with you, and it will not be long before we solve the mystery.'

We were as good as our word, for it was just seven when we reached the Copper Beeches, having put up our trap at a wayside public-house. The group of trees, with their dark leaves shining like burnished metal in the light of the setting sun, were sufficient to mark the house even had Miss Hunter not been standing smiling on the door-step.

'Have you managed it?' asked Holmes.

A loud thudding noise came from somewhere downstairs. 'That is Mrs Toller in the cellar,' said she. 'Her husband lies snoring on the kitchen rug. Here are his keys, which are the duplicates of Mr Rucastle's.'

'You have done well indeed!' cried Holmes with enthusiasm. 'Now lead the way, and we shall soon see the end of this black business.'

We passed up the stair, unlocked the door, followed on down a passage, and found ourselves in front of the barricade which Miss Hunter had described. Holmes cut the cord and removed the transverse bar. Then he tried the various keys in the lock, but without success. No sound came from within, and at the silence Holmes's face clouded over.

'I trust that we are not too late,' said he. 'I think, Miss Hunter, that we had better go in without you. Now, Watson, put your shoulder to it, and we shall see whether we cannot make our way in.'

It was an old rickety door and gave at once before our united strength. Together we rushed into the room. It was empty. There was no furniture save a little pallet bed, a small table, and a basketful of linen. The skylight above was open, and the prisoner gone.

'There has been some villainy here,' said Holmes, 'this beauty has guessed Miss Hunter's intentions and has carried his victim off.'

'But how?'

'Through the skylight. We shall soon see how he managed it.' He swung himself up onto the roof. 'Ah, yes,' he cried, 'here's the end of a long light ladder against the eaves. That is how he did it.'

'But it is impossible,' said Miss Hunter; 'the ladder was not there when the Rucastles went away.'

'He has come back and done it. I tell you that he is a clever and dangerous man. I should not be very much surprised if this were he whose step I hear now upon the stair. I think, Watson, that it would be as well for you to have your pistol ready.'

The words were hardly out of his mouth before a man appeared at the door of the room, a very fat and burly man, with a heavy stick in his hand. Miss Hunter screamed and shrunk against the wall at the sight of him, but Sherlock Holmes sprang forward and confronted him.

'You villain!' said he, 'where's your daughter?'

The fat man cast his eyes round, and then up at the open skylight.

'It is for me to ask you that,' he shrieked, 'you thieves! Spies and thieves! I have caught you, have I? You are in my power. I'll serve you!' He turned and clattered down the stairs as hard as he could go.

'He's gone for the dog!' cried Miss Hunter.

'I have my revolver,' said I.

'Better close the front door,' cried Holmes, and we all rushed down the stairs together. We had hardly reached the hall when we heard the baying of a hound, and then a scream of agony, with a horrible worrying sound which it was dreadful to listen to. An elderly man with a red face and shaking limbs came staggering out at a side door.

'My God!' he cried. 'Someone has loosed the dog. It's not been fed for two days. Quick, quick, or it'll be too late!'

Holmes and I rushed out and round the angle of the house, with Toller hurrying behind us. There was the huge famished brute, its black muzzle buried in Rucastle's throat, while he writhed and screamed upon the ground. Running up, I blew its brains out, and it fell over with its keen white teeth still meeting in the great creases of his neck. With much labour we separated them and carried him, living but horribly mangled, into the house. We laid him upon the drawing-room sofa, and having dispatched the sobered Toller to bear the news to his wife, I did what I could to relieve his pain. We were all assembled round him when the door opened, and a tall, gaunt woman entered the room.

'Mrs Toller!' cried Miss Hunter.

'Yes, miss. Mr Rucastle let me out when he came back before he went up to you. Ah, miss, it is a pity you didn't let me know what you were planning, for I would have told you that your pains were wasted.'

'Ha!' said Holmes, looking keenly at her. 'It is clear that Mrs Toller knows more about this matter than anyone else.'

'Yes, sir, I do, and I am ready enough to tell what I know.'

'Then, pray, sit down, and let us hear it, for there are several points on which I must confess that I am still in the dark.'

'I will soon make it clear to you,' said she; 'and I'd have done so before now if I could ha' got out from the cellar. If there's police-court business over this, you'll remember that I was the one that stood your friend, and that I was Miss Alice's friend too.

'She was never happy at home, Miss Alice wasn't, from the time that her father married again. She was slighted like and had no say in anything, but it never really became bad for her until after she met Mr Fowler at a friend's house. As well as I could learn, Miss Alice had rights of her own by will, but she was so quiet and patient, she was, that she never said a word about them, but just left everything in Mr Rucastle's hands. He knew he was safe with her; but when there was a chance of a husband coming forward, who would ask for all that the law would give him, then her father thought it time to put a stop on it. He wanted her to sign a paper, so that whether she married or not, he could use her money. When she wouldn't do it, he kept on worrying her until she got brain-fever, and for six weeks was at death's door. Then she got better at last, all worn to a shadow, and with her beautiful hair cut off; but that didn't make no change in her young man, and he stuck to her as true as man could be.'

'Ah,' said Holmes, 'I think that what you have been good enough to tell us makes the matter fairly clear, and that I can deduce all that remains. Mr Rucastle then, I presume, took to this system of imprisonment?'

'Yes, sir.'

'And brought Miss Hunter down from London in order to get rid of the disagreeable persistence of Mr Fowler.'

'That was it, sir.'

'But Mr Fowler being a persevering man, as a good seaman should be, blockaded the house, and having met you succeeded by certain arguments, metallic or otherwise, in convincing you that your interests were the same as his.'

'Mr Fowler was a very kind-spoken, free-handed gentleman,' said Mrs Toller serenely.

'And in this way he managed that your good man should have no want of drink and that a ladder should be ready at the moment when your master had gone out.

'You have it, sir, just as it happened.'

'I am sure we owe you an apology, Mrs Toller,' said Holmes, 'for you have certainly cleared up everything which puzzled us. And here comes the country surgeon and Mrs Rucastle, so I think, Watson, that we had best escort Miss Hunter back to Winchester, as it seems to me that our *locus standi* now is rather a questionable one.'

And thus was solved the mystery of the sinister house with

the copper beeches in front of the door. Mr Rucastle survived, but was always a broken man, kept alive solely through the care of his devoted wife. They still live with their old servants, who probably know so much of Rucastle's past life that he finds it difficult to part from them. Mr Fowler and Miss Rucastle were married, by special licence, in Southampton the day after their flight, and he is now the holder of a government appointment in the island of Mauritius. As to Miss Violet Hunter, my friend Holmes, rather to my disappointment, manifested no further interest in her when once she had ceased to be the centre of one of his problems, and she is now the head of a private school at Walsall, where I believe that she has met with considerable success.

THE BITER BIT

William Wilkie Collins

[Extracted from the Correspondence of the London Police]

FROM CHIEF INSPECTOR THEAKSTONE, OF THE DETECTIVE POLICE, TO SERGEANT BULMER OF THE SAME FORCE

LONDON, *4 July, 18—*.

SERGEANT Bulmer, – This is to inform you that you are wanted to assist in looking up a case of importance, which will require all the attention of an experienced member of the force. The matter of the robbery on which you are now engaged, you will please to shift over to the young man who brings you this letter. You will tell him all the circumstances of the case, just as they stand; you will put him up to the progress you have made (if any) towards detecting the person or persons by whom the money has been stolen; and you will leave him to make the best he can of the matter now in his hands. He is to have the whole responsibility of the case, and the whole credit of his success, if he brings it to a proper issue.

So much for the orders that I am desired to communicate to you.

A word in your ear, next, about this new man who is to take your place. His name is Matthew Sharpin; and he is to have the chance given him of dashing into our office at a jump – supposing he turns out strong enough to take it. You will naturally ask me how he comes by this privilege. I can only tell you that he has some uncommonly strong interest to back him in certain high quarters which you and I had better not mention except under our breaths. He has been a lawyer's clerk; and he is wonderfully conceited in his opinion of himself, as well as mean and underhand to look at. According to his own account, he leaves his old trade, and joins ours, of his own free will and preference. You will no more believe that than I do. My notion is, that he has managed to ferret out some private information in connection with the affairs of one of his master's clients, which makes him rather an awkward customer to keep in the office for the future, and which, at the same time, gives him hold enough over his employer to make it dangerous to drive him into a corner by turning him away. I think the giving him this unheard-of chance among us, is, in plain words, pretty much like giving him hush-money to keep him quiet. However that may be, Mr Matthew Sharpin is to have the case now in your hands; and if he succeeds with it, he pokes his ugly nose into our office, as sure as fate. I put you up to this, Sergeant, so that you may not stand in your own light by giving the new man any cause to complain of you at headquarters, and remain yours,

Francis Theakstone

FROM MR MATTHEW SHARPIN TO CHIEF INSPECTOR THEAKSTONE

LONDON, *5 July, 18–*.

DEAR SIR, – Having now been favoured with the necessary instructions from Sergeant Bulmer, I beg to remind you of certain directions which I have received, relating to the report of my future proceedings which I am to prepare for examination at headquarters.

The object of my writing, and of your examining what I have written, before you send it in to the higher authorities, is, I am informed, to give me, as an untried hand, the benefit of your advice, in case I want it (which I venture to think I shall not) at any stage of my proceedings. As the extraordinary circumstances of the case on which I am now engaged make it impossible for me to absent myself from the place where the robbery was committed, until I have made some progress towards discovering the thief, I am necessarily precluded from consulting you personally. Hence the necessity of my writing down the various details, which might, perhaps, be better communicated by word of mouth. This, if I am not mistaken, is the position in which we are now placed. I state my own impressions on the subject, in writing, in order that we may clearly understand each other at the outset; and have the honour to remain, your obedient servant,

Matthew Sharpin

FROM CHIEF INSPECTOR THEAKSTONE TO MR MATTHEW SHARPIN

LONDON, *5 July, 18–.*

Sir, – You have begun by wasting time, ink, and paper. We both of us perfectly well knew the position we stood in towards each other, when I sent you with my letter to Sergeant Bulmer. There was not the least need to repeat it in writing. Be so good as to employ your pen, in future, on the business actually in hand.

You have now three separate matters on which to write to me. First, you have to draw up a statement of your instructions received from Sergeant Bulmer, in order to show us that nothing has escaped your memory, and that you are thoroughly acquainted with all the circumstances of the case which has been entrusted to you. Secondly, you are to inform me what it is you propose to do. Thirdly, you are to report every inch of your progress (if you make any) from day to day, and, if need be, from hour to hour as well. This is *your* duty. As to what *my* duty may be, when I want you to remind me of it, I will write and tell you so. In the meantime, I remain, yours,

Francis Theakstone

FROM MR MATTHEW SHARPIN TO CHIEF INSPECTOR THEAKSTONE

LONDON, *6 July, 18–.*

SIR, – You are rather an elderly person, and, as such, naturally inclined to be a little jealous of men like me, who are in the prime of their lives and their faculties. Under these circumstances, it is my duty to be considerate towards you, and not to bear too hardly on your small failings. I decline, therefore, altogether, to take offence at the tone of your letter; I give you the full benefit of the natural generosity of my nature; I sponge the very existence of your surly communication out of my memory – in short, Chief Inspector Theakstone, I forgive you, and proceed to business.

My first duty is to draw up a full statement of the instructions I have received from Sergeant Bulmer. Here they are at your service, according to my version of them.

At number 13 Rutherford Street, Soho, there is a stationer's shop. It is kept by one Mr Yatman. He is a married man, but has no family. Besides Mr and Mrs Yatman, the other inmates in the house are a young single man named Jay, who lodges in the front room on the second floor – a shopman, who sleeps in one of the attics, – and a servant-of-all-work, whose bed is in the back-kitchen. Once a week a charwoman comes for a few hours in the morning only, to help this servant. These are all the persons who, on ordinary occasions, have means of access to the interior of the house, placed, as a matter of course, at their disposal.

Mr Yatman has been in business for many years, carrying on his affairs prosperously enough to realize a handsome independence for a person in his position. Unfortunately for himself, he endeavoured to increase the amount of his property by speculating. He ventured boldly in his investments, luck went against him, and rather less than two years ago he found himself a poor man again. All that was saved out of the wreck of his property was the sum of two hundred pounds.

Although Mr Yatman did his best to meet his altered circumstances, by giving up many of the luxuries and comforts to which he and his wife had been accustomed, he found it impossible to retrench so far as to allow of putting by any money from the income produced by his shop. The business has been declining of late years – the cheap advertising stationers having done it injury with the public. Consequently, up to the last week the only surplus property possessed by Mr Yatman consisted of the two hundred pounds which had been recovered from the wreck of his fortune. This sum was placed as a deposit in a joint-stock bank of the highest possible character.

Eight days ago, Mr Yatman and his lodger, Mr Jay, held a conversation on the subject of the commercial difficulties which are hampering trade in all directions at the present time. Mr Jay (who lives by supplying the newspapers with short paragraphs relating to accidents, offences, and brief records of remarkable occurrences in general – who is, in short, what they call a penny-a-liner) told his landlord that he had been in the city that day, and had heard unfavourable rumours on the subject of the joint-stock banks. The rumours to which he alluded had already reached the ears of Mr Yatman from other quarters; and the confirmation of them by his lodger had such an effect on his mind – predisposed as it was to alarm by the experience of his former losses – that he resolved to go at once to the bank and withdraw his deposit.

It was then getting on towards the end of the afternoon; and he arrived just in time to receive his money before the bank closed.

He received the deposit in bank-notes of the following amounts; – one fifty-pound note, three twenty-pound notes, six ten-pound notes, and six five-pound notes. His object in drawing the money in this form was to have it ready to lay out immediately in trifling loans, on good security, among the small tradespeople of his district, some of whom are sorely pressed for the very means of existence at the present time. Investments of this kind seemed to Mr Yatman to be the most safe and the most profitable on which he could now venture.

He brought the money back in an envelope placed in his breast-pocket; and asked his shopman, on getting home, to look for a small flat tin cash-box, which had not been used for years, and which, as Mr Yatman remembered it, was exactly of the right size to hold the bank-notes. For some time the cash-box was searched for in vain. Mr Yatman called to his wife to know if she had any idea where it was. The question was overheard by the servant-of-all-work, who was taking up the tea-tray at the time, and by Mr Jay, who was coming downstairs on his way out to the theatre. Ultimately the cash-box was found by the shopman. Mr Yatman placed the bank-notes in it, secured them by a padlock, and put the box in his coat-pocket. It stuck out of the coat pocket a very little, but enough to be seen. Mr Yatman remained at home, upstairs, all the evening. No visitors called. At eleven o'clock he went to bed, and put the cash-box along with his clothes, on a chair by the bedside.

When he and his wife woke the next morning, the box was gone. Payment of the notes was immediately stopped at the Bank of England; but no news of the money has been heard of since that time.

So far, the circumstances of the case are perfectly clear. They point unmistakably to the conclusion that the robbery must have been committed by some person living in the house. Suspicion falls, therefore, upon the servant-of-all-work, upon the shopman, and upon Mr Jay. The two first knew that the cash-box was being inquired for by their master, but did not know what it was he wanted to put into it. They would assume, of course that it was money. They both had opportunities (the servant, when she took away the tea – and the shopman, when he came, after shutting up, to give the keys of the till to his master) of seeing the cash-box in Mr Yatman's pocket, and of inferring naturally, from its position there, that he intended to take it into his bedroom with him at night.

Mr Jay, on the other hand, had been told, during the afternoon's conversation on the subject of joint-stock banks, that his landlord had a deposit of two hundred pounds in one of them. He also knew that Mr Yatman left him with the intention of drawing that money out; and he heard the inquiry for the cash-box, afterwards, when he was coming downstairs. He must, therefore, have inferred that the money was in the house, and that the cash-box was the receptacle intended to contain it. That he could have had any idea, however, of the place in which Mr Yatman intended to keep it for the night, is impossible, seeing that he went out before the box was found, and did not return till his landlord was in bed. Consequently, if he committed the robbery, he must have gone into the bedroom purely on speculation.

Speaking of the bedroom reminds me of the necessity of

noticing the situation of it in the house, and the means that exist of gaining easy access to it any hour of the night.

The room in question is the back-room on the first-floor. In consequence of Mrs Yatman's constitutional nervousness on the subject of fire (which makes her apprehend being burnt alive in her room, in case of accident, by the hampering of the lock if the key is turned in it) her husband has never been accustomed to lock the bedroom door. Both he and his wife are, by their own admission, heavy sleepers. Consequently the risk to be run by any evil-disposed persons wishing to plunder the bedroom, was of the most trifling kind. They could enter the room by merely turning the handle of the door; and if they moved with ordinary caution, there was no fear of their waking the sleepers inside. This fact is of importance. It strengthens our conviction that the money must have been taken by one of the inmates of the house, because it tends to show that the robbery, in this case, might have been committed by persons not possessed of the superior vigilance and cunning of the experienced thief.

Such are the circumstances, as they were related to Sergeant Bulmer, when he was first called in to discover the guilty parties, and, if possible, to recover the lost bank-notes. The strictest inquiry which he could institute, failed of producing the smallest fragment of evidence against any of the persons on whom suspicion naturally fell. Their language and behaviour, on being informed of the robbery, was perfectly consistent with the language and behaviour of innocent people. Sergeant Bulmer felt from the first that this was a case for private inquiry and secret observation. He began by recommending Mr and Mrs Yatman to affect a feeling of perfect confidence in the innocence of the persons living under their roof; and he then opened the campaign by employing himself in following the goings and comings, and in discovering the friends, the habits, and the secrets of the maid-of-all work.

Three days and nights of exertion on his own part, and on that of others who were competent to assist his investigations, were enough to satisfy him that there was no sound cause for suspicion against the girl.

He next practised the same precaution in relation to the

shopman. There was more difficulty and uncertainty in privately clearing up this person's character without his knowledge, but the obstacles were at last smoothed away with tolerable success; and though there is not the same amount of certainty, in this case, which there was in that of the girl, there is still fair reason for supposing that the shopman has had nothing to do with the robbery of the cash-box.

As a necessary consequence of these proceedings, the range of suspicion now becomes limited to the lodger, Mr Jay.

When I presented your letter of introduction to Sergeant Bulmer, he had already made some inquiries on the subject of this young man. The result, so far, has not been at all favourable. Mr Jay's habits are irregular; he frequents public houses, and seems to be familiarly acquainted with a great many dissolute characters; he is in debt to most of the tradespeople whom he employs; he has not paid his rent to Mr Yatman for the last month; yesterday evening he came home excited by liquor, and last week he was seen talking to a prize-fighter. In short, though Mr Jay does call himself a journalist, in virtue of his penny-a-line contributions to the newspapers, he is a young man of low tastes, vulgar manners, and bad habits. Nothing has yet been discovered in relation to him, which resounds to his credit in the smallest degree.

I have now reported, down to the very last details, all the particulars communicated to me by Sergeant Bulmer. I believe you will not find an omission anywhere; and I think you will admit, though you are prejudiced against me, that a clearer statement of facts was never laid before you than the statement I have now made. My next duty is to tell you what I propose to do, now that the case is confided to my hands.

In the first place, it is clearly my business to take up the case at the point where Sergeant Bulmer has left it. On his authority, I am justified in assuming that I have no need to trouble myself about the maid-of-all-work and the shopman. Their characters are now to be considered as cleared up. What remains to be privately investigated is the question of the guilt or innocence of Mr Jay. Before we give up the notes for lost, we must make sure, if we can, that he knows nothing about them.

This is the plan that I have adopted, with the full approval of Mr and Mrs Yatman, for discovering whether Mr Jay is or is not the person who has stolen the cash-box:

I propose, today, to present myself at the house in the character of a young man who is looking for lodgings. The back room on the second-floor will be shown to me as the room to let; and I shall establish myself there tonight, as a person from the country who has come to London to look for a situation in a respectable shop or office.

By this means I shall be living next to the room occupied by Mr Jay. The partition between us is mere lath and plaster. I shall make a small hole in it, near the cornice, through which I can see what Mr Jay does in his room, and hear every word that is said when any friend happens to call on him. Whenever he is at home, I shall be at my post of observation. Whenever he goes out, I shall be after him. By employing these means of watching him, I believe I may look forward to the discovery of his secret – if he knows anything about the lost bank-notes – as to a dead certainty.

What you may think of my plan of observation I cannot undertake to say. It appears to me to unite the invaluable merits of boldness and simplicity. Fortified by this conviction, I close the present communication with feelings of the most sanguine description in regard to the future, and remain your obedient servant,

Matthew Sharpin.

FROM THE SAME TO THE SAME

7 July.

SIR, – As you have not honoured me with an answer to my last communication, I assume that, in spite of your prejudices against me, it has produced the favourable impression on your mind which I ventured to anticipate. Gratified beyond measure by the token of approval which your eloquent silence conveys to me, I proceed to report the progress that has been made in the course of the last twenty-four hours.

I am now comfortably established next door to Mr Jay; and I am delighted to say that I have two holes in the partition, instead of one. My natural sense of humour has led me into the pardonable extravagance of giving them appropriate names. One I call my peep-hole, and the other my pipe-hole. The name of the first explains itself, the name of the second refers to a small tin pipe, or tube, inserted in the hole, and twisted so that the mouth of it comes close to my ear, while I am standing at my post of observation. Thus, while I am looking at Mr Jay through my peep-hole, I can hear every word that may be spoken in his room through my pipe-hole.

Perfect candour – a virtue which I have possessed from my childhood – compels me to acknowledge, before I go any further, that the ingenious notion of adding a pipe-hole to my proposed peep-hole originated with Mrs Yatman. This lady – a most intelligent and accomplished person, simple, and yet distinguished, in her manners – has entered into all my little plans with an enthusiasm and intelligence which I cannot too highly praise. Mr Yatman is so cast down by his loss, that he is quite incapable of affording me any assistance. Mrs Yatman, who is evidently most tenderly attached to him, feels her husband's sad condition of mind even more acutely than she feels the loss of the money; and is mainly stimulated to exertion by her desire to assist in raising him from the miserable state of prostration into which he has now fallen.

'The money, Mr Sharpin,' she said to me yesterday evening, with tears in her eyes, 'the money may be regained by rigid economy and strict attention to business. It is my husband's wretched state of mind that makes me so anxious for the discovery of the thief. I may be wrong, but I felt hopeful of success as soon as you entered the house; and I believe, if the wretch who has robbed us is to be found, you are the man to discover him. I accepted this gratifying compliment in the spirit in which it was offered – firmly believing that I shall be found, sooner or later, to have thoroughly deserved it.

Let me now return to business; that is to say, to my peep-hole and my pipe-hole.

I have enjoyed some hours of calm observation of Mr Jay. Though rarely at home, as I understand from Mrs Yatman, on ordinary occasions, he has been indoors the whole of this day. That is suspicious, to begin with. I have to report, further that he rose at a late hour this morning (always a bad sign in a young man), and that he lost a great deal of time, after he was up, in yawning and complaining to himself of headache. Like other debauched characters, he ate little or nothing for breakfast. His next proceeding was to smoke a pipe – a dirty clay pipe, which a gentleman would have been ashamed to put between his lips. When he had done smoking, he took out pen, ink, and paper, and sat down to write with a groan – whether of remorse for having taken the bank-notes, or of disgust at the task before him, I am unable to say. After writing a few lines (too far away from my peep-hole to give me a chance of reading over his shoulder), he leaned back in his chair, and amused himself by humming the tunes of certain popular songs. Whether these do, or do not, represent secret signals by which he communicates with his accomplices remains to be seen. After he had amused himself for some time by humming, he got up and began to walk about the room, occasionally stopping to add a sentence to the paper on his desk. Before long, he went to a locked cupboard and opened it. I strained my eyes eagerly, in expectation of making a discovery. I saw him take something carefully out of the cupboard – he turned round – and it was only a pint bottle of brandy! Having drunk some of the liquor, this extremely indolent reprobate lay down on his bed again, and in five minutes was fast asleep.

After hearing him snoring for at least two hours, I was recalled to my peep-hole by a knock at his door. He jumped up and opened it with suspicious activity.

A very small boy, with a very dirty face, walked in, said, 'Please, sir, they're waiting for you,' sat down on a chair, with his legs a long way from the ground, and instantly fell asleep! Mr Jay swore an oath, tied a wet towel round his head, and going back to his paper, began to cover it with writing as fast as his fingers could move the pen. Occasionally getting up to dip the towel in water and tie it on again, he continued at this employment for nearly three hours; then folded up the leaves of writing, woke the boy, and gave them to him, with this remarkable expression: 'Now then, young sleepy-head, quick – march! If you see the governor, tell him to have the money ready when I call for it.' The boy grinned, and disappeared. I was sorely tempted to follow 'sleepy-head,' but, on reflection, considered it safest still to keep my eye on the proceedings of Mr Jay.

In half an hour's time, he put on his hat and walked out. Of course, I put on my hat and walked out also. As I went down stairs, I passed Mrs Yatman going up. The lady has been kind enough to undertake, by previous arrangement between us, to search Mr Jay's room, while he is out of the way, and while I am necessarily engaged in the pleasing duty of following him wherever he goes. On the occasion to which I refer, he walked straight to the nearest tavern, and ordered a couple of mutton chops for his dinner. I placed myself in the next box to him, and ordered a couple of mutton chops for my dinner. Before I had been in the room a minute, a young man of highly suspicious manners and appearance, sitting at a table opposite, took his glass of porter in his hand and joined Mr Jay. I pretended to be reading the newspaper, and listened, as in duty bound, with all my might.

'Jack has been here inquiring after you,' says the young man.

'Did he leave any message?' asks Mr Jay.

'Yes,' says the other. 'He told me, if I met with you, to say that he wished very particularly to see you tonight; and that he would give you a look in, at Rutherford Street, at seven o'clock.'

'All right,' says Mr Jay. 'I'll get back in time to see him.'

Upon this, the suspicious-looking young man finished his porter, and saying that he was rather in a hurry, took leave of his friend (perhaps I should not be wrong if I said his accomplice) and left the room.

At twenty-five minutes and a half past six – in these serious cases it is important to be particular about time – Mr Jay finished his chops and paid his bill. At twenty-six minutes and three-quarters I finished my chops and paid mine. In ten minutes more I was inside the house in Rutherford Street, and was received by Mrs Yatman in the passage. That charming woman's face exhibited an expression of melancholy and disappointment which it quite grieved me to see.

'I am afraid, Ma'am,' says I, 'that you have not hit on any little criminating discovery in the lodger's room?'

She shook her head and sighed. It was a soft, languid, fluttering sigh; – and, upon my life, it quite upset me. For the moment I forgot business, and burned with envy of Mr Yatman.

'Don't despair, Ma'am,' I said, with an insinuating mildness which seemed to touch her. 'I have heard a mysterious conversation – I know of a guilty appointment – and I expect great things from my peep-hole and my pipe-hole tonight. Pray, don't be alarmed, but I think we are on the brink of a discovery.'

Here my enthusiastic devotion to business got the better of my tender feelings. I looked – winked – nodded – left her.

When I got back to my observatory, I found Mr Jay digesting his mutton chops in an arm-chair, with his pipe in his mouth. On his table were two tumblers, a jug of water, and the pint bottle of brandy. It was then close upon seven o'clock. As the hour struck, the person described as 'Jack' walked in.

He looked agitated – I am happy to say he looked violently agitated. The cheerful glow of anticipated success diffused itself (to use a strong expression) all over me, from head to foot. With breathless interest I looked through my peep-hole, and saw the visitor – the 'Jack' of this delightful case – sit down, facing me, at the opposite side of the table to Mr Jay. Making allowance for the difference in expression which their countenances just now happened to exhibit, these two abandoned villains were so much alike in other respects as to lead at once to the conclusion that they were brothers. Jack was the cleaner man and the better dressed of the two. I admit that, at the outset. It is, perhaps, one of my failings to push justice and impartiality to their utmost limits. I am no Pharisee; and where vice has its redeeming point, I say, let vice have its due – yes, yes, by all manner of means, let vice have its due.

'What's the matter now, Jack?' says Mr Jay.

'Can't you see it in my face?' says Jack. 'My dear fellow, delays are dangerous. Let us have done with suspense, and risk it the day after tomorrow.'

'So soon as that?' cried Mr Jay, looking very much astonished. 'Well, I'm ready, if you are. But, I say, Jack, is Somebody Else ready too? Are you quite sure of that?'

He smiled as he spoke – a frightful smile – and laid a very strong emphasis on those two words, 'Somebody Else.' There is evidently a third ruffian, a nameless desperado, concerned in the business.

'Meet us tomorrow,' says Jack, 'and judge for yourself. Be in the Regent's Park at eleven in the morning, and look out for us at the turning that leads to the Avenue Road.'

'I'll be there,' says Mr Jay. 'Have a drop of brandy and water? What are you getting up for? You're not going already?'

'Yes, I am,' says Jack. 'The fact is, I'm so excited and agitated that I can't sit still anywhere for five minutes together. Ridiculous as it may appear to you, I'm in a perpetual state of nervous flutter. I can't, for the life of me, help fearing that we shall be found out. I fancy that every man who looks twice at me in the street is a spy–'

At those words, I thought my legs would have given way under me. Nothing but strength of mind kept me at my peephole – nothing else, I give you my word of honour.

'Stuff and nonsense!' cried Mr Jay, with all the effrontery of a veteran in crime. 'We have kept the secret up to this time, and we will manage cleverly to the end. Have a drop of brandy and water, and you will feel as certain about it as I do.'

Jack steadily refused the brandy and water, and steadily persisted in taking his leave.

'I must try if I can't walk it off,' he said. 'Remember tomorrow morning – eleven o'clock, Avenue Road side of the Regent's Park.'

With those words he went out. His hardened relative laughed desperately, and resumed the dirty clay pipe.

I sat down on the side of my bed, actually quivering with excitement.

It is clear to me that no attempt has yet been made to change the stolen bank-notes; and I may add that Sergeant Bulmer was of that opinion also, when he left the case in my hands. What is the natural conclusion to draw from the conversation which I have just set down? Evidently, that the confederates meet tomorrow to take their respective shares in the stolen money, and to decide on the safest means of getting the notes changed the day after. Mr Jay is, beyond a doubt, the leading criminal in this business, and he will probably run the chief risk – that of changing the fifty-pound note. I shall, therefore, still make it my business to follow him – attending at the Regent's Park tomorrow, and doing my best to hear what is said there. If another appointment is made for the day after, I shall, of course, go to it. In the meantime, I shall want the immediate assistance of two competent persons (supposing the rascals separate after their meeting) to follow the two minor criminals. It is only fair to add, that, if the rogues all retire together, I shall probably keep my subordinates in reserve. Being naturally ambitious, I desire, if possible, to have the whole credit of discovering this robbery to myself.

8 July.

I have to acknowledge, with thanks, the speedy arrival of my two subordinates – men of very average abilities, I am afraid; but, fortunately, I shall always be on the spot to direct them.

My first business this morning was, necessarily, to prevent mistakes by accounting to Mr and Mrs Yatman for the presence of two strangers on the scene. Mr Yatman (between ourselves, a poor feeble man) only shook his head and groaned. Mrs Yatman (that superior woman) favoured me with a charming look of intelligence.

'Oh, Mr Sharpin!' she said, 'I am so sorry to see those two men! Your sending for their assistance looks as if you were beginning to be doubtful of success.'

I privately winked at her (she is very good in allowing me to do so without taking offence), and told her, in my facetious way, that she laboured under a slight mistake.

'It is because I am sure of success, Ma'am, that I send for them. I am determined to recover the money, not for my own sake only, but for Mr Yatman's sake – and for yours.'

I laid a considerable amount of stress on those last three words. She said, 'Oh, Mr Sharpin!' again – and blushed of a heavenly red – and looked down at her work. I could go to the world's end with that woman, if Mr Yatman would only die.

I sent off the two subordinates to wait, until I wanted them, at the Avenue Road gate of the Regent's Park. Half an hour afterwards I was following in the same direction myself, at the heels of Mr Jay.

The two confederates were punctual to the appointed time, I blush to record it, but it is nevertheless necessary to state, that the third rogue – the nameless desperado of my report, or if you prefer it, the mysterious 'Somebody Else' of the conversation between the two brothers – is a Woman! and, what is worse, a young woman! and what is more lamentable still, a nice-looking woman! I have long resisted a growing conviction, that, wherever there is mischief in this world, an individual of the fair sex is inevitably certain to be mixed up in it. After the experience of this morning, I can struggle against that sad conclusion no longer. – I give up the sex – excepting Mrs Yatman, I give up the sex.

The man named 'Jack' offered the woman his arm. Mr Jay placed himself on the other side of her. The three then walked away slowly among the trees. I followed them at a respectful distance. My two subordinates, at a respectful distance also, followed me.

It was, I deeply regret to say, impossible to get near enough to them to overhear their conversation, without running too great a risk of being discovered. I could only infer from their gestures and actions that they were all three talking with extraordinary earnestness on some subject which deeply interested them. After having been engaged in this way a full quarter of an hour, they suddenly turned round to retrace their steps. My presence of mind did not forsake me in this emergency. I signed to the two subordinates to walk on carelessly and pass them, while I myself slipped dexterously behind a tree. As they came by me, I heard 'Jack' address these words to Mr Jay:

'Let us say half-past ten tomorrow morning. And mind you come in a cab. We had better not risk taking one in this neighbourhood.'

Mr Jay made some brief reply, which I could not overhear. They walked back to the place at which they had met, shaking hands there with an audacious cordiality which it quite sickened me to see. They then separated. I followed Mr Jay. My subordinates paid the same delicate attention to the other two.

Instead of taking me back to Rutherford Street, Mr Jay led me to the Strand. He stopped at a dingy, disreputable-looking house, which, according to the inscription over the door, was a newspaper office, but which, in my judgment, had all the external appearance of a place devoted to the reception of stolen goods.

After remaining inside for a few minutes, he came out whistling, with his finger and thumb in his waistcoat pocket. A less discreet man than myself would have arrested him on the spot. I remembered the necessity of catching the two confederates, and the importance of not interfering with the appointment that had been made for the next morning. Such coolness as this, under trying circumstances, is rarely to be found, I should imagine, in a young beginner, whose reputation as a detective policeman is still to make.

From the house of suspicious appearance, Mr Jay betook himself to a cigar-divan, and read the magazines over a cheroot. I sat at a table near him, and read the magazines likewise over a cheroot. From the divan he strolled to the tavern and had his chops. I strolled to the tavern and had my chops. When he had done, he went back to his lodging. When I had done, I went back to mine. He was overcome with drowsiness early in the evening, and went to bed. As soon as I heard him snoring, I was overcome with drowsiness, and went to bed also.

Early in the morning my two subordinates came to make their report.

They had seen the man named 'Jack' leave the woman near the gate of an apparently respectable villa-residence, not far from the Regent's Park. Left to himself, he took a turning to the right, which led to a sort of suburban street, principally inhabited by shopkeepers. He stopped at the private door of one of the houses, and let himself in with his own key – looking about him as he opened the door, and staring suspiciously at my men as they lounged along on the opposite side of the way. These were all the particulars which the subordinates had to communicate. I kept them in my room to attend on me, if needful, and mounted to my peep-hole to have a look at Mr Jay.

He was occupied in dressing himself, and was taking extraordinary pains to destroy all traces of the natural slovenliness of his appearance. This was precisely what I expected. A vagabond like Mr Jay knows the importance of giving himself a respectable look when he is going to run the risk of changing a stolen banknote. At five minutes past ten o'clock, he had given the last brush to his shabby hat and the last scouring with bread-crumbs to his dirty gloves. At ten minutes past ten he was in the street, on his way to the nearest cab-stand, and I and my subordinates were close on his heels.

He took a cab, and we took a cab. I had not overheard them appoint a place of meeting, when following them in the Park on the previous day; but I soon found that we were proceeding in the old direction of the Avenue Road gate.

The cab in which Mr Jay was riding turned into the Park slowly. We stopped outside, to avoid exciting suspicion. I got out to follow the cab on foot. Just as I did so, I saw it stop, and detected the two confederates approaching it from among the trees. They got in, and the cab was turned about directly. I ran back to my own cab, and told the driver to let them pass him, and then to follow as before.

The man obeyed my directions, but so clumsily as to excite their suspicions. We had been driving after them about three minutes (returning along the road by which we had advanced) when I looked out of the window to see how far they might be ahead of us. As I did this, I saw two hats popped out of the windows of their cab, and two faces looking back at me. I sank into my place in a cold sweat; the expression is coarse, but no other form of words can describe my condition at that trying moment.

'We are found out!' I said faintly to my two subordinates. They stared at me in astonishment. My feelings changed instantly from the depth of despair to the height of indignation.

'It is the cabman's fault. Get out, one of you,' I said, with dignity – 'get out and punch his head.'

Instead of following my directions (I should wish this act of disobedience to be reported at head-quarters) they both looked out of the window. Before I could pull them back, they both sat down again. Before I could express my just indignation, they both grinned, and said to me, 'Please to look out, sir!'

I did look out. The thieves' cab had stopped.

Where?

At a church door!!!

What effect this discovery might have had upon the ordinary run of men, I don't know. Being of a strong religious turn myself, it filled me with horror. I have often read of the unprincipled cunning of criminal persons; but I never before heard of three thieves attempting to double on their pursuers by entering a church! The sacrilegious audacity of that proceeding is, I should think, unparalleled in the annals of crime.

I checked my grinning subordinates by a frown. It was easy to see what was passing in their superficial minds. If I had not been able to look below the surface, I might, on observing two nicely-dressed men and one nicely-dressed woman enter a church before eleven in the morning on a weekday, have come to the same hasty conclusion at which my inferiors had evidently arrived. As it was, appearances had no power to impose on *me*. I got out, and, followed by one of my men, entered the church. The other man I sent round to watch the vestry door. You may catch a weasel asleep – but not your humble servant, Matthew Sharpin!

We stole up the gallery stairs, diverged to the organ loft and peered through the curtains in front. There they were all three, sitting in a pew below – yes, incredible as it may appear, sitting in a pew below!

Before I could determine what to do, a clergyman made his appearance in full canonicals, from the vestry door, followed by a clerk. My brain whirled, and my eyesight grew dim. Dark remembrances of robberies committed in vestries floated through my mind. I trembled for the excellent man in full canonicals – I even trembled for the clerk.

The clergyman placed himself inside the altar rails. The three desperadoes approached him. He opened his book, and began to read. What? – you will ask.

I answer, without the slightest hesitation, the first lines of the Marriage Service.

My subordinate had the audacity to look at me, and then to stuff his pocket-handkerchief into his mouth. I scorned to pay any attention to him. After I had discovered that the man 'Jack' was the bridegroom, and that the man Jay acted the part of father, and gave away the bride, I left the church, followed by my man, and joined the other subordinate outside the vestry door. Some people in my position would now have felt rather crestfallen, and would have begun to think that they had made a very foolish mistake. Not the faintest misgiving of any kind troubled me. I did not feel in the slightest degree depreciated in my own estimation. And even now, after a lapse of three hours, my mind remains, I am happy to say, in the same calm and hopeful condition.

As soon as I and my subordinates were assembled together outside the church, I intimated my intention of still following the other cab, in spite of what had occurred. My reason for deciding on this course will appear presently. The two subordinates were astonished at my resolution. One of them had the impertinence to say to me:

'If you please, sir, who is it that we are after? A man who has stolen money, or a man who has stolen a wife?'

The other low person encouraged him by laughing. Both have deserved an official reprimand; and both, I sincerely trust, will be sure to get it.

When the marriage ceremony was over, the three got into their cab; and once more our vehicle (neatly hidden round the corner of the church, so that they could not suspect it to be near them) started to follow theirs.

We traced them to the terminus of the South-Western Railway. The newly-married couple took tickets for Richmond – paying their fare with a half-sovereign, and so depriving me of the pleasure of arresting them, which I should certainly have done, if they had offered a bank-note. They parted from Mr Jay, saying, 'Remember the address, – 14 Babylon Terrace. You dine with us tomorrow week.' Mr Jay accepted the invitation, and added, jocosely, that he was going home at once to get off his clean clothes, and to be comfortable and dirty again for the rest of the day. I have to report that I saw him home safely, and that he is comfortable and dirty again (to use his own disgraceful language) at the present moment.

Here the affair rests, having by this time reached what I may call its first stage.

I know very well what persons of hasty judgment will be inclined to say of my proceedings thus far. They will assert that I have been deceiving myself all through, in the most absurd way; they will declare that the suspicious conversations which I have reported, referred solely to the difficulties and dangers of successfully carrying out a runaway match; and they will appeal to the scene in the church, as offering undeniable proof of the correctness of their assertions. So let it be. I dispute nothing up to this point. But I ask a question, out of the depths of my own sagacity as a man of the world, which the bitterest of my enemies will not, I think, find it particularly easy to answer.

Granted the fact of the marriage, what proof does it afford me of the innocence of the three persons concerned in that clandestine transaction? It gives me none. On the contrary, it strengthens my suspicions against Mr Jay and his confederates, because it suggests a distinct motive for their stealing the money. A gentleman who is going to spend his honeymoon at Richmond wants money; and a gentleman who is in debt to all his tradespeople wants money. Is this an unjustifiable imputation of bad motives? In the name of outraged morality, I deny it. These men have combined together, and have stolen a woman. Why should they not combine together, and steal a cash-box? I take my stand on the logic of rigid virtue; and I defy all the sophistry of vice to move me an inch out of my position.

Speaking of virtue, I may add that I have put this view of the case to Mr and Mrs Yatman. That accomplished and charming woman found it difficult, at first, to follow the close chain of my reasoning. I am free to confess that she shook her head, and shed tears, and joined her husband in premature lamentation over the loss of the two hundred pounds. But a little careful explanation on my part, and a little attentive listening on hers, ultimately changed her opinion. She now agrees with me, that there is nothing in this unexpected circumstance of the clandestine marriage which absolutely tends to divert suspicion from Mr Jay, or Mr 'Jack,' or the runaway lady. 'Audacious hussy' was the term my fair friend used in speaking of her, but let that pass. It is more to the purpose to record that Mrs Yatman has not lost confidence in me and that Mr Yatman promises to follow her example, and do his best to look hopefully for future results.

I have now, in the new turn that circumstances have taken, to await advice from your office. I pause for fresh orders with all the composure of a man who has got two strings to his bow. When I traced the three confederates from the church to the railway terminus, I had two motives for doing so. First, I followed them as a matter of official business, believing them still to have been guilty of the robbery. Secondly, I followed them as a matter of private speculation, with a view of discovering the place of refuge to which the runaway couple intended to retreat, and of making my information a marketable commodity to offer to the young lady's family and friends. Thus, whatever happens, I may congratulate myself beforehand on not having wasted my time. If the office approves of my conduct, I have my plan ready for further proceedings. If the office blames me, I shall take myself off, with my marketable information, to the genteel villa-residence in the neighbourhood of the Regent's Park. Anyway, the affair puts money into my pocket, and does credit to my penetration as an uncommonly sharp man.

I have only one word more to add, and it is this: If any individual ventures to assert that Mr Jay and his confederates are innocent of all share in the stealing of the cash-box, I, in return, defy that individual – though he may even be Chief Inspector Theakstone himself – to tell me who has committed the robbery at Rutherford Street, Soho.

I have the honour to be,

Your very obedient servant,

Matthew Sharpin.

FROM CHIEF INSPECTOR THEAKSTONE TO SERGEANT BULMER

BIRMINGHAM, *9 July*

Sergeant Bulmer, – That empty-headed puppy, Mr Matthew Sharpin, has made a mess of the case at Rutherford Street, exactly as I expected he would. Business keeps me in this town; so I write to you to set the matter straight. I enclose, with this, the pages of feeble scribble-scrabble which the creature, Sharpin, calls a report. Look them over; and when you have made your way through all the gabble, I think you will agree with me that the conceited booby has looked for the thief in every direction but the right one. You can lay your hand on the guilty person in five minutes, now. Settle the case at once; forward your report to me at this place; and tell Mr Sharpin that he is suspended till further notice.

Yours,

Francis Theakstone.

FROM SERGEANT BULMER TO CHIEF INSPECTOR THEAKSTONE

LONDON, *10 July*

Inspector Theakstone, – Your letter and enclosure came safe to hand. Wise men, they say, may always learn something, even from a fool. By the time I had got through Sharpin's maundering report of his own folly, I saw my way clear enough to the end of the Rutherford Street case, just as you thought I should. In half an hour's time I was at the house. The first person I saw there was Mr Sharpin himself.

'Have you come to help me?' says he.

'Not exactly,' says I. 'I've come to tell you that you are suspended till further notice.'

'Very good,' says he, not taken down, by so much as a single peg, in his own estimation. 'I thought you would be jealous of me. It's very natural; and I don't blame you. Walk in, pray, and make yourself at home. I'm off to do a little detective business on my own account, in the neighbourhood of the Regent's Park. Ta-ta, sergeant, ta-ta!'

With those words he took himself out of the way – which was exactly what I wanted him to do.

As soon as the maid-servant had shut the door, I told her to inform her master that I wanted to say a word to him in private. She showed me into the parlour behind the shop; and there was Mr Yatman, all alone, reading the newspaper.

'About this matter of the robbery, sir,' says I.

He cut me short, peevishly enough – being naturally a poor, weak, womanish sort of man. 'Yes, yes, I know,' says he. 'You have come to tell me that your wonderfully clever man, who has bored holes in my second-floor partition, has made a mistake, and is off the scent of the scoundrel who has stolen my money.'

'Yes, sir,' says I. 'That *is* one of the things I came to tell you. But I have got something else to say, besides that.'

'Can you tell me who the thief is?' says he, more pettish than ever.

'Yes, sir,' said I, 'I think I can.'

He put down the newspaper, and began to look rather anxious and frightened.

'Not my shopman?' says he. 'I hope, for the man's own sake, it's not my shopman.'

'Guess again, sir,' says I.

'That idle slut, the maid?' says he.

'She is idle, sir,' says I, 'and she is also a slut; my first inquiries about her proved as much as that. But she's not the thief.'

'Then in the name of heaven, who is?' says he.

'Will you please prepare yourself for a very disagreeable surprise, sir?' says I. 'And in case you lose your temper, will you excuse my remarking that I am the stronger man of the two, and that, if you allow yourself to lay hands on me, I may unintentionally hurt you, in pure self-defence?'

He turned as pale as ashes, and pushed his chair two or three feet away from me.

'You have asked me to tell you, sir, who has taken your money,' I went on. 'If you insist on my giving you an answer–'

'I do insist,' he said, faintly. 'Who has taken it?'

'Your wife has taken it,' I said very quietly, and very positively at the same time.

He jumped out of the chair as if I had put a knife into him, and struck his fist on the table, so heavily that the wood cracked again.

'Steady, sir,' says I. 'Flying into a passion won't help you to the truth.'

'It's a lie!' says he, with another smack of his fist on the table – 'a base, vile, infamous lie! How dare you–'

He stopped, and fell back into the chair again, looked about him in a bewildered way, and ended by bursting out crying.

'When your better sense comes back to you, sir,' says I, 'I am sure you will be gentleman enough to make an apology for the language you have just used. In the meantime, please to listen, if you can, to a word of explanation. Mr Sharpin has sent in a report to our inspector, of the most irregular and ridiculous kind; setting down, not only all his own foolish doings and sayings, but the doings and sayings of Mrs Yatman as well. In most cases, such a document would have been fit for the waste-paper basket; but, in this particular case, it so happens that Mr Sharpin's budget of nonsense leads to a certain conclusion, which the simpleton of a writer has been quite innocent of suspecting from the beginning to the end. Of that conclusion I am so sure, that I will forfeit my place, if it does not turn out that Mrs Yatman has been practising upon the folly and conceit of this young man, and that she has tried to shield herself from discovery by purposely encouraging him to suspect the wrong persons. I tell you that confidently; and I will even go further. I will undertake to give a decided opinion as to why Mrs Yatman took the money, and what she has done with it, or with a part of it. Nobody can look at that lady, sir, without being struck by the great taste and beauty of her dress–'

As I said those last words, the poor man seemed to find his powers of speech again. He cut me short directly, as haughtily as if he had been a duke instead of a stationer.

'Try some other means of justifying your vile calumny against my wife,' says he. 'Her milliner's bill for the past year is on my file of receipted accounts at this moment.'

'Excuse me, sir,' says I, 'but that proves nothing. Milliners, I must tell you, have a certain rascally custom which comes within the daily experience of our office. A married lady who wishes it, can keep two accounts at her dressmaker's; one is the account which her husband sees and pays; the other is the private account, which contains all the extravagant items, and which the wife pays secretly, by instalments, whenever she can. According to our usual experience, these instalments are mostly squeezed out of the housekeeping money. In your case, I suspect no instalments have been paid; proceedings have been threatened; Mrs Yatman, knowing your altered circumstances, has felt herself driven into a corner; and she has paid her private account out of your cash-box.'

'I won't believe it,' says he. 'Every word you speak is an abominable insult to me and to my wife.'

'Are you man enough, sir,' says I, taking him up short, in order to save time and words, 'to get that receipted bill you spoke of just now off the file, and come with me at once to the milliner's shop where Mrs Yatman deals?'

He turned red in the face at that, got the bill directly, and put on his hat. I took out of my pocket-book the list containing the numbers of the lost notes, and we left the house together immediately.

Arrived at the milliner's (one of the expensive West-end houses, as I expected), I asked for a private interview, on important business, with the mistress of the concern. It was not the first time that she and I had met over the same delicate investigation. The moment she set eyes on me, she sent for her husband. I mentioned who Mr Yatman was, and what we wanted.

'This is strictly private?' inquires her husband. I nodded my head.

'And confidential?' says the wife. I nodded again.

'Do you see any objection, dear, to obliging the sergeant with a sight of the books?' says her husband.

'None in the world, love, if you approve of it,' says the wife.

All this while poor Mr Yatman sat looking the picture of astonishment and distress, quite out of place at our polite conference. The books were brought – and one minute's look at the pages in which Mrs Yatman's name figured was enough, and more than enough, to prove the truth of every word I had spoken.

There, in one book, was the husband's account, which Mr Yatman had settled. And there, in the other, was the private account, crossed off also; the date of settlement being the very day after the loss of the cash-box. This said private account amounted to the sum of a hundred and seventy-five pounds, odd shillings; and it extended over a period of three years. Not a single instalment had been paid on it. Under the last line was an entry to this effect: 'Written to for the third time, June 23rd.' I pointed to it, and asked the milliner if that meant 'last June.' Yes, it did mean last June; and she now deeply regretted to say that it had been accompanied by a threat of legal proceedings.

'I thought you gave good customers more than three years credit?' says I.

The milliner looks at Mr Yatman, and whispers to me – 'Not when a lady's husband gets into difficulties.'

She pointed to the account as she spoke. The entries after the time when Mr Yatman's circumstances became involved were just as extravagant, for a person in his wife's situation, as the entries for the year before that period. If the lady had economized in other things, she had certainly not economized in the matter of dress.

There was nothing left now but to examine the cash-book, for form's sake. The money had been paid in notes, the amounts and numbers of which exactly tallied with the figures set down in my list.

After that, I thought it best to get Mr Yatman out of the house immediately. He was in such a pitiable condition, that I called a cab and accompanied him home in it. At first he cried and raved like a child: but I soon quieted him – and I must add, to his credit, that he made me a most handsome apology for his language, as the cab drew up at his house door. In return, I tried to give him some advice about how to set matters right, for the future, with his wife. He paid very little attention to me, and went upstairs muttering to himself about a separation. Whether Mrs Yatman will come cleverly out of the scrape or not, seems doubtful. I should say, myself, that she will go into screeching hysterics, and so frighten the poor man into forgiving her. But this is no business of ours. So far as we are concerned, the case is now at an end; and the present report may come to a conclusion along with it.

I remain, accordingly, yours to command,

Thomas Bulmer.

P.S. – I have to add, that, on leaving Rutherford Street, I met Mr Matthew Sharpin coming to pack up his things.

'Only think!' says he, rubbing his hands in great spirits, 'I've been to the genteel villa-residence; and the moment I mentioned my business, they kicked me out directly. There were two witnesses of the assault; and it's worth a hundred pounds to me, if it's worth a farthing.'

'I wish you joy of your luck,' says I.

'Thank you,' says he. 'When may I pay you the same compliment on finding the thief?'

'Whenever you like,' says I, 'for the thief is found.'

'Just what I expected,' says he. 'I've done all the work; and now you cut in, and claim all the credit – Mr Jay of course?'

'No,' says I.

'Who is it then?' says he.

'Ask Mrs Yatman,' says I. 'She's waiting to tell you.'

'All right! I'd much rather hear it from that charming woman than from you,' says he, and goes into the house in a mighty hurry.

What do you think of that, Inspector Theakstone? Would you like to stand in Mr Sharpin's shoes? I shouldn't, I can promise you!

FROM CHIEF INSPECTOR THEAKSTONE TO MR MATTHEW SHARPIN

12 July

Sir, – Sergeant Bulmer has already told you to consider yourself suspended until further notice. I have now authority to add, that your services as a member of the Detective Police are positively declined. You will please to take this letter as notifying officially your dismissal from the force.

I may inform you, privately, that your rejection is not

intended to cast any reflections on your character. It merely implies that you are not quite sharp enough for our purpose. If we *are* to have a new recruit among us, we should infinitely prefer Mrs Yatman.

Your obedient servant,

Francis Theakstone.

NOTE ON THE PRECEDING CORRESPONDENCE, ADDED BY MR THEAKSTONE

The Inspector is not in a position to append any explanations of importance to the last of the letters. It has been discovered that Mr Matthew Sharpin left the house in Rutherford Street five minutes after his interview outside of it with Sergeant Bulmer – his manner expressing the liveliest emotions of terror and astonishment, and his left cheek displaying a bright patch of red, which might have been the result of a slap on the face from a female hand. He was also heard, by the shopman at Rutherford Street, to use a very shocking expression in reference to Mrs Yatman; and was seen to clench his fist vindictively, as he ran round the corner of the street. Nothing more has been heard of him; and it is conjectured that he has left London with the intention of offering his valuable services to the provincial police.

On the interesting domestic subject of Mr and Mrs Yatman still less is known. It has, however, been positively ascertained that the medical attendant of the family was sent for in a great hurry, on the day when Mr Yatman returned from the milliner's shop. The neighbouring chemist received, soon afterwards, a prescription of a soothing nature to make up for Mrs Yatman. The day after, Mr Yatman purchased some smelling-salts at the shop, and afterwards appeared at the circulating library to ask for a novel, descriptive of high life, that would amuse an invalid lady. It has been inferred from these circumstances, that he has not thought it desirable to carry out his threat of separating himself from his wife – at least in the present (presumed) condition of that lady's sensitive nervous system.

THE PURLOINED LETTER

Edgar Allan Poe

Nil sapientiæ odiosius acumine nimio. – *Seneca*

At Paris, just after dark one gusty evening in the autumn of 18–, I was enjoying the twofold luxury of meditation and a meerschaum, in company with my friend, C. Auguste Dupin, in his little back library, or book-closet, *au troisième*, No. 33 *Rue Dunôt, Faubourg St. Germain.* For one hour at least we had maintained a profound silence; while each, to any casual observer, might have seemed intently and exclusively occupied with the curling eddies of smoke that oppressed the atmosphere of the chamber. For myself, however, I was mentally discussing certain topics which had formed matter for conversation between us at an earlier period of the evening; I mean the affair of the Rue Morgue, and the mystery attending the murder of Marie Rogêt. I looked upon it, therefore, as something of a coincidence, when the door of our apartment was thrown open and admitted our old acquaintance, Monsieur G–, the Prefect of the Parisian police.

We gave him a hearty welcome; for there was nearly half as much of the entertaining as of the contemptible about the man, and we had not seen him for several years. We had been sitting in the dark, and Dupin now arose for the purpose of lighting a lamp, but sat down again, without doing so, upon G.'s saying that he had called to consult us, or rather to ask the opinion of my friend, about some official business which had occasioned a great deal of trouble.

'If it is any point requiring reflection,' observed Dupin, as he forbore to enkindle the wick, 'we shall examine it to better purpose in the dark.'

'That is another of your odd notions,' said the Prefect, who had the fashion of calling everything 'odd' that was beyond his comprehension, and thus lived amid an absolute legion of 'oddities'.

'Very true,' said Dupin, as he supplied his visitor with a pipe, and rolled toward him a comfortable chair.

'And what is the difficulty now?' I asked. 'Nothing more in the assassination way I hope?'

'Oh, no; nothing of that nature. The fact is, the business is *very* simple indeed, and I make no doubt that we can manage it sufficiently well ourselves; but then I thought Dupin would like to hear the details of it, because it is so excessively *odd*.'

'Simple and odd,' said Dupin.

'Why, yes; and not exactly that either. The fact is, we have all been a good deal puzzled because the affair *is* so simple, and yet baffles us altogether.'

'Perhaps it is the very simplicity of the thing which puts you at fault,' said my friend.

'What nonsense you *do* talk!' replied the Prefect, laughing heartily.

'Perhaps the mystery is a little *too* plain,' said Dupin.

'Oh, good heavens! who ever heard of such an idea?'

'A little *too* self-evident.'

'Ha! ha! ha! – ha! ha! ha! – ho! ho! ho!' roared our visitor, profoundly amused, 'oh, Dupin, you will be the death of me yet!'

'And what, after all *is* the matter on hand?' I asked.

'Why, I will tell you,' replied the Prefect, as he gave a long, steady, and contemplative puff, and settled himself in his chair. 'I will tell you in a few words; but, before I begin, let me caution you that this is an affair demanding the greatest secrecy, and that I should most probably lose the position I now hold, were it known that I confided it to any one.'

'Proceed,' said I.

'Or not,' said Dupin.

'Well, then; I have received personal information, from a very high quarter, that a certain document of the last importance has been purloined from the royal apartments. The individual who purloined it is known; this beyond a doubt; he was seen to take it. It is known, also, that it still remains in his possession.'

'How is this known?' asked Dupin.

'It is clearly inferred,' replied the Prefect, 'from the nature of the document, and from the non-appearance of certain results which would at once arise from its passing *out* of the robber's possession – that is to say, from his employing it as he must design in the end to employ it.'

'Be a little more explicit,' I said.

'Well, I may venture so far as to say that the paper gives its holder a certain power in a certain quarter where such power is immensely valuable.' The Prefect was fond of the cant of diplomacy.

'Still I do not quite understand,' said Dupin.

'No? Well; the disclosure of the document to a third person, who shall be nameless, would bring in question the honor of a personage of most exalted station; and this fact gives the holder of the document an ascendancy over the illustrious personage whose honor and peace are so jeopardized.'

'But this ascendancy,' I interposed, 'would depend upon the robber's knowledge of the loser's knowledge of the robber. Who would dare–'

'The thief,' said G., 'is the Minister D–, who dares all things, those unbecoming as well as those becoming a man. The method of the theft was not less ingenious than bold. The document in question – a letter, to be frank – had been received by the personage robbed while alone in the royal *boudoir*. During its perusal she was suddenly interrupted by the entrance of the other exalted personage from whom especially it was her wish to conceal it. After a hurried and vain endeavour to thrust it in a drawer, she was forced to place it, open as it was, upon a table. The address, however, was uppermost, and, the contents thus unexposed, the letter escaped notice. At this juncture enters the Minister D–. His lynx eye immediately perceives the paper, recognizes the handwriting of the address, observes the confusion of the personage addressed, and fathoms her secret. After some business transactions, hurried through in his ordinary manner, he produces a letter somewhat similar to the one in question, opens it, to read it, and then places it in close juxtaposition to the other. Again he converses, for some fifteen minutes, upon the public affairs. At length, in taking leave, he takes also from the table the letter to which he had no claim. Its rightful owner saw, but, of course, dared not call attention to the act, in the presence of the third personage who stood at her elbow. The Minister decamped; leaving his own letter – one of no importance – upon the table.'

'Here, then,' said Dupin to me, 'you have precisely what you demand to make the ascendancy complete – the robber's knowledge of the loser's knowledge of the robber.'

'Yes,' replied the Prefect; 'and the power thus attained has, for some months past, been wielded, for political purposes, to a very dangerous extent. The personage robbed is more thoroughly convinced, every day, of the necessity of reclaiming her letter. But this, of course, cannot be done openly. In fine, driven to despair, she has committed the matter to me.'

'Than whom,' said Dupin, amid a perfect whirlwind of smoke, 'no more sagacious agent could, I suppose, be desired, or even imagined.'

'You flatter me,' replied the Prefect; 'but it is possible that some such opinion may have been entertained.'

'It is clear,' said I, 'as you observe, that the letter is still in the possession of the Minister; since it is this position, and not any employment of the letter, which bestows the power. With the employment the power departs.'

'True,' said G.; 'and upon this conviction I proceeded. My first care was to make thorough search of the Minister's hotel; and here my chief embarrassment lay in the necessity of searching without his knowledge. Beyond all things, I have been warned of the danger which would result from giving him reason to suspect our design.'

'But,' said I, 'you are quite *au fait* in these investigations. The Parisian police have done this thing often before.'

'Oh, yes; and for this reason I did not despair. The habits of the Minister gave me, too, a great advantage. He is frequently absent from home all night. His servants are by no means numerous. They sleep at a distance from their master's apartment, and, being chiefly Neapolitans, are readily made drunk. I have keys, as you know, with which I can open any chamber or cabinet in Paris. For three months a night has not passed, during the greater part of which I have not been engaged, personally, in ransacking the D– Hotel. My honour is interested, and, to mention a great secret, the reward is enormous. So I did not abandon the search until I had become fully satisfied that the thief is a more astute man than myself. I fancy that I have investigated every nook and corner of the premises in which it is possible that the paper can be concealed.'

'But is it not possible,' I suggested, 'that although the letter may be in possession of the Minister, as it unquestionably is, he may have concealed it elsewhere than upon his own premises?'

'This is barely possible,' said Dupin. 'The present peculiar condition of affairs at court, and especially of those intrigues in which D– is known to be involved, would render the instant availability of the document – its susceptibility of being produced at a moment's notice – a point of nearly equal importance with its possession.'

'Its susceptibility of being produced?' said I.

'That is to say, of being *destroyed*,' said Dupin.

'True,' I observed; 'the paper is clearly then upon the premises. As for its being upon the person of the Minister, we may consider that as out of the question.'

'Entirely,' said the Prefect. 'He has been twice waylaid, as if by footpads, and his person rigidly searched under my own inspection.'

'You might have spared yourself the trouble,' said Dupin. 'D–, I presume, is not altogether a fool, and, if not, must have anticipated these waylayings, as a matter of course.'

'Not *altogether* a fool,' said G.; 'but then he is a poet, which I take to be only one remove from a fool.'

'True,' said Dupin, after a long and thoughtful whiff from his meerschaum, 'although I have been guilty of certain doggerel myself.'

'Suppose you detail,' said I, 'the particulars of your search.'

'Why, the fact is, we took our time, and we searched *everywhere*. I have had long experience in these affairs. I took the entire building, room by room; devoting the nights of a whole week to each. We examined, first, the furniture of each apartment. We opened every possible drawer; and I presume you know that, to a properly trained police-agent, such a thing as a '*secret*' drawer is impossible. Any man is a dolt who permits a 'secret' drawer to escape him in a search of this kind. The thing is *so* plain. There is a certain amount of bulk – of space – to be accounted for in every cabinet. Then we have accurate rules. The fiftieth part of a line could not escape us. After the cabinets we took the chairs. The cushions we probed with the fine long needles you have seen me employ. From the tables we removed the tops.'

'Why so?'

'Sometimes the top of a table, or other similarly arranged piece of furniture, is removed by the person wishing to conceal an article; then the leg is excavated, the article deposited within the cavity, and the top replaced. The bottoms and tops of bedposts are employed in the same way.'

'But could not the cavity be detected by sounding?' I asked.

'By no means, if, when the article is deposited, a sufficient wadding of cotton be placed around it. Besides, in our case, we were obliged to proceed without noise.'

'But you could not have removed – you could not have taken to pieces *all* articles of furniture in which it would have been possible to make a deposit in the manner you mention. A letter may be compressed into a thin spiral roll, not differing much in shape or bulk from a large knitting-needle, and in this form it might be inserted into the rung of a chair, for example. You did not take to pieces all the chairs?'

'Certainly not; but we did better – we examined the rungs of every chair in the hotel, and, indeed, the jointings of every description of furniture, by the aid of a most powerful microscope. Had there been any traces of recent disturbance we should not have failed to detect it instantly. A single grain of gimlet-dust, for example, would have been as obvious as an apple. Any disorder in the gluing – any unusual gaping in the joints – would have sufficed to insure detection.'

'I presume you looked to the mirrors, between the boards

and the plates, and you probed the beds and the bedclothes, as well as the curtains and carpets.'

'That of course; and when we had absolutely completed every particle of the furniture in this way, then we examined the house itself. We divided its entire surface into compartments, which we numbered, so that none might be missed; then we scrutinized each individual square inch throughout the premises, including the two houses immediately adjoining, with the microscope, as before.'

'The two houses adjoining!' I exclaimed; 'you must have had a great deal of trouble.'

'We had; but the reward offered is prodigious.'

'You include the *grounds* about the houses?'

'All the grounds are paved with brick. They gave us comparatively little trouble. We examined the moss between the bricks, and found it undisturbed.'

'You looked among D–'s papers, of course, and into the books of the library?'

'Certainly; we opened every package and parcel; we not only opened every book, but we turned over every leaf in each volume, not contenting ourselves with a mere shake, according to the fashion of some of our police officers. We also measured the thickness of every book-*cover*, with the most accurate admeasurement, and applied to each the most jealous scrutiny of the microscope. Had any of the bindings been recently meddled with, it would have been utterly impossible that the fact should have escaped observation. Some five or six volumes, just from the hands of the binder, we carefully probed, longitudinally, with the needles.'

'You explored the floors beneath the carpets?'

'Beyond doubt. We removed every carpet, and examined the boards with the microscope.'

'And the paper on the walls?'

'Yes.'

'You looked into the cellars?'

'We did.'

'Then,' I said, 'you have been making a miscalculation, and the letter is *not* upon the premises, as you suppose.'

'I fear you are right there,' said the Prefect. 'And now, Dupin, what would you advise me to do?'

'To make a thorough research of the premises.'

'That is absolutely needless,' replied G–. 'I am not more sure that I breathe than I am that the letter is not at the hotel.'

'I have no better advice to give you,' said Dupin. 'You have, of course, an accurate description of the letter?'

'Oh, yes!' – And here the Prefect, producing a memorandum-book, proceeded to read aloud a minute account of the internal, and especially of the external, appearance of the missing document. Soon after finishing the perusal of this description, he took his departure, more entirely depressed in spirits than I had ever known the good gentleman before.

In about a month afterward he paid us another visit, and found us occupied very nearly as before. He took a pipe and a chair and entered into some ordinary conversation. At length I said:

'Well, but G., what of the purloined letter? I presume you have at last made up your mind that there is no such thing as overreaching the Minister?'

'Confound him, say I – yes; I made the re-examination however, as Dupin suggested – but it was all labor lost, as I knew it would be.'

'How much was the reward offered, did you say?' asked Dupin.

'Why, a very great deal – a *very* liberal reward – I don't like to say how much, precisely; but one thing I *will* say, that I wouldn't mind giving my individual check for fifty thousand francs to any one who could obtain me that letter. The fact is, it is becoming of more and more importance every day; and the reward has been lately doubled. If it were trebled, however, I could do no more than I have done.'

'Why, yes,' said Dupin, drawlingly, between the whiffs of his meerschaum, 'I really – think, G., you have not exerted yourself – to the utmost in this matter. You might – do a little more, I think, eh?'

'How? – in what way?'

'Why – puff, puff – you might – puff, puff – employ counsel

in the matter, eh? – puff, puff, puff. Do you remember the story they tell of Abernethy?'

'No; hang Abernethy!'

'To be sure! hang him and welcome. But, once upon a time, a certain rich miser conceived the design of spunging upon this Abernethy for a medical opinion. Getting up, for this purpose, an ordinary conversation in a private company, he insinuated his case to the physician, as that of an imaginary individual.

' "We will suppose," said the miser, "that his symptoms are such and such; now, doctor, what would *you* have directed him to take?'

' "Take!" said Abernethy, "why, take *advice*, to be sure." '

'But,' said the Prefect, a little discomposed, '*I* am *perfectly* willing to take advice, and to pay for it. I would *really* give fifty thousand francs to any one who would aid me in the matter.'

'In that case,' replied Dupin, opening a drawer, and producing a check-book, 'you may as well fill me up a check for the amount mentioned. When you have signed it, I will hand you the letter.'

I was astounded. The Prefect appeared absolutely thunder-stricken. For some minutes he remained speechless and motionless, looking incredulously at my friend with open mouth, and eyes that seemed starting from their sockets; then apparently recovering himself in some measure, he seized a pen, and after several pauses and vacant stares, finally filled up and signed a check for fifty thousand francs, and handed it across the table to Dupin. The latter examined it carefully and deposited it in his pocket-book; then, unlocking an *escritoire*, took thence a letter and gave it to the Prefect. This functionary grasped it in a perfect agony of joy, opened it with a trembling hand, cast a rapid glance at its contents, and then, scrambling and struggling to the door, rushed at length unceremoniously from the room and from the house, without having uttered a syllable since Dupin had requested him to fill up the check.

When he had gone, my friend entered into some explanations.

'The Parisian police,' he said, 'are exceedingly able in their way. They are persevering, ingenious, cunning, and thoroughly versed in the knowledge which their duties seem chiefly to demand. Thus, when G– detailed to us his mode of searching the premises at the Hotel D–, I felt entire confidence in his having made a satisfactory investigation – so far as his labors extended.'

'So far as his labors extended?' said I.

'Yes,' said Dupin. 'The measures adopted were not only the best of their kind, but carried out to absolute perfection. Had the letter been deposited within the range of their search, these fellows would, beyond a question, have found it.'

I merely laughed – but he seemed quite serious in all that he said.

'The measures, then,' he continued, 'were good in their kind, and well executed; their defect lay in their being inapplicable to the case and to the man. A certain set of highly ingenious resources are, with the Prefect, a sort of Procrustean bed, to which he forcibly adapts his designs. But he perpetually errs by being too deep or too shallow for the matter in hand; and many a school-boy is a better reasoner than he. I knew one about eight years of age, whose success at guessing the game of "even and odd" attracted universal admiration. This game is simple, and is played with marbles. One player holds in his hand a number of these toys, and demands of another whether that number is even or odd. If the guess is right, the guesser wins one; if wrong, he loses one. The boy to whom I allude won all the marbles of the school. Of course he had some principle of guessing; and this lay in mere observation and admeasurement of the astuteness of his opponents. For example, an arrant simpleton is his opponent, and, holding up his closed hand, asks, "Are they even or odd?" Our school-boy replies, "Odd," and loses; but upon the second trial he wins, for he then says to himself: "The simpleton had them even upon the first trial, and his amount of cunning is just sufficient to make him have them odd upon the second; I will therefore guess odd"; – he guesses odd, and wins. Now, with a simpleton a degree above the first, he would have reasoned thus: "This fellow finds that in the first instance I guessed odd, and, in the second, he will propose to himself, upon the first impulse, a simple variation from even to odd, as did the first simpleton; but then a second thought will suggest that this is too simple a variation, and finally he will decide upon putting it even as before. I will therefore guess even"; – he guesses even, and wins. Now this mode of reasoning in the school-boy, whom his fellows termed "lucky", – what, in its last analysis, is it?'

'It is merely,' I said, 'an identification of the reasoner's intellect with that of his opponent.'

'It is,' said Dupin; 'and, upon inquiring of the boy by what means he effected the *thorough* identification in which his success consisted, I received answer as follows: "When I wish to find out how wise, or how stupid, or how good, or how wicked is any one, or what are his thoughts at the moment, I fashion the expression of my face, as accurately as possible, in accordance with the expression of his, and then wait to see what thoughts or sentiments arise in my mind or heart, as if to match or correspond with the expression." This response of the school-boy lies at the bottom of all the spurious profundity which has been attributed to Rochefoucault, to La Bougive, to Machiavelli, and to Campanella.'

'And the identification,' I said, 'of the reasoner's intellect with that of his opponent, depends, if I understand you aright, upon the accuracy with which the opponent's intellect is admeasured.'

'For its practical value it depends upon this,' replied Dupin; 'and the Prefect and his cohort fail so frequently, first, by default of this identification, and, secondly, by ill-admeasurement, or rather through non-admeasurement, of the intellect with which they are engaged. They consider only their *own* ideas of ingenuity; and, in searching for any thing hidden, advert only to the modes in which *they* would have hidden it. They are right in this much – that their own ingenuity is a faithful representative of that of *the mass*; but when the cunning of the individual felon is diverse in character from their own, the felon foils them, of course. This always happens when it is above their own, and very usually when it is below. They have no variation of principle in their investigations; at best, when urged by some unusual emergency – by some extraordinary reward – they extend or exaggerate their old modes of *practice*, without touching their principles. What, for example, in this case of D–, has been done to vary the principle of action? What is all this boring, and probing, and sounding, and scrutinizing with the microscope, and dividing the surface of the building into registered square inches – what is it all but an exaggeration of *the application* of the one principle or set of principles of search, which are based upon the one set of notions regarding human ingenuity, to which the Prefect, in the long routine of his duty, has been accustomed? Do you not see he has taken it for granted that *all* men proceed to conceal a letter, not exactly in a gimlet-hole bored in a chair-leg, but, at least, in *some* out-of-the-way hole or corner suggested by the same tenor of thought which would urge a man to secrete a letter in a gimlet-hole bored in a chair-leg? And do you not see also, that such *recherchés* nooks for concealment are adapted only for ordinary occasions, and would be adopted only by ordinary intellects; for, in all cases of concealment, a disposal of the article concealed – a disposal of it in this *recherché* manner, – is, in the very first instance, presumable and presumed; and thus its discovery depends, not at all upon the acumen, but altogether upon the mere care, patience, and determination of the seekers; and where the case is of importance – or, what amounts to the same thing in the political eyes, when the reward is of magnitude, – the qualities in question have *never* been known to fail. You will now understand what I meant in suggesting that, had the purloined letter been hidden anywhere within the limits of the Prefect's examination – in other words, had the principle of its concealment been comprehended within the principles of the Prefect – its discovery would have been a matter altogether beyond question. This functionary, however, has been thoroughly mystified; and the remote source of his defeat lies in the supposition that the Minister is a fool, because he has acquired renown as a poet. All fools are poets; this the Prefect *feels*; and he is merely guilty of a *non distributio medii* in thence inferring that all poets are fools.'

'But is this really the poet?' I asked. 'There are two brothers, I know; and both have attained reputation in letters. The Minister I believe has written learnedly on the Differential Calculus. He is a mathematician, and no poet.'

'You are mistaken; I know him well; he is both. As poet *and* mathematician, he would reason well; as mere mathematician, he could not have reasoned at all, and thus would have been at the mercy of the Prefect.'

'You surprise me,' I said, 'by these opinions, which have been contradicted by the voice of the world. You do not mean to set at naught the well-digested idea of centuries. The mathematical reason has long been regarded as *the* reason *par excellence.*'

' "*Il y a à parier,*" ' replied Dupin, quoting from Chamfort, ' "*que toute idée publique, toute convention reçue, est une sottise, car elle a convenue au plus grand nombre.*" The mathematicians, I grant you, have done their best to promulgate the popular error to which you allude, and which is none the less an error for its promulgation as truth. With an art worthy a better cause, for example, they have insinuated the term "analysis" into application to algebra. The French are the originators of this particular deception; but if a term is of any importance – if words derive any value from applicability – then "analysis" conveys "algebra" about as much as, in Latin, "*ambitus*" implies "ambition" "*religio*" "religion", or "*homines honesti*" a set of *honorable* men.'

'You have a quarrel on hand, I see,' said I, 'with some of the algebraists of Paris; but proceed.'

'I dispute the availability, and thus the value, of that reason which is cultivated in any especial form other than the abstractly logical. I dispute, in particular, the reason educed by mathematical study. The mathematics are the science of form and quantity; mathematical reasoning is merely logic applied to observation upon form and quantity. The great error lies in supposing that even the truths of what is called *pure* algebra are abstract or general truths. And this error is so egregious that I am confounded at the universality with which it has been received. Mathematical axioms are *not* axioms of general truth. What is true of *relation* – of form and quantity – is often grossly false in regard to morals, for example. In this latter science it is very usually *un*true that the aggregated parts are equal to the whole. In chemistry also the axiom fails. In the consideration of motive it fails; for two motives, each of a given value, have not, necessarily, a value when united, equal to the sum of their values apart. There are numerous other mathematical truths which are only truths within the limits of *relation*. But the mathematician argues from his *finite truths*, through habit, as if they were of an absolutely general applicability – as the world indeed imagines them to be. Bryant, in his very learned "Mythology," mentions an analogous source of error, when he says that "although the pagan fables are not believed, yet we forget ourselves continually, and make inferences from them as existing realities." With the algebraists, however, who are pagans themselves, the "pagan fables" *are* believed, and the inferences are made, not so much through lapse of memory as through an unaccountable addling of the brains. In short, I never yet encountered the mere mathematician who would be trusted out of equal roots, or one who did not clandestinely hold it as a point of his faith that $x^2 + px$ was absolutely and unconditionally equal to q. Say to one of these gentlemen, by way of experiment, if you please, that you believe occasions may occur where $x^2 + px$ is *not* altogether equal to q, and, having made him understand what you mean, get out of his reach as speedily as convenient, for, beyond doubt, he will endeavor to knock you down.

'I mean to say,' continued Dupin, while I merely laughed at his last observations, 'that if the Minister had been no more than a mathematician, the Prefect would have been under no necessity of giving me this check. I knew him, however, as both mathematician and poet, and my measures were adapted to his capacity, with reference to the circumstances by which he was surrounded. I knew him as a courtier, too, and as a bold *intriguant*. Such a man, I considered, could not fail to be aware of the ordinary policial modes of action. He could not have failed to anticipate – and events have proved that he did not fail to anticipate – the waylayings to which he was subjected. He must have foreseen, I reflected, the secret investigations of his premises. His frequent absences from home at night, which were hailed by the Prefect as certain aids to his success, I regarded only as *ruses*, to afford opportunity for horough search to the police, and thus the sooner to impress them with the conviction to which G–, in fact, did finally arrive – the conviction that the letter was not upon the premises. I felt, also, that the whole train of thought which I was at some pains in detailing to you just now, concerning the invariable principle of policial action in searches for articles concealed – I felt that this whole train of thought would necessarily pass through the mind of the Minister. It would imperatively lead him to despise all the ordinary *nooks* of concealment. *He* could not, I reflected, be so weak as not to see that the most intricate and remote recess of his hotel would be as open as his commonest closets to the eyes, to the probes, to the gimlets, and to the microscopes of the Prefect. I saw, in fine, that he would be driven, as a matter of course, to *simplicity*, if not deliberately induced to it as a matter of choice. You will remember, perhaps, how desperately the Prefect laughed when I suggested, upon our first interview, that it was just possible this mystery troubled him so much on account of its being so *very* self-evident.'

'Yes,' said I, 'I remember his merriment well. I really thought he would have fallen into convulsions.'

'The material world,' continued Dupin, 'abounds with very strict analogies to the immaterial; and thus some color of truth has been given to the rhetorical dogma, that metaphor, or simile, may be made to strengthen an argument as well as to embellish a description. The principle of the *vis inertiæ*, for example, seems to be identical in physics and metaphysics. It is not more true in the former, that a large body is with more difficulty set in motion than a smaller one, and that its subsequent *momentum* is commensurate with this difficulty, than it is, in the latter, that intellects of the vaster capacity, while more forcible, more constant, and more eventful in their movements than those of inferior grade, are yet the less readily moved, and more embarrassed, and full of hesitation in the first few steps of their progress. Again: have you ever noticed which of the street signs, over the shop doors, are the most attractive of attention?'

'I have never given the matter a thought,' I said.

'There is a game of puzzles,' he resumed, 'which is played

upon a map. One party playing requires another to find a given word – the name of town, river, state, or empire – any word, in short, upon the motley and perplexed surface of the chart. A novice in the game generally seeks to embarrass his opponents by giving them the most minutely lettered names; but the adept selects such words as stretch, in large characters, from one end of the chart to the other. These, like the over-largely lettered signs and placards of the street, escape observation by dint of being excessively obvious; and here the physical oversight is precisely analogous with the moral inapprehension by which the intellect suffers to pass unnoticed those considerations which are too obtrusively and too palpably self-evident. But this is a point, it appears, somewhat above or beneath the understanding of the Prefect. He never once thought it probable, or possible, that the Minister had deposited the letter immediately beneath the nose of the whole world, by way of best preventing any portion of that world from perceiving it.

'But the more I reflected upon the daring, dashing, and discriminating ingenuity of D–; upon the fact that the document must always have been *at hand*, if he intended to use it to good purpose; and upon the decisive evidence, obtained by the Prefect, that it was not hidden within the limits of that dignitary's ordinary search – the more satisfied I became that, to conceal this letter, the Minister had resorted to the comprehensive and sagacious expedient of not attempting to conceal it at all.

'Full of these ideas, I prepared myself with a pair of green spectacles, and called one fine morning, quite by accident, at the Ministerial hotel. I found D– at home, yawning, lounging, and dawdling, as usual, and pretending to be in the last extremity of *ennui*. He is, perhaps, the most really energetic human being now alive – but that is only when nobody sees him.

'To be even with him, I complained of my weak eyes, and lamented the necessity of the spectacles, under cover of which I cautiously and thoroughly surveyed the whole apartment, while seemingly intent only upon the conversation of my host.

'I paid especial attention to a large writing-table near which he sat, and upon which lay confusedly, some miscellaneous letters and other papers, with one or two musical instruments and a few books. Here, however, after a long and very deliberate scrutiny, I saw nothing to excite particular suspicion.

'At length my eyes, in going the circuit of the room, fell upon a trumpery filigree card-rack of pasteboard, that hung dangling by a dirty blue ribbon, from a little brass knob just beneath the middle of the mantelpiece. In this rack, which had three or four compartments, were five or six visiting cards and a solitary letter. This last was much soiled and crumpled. It was torn nearly in two, across the middle – as if a design, in the first instance, to tear it entirely up as worthless, had been altered, or stayed, in the second. It had a large black seal, bearing the D– cipher *very* conspicuously, and was addressed, in a diminutive female hand, to D–, the Minister, himself. It was thrust carelessly, and even, as it seemed, contemptuously, into one of the uppermost divisions of the rack.

'No sooner had I glanced at this letter than I concluded it to be that of which I was in search. To be sure, it was, to all appearance, radically different from the one of which the Prefect had read us so minute a description. Here the seal was large and black, with the D– cipher; there it was small and red, with the ducal arms of the S– family. Here, the address, to the Minister, was diminutive and feminine; there the superscription, to a certain royal personage, was markedly bold and decided; the size alone formed a point of correspondence. But, then, the *radicalness* of these differences, which was excessive; the dirt; the soiled and torn condition of the paper, so inconsistent with the *true* methodical habits of D–, and so suggestive of a design to delude the beholder into an idea of the worthlessness of the document; – these things, together with the hyperobtrusive situation of this document, full in the view of every visitor, and thus exactly in accordance with the conclusions to which I had previously arrived; these things, I say, were strongly corroborative of suspicion, in one who came with the intention to suspect.

'I protracted my visit as long as possible, and, while I maintained a most animated discussion with the Minister, upon a topic which I knew well had never failed to interest and excite him, I kept my attention really riveted upon the letter. In this examination, I committed to memory its external appearance and arrangement in the rack; and also fell, at length, upon a discovery which set at rest whatever trivial doubt I might have entertained. In scrutinizing the edges of the paper, I observed them to be more *chafed* than seemed necessary. They presented the *broken* appearance which is manifested when a stiff paper, having been once folded and pressed with a folder, is refolded in a reversed direction, in the same creases or edges which had formed the original fold. This discovery was sufficient. It was clear to me that the letter had been turned, as a glove, inside out, re-directed and re-sealed. I bade the Minister good-morning, and took my departure at once, leaving a gold snuff-box upon the table.

'The next morning I called for the snuff-box, when we resumed, quite eagerly, the conversation of the preceding day. While thus engaged, however, a loud report, as if of a pistol, was heard immediately beneath the windows of the hotel, and was succeeded by a series of fearful screams, and the shoutings of a terrified mob. D– rushed to a casement, threw it open, and looked out. In the meantime I stepped to the card-rack, took the letter, put it in my pocket, and replaced it by a *fac-simile*, (so far as regards externals) which I had carefully prepared at my lodgings – imitating the D– cipher, very readily, by means of a seal formed of bread.

'The disturbance in the street had been occasioned by the frantic behavior of a man with a musket. He had fired it among a crowd of women and children. It proved, however, to have been without ball, and the fellow was suffered to go his way as a lunatic or a drunkard. When he had gone, D– came from the window, whither I had followed him immediately upon securing the object in view. Soon afterward I bade him farewell. The pretended lunatic was a man in my own pay.'

'But what purpose had you,' I asked, 'in replacing the letter by a *fac-simile*? Would it not have been better, at the first visit, to have seized it openly, and departed?'

'D–,' replied Dupin, 'is a desperate man, and a man of nerve. His hotel, too, is not without attendants devoted to his interests. Had I made the wild attempt you suggest, I might never have left the Ministerial presence alive. The good people of Paris might have heard of me no more. But I had an object apart from these considerations. You know my political prepossessions. In this matter, I act as a partisan of the lady concerned. For eighteen months the Minister has had her in his power. She has now him in hers – since, being unaware that the letter is not in his possession, he will proceed with his exactions as if it was. Thus will he inevitably commit himself, at once, to his political destruction. His downfall, too, will not be more precipitate than awkward. It is all very well to talk about the *facilis descensus Averni*; but in all kinds of climbing, as Catalani said of singing, it is far more easy to get up than to come down. In the present instance I have no sympathy – at least no pity – for him who descends. He is that *monstrum horrendum*, an unprincipled man of genius. I confess, however, that I should like very well to know the precise character of his thoughts, when, being defied by her whom the Prefect terms "à certain personage," he is reduced to opening the letter which I left for him in the card-rack.'

'How? did you put anything particular in it?'

'Why – it did not seem altogether right to leave the interior blank – that would have been insulting. D–, at Vienna once, did me an evil turn, which I told him, quite good-humouredly, that I should remember. So, as I knew he would feel some curiosity in regard to the identity of the person who had outwitted him, I thought it a pity not to give him a clue. He is well acquainted with my MS, and I just copied into the middle of the blank sheet the words–

"– Un dessein si funeste,
S'il n'est digne d'Atrée, est digne de Thyeste."

They are to be found in Crébillon's "Atrée." '

MURDER

Arnold Bennett

I

MANY great ones of the earth have justified murder as a social act, defensible, and even laudable in certain instances. There is something to be said for murder, though perhaps not much. All of us, or nearly all of us, have at one time or another had the desire and the impulse to commit murder. At any rate, murder is not an uncommon affair. On an average, two people are murdered every week in England, and probably about two hundred every week in the United States. And forty per cent of the murderers are not brought to justice. These figures take no account of the undoubtedly numerous cases where murder has been done but never suspected. Murders and murderesses walk safely abroad among us, and it may happen to us to shake hands with them. A disturbing thought! But such is life, and such is homicide.

II

Two men, named respectively Lomax Harder and John Franting, were walking side by side one autumn afternoon, on the Marine Parade of the seaside resort and port of Quangate (English Channel). Both were well-dressed and had the air of moderate wealth, and both were about thirty-five years of age. At this point the resemblances between them ceased. Lomax Harder had refined features, an enormous forehead, fair hair, and a delicate, almost apologetic manner. John Franting was low-browed, heavy-chinned, scowling, defiant, indeed what is called a tough customer. Lomax Harder corresponded in appearance with the popular notion of a poet – save that he was carefully barbered. He was in fact a poet, and not unknown in the tiny, trifling, mad world where poetry is a matter of first-rate interest. John Franting corresponded in appearance with the popular notion of a gambler, an amateur boxer, and, in spare time, a deluder of women. Popular notions sometimes fit the truth.

Lomax Harder, somewhat nervously buttoning his overcoat, said in a quiet but firm and insistent tone:

'Haven't you got anything to say?'

John Franting stopped suddenly in front of a shop whose façade bore the sign: 'Gontle. Gunsmith.'

'Not in words,' answered Franting. 'I'm going in here.'

And he brusquely entered the small, shabby shop.

Lomax Harder hesitated half a second, and then followed his companion.

The shopman was a middle-aged gentleman wearing a black velvet coat.

'Good afternoon,' he greeted Franting, with an expression and in a tone of urbane condescension which seemed to indicate that Franting was a wise as well as a fortunate man in that he knew of the excellence of Gontle's and had the wit to come into Gontle's.

For the name of Gontle was favourably and respectfully known wherever triggers are pressed. Not only along the whole length of the Channel coast, but throughout England, was Gontle's renowned. Sportsmen would travel to Quangate from the far north, and even from London, to buy guns. To say: 'I bought it at Gontle's,' or 'Old Gontle recommended it,' was sufficient to silence any dispute concerning the merits of a fire-arm. Experts bowed the head before the unique reputation of Gontle. As for old Gontle, he was extremely and pardonably conceited. His conviction that no other gunsmith in the wide world could compare with him was absolute. He sold guns and rifles with the gesture of a monarch conferring an honour. He never argued; he stated; and the customer who contradicted him was as likely as not to be courteously and icily informed by Gontle of the geographical situation of the shop-door. Such shops exist in the English provinces, and nobody knows how they have achieved their renown. They could exist nowhere else.

''d afternoon,' said Franting gruffly, and paused.

'What can I do for you?' asked Mr Gontle, as if saying: 'Now don't be afraid. This shop is tremendous, and I am tremendous; but I shall not eat you.'

'I want a revolver,' Franting snapped.

'Ah! A revolver!' commented Mr Gontle, as if saying: 'A gun or a rifle, yes! But a revolver – an arm without individuality, manufactured wholesale! . . . However, I suppose I must deign to accommodate you.'

'I presume you know something about revolvers?' asked Mr Gontle, as he began to produce the weapons.

'A little.'

'Do you know the Webley Mark III?'

'Can't say that I do.'

'Ah! It is the best for all common purposes.' And Mr Gontle's glance said: 'Have the goodness not to tell me it isn't.'

Franting examined the Webley Mark III.

'You see,' said Mr Gontle. 'The point about it is that until the breech is properly closed it cannot be fired. So that it can't blow open and maim or kill the would-be murderer.' Mr Gontle smiled archly at one of his oldest jokes.

'What about suicides?' Franting grimly demanded.

'Ah!'

'You might show me just how to load it,' said Franting.

Mr Gontle, having found ammunition, complied with this reasonable request.

'The barrel's a bit scratched,' said Franting.

Mr Gontle inspected the scratch with pain. He would have denied the scratch, but could not.

'Here's another one,' said he, 'since you're so particular.' He simply had to put customers in their place.

'You might load it,' said Franting.

Mr Gontle loaded the second revolver.

'I'd like to try it,' said Franting.

'Certainly,' said Mr Gontle, and led Franting out of the shop by the back, and down to a cellar where revolvers could be experimented with.

Lomax Harder was now alone in the shop. He hesitated a long time and then picked up the revolver rejected by Franting, fingered it, put it down, and picked it up again. The back-door of the shop opened suddenly, and, startled, Harder dropped the revolver into his overcoat pocket: a thoughtless, quite unpremeditated act. He dared not remove the revolver. The revolver was as fast in his pocket as though the pocket had been sewn up.

'And cartridges?' asked Mr Gontle of Franting.

'Oh,' said Franting, 'I've only had one shot. Five'll be more than enough for the present. What does it weigh?'

'Let me see. Four inch barrel? Yes. One pound four ounces.'

Franting paid for the revolver, receiving thirteen shillings in change from a five-pound note, and strode out of the shop, weapon in hand. He was gone before Lomax Harder decided upon a course of action.

'And for you, sir?' said Mr Gontle, addressing the poet.

Harder suddenly comprehended that Mr Gontle had mistaken him for a separate customer, who had happened to enter the shop a moment after the first one. Harder and Franting had said not a word to one another during the purchase, and Harder well knew that in the most exclusive shops it is the custom utterly to ignore a second customer until the first one has been dealt with.

'I want to see some foils.' Harder spoke stammeringly the only words that came into his head.

'Foils!' exclaimed Mr Gontle, shocked, as if to say: 'Is it conceivable that you should imagine that I, Gontle, gunsmith, sell such things as foils?'

After a little talk Harder apologized and departed – a thief.

'I'll call later and pay the fellow,' said Harder to his restive conscience. 'No. I can't do that. I'll send him some anonymous postal orders.'

He crossed the Parade and saw Franting, a small left-handed figure all alone far below on the deserted sands, pointing the revolver. He thought that his ear caught the sound of a discharge, but the distance was too great for him to be sure. He continued to watch, and at length Franting walked westward diagonally across the beach.

'He's going back to the Bellevue,' thought Harder, the Bellevue being the hotel from which he had met Franting coming out half an hour earlier. He strolled slowly towards the white hotel. But Franting, who had evidently come up the face of the cliff in the penny lift, was before him. Harder, standing outside, saw Franting seated in the lounge. Then Franting rose and vanished down a long passage at the rear of the lounge. Harder entered the hotel rather guiltily. There was no hall-porter at the door, and not a soul in the lounge or in sight of the lounge. Harder went down the long passage.

III

At the end of the passage Lomax Harder found himself in a billiard-room – an apartment built partly of brick and partly of wood on a sort of courtyard behind the main structure of the hotel. The roof, of iron and grimy glass, rose to a point in the middle. On two sides the high walls of the hotel obscured the light. Dusk was already closing in. A small fire burned feebly in the grate. A large radiator under the window was steel-cold, for though summer was finished, winter had not officially begun in the small economically-run hotel: so that the room was chilly; nevertheless, in deference to the English passion for fresh air and discomfort, the window was wide open.

Franting, in his overcoat, and an unlit cigarette between his lips, stood lowering with his back to the bit of fire. At sight of Harder he lifted his chin in a dangerous challenge.

'So you're still following me about,' he said resentfully to Harder.

'Yes,' said the latter, with his curious gentle primness of manner. 'I came down here specially to talk to you. I should have said all I had to say earlier, only you happened to be going out of the hotel just as I was coming in. You didn't seem to want to talk in the street; but there's some talking has to be done. I've a few things I must tell you.' Harder appeared to be perfectly calm, and he felt perfectly calm. He advanced from the door towards the billiard-table.

Franting raised his hand, displaying his square-ended, brutal fingers in the twilight.

'Now listen to me,' he said with cold, measured ferocity. 'You can't tell me anything I don't know. If there's some talking to be done I'll do it myself, and when I've finished you can get out. I know that my wife has taken a ticket for Copenhagen by the steamer from Harwich, and that she's been seeing to her passport, and packing. And of course I know that you have interests in Copenhagen and spend about half your precious time there. I'm not worrying to connect the two things. All that's got nothing to do with me. Emily has always seen a great deal of you, and I know that the last week or two she's been seeing you more than ever. Not that I mind that. I know that she objects to my treatment of her and my conduct generally. That's all right, but it's a matter that only concerns her and me. I mean that it's no concern of yours, for instance, or anybody else's. If she objects enough she can try and divorce me. I doubt if she'd succeed, but you can never be sure – with these new laws. Anyhow she's my wife till she does divorce me, and so she has the usual duties and responsibilities towards me – even though I was the worst husband in the world. That's how I look at it, in my old-fashioned way. I've just had a letter from her – she knew I was here, and I expect that explains how you knew I was here.'

'It does,' said Lomax Harder quietly.

Franting pulled a letter out of his inner pocket and unfolded it.

'Yes,' he said, glancing at it, and read some sentences aloud: ' "I have absolutely decided to leave you, and I won't hide from you that I know you know who is doing what he can to help me. I can't live with you any longer. You may be very fond of me, as you say, but I find your way of showing your fondness too humiliating and painful. I've said this to you before, and now I'm saying it for the last time." And so on and so on.'

Franting tore the letter in two, dropped one half on the floor, twisted the other half into a spill, turned to the fire, and lit his cigarette.

'That's what I think of her letter,' he proceeded, the cigarette between his teeth. 'You're helping her, are you? Very well. I don't say you're in love with her, or she with you. I'll make no wild statements. But if you aren't in love with her I wonder why you're taking all this trouble over her. Do you go about the world helping ladies who say they're unhappy just for the pure sake of helping? Never mind. Emily isn't going to leave me. Get that into your head. I shan't let her leave me. She has money, and I haven't. I've been living on her, and it would be infernally awkward for me if she left me for good. That's a reason for keeping her, isn't it? But you may believe me or not – it isn't my reason. She's right enough when she says I'm very fond of her. That's a reason for keeping her too. But it isn't my reason. My reason is that a wife's a wife, and she can't break her word just because everything isn't lovely in the garden. I've heard it said I'm unmoral. I'm not all unmoral. And I feel particularly strongly about what's called the marriage tie.' He drew the revolver from his overcoat pocket, and held it up to view. 'You see this thing. You saw me buy it. Now you needn't be afraid. I'm not threatening you; and it's no part of my game to shoot you. I've nothing to do with your goings-on. What I have to do with is the goings-on of my wife. If she deserts me – for you or for anybody or for nobody – I shall follow her, whether it's to Copenhagen or Bangkok or the North Pole, and I shall kill her – with just this very revolver that you saw me buy. And now you can get out.'

Franting replaced the revolver, and began to consume the cigarette with fierce and larger puffs.

Lomax Harder looked at the grim, set, brutal, scowling bitter face, and knew that Franting meant what he had said. Nothing would stop him from carrying out his threat. The fellow was not an argufier; he could not reason; but he had unmistakable grit and would never recoil from the fear of consequences. If Emily left him, Emily was a dead woman; nothing in the end could protect her from the execution of her husband's menace. On the other hand, nothing would persuade her to remain with her husband. She had decided to go, and she would go. And indeed the mere thought of this lady to whom he, Harder, was utterly devoted, staying with her husband and continuing to suffer the tortures and humiliations which she had been suffering for years – this thought revolted him. He could not think it.

He stepped forward along the side of the billiard-table, and simultaneously Franting stepped forward to meet him. Lomax Harder snatched the revolver which was in his pocket, aimed, and pulled the trigger.

Franting collapsed, with the upper half of his body somehow balanced on the edge of the billiard-table. He was dead. The sound of the report echoed in Harder's ear like the sound of a violin string loudly twanged by a finger. He saw a little reddish hole in Franting's bronzed right temple.

'Well,' he thought, 'somebody had to die. And it's better him than Emily.' He felt that he had performed a righteous act. Also he felt a little sorry for Franting.

Then he was afraid. He was afraid for himself, because he wanted not to die, especially on the scaffold; but also for Emily Franting who would be friendless and helpless without him; he could not bear to think of her alone in the world – the central point of a terrific scandal. He must get away instantly . . .

Not down the corridor back into the hotel-lounge! No! That would be fatal! The window. He glanced at the corpse. It was more odd, curious, than affrighting. He had made the corpse. Strange! He could not unmake it. He had accomplished the irrevocable. Impressive! He saw Franting's cigarette glowing on the linoleum in the deepening dusk, and picked it up and threw it into the fender.

Lace curtains hung across the whole width of the window. He drew one aside, and looked forth. The light was much stronger in the courtyard than within the room. He put his gloves on. He gave a last look at the corpse, straddled the window-sill, and was on the brick pavement of the courtyard. He saw that the curtain had fallen back into the perpendicular.

He gazed around. Nobody! Not a light in any window! He saw a green wooden gate, pushed it; it yielded; then a sort of entry-passage . . . In a moment, after two half-turns, he was on the Marine Parade again. He was a fugitive. Should he fly to the right, to the left? Then he had an inspiration. An idea of genius for baffling pursuers. He would go into the hotel by the main-entrance. He went slowly and deliberately into the portico, where a middle-aged hall-porter was standing in the gloom.

'Good evening, sir.'

'Good evening. Have you got any rooms?'

'I think so, sir. The housekeeper is out, but she'll be back in a moment – if you'd like a seat. The manager's away in London.'

The hall-porter suddenly illuminated the lounge, and Lomax Harder, blinking, entered and sat down.

'I might have a cocktail while I'm waiting,' the murderer suggested with a bright and friendly smile. 'A Bronx.'

'Certainly, sir. The page is off duty. He sees to orders in the lounge, but I'll attend to you myself.'

'What a hotel!' thought the murderer, solitary in the chilly lounge, and gave a glance down the long passage. 'Is the whole place run by the hall-porter? But of course it's the dead season.'

Was it conceivable that nobody had heard the sound of the shot?

Harder had a strong impulse to run away. But no! To do so would be highly dangerous. He restrained himself.

'How much?' he asked of the hall-porter, who had arrived with surprising quickness, tray in hand and glass on tray.

'A shilling, sir.'

The murderer gave him eighteenpence, and drank off the cocktail.

'Thank you very much, sir.' The hall-porter took the glass.

'See here!' said the murderer. 'I'll look in again. I've got one or two little errands to do.'

And he went, slowly, into the obscurity of the Marine Parade.

IV

Lomax Harder leant over the left arm of the sea-wall of the man-made port of Quangate. Not another soul was there. Night had fallen. The lighthouse at the extremity of the right arm was occulting. The lights – some red, some green, many white – of ships at sea passed in both directions in endless processions. Waves plashed gently against the vast masonry of the wall. The wind, blowing steadily from the north-west, was not cold. Harder, looking about – though he knew he was absolutely alone, took his revolver from his overcoat pocket and stealthily dropped it into the sea. Then he turned round and gazed across the small harbour at the mysterious amphitheatre of the lighted town, and heard public clocks and religious clocks striking the hour.

He was a murderer, but why should he not successfully escape detection? Other murderers had done so. He had all his wits. He was not excited. He was not morbid. His perspective of things was not askew. The hall-porter had not seen his first entrance into the hotel, nor his exit after the crime. Nobody had seen them. He had left nothing behind in the billiard-room. No finger marks on the window-sill. (The putting-on of his gloves was in itself a clear demonstration that he had fully kept his presence of mind.) No footmarks on the hard, dry pavement of the courtyard.

Of course there was the possibility that some person unseen had seen him getting out of the window. Slight: but still a possibility! And there was also the possibility that someone who knew Franting by sight had noted him walking by Franting's side in the streets. If such a person informed the police and gave a description of him, inquiries might be made . . . No! Nothing in it. His appearance offered nothing remarkable to the eye of a casual observer – except his forehead, of which he was rather proud, but which was hidden by his hat.

It was generally believed that criminals always did something silly. But so far he had done nothing silly, and he was convinced that, in regard to the crime, he never would do anything silly. He had none of the desire, supposed to be common among murderers, to revisit the scene of the crime or to look upon the corpse once more. Although he regretted the necessity for his act, he felt no slightest twinge of conscience. Somebody had to die, and surely it was better that a brute should die than the heavenly, enchanting, martyrized creature whom his act had rescued for ever from the brute! He was aware within himself of an ecstasy of devotion to Emily Franting – now a widow and free. She was a unique woman. Strange that a woman of such gifts should have come under the sway of so obvious a scroundrel as Franting. But she was very young at the time, and such freaks of sex had happened before and would happen again; they were a widespread phenomenon in the history of the relations of men and women. He would have killed a hundred men if a hundred men had threatened her felicity. His heart was pure; he wanted nothing from Emily in exchange for what he had done in her defence. He was passionate in her defence. When he reflected upon the coarseness and cruelty of the gesture by which Franting had used Emily's letter to light his cigarette, Harder's cheeks grew hot with burning resentment.

A clock struck the quarter. Harder walked quickly to the harbour front, where was a taxi-rank, and drove to the station . . . A sudden apprehension! The crime might have been discovered! Police might already be watching for suspicious-looking travellers! Absurd! Still, the apprehension remained despite its absurdity. The taxi-driver looked at him queerly. No! Imagination! He hesitated on the threshold of the station, then walked boldly in, and showed his return ticket to the ticket-inspector. No sign of a policeman. He got into the Pullman car, where five other passengers were sitting. The train started.

V

He nearly missed the boat-train at Liverpool Street because according to its custom the Quangate flyer arrived twenty minutes late at Victoria. And at Victoria the foolish part of him, as distinguished from the common-sense part, suffered another spasm of fear. Would detectives, instructed by telegraph, be waiting for the train? No! An absurd idea! The boat-train from Liverpool Street was crowded with travellers, and the platform crowded with senders-off. He gathered from scraps of talk overhead that an international conference was about to take place at Copenhagen. And he had known nothing of it – not seen a word of it in the papers! Excusable perhaps; graver matters had held his attention.

Useless to look for Emily in the vast bustle of the compartments! She had her through ticket (which she had taken herself, in order to avoid possible complications), and she happened to be the only woman in the world who was never late and never in a hurry. She was certain to be in the train. But was she in the train? Something sinister might have come to pass. For instance, a telephone message to the flat that her husband had been found dead with a bullet in his brain.

The swift two-hour journey to Harwich was terrible for Lomax Harder. He remembered that he had left the unburnt part of the letter lying under the billiard-table. Forgetful! Silly! One of the silly things that criminals did! And on Parkeston Quay the confusion was enormous. He did not walk, he was swept, on to the great shaking steamer whose dark funnels rose amid wisps of steam into the starry sky. One advantage: detectives would have no chance in that multitudinous scene, unless indeed they held up the ship.

The ship roared a warning, and slid away from the quay, groped down the tortuous channel to the harbour mouth, and was in the North Sea; and England dwindled to naught but a string of lights. He searched every deck from stem to stern, and could not find Emily. She had not caught the train, or, if she had caught the train, she had not boarded the steamer because he had failed to appear. His misery was intense. Everything was going wrong. And on the arrival at Esbjerg would not detectives be lying in wait for the Copenhagen train? . . .

Then he descried her, and she him. She too had been searching. Only chance had kept them apart. Her joy at finding him was ecstatic; tears came into his eyes at sight of it. He was everything to her, absolutely everything. He clasped her right hand in both his hands and gazed at her in the dim, diffused light blended of stars, moon and electricity. No woman was ever like her: mature, innocent, wise, trustful, honest. And the touching beauty of her appealing, sad, happy face, and the pride of her carriage! A unique jewel – snatched from the brutal grasp of that fellow – who had ripped her solemn letter in two and used it as a spill for his cigarette! She related her movements; and he his. Then she said:

'Well?'

'I didn't go,' he answered. 'Thought it best not to. I'm convinced it wouldn't have been any use.'

He had not intended to tell her this lie. Yet when it came to the point, what else could he say? He told one lie instead of twenty. He was deceiving her, but for her sake. Even if the worst occurred, she was for ever safe from that brutal grasp. And he had saved her. As for the conceivable complications of the future, he refused to front them; he could live in the marvellous present. He felt suddenly the amazing beauty of the night at sea, and beneath all his other sensations was the obscure sensation of a weight at his heart.

'I expect you were right,' she angelically acquiesced.

VI

The Superintendent of Police (Quangate was the county town of the western half of the county), and a detective-sergeant were in the billiard-room of the Bellevue. Both wore mufti. The powerful green-shaded lamps usual in billiard-rooms shone down ruthlessly on the green table, and on the reclining body of John Franting, which had not moved and had not been moved.

A charwoman was just leaving these officers when a stout gentleman, who had successfully beguiled a policeman guarding the other end of the long corridor, squeezed past her, greeted the two officers, and shut the door.

The Superintendent, a thin man, with lips to match, and a moustache, stared hard at the arrival.

'I am staying with my friend Dr Furnival,' said the arrival cheerfully. 'You telephoned for him, and as he had to go out to one of those cases in which nature will not wait, I offered to come in his place. I've met you before, Superintendent, at Scotland Yard.'

'Dr Austin Bond!' exclaimed the Superintendent.

'He,' said the other.

They shook hands, Dr Bond genially, the Superintendent half-consequential, half-deferential, as one who had his dignity to think about; also as one who resented an intrusion, but dared not show resentment.

The detective-sergeant recoiled at the dazzling name of the great amateur detective, a genius who had solved the famous mysteries of 'The Yellow Hat,' 'The Three Towns,' 'The Three Feathers,' 'The Gold Spoon,' etc., etc., etc., whose devilish perspicacity had again and again made professional detectives both look and feel foolish, and whose notorious friendship with the loftiest heads of Scotland Yard compelled all police forces to treat him very politely indeed.

'Yes,' said Dr Austin Bond, after detailed examination. 'Been shot about ninety minutes, poor fellow! Who found him?'

'That woman who's just gone out. Some servant here. Came in to look after the fire.'

'How long since?'

'Oh! About an hour ago.'

'Found the bullet? I see it hit the brass on that cue-rack there.'

The detective-sergeant glanced at the Superintendent, who, however, resolutely remained unastonished.

'Here's the bullet,' said the Superintendent.

'Ah!' commented Dr Austin Bond, glinting through his spectacles at the bullet as it lay in the Superintendent's hand. 'Decimal 38, I see. Flattened. It would be.'

'Sergeant,' said the Superintendent. 'You can get help and have the body moved, now Dr Bond has made his examination. Eh, Doctor?'

'Certainly,' answered Dr Bond, at the fireplace. 'He was smoking a cigarette, I see.'

'Either he or his murderer.'

'You've got a clue?'

'Oh yes,' the Superintendent answered, not without pride. 'Look here. Your torch, sergeant.'

The detective-sergeant produced a pocket electric-lamp, and the Superintendent turned to the window-sill.

'I've got a stronger one than that,' said Dr Austin Bond, producing another torch.

The Superintendent displayed finger-prints on the window-frame, footmarks on the sill, and a few strands of inferior blue cloth. Dr Austin Bond next produced a magnifying glass, and inspected the evidence at very short range.

'The murderer must have been a tall man – you can judge that from the angle of fire; he wore a blue suit, which he tore slightly on this splintered wood of the window-frame; one of his boots had a hole in the middle of the sole, and he'd only three fingers on his left hand. He must have come in by the window and gone out by the window, because the hall-porter is sure that nobody except the dead man entered the lounge by any door within an hour of the time when the murder must have been committed.' The Superintendent proudly gave many more details, and ended by saying that he had already given instructions to circulate a description.

'Curious,' said Dr Austin Bond, 'that a man like John Franting should let anyone enter the room by the window! Especially a shabby-looking man!'

'You knew the deceased personally then?'

'No! But I know he was John Franting.'

'How, Doctor?'

'Luck.'

'Sergeant,' said the Superintendent, piqued. 'Tell the constable to fetch the hall-porter.'

Dr Austin Bond walked to and fro, peering everywhere, and picked up a piece of paper that had lodged against the step of the platform which ran round two sides of the room for the raising of the spectators' benches. He glanced at the paper casually, and dropped it again.

'My man,' the Superintendent addressed the hall-porter. 'How can you be sure that nobody came in here this afternoon?'

'Because I was in my cubicle all the time, sir.'

The hall-porter was lying. But he had to think of his own

welfare. On the previous day he had been reprimanded for quitting his post against the rule. Taking advantage of the absence of the manager, he had sinned once again, and he lived in fear of dismissal if found out.

'With a full view of the lounge?'

'Yes, sir.'

'Might have been in there beforehand,' Dr Austin Bond suggested.

'No,' said the Superintendent. 'The charwoman came in twice. Once just before Franting came in. She saw the fire wanted making up and she went for some coal, and then returned later with some coal. But the look of Franting frightened her, and she went back with her coal.'

'Yes,' said the hall-porter. 'I saw that.'

Another lie.

At a sign from the Superintendent he withdrew.

'I should like to have a word with that charwoman,' said Dr Austin Bond.

The Superintendent hesitated. Why should the great amateur meddle with what did not concern him? Nobody had asked his help. But the Superintendent thought of the amateur's relations with Scotland Yard, and sent for the charwoman.

'Did you clean the window here today?' Dr Austin Bond interrogated her.

'Yes, please, sir.'

'Show me your left hand.' The slattern obeyed. 'How did you lose your little finger?'

'In a mangle accident, sir.'

'Just come to the window, will you, and put your hands on it. But take off your left boot first.'

The slattern began to weep.

'It's quite all right, my good creature.' Dr Austin Bond reassured her. 'Your skirt is torn at the hem, isn't it?'

When the slattern was released from her ordeal and had gone, carrying one boot in her grimy hand, Dr Austin Bond said genially to the Superintendent:

'Just a fluke. I happened to notice she'd only three fingers on her left hand when she passed me in the corridor. Sorry I've destroyed your evidence. But I felt sure almost from the first that the murderer hadn't either entered or decamped by the window.'

'How?'

'Because I think he's still here in the room.'

The two police officers gazed about them as if exploring the room for the murderer.

'I think he's there.'

Dr Austin Bond pointed to the corpse.

'And where did he hide the revolver after he'd killed himself?' demanded the thin-lipped Superintendent icily, when he had somewhat recovered his aplomb.

'I'd thought of that, too,' said Dr Austin Bond, beaming. 'It is always a very wise course to leave a dead body absolutely untouched until a professional man has seen it. But *looking* at the body can do no harm. You see the left-hand pocket of the overcoat. Notice how it bulges. Something unusual in it. Something that has the shape of a – Just feel inside it, will you?'

The Superintendent, obeying, drew a revolver from the overcoat pocket of the dead man.

'Ah! Yes!' said Dr Austin Bond. 'A Webley Mark III. Quite new. You might take out the ammunition.' The Superintendent dismantled the weapon. 'Yes, yes! Three chambers empty. Wonder how he used the other two! Now, where's that bullet? You see? He fired. His arm dropped, and the revolver happened to fall into the pocket.'

'Fired with his left hand, did he?' asked the Superintendent, foolishly ironic.

'Certainly. A dozen years ago Franting was perhaps the finest amateur light-weight boxer in England. And one reason for it was that he bewildered his opponents by being left-handed. His lefts were much more fatal than his rights. I saw him box several times.'

Whereupon Dr Austin Bond strolled to the step of the platform near the door and picked up the fragment of very thin paper that was lying there.

'This,' said he, 'must have blown from the hearth to here by the draught from the window when the door was opened. It's part of a letter. You can see the burnt remains of the other part in the corner of the fender. He probably lighted the cigarette with it. Out of bravado! His last bravado! Read this.'

The Superintendent read:

'. . . repeat that I realize how fond you are of me, but you have killed my affection for you, and I shall leave our home tomorrow. This is absolutely final. E.'

Dr Austin Bond, having for the nth time satisfactorily demonstrated in his own unique, rapid way, that police-officers were a set of numskulls, bade the Superintendent a most courteous good evening, nodded amicably to the detective-sergeant, and left in triumph.

VII

'I must get some mourning and go back to the flat,' said Emily Franting.

She was sitting one morning in the lobby of the Palads Hotel, Copenhagen. Lomax Harder had just called on her with an English newspaper containing an account of the inquest at which the jury had returned a verdict of suicide upon the body of her late husband. Her eyes filled with tears.

'Time will put her right,' thought Lomax Harder, tenderly watching her. 'I was bound to do what I did. And I can keep a secret for ever.'

THE KING IN YELLOW

Raymond Chandler

I

GEORGE Millar, night auditor at the Carlton Hotel, was a dapper wiry little man, with a soft deep voice like a torch-singer's. He kept it low, but his eyes were sharp and angry, as he said into the PBX mouthpiece: 'I'm very sorry. It won't happen again. I'll send up at once.'

He tore off the head-piece, dropped it on the keys of the switchboard and marched swiftly from behind the pebbled screen and out into the entrance lobby. It was past one and the Carlton was two-thirds residential. In the main lobby, down three shallow steps, lamps were dimmed and the night porter had finished tidying up. The place was deserted – a wide space of dim furniture, rich carpet. Faintly in the distance a radio sounded. Millar went down the steps and walked quickly towards the sound, turned through an archway and looked at a man stretched out on a pale-green davenport and what looked like all the loose cushions in the hotel. He lay on his side, dreamy-eyed and listened to the radio two yards away from him.

Millar barked: 'Hey, you! Are you the house dick here or the house cat?'

Steve Grayce turned his head slowly and looked at Millar. He was a long black-haired man, about twenty-eight, with deep-set silent eyes and a rather gentle mouth. He jerked a thumb at the radio and smiled. 'King Leopardi, George. Hear that trumpet tone. Smooth as an angel's wing, boy.'

'Swell! Go on back upstairs and get him out of the corridor!'

Steve Grayce looked shocked. 'What – again? I thought I had those birds put to bed long ago.' He swung his feet to the floor and stood up. He was at least a foot taller than Millar.

'Well, Eight-sixteen says no. Eight-sixteen says he's out in the hall with two of his stooges. He's dressed in yellow satin shorts and a trombone and he and his pals are putting on a jam session. And one of those hustlers Quillan registered in Eight-eleven is out there truckin' for them. Now get on to it, Steve – and this time make it stick.'

Steve Grayce smiled wryly. He said: 'Leopardi doesn't belong here anyway. Can I use chloroform or just my blackjack?'

He stepped long legs over the pale-green carpet, through the arch and across the main lobby to the single elevator that was open and lighted. He slid the doors shut and ran it up to Eight, stopped it roughly and stepped out into the corridor.

The noise hit him like a sudden wind. The walls echoed with it. Half a dozen doors were open and angry guests in night robes stood in them peering.

'It's O.K. folks,' Steve Grayce said rapidly. 'This is absolutely the last act. Just relax.'

He rounded a corner and the hot music almost took him off his feet. Three men were lined up against the wall, near an open door from which light streamed. The middle one, the one with the trombone, was six feet tall, powerful and graceful, with a hairline mustache. His face was flushed and his eyes had an alcoholic glitter. He wore yellow satin shorts with large initials embroidered in black on the left leg – nothing more. His torso was tanned and naked.

The two with him were in pajamas, the usual halfway-good-looking band boys, both drunk, but not staggering drunk. One jittered madly on a clarinet and the other on a tenor saxophone.

Back and forth in front of them, strutting, trucking, preening herself like a magpie, arching her arms and her eyebrows, bending her fingers back until the carmine nails almost touched her arms, a metallic blonde swayed and went to town on the music. Her voice was a throaty screech, without melody, as false as her eyebrows and as sharp as her nails. She wore high-heeled slippers and black pajamas with a long purple sash.

Steve Grayce stopped dead and made a sharp downward motion with his hand. 'Wrap it up!' he snapped. 'Can it. Put it on ice. Take it away and bury it. The show's out. Scram, now – scram!'

King Leopardi took the trombone from his lips and bellowed: 'Fanfare to a house dick!'

The three drunks blew a stuttering note that shook the walls. The girl laughed foolishly and kicked out. Her slipper caught Steve Grayce in the chest. He picked it out of the air, jumped towards the girl and took hold of her wrist.

'Tough, eh?' he grinned. 'I'll take you first.'

'Get him!' Leopardi yelled. 'Sock him low! Dance the gum-heel on his neck!'

Steve swept the girl off her feet, tucked her under his arm and ran. He carried her as easily as a parcel. She tried to kick his legs. He laughed and shot a glance through a lighted doorway. A man's brown brogues lay under a bureau. He went on past that to a second lighted doorway, slammed through and kicked the door shut, turned far enough to twist the tabbed key in the lock. Almost at once a fist hit the door. He paid no attention to it.

He pushed the girl along the short passage past the bathroom, and let her go. She reeled away from him and put her back to the bureau, panting, her eyes furious. A lock of damp gold-dipped hair swung down over one eye. She shook her head violently and bared her teeth.

'How would you like to get vagged, sister?'

'Go to hell!' she spit out. 'The King's a friend of mine, see? You better keep your paws off me, copper.'

'You run the circuit with the boys?'

She spat at him again.

'How'd you know they'd be here?'

Another girl was sprawled across the bed, her head to the wall, tousled black hair over a white face. There was a tear in the leg of her pajamas. She lay limp and groaned.

Steve said harshly: 'Oh, oh, the torn-pajama act. It flops here, sister, it flops hard. Now listen, you kids. You can go to bed and stay till morning or you can take the bounce. Make up your minds.'

The black-haired girl groaned. The blonde said: 'You get out of my room, you damned gum-heel!'

She reached behind her and threw a hand mirror. Steve ducked. The mirror slammed against the wall and fell without breaking. The black-haired girl rolled over on the bed and said wearily: 'Oh lay off. I'm sick.'

She lay with her eyes closed, the lids fluttering.

The blonde swiveled her hips across the room to a desk by the window, poured herself a full half-glass of Scotch in a water glass and gurgled it down before Steve could get to her. She choked violently, dropped the glass and went down on her hands and knees.

Steve said grimly: 'That's the one that kicks you in the face, sister.'

The girl crouched, shaking her head. She gagged once, lifted the carmine nails to paw at her mouth. She tried to get up, and her foot skidded out from under her and she fell down on her side and went fast asleep.

Steve sighed, went over, and shut the window and fastened it. He rolled the black-haired girl over and straightened her on the bed and got the bedclothes from under her, tucked a pillow under her head. He picked the blonde bodily off the floor and dumped her on the bed and covered both girls to the chin. He opened the transom, switched off the ceiling-light and unlocked the door. He relocked it from the outside with a master-key on a chain.

'Hotel business,' he said under his breath. 'Phooey.'

The corridor was empty now. One lighted door still stood open. Its number was 815, two doors from the room the girls were in. Trombone music came from it softly – but not softly enough for 1:25 a.m.

Steve Grayce turned into the room, crowded the door shut with his shoulder and went along past the bathroom. King Leopardi was alone in the room.

The bandleader was sprawled out in an easy chair, with a tall misted glass at his elbow. He swung the trombone in a tight circle as he played it and the lights danced in the horn.

Steve lit a cigarette, blew a plume of smoke and stared through it at Leopardi with a queer, half-admiring, half-contemptuous expression.

He said softly: 'Lights out, yellow-pants. You play a sweet trumpet and your trombone don't hurt either. But we can't use it here. I already told you that once. Lay off. Put that thing away.'

Leopardi smiled nastily and blew a stuttering raspberry that sounded like a devil laughing.

'Says you,' he sneered. 'Leopardi does what he likes, where he likes when he likes. Nobody's stopped him yet, gum-shoe. Take the air.'

Steve hunched his shoulders and went close to the tall dark man. He said patiently: 'Put that bazooka down, big-stuff. People are trying to sleep. They're funny that way. You're a great guy on a bandshell. Everywhere else you're just a guy with a lot of jack and a personal reputation that stinks from here to Miami and back. I've got a job to do and I'm doing it. Blow that thing again and I'll wrap it around your neck.'

Leopardi lowered the trombone and took a long drink from the glass at his elbow. His eyes glinted nastily. He lifted the trombone to his lips again, filled his lungs with air and blew a blast that rocked the walls. Then he stood up very suddenly and smoothly and smashed the instrument down on Steve's head.

'I never did like house-peepers,' he sneered. 'They smell like public toilets.'

Steve took a short step back and shook his head. He leered, slid forward on one foot and smacked Leopardi open-handed. The blow looked light, but Leopardi reeled all the way across the room and sprawled at the foot of the bed, sitting on the floor, his right arm draped in an open suitcase.

For a moment neither man moved. Then Steve kicked the trombone away from him and squashed his cigarette in a glass tray. His black eyes were empty but his mouth grinned whitely.

'If you want trouble,' he said, 'I come from where they make it.'

Leopardi smiled, thinly, tautly, and his right hand came up

out of the suitcase with a gun in it. His thumb snicked the safety catch. He held the gun steady, pointing.

'Make some with this,' he said, and fired.

The bitter roar of the gun seemed a tremendous sound in the closed room. The bureau mirror splintered and glass flew. A sliver cut Steve's cheek like a razor blade. Blood oozed in a small narrow line on his skin.

He left his feet in a dive. His right shoulder crashed against Leopardi's bare chest and his left hand brushed the gun away from him, under the bed. He rolled swiftly to his right and came up on his knees spinning.

He said thickly, harshly: 'You picked the wrong gee, brother.'

He swarmed on Leopardi and dragged him to his feet by his hair, by main strength. Leopardi yelled and hit him twice on the jaw and Steve grinned and kept his left hand twisted in the bandleader's long sleek black hair. He turned his hand and the head twisted with it and Leopardi's third punch landed on Steve's shoulder. Steve took hold of the wrist behind the punch and twisted that and the bandleader went down on his knees yowling. Steve lifted him by the hair again, let go of his wrist and punched him three times in the stomach, short terrific jabs. He let go of the hair then as he sank the fourth punch almost to his wrist.

Leopardi sagged blindly to his knees and vomited.

Steve stepped away from him and went into the bathroom and got a towel off the rack. He threw it at Leopardi, jerked the open suitcase onto the bed and started throwing things into it.

Leopardi wiped his face and got to his feet still gagging. He swayed, braced himself on the end of the bureau. He was white as a sheet.

Steve Grayce said: 'Get dressed, Leopardi. Or go out the way you are. It's all one to me.'

Leopardi stumbled into the bathroom, pawing the wall like a blind man.

II

Millar stood very still behind the desk as the elevator opened. His face was white and scared and his cropped black mustache was a smudge across his upper lip. Leopardi came out of the elevator first, a muffler around his neck, a lightweight coat tossed over his arm, a hat tilted on his head. He walked stiffly, bent forward a little, his eyes vacant. His face had a greenish pallor.

Steve Grayce stepped out behind him carrying a suitcase, and Carl, the night porter came last with two more suitcases and two instrument cases in black leather. Steve marched over to the desk and said harshly: 'Mr Leopardi's bill – if any. He's checking out.'

Millar goggled at him across the marble desk. 'I – I don't think, Steve – '

'O.K. I thought not.'

Leopardi smiled very thinly and unpleasantly and walked out through the brass-edged swing-doors the porter held open for him. There were two nighthawk cabs in the line. One of them came to life and pulled up to the canopy and the porter loaded Leopardi's stuff into it. Leopardi got into the cab and leaned forward to put his head to the open window. He said slowly and thickly: 'I'm sorry for you, gum-heel. I mean sorry.'

Steve Grayce stepped back and looked at him woodenly. The cab moved off down the street, rounded a corner and was gone. Steve turned on his heel, took a quarter from his pocket and tossed it up in the air. He slapped it into the night porter's hand.

'From the King,' he said. 'Keep it to show your grandchildren.'

He went back into the hotel, got into the elevator without looking at Millar, shot it up to Eight again and went along the corridor, master-keyed his way into Leopardi's room. He relocked it from the inside, pulled the bed out from the wall and went in behind it. He got a .32 automatic off the carpet, put it in his pocket and prowled the floor with his eyes looking for the ejected shell. He found it against the wastebasket, reached to pick it up, and stayed bent over, staring into the wastebasket. His mouth tightened. He picked up the shell and dropped it absently into his pocket, then reached a questing finger into the basket and lifted out a torn scrap of paper on which a piece of newsprint had been pasted. Then he picked up the basket, pushed the bed back against the wall and dumped the contents of the basket out on it.

From the trash of torn papers and matches he separated a number of pieces with newsprint pasted to them. He went over to the desk with them and sat down. A few minutes later he had the torn scraps put together like a jigsaw puzzle and could read the message that had been made by cutting words and letters from magazines and pasting them on a sheet.

> TEN GRAND BY THURSDAY NIGHT, LEOPARDI. DAY AFTER YOU OPEN AT THE CLUB SHALOTTE. OR ELSE – CURTAINS. FROM HER BROTHER.

Steve Grayce said: 'Huh.' He scooped the torn pieces into a hotel envelope, put that in his inside breast pocket and lit a cigarette. 'The guy had guts,' he said. 'I'll grant him that – and his trumpet.'

He locked the room, listened a moment in the now silent corridor, then went along to the room occupied by the two girls. He knocked softly and put his ear to the panel. A chair squeaked and feet came towards the door.

'What is it?' The girl's voice was cool, wide-awake. It was not the blonde's voice.

'The house man. Can I speak to you a minute?'

'You're speaking to me.'

'Without the door between, lady.'

'You've got the pass-key. Help yourself.' The steps went away. He unlocked the door with his master key, stepped quietly inside, and shut it. There was a dim light in a lamp with a shirred shade on the desk. On the bed the blonde snored heavily, one hand clutched in her brilliant metallic hair. The black-haired girl sat in the chair by the window, her legs crossed at right angles like a man's and stared at Steve emptily.

He went close to her and pointed to the long tear in her pajama leg. He said softly: 'You're not sick. You were not drunk. That tear was done a long time ago. What's the racket? A shakedown on the King?'

The girl stared at him coolly, puffed at a cigarette and said nothing.

'He checked out,' Steve said. 'Nothing doing in that direction now, sister.' He watched her like a hawk, his black eyes hard and steady on her face.

'Aw, you house dicks make me sick!' the girl said with sudden anger. She surged to her feet and went past him into the bathroom, shut and locked the door.

Steve shrugged and felt the pulse of the girl asleep in the bed – a thumpy, draggy pulse, a liquor pulse.

'Poor damn hustlers,' he said under his breath.

He looked at a large purple bag that lay on the bureau, lifted it idly and let it fall. His face stiffened again. The bag made a heavy sound on the glass top, as if there were a lump of lead inside it. He snapped it open quickly and plunged a hand in. His fingers touched the cold metal of a gun. He opened the bag wide and stared down into it at a small .25 automatic. A scrap of white paper caught his eye. He fished it out and held it to the light – a rent receipt with a name and address. He stuffed it into his pocket, closed the bag and was standing by the window when the girl came out of the bathroom.

'Hell, are you still haunting me?' she snapped. 'You know what happens to hotel dicks that master-key their way into ladies' bedrooms at night?'

Steve said loosely: 'Yeah. They get in trouble. They might even get shot at.'

The girl's face became set, but her eyes crawled sideways and looked at the purple bag. Steve looked at her. 'Know Leopardi in Frisco?' he asked. 'He hasn't played here in two years. Then he was just a trumpet player in Vane Utigore's band – a cheap outfit.'

The girl curled her lip, went past him and sat down by the window again. Her face was white, stiff. She said dully: 'Blossom did. That's Blossom on the bed.'

'Know he was coming to this hotel tonight?'

'What makes it your business?'

'I can't figure him coming here at all,' Steve said. 'This is a quiet place. So I can't figure anybody coming here to put the bite on him.'

'Go somewhere else and figure. I need sleep.'

Steve said: 'Good-night, sweetheart – and keep your door locked.'

A thin man with thin blond hair and thin face was standing by the desk, tapping on the marble with thin fingers. Millar was still behind the desk and he still looked white and scared. The thin man wore a dark gray suit with a scarf inside the collar of the coat. He had a look of having just got up. He turned sea-green eyes slowly on Steve as he got out of the elevator, waited for him to come up to the desk and throw a tabbed key on it.

Steve said: 'Leopardi's key, George. There's a busted mirror in his room and the carpet has his dinner on it – mostly Scotch.' He turned to the thin man. 'You want to see me, Mr Peters?'

'What happened, Grayce?' The thin man had a tight voice that expected to be lied to.

'Leopardi and two of his boys were on Eight, the rest of the gang on Five. The bunch on Five went to bed. A couple of obvious hustlers managed to get themselves registered just two rooms from Leopardi. They managed to contact him and everybody was having a lot of nice noisy fun out in the hall. I could only stop it by getting a little tough.'

'There's blood on your cheek,' Peters said coldly. 'Wipe it off.'

Steve scratched at his cheek with a handkerchief. The thin thread of blood had dried. 'I got the girls tucked away in their room,' he said. 'The two stooges took the hint and holed up, but Leopardi still thought the guests wanted to hear trombone music. I threatened to wrap it around his neck and he beaned me with it. I slapped him open-handed and he pulled a gun and took a shot at me. Here's the gun.'

He took the .32 automatic out of his pocket and laid it on the desk. He put the used shell beside it. 'So I beat some sense into him and threw him out,' he added.

Peters tapped on the marble. 'Your usual tact seems to have been well in evidence.'

Steve stared at him. 'He shot at me,' he repeated quietly.

'With a gun. This gun. I'm tender to bullets. He missed, but suppose he hadn't? I like my stomach the way it is, with just one way in and one way out.'

Peters narrowed his tawny eyebrows. He said very politely: 'We have you down on the payroll here as a night clerk, because we don't like the name house detective. But neither night clerks nor house detectives put guests out of the hotel without consulting me. Not ever, Mr Grayce.'

Steve said: 'The guy shot at me, pal. With a gun. Catch on? I don't have to take that without a kickback, do I?' His face was a little white.

Peters said: 'Another point for your consideration. The controlling interest in this hotel is owned by Mr Halsey G. Walters. Mr Walters also owns the Club Shalotte, where King Leopardi is opening on Wednesday night. And that, Mr Grayce, is why Leopardi was good enough to give us his business. Can you think of anything else I should like to say to you?'

'Yeah. I'm canned,' Steve said mirthlessly.

'Very correct, Mr Grayce. Good-night, Mr Grayce.'

The thin blond man moved to the elevator and the night porter took him up.

Steve looked at Millar.

'Jumbo Walters, huh?' he said softly. 'A tough, smart guy. Much too smart to think this dump and the Club Shalotte belong to the same sort of customers. Did Peters write Leopardi to come here?'

'I guess he did, Steve.' Millar's voice was low and gloomy.

'Then why wasn't he put in a tower suite with a private balcony to dance on, at eighteen bucks a day? Why was he put on a medium-priced transient floor? And why did Quillan let those girls get so close to him?'

Millar pulled at his black mustache. 'Tight with money – as well as with Scotch, I suppose. As to the girls, I don't know.'

Steve slapped the counter open-handed. 'Well, I'm canned, for not letting a drunken heel make a parlor-house and a shooting-gallery out of the eighth floor. Nuts! Well, I'll miss the joint at that.'

'I'll miss you too, Steve,' Millar said gently. 'But not for a week. I take a week off starting tomorrow. My brother has a cabin at Crestline.'

'Didn't know you had a brother,' Steve said absently. He opened and closed his fist on the marble desk-top.

'He doesn't come into town much. A big guy. Used to be a fighter.'

Steve nodded and straightened from the counter. 'Well, I might as well finish out the night,' he said. 'On my back. Put this gun away somewhere, George.'

He grinned coldly and walked away, down the steps into the dim main lobby and across to the room where the radio was. He punched the pillows into shape on the pale-green davenport, then suddenly reached into his pocket and took out the scrap of white paper he had lifted from the black-haired girl's purple handbag. It was a receipt for a week's rent, to a Miss Marilyn Delorme, Apt. 211, Ridgeland Apartments, 118 Court Street.

He tucked it into his wallet and stood staring at the silent radio. 'Steve, I think you got another job,' he said under his breath. 'Something about this set-up smells.'

He slipped into a closet-like phone-booth in the corner of the room, dropped a nickel and dialed an all-night radio station. He had to dial four times before he got a clear line to the Owl Program announcer.

'How's to play King Leopardi's record of *Solitude* again?' he asked him.

'Got a lot of requests piled up. Played it twice already. Who's calling?'

'Steve Grayce, night man at the Carlton Hotel.'

'Oh, a sober guy on his job. For you, pal, anything.

Steve went back to the davenport, snapped the radio on and lay down on his back, with his hands clasped behind his head.

Ten minutes later the high, piercingly sweet trumpet notes of King Leopardi came softly from the radio, muted almost to a whisper, and sustaining E in Alt for an almost incredible period of time.

'Shucks,' Steve grumbled, when the record ended. 'A guy that can play like that – maybe I was too tough with him.'

III

Court Street was old town, wop town, crook town, arty town. It lay across the top of Bunker Hill and you could find anything there from down-at-heels ex-Greenwich Villagers to crooks on the lam, from ladies of anybody's evening to County Relief clients brawling with haggard landladies in grand old houses with scrolled porches, parquetry floors, and immense sweeping banisters of white oak, mahogany and Circassian walnut.

It had been a nice place once, had Bunker Hill, and from the days of its niceness there still remained the funny little funicular railway, called the Angel's Flight, which crawled up and down a yellow clay bank from Hill Street. It was afternoon when Steve Grayce got off the car at the top, its only passenger. He walked along in the sun, a tall, wide-shouldered, rangy-looking man in a well-cut blue suit.

He turned west at Court and began to read the numbers. The one he wanted was two from the corner, across the street from a red brick funeral parlor with a sign in gold over it – *Paolo Perrugini Funeral Home*. A swarthy iron-gray Italian in a cutaway coat stood in front of the curtained door of the red brick building, smoking a cigar and waiting for somebody to die.

118 was a three-storied frame apartment house. It had a glass door, well masked by a dirty net curtain, a hall runner eighteen inches wide, dim doors with numbers painted on them with dim paint, a staircase halfway back. Brass stair rods glittered in the dimness of the hallway.

Steve Grayce went up the stairs and prowled back to the front. Apartment 211, Miss Marilyn Delorme, was on the right, a front apartment. He tapped lightly on the wood, waited, tapped again. Nothing moved beyond the silent door, or in the hallway. Behind another door across the hall somebody coughed and kept on coughing.

Standing there in the half-light Steve Grayce wondered why he had come. Miss Delorme had carried a gun. Leopardi had received some kind of a threat letter and torn it up and thrown it away. Miss Delorme had checked out of the Carlton about an hour after Steve told her Leopardi was gone. Even at that –

He took out a leather keyholder and studied the lock of the door. It looked as if it would listen to reason. He tried a pick on it, snicked the bolt back and stepped softly into the room. He shut the door, but the pick wouldn't lock it.

The room was dim with drawn shades across two front windows. The air smelled of face powder. There was light-painted furniture, a pull-down double bed which was pulled down but had been made up. There was a magazine on it, a glass tray full of cigarette butts, a pint bottle half full of whiskey, and a glass on a chair beside the bed. Two pillows had been used for a back rest and were still crushed in the middle.

On the dresser there was a composition toilet set, neither cheap nor expensive, a comb with black hair in it, a tray of manicuring stuff, plenty of spilled powder – in the bathroom nothing. In a closet behind the bed a lot of clothes and two suitcases. The shoes were all one size.

Steve stood beside the bed and pinched his chin. 'Blossom, the spitting blonde, doesn't live here,' he said under his breath. 'Just Marilyn the torn-pants brunette.'

He went back to the dresser and pulled drawers out. In the bottom drawer, under the piece of wall paper that lined it, he found a box of .25 copper-nickel automatic shells. He poked at the butts in the ash tray. All had lipstick on them. He pinched his chin again, then feathered the air with the palm of his hand, like an oarsman with a scull.

'Bunk,' he said softly. 'Wasting your time, Stevie.'

He walked over to the door and reached for the knob, then turned back to the bed and lifted it by the footrail.

Miss Marilyn Delorme was in.

She lay on her side on the floor under the bed, long legs scissored out as if in running. One mule was on, one off. Garters and skin showed at the tops of her stockings, and a blue rose on something pink. She wore a square-necked, beige-sleeved dress that was not too clean. Her neck above the dress was blotched with purple bruises.

Her face was a dark plum color, her eyes had the faint stale glitter of death, and her mouth was open so far that it foreshortened her face. She was colder than ice, and still quite limp. She had been dead two or three hours at least, six hours at most.

The purple bag was beside her, gaping like her mouth. Steve didn't touch any of the stuff that had been emptied out on the floor. There was no gun and there were no papers.

He let the bed down over her again, then made the rounds of the apartment, wiping everything he had touched and a lot of things he couldn't remember whether he had touched or not.

He listened at the door and stepped out. The hall was still empty. The man behind the opposite door still coughed. Steve went down the stairs, looked at the mailboxes and went back along the lower hall to a door.

Behind this door a chair creaked monotonously. He knocked and a woman's sharp voice called out. Steve opened the door with his handkerchief and stepped in.

In the middle of the room a woman rocked in an old Boston rocker, her body in the slack boneless attitude of exhaustion. She had a mud-colored face, stringy hair, gray cotton stockings – everything a Bunker Hill landlady should have. She looked at Steve with the interested eye of a dead goldfish.

'Are you the manager?'

The woman stopped rocking, screamed, 'Hi, Jake! Company!' at the top of her voice, and started rocking again.

An icebox door thudded shut behind a partly open inner door and a very big man came into the room carrying a can of beer. He had a doughy mooncalf face, a tuft of fuzz on top of an otherwise bald head, a thick brutal neck and chin, and brown pig eyes about as expressionless as the woman's. He needed a shave – had needed one the day before – and his colorless shirt gaped over a big hard hairy chest. He wore scarlet suspenders with large gilt buckles on them.

He held the can of beer out to the woman. She clawed it out of his hand and said bitterly: 'I'm so tired I ain't got no sense.'

The man said: 'Yah. You ain't done the halls so good at that.'

The woman snarled: 'I done 'em as good as I aim to.' She sucked the beer thirstily.

Steve looked at the man and said: 'Manager?'

'Yah. 'S me. Jake Stoyanoff. Two hun'erd eighty-six stripped, and still plenty tough.'

Steve said: 'Who lives in Two-eleven?'

The big man leaned forward a little from the waist and snapped his suspenders. Nothing changed in his eyes. The skin along his big jaw may have tightened a little. 'A dame,' he said.

'Alone?'

'Go on – ask me,' the big man said. He stuck his hand out and lifted a cigar off the edge of a stained-wood table. The cigar was burning unevenly and it smelled as if somebody had set fire to the doormat. He pushed it into his mouth with a hard, thrusting motion, as if he expected his mouth wouldn't want it to go in.

'I'm asking you,' Steve said.

'Ask me out in the kitchen,' the big man drawled.

He turned and held the door open. Steve went past him.

The big man kicked the door shut against the squeak of the rocking-chair, opened up the icebox and got out two cans of beer. He opened them and handed one to Steve.

'Dick?'

Steve drank some of the beer, put the can down on the sink, got a brand-new card out of his wallet – a business card printed that morning. He handed it to the man.

The man read it, put it down on the sink, picked it up and read it again. 'One of them guys,' he growled over his beer. 'What's she pulled this time?'

Steve shrugged and said: 'I guess it's the usual. The torn-pajama act. Only there's a kickback this time.'

'How come? You handling it, huh? Must be a nice cozy one.'

Steve nodded. The big man blew smoke from his mouth. 'Go ahead and handle it,' he said.

'You don't mind a pinch here?'

The big man laughed heartily. 'Nuts to you, brother,' he said pleasantly enough. 'You're a private dick. So it's a hush. O.K. Go out and hush it. And if it *was* a pinch – that bothers me like a quart of milk. Go into your act. Take all the room you want. Cops don't bother Jake Stoyanoff.'

Steve stared at the man. He didn't say anything. The big man talked it up some more, seemed to get more interested. 'Besides,' he went on, making motions with his cigar, 'I'm soft-hearted. I never turn up a dame. I never put a frill in the middle.' He finished his beer and threw the can in a basket under the sink, and pushed his hand out in front of him, revolving the large thumb slowly against the next two fingers. 'Unless there's some of that,' he added.

Steve said softly: 'You've got big hands. You could have done it.'

'Huh?' His small brown leathery eyes got silent and stared.

Steve said: 'Yeah. You might be clean as an angel's wing. But with those hands the cops'd go round and round with you just the same.'

The big man moved a little to his left, away from the sink. He let his right hand hang down at his side, loosely. His mouth got so tight that the cigar almost touched his nose.

'What's the beef, huh?' he barked. 'What you shovin' at me, guy? What – '

'Cut it,' Steve drawled. 'She's been croaked. Strangled. Upstairs, on the floor under her bed. About midmorning, I'd say. Big hands did it – hands like yours.'

The big man did a nice job of getting the gun off his hip. It arrived so suddenly that it seemed to have grown in his hand and been there all the time.

Steve frowned at the gun and didn't move. The big man looked him over. 'You're tough,' he said. 'I been in the ring long enough to size up a guy's meat. You're plenty hard, boy. But you ain't as hard as lead. Talk it up fast.'

'I knocked at her door. No answer. The lock was a pushover. I went in. I almost missed her because the bed was pulled down and she had been sitting on it, reading a magazine. There was no sign of struggle. I lifted the bed just before I left – and there she was. Very dead, Mr Stoyanoff. Put the gat away. Cops don't bother you, you said a minute ago.'

The big man whispered: 'Yes and no. They don't make me

happy neither. I get a bump once'n a while. Mostly a Dutch. You said something about my hands, mister.'

Steve shook his head. 'That was a gag,' he said. 'Her neck has nail marks. You bite your nails down close. You're clean.'

The big man didn't look at his fingers. He was very pale. There was sweat on his lower lip, in the black stubble of his beard. He was still leaning forward, still motionless, when there was a knocking beyond the kitchen door, the door from the living-room to the hallway. The creaking chair stopped and the woman's sharp voice screamed: 'Hi, Jake! Company!'

The big man cocked his head. 'That old slut wouldn't climb off'n her fanny if the house caught fire,' he said thickly.

He stepped to the door and slipped through it, locking it behind him.

Steve ranged the kitchen swiftly with his eyes. There was a small high window beyond the sink, a trap low down for a garbage pail and parcels, but no other door. He reached for his card Stoyanoff had left lying on the drainboard and slipped it back into his pocket. Then he took a short-barreled Detective Special out of his left breast pocket where he wore it nose down, as in a holster.

He had got that far when the shots roared beyond the wall – muffled a little, but still loud – four of them blended in a blast of sound.

Steve stepped back and hit the kitchen door with his leg out straight. It held and jarred him to the top of his head and in his hip joint. He swore, took the whole width of the kitchen and slammed into it with his left shoulder. It gave this time. He pitched into the living-room. The mud-faced woman sat leaning forward in her rocker, her head to one side and a lock of mousy hair smeared down over her bony forehead.

'Backfire, huh?' she said stupidly. 'Sounded kinda close. Musta been in the alley.'

Steve jumped across the room, yanked the outer door open and plunged out into the hall.

The big man was still on his feet, a dozen feet down the hallway, in the direction of a screen door that opened flush on an alley. He was clawing at the wall. His gun lay at his feet. His left knee buckled and he went down on it.

A door was flung open and a hard-looking woman peered out, and instantly slammed her door shut again. A radio suddenly gained in volume beyond her door.

The big man got up off his left knee and the leg shook violently inside his trousers. He went down on both knees and got the gun into his hand and began to crawl towards the screen door. Then, suddenly he went down flat on his face and tried to crawl that way, grinding his face into the narrow hall runner.

Then he stopped crawling and stopped moving altogether. His body went limp and the hand holding the gun opened and the gun rolled out of it.

Steve hit the screen door and was out in the alley. A gray sedan was speeding towards the far end of it. He stopped, steadied himself and brought his gun up level, and the sedan whisked out of sight around the corner.

A man boiled out of another apartment house across the alley. Steve ran on, gesticulating back at him and pointing ahead. As he ran he slipped the gun back into his pocket. When he reached the end of the alley, the gray sedan was out of sight. Steve skidded around the wall onto the sidewalk, slowed to a walk and then stopped.

Half a block down a man finished parking his car, got out and went across the sidewalk to a lunchroom. Steve watched him go in, then straightened his hat and walked along the wall to the lunchroom.

He went in, sat at the counter and ordered coffee. In a little while there were sirens.

Steve drank his coffee, asked for another cup and drank that. He lit a cigarette and walked down the long hill to Fifth, across to Hill, back to the foot of the Angel's Flight, and got his convertible out of a parking lot.

He drove out west, beyond Vermont, to the small hotel where he had taken a room that morning.

IV

Bill Dockery, floor manager of the Club Shalotte, teetered on his heels and yawned in the unlighted entrance to the dining-room. It was a dead hour for business, late cocktail time, too early for dinner, and much too early for the real business of the club, which was high-class gambling.

Dockery was a handsome mug in a midnight-blue dinner jacket and a maroon carnation. He had a two-inch forehead under black lacquer hair, good features a little on the heavy side, alert brown eyes and very long curly eyelashes which he liked to let down over his eyes, to fool troublesome drunks into taking a swing at him.

The entrance door of the foyer was opened by the uniformed doorman and Steve Grayce came in.

Dockery said, 'Ho, hum,' tapped his teeth and leaned his weight forward. He walked across the lobby slowly to meet the guest. Steve stood just inside the doors and ranged his eyes over the high foyer walled with milky glass, lighted softly from behind. Molded in the glass were etchings of sailing-ships, beasts of the jungle, Siamese pagodas, temples of Yucatan. The doors were square frames of chromium, like photo frames. The Club Shalotte had all the class there was, and the mutter of voices from the bar lounge on the left was not noisy. The faint Spanish music behind the voices was delicate as a carved fan.

Dockery came up and leaned his sleek head forward an inch. 'May I help you?'

'King Leopardi around?'

Dockery leaned back again. He looked less interested. 'The bandleader? He opens tomorrow night.'

'I thought he might be around – rehearsing or something.'

'Friend of his?'

'I know him. I'm not job-hunting, and I'm not a song-plugger if that's what you mean.'

Dockery teetered on his heels. He was tone deaf and Leopardi meant no more to him than a bag of peanuts. He half smiled. 'He was in the bar lounge a while ago.' He pointed with his square rock-like chin. Steve Grayce went into the bar lounge.

It was about a third full, warm and comfortable and not too dark nor too light. The little Spanish orchestra was in an archway, playing with muted strings small seductive melodies that were more like memories than sounds. There was no dance floor. There was a long bar with comfortable seats, and there were small round composition-top tables, not too close together. A wall seat ran around three sides of the room. Waiters flitted among the tables like moths.

Steve Grayce saw Leopardi in the far corner, with a girl. There was an empty table on each side of him. The girl was a knockout.

She looked tall and her hair was the color of a brush-fire seen through a dust cloud. On it, at the ultimate rakish angle, she wore a black velvet double-pointed beret with two butterflies made of polka-dotted feathers and fastened on with tall silver pins. Her dress was burgundy-red wool and the blue fox draped over one shoulder was at least a foot wide. Her eyes were large, smoke-blue, and looked bored. She slowly turned a small glass on the tabletop with a gloved left hand.

Leopardi faced her, leaning forward, talking. His shoulders looked very big in a shaggy, cream-colored sports coat. Above the neck of it his hair made a point on his brown neck. He laughed across the table as Steve came up, and his laugh had a confident, sneering sound.

Steve stopped, then moved behind the next table. The movement caught Leopardi's eye. His head turned, he looked annoyed, and then his eyes got very wide and brilliant and his whole body turned slowly, like a mechanical toy.

Leopardi put both his rather small well-shaped hands down on the table, on either side of a highball glass. He smiled. Then he pushed his chair back and stood up. He put one finger up and touched his hair-line mustache, with theatrical delicacy. Then he said drawlingly, but distinctly: 'You———————!'

A man at a near-by table turned his head and scowled. A waiter who had started to come over stopped in his tracks, then faded back among the tables. The girl looked at Steve Grayce and then leaned back against the cushion of the wall seat and moistened the end of one bare finger on her right hand and smoothed a chestnut eyebrow.

Steve stood quite still. There was a sudden high flush on his cheek-bones. He said softly: 'You left something at the hotel last night. I think you ought to do something about it. Here.'

He reached a folded paper out of his pocket and held it out. Leopardi took it, still smiling, opened it and read it. It was a sheet of yellow paper with torn pieces of white paper pasted on it. Leopardi crumpled the sheet and let it drop at his feet.

He took a smooth step towards Steve and repeated more loudly: 'You———————!'

The man who had first looked around stood up sharply and turned. He said clearly: 'I don't like that sort of language in front of my wife.'

Without even looking at the man Leopardi said: 'To hell with you and your wife.'

The man's face got a dusky red. The woman with him stood up and grabbed a bag and a coat and walked away. After a moment's indecision the man followed her. Everybody in the place was staring now. The waiter who had faded back among the tables went through the doorway into the entrance foyer, walking very quickly.

Leopardi took another, longer step and slammed Steve Grayce on the jaw. Steve rolled with the punch and stepped back and put his hand down on another table and upset a glass. He turned to apologize to the couple at the table. Leopardi jumped forward very fast and hit him behind the ear.

Dockery came through the doorway, split two waiters like a banana skin and started down the room showing all his teeth.

Steve gagged a little and ducked away. He turned and said thickly: 'Wait a minute, you fool – that isn't all of it – there's – '

Leopardi closed in fast and smashed him full on the mouth. Blood oozed from Steve's lip and crawled down the line at the corner of his mouth and glistened on his chin. The girl with the red hair reached for her bag, white-faced with anger, and started to get up from behind her table.

Leopardi turned abruptly on his heel and walked away. Dockery put out a hand to stop him. Leopardi brushed it aside and went on, went out of the lounge.

The tall red-haired girl put her bag down on the table again and dropped her handkerchief on the floor. She looked at Steve quietly, spoke quietly. 'Wipe the blood off your chin before it drips on your shirt.' She had a soft, husky voice with a trill in it.

Dockery came up harsh-faced, took Steve by the arm and put weight on the arm. 'All right, you! Let's go!'

Steve stood quite still, his feet planted, staring at the girl. He dabbed at his mouth with a handkerchief. He half smiled. Dockery couldn't move him an inch. Dockery dropped his hand, signaled two waiters and they jumped behind Steve, but didn't touch him.

Steve felt his lip carefully and looked at the blood on his handkerchief. He turned to the people at the table behind him and said: 'I'm terribly sorry. I lost my balance.'

The girl whose drink he had spilled was mopping her dress with a small fringed napkin. She smiled up at him and said: 'It wasn't your fault.'

The two waiters suddenly grabbed Steve's arms from behind. Dockery shook his head and they let go again. Dockery said tightly: 'You hit him?'

'No.'

'You say anything to make him hit you?'

'No.'

The girl at the corner table bent down to get her fallen handkerchief. It took her quite a time. She finally got it and slid into the corner behind the table again. She spoke coldly.

'Quite right, Bill. It was just some more of the King's sweet way with his public.'

Dockery said 'Huh?' and swiveled his head on his thick hard neck. Then he grinned and looked back at Steve.

Steve said grimly: 'He gave me three good punches, one from behind, without a return. You look pretty hard. See can you do it.'

Dockery measured him with his eyes. He said evenly: 'You win. I couldn't . . . Beat it!' he added sharply to the waiters. They went away. Dockery sniffed his carnation, and said quietly: 'We don't go for brawls in here.' He smiled at the girl again and went away, saying a word here and there at the tables. He went out through the foyer doors.

Steve tapped his lip, put his handkerchief in his pocket and stood searching the floor with his eyes.

The red-haired girl said calmly: 'I think I have what you want – in my handkerchief. Won't you sit down?'

Her voice had a remembered quality, as if he had heard it before.

He sat down opposite her, in the chair where Leopardi had been sitting.

The red-haired girl said: 'The drink's on me. I was with him.'

Steve said, 'Coke with a dash of bitters,' to the waiter.

The waiter said: 'Madame?'

'Brandy and soda. Light on the brandy, please.' The waiter bowed and drifted away. The girl said amusedly: 'Coke with a dash of bitters. That's what I love about Hollywood. You meet so many neurotics.'

Steve stared into her eyes and said softly: 'I'm an occasional drinker, the kind of guy who goes out for a beer and wakes up in Singapore with a full beard.'

'I don't believe a word of it. Have you known the King long?'

'I met him last night. I didn't get along with him.'

'I sort of noticed that.' She laughed. She had a rich low laugh, too.

'Give me that paper, lady.'

'Oh, one of these impatient men. Plenty of time.' The handkerchief with the crumpled yellow sheet inside it was clasped tightly in her gloved hand. Her middle right finger played with an eyebrow. 'You're not in pictures, are you?'

'Hell, no.'

'Same here. Me, I'm too tall. The beautiful men have to wear stilts in order to clasp me to their bosoms.'

The waiter set the drinks down in front of them, made a few grace notes in the air with his napkin and went away.

Steve said quietly, stubbornly: 'Give me that paper, lady.'

'I don't like that "lady" stuff. It sounds like a cop to me.'

'I don't know your name.'

'I don't know yours. Where did you meet Leopardi?'

Steve sighed. The music from the little Spanish orchestra had a melancholy minor sound now and the muffled clicking of gourds dominated it.

Steve listened to it with his head on one side. He said: 'The E string is a half-tone flat. Rather cute effect.'

The girl stared at him with new interest. 'I'd never have noticed that,' she said. 'And I'm supposed to be a pretty good singer. But you haven't answered my question.'

He said slowly: 'Last night I was house dick at the Carlton Hotel. They called me night clerk, but house dick was what I was. Leopardi stayed there and cut up too rough. I threw him out and got canned.'

The girl said: 'Ah, I begin to get the idea. He was being the King and you were being – if I might guess – a pretty tough order of house detective.'

'Something like that. Now will you please – '

'You still haven't told me your name.'

He reached for his wallet, took one of the brand-new cards out of it and passed it across the table. He sipped his drink while she read it.

'A nice name,' she said slowly. 'But not a very good address. And *Private Investigator* is bad. It should have been *Investigations*, very small, in the lower left-hand corner.'

'They'll be small enough,' Steve grinned. 'Now will you please – '

She reached suddenly across the table and dropped the crumpled ball of paper in his hand.

'Of course I haven't read it – and of course I'd like to. You do give me that much credit, I hope' – she looked at the card again, and added – 'Steve. Yes, and your office should be in a Georgian or very modernistic building in the Sunset Eighties. Suite Something-or-other. And your clothes should be very jazzy. Very jazzy indeed, Steve. To be inconspicuous in this town is to be a busted flush.'

He grinned at her. His deep-set black eyes had lights in them. She put the card away in her bag, gave her fur piece a yank, and drank about half of her drink. 'I have to go.' She signaled the waiter and paid the check. The waiter went away and she stood up.

Steve said sharply: 'Sit down.'

She stared at him wonderingly. Then she sat down again and leaned against the wall, still staring at him. Steve leaned across the table, asked: 'How well do *you* know Leopardi?'

'Off and on for years. If it's any of your business. Don't go masterful on me, for God's sake. I loathe masterful men. I once sang for him, but not for long. You can't just sing for Leopardi – if you get what I mean.'

'You were having a drink with him.'

She nodded slightly and shrugged. 'He opens here tomorrow night. He was trying to talk me into singing for him again. I said no, but I may have to, for a week or two anyway. The man who owns the Club Shalotte also owns my contract – and the radio station where I work a good deal.'

'Jumbo Walters,' Steve said. 'They say he's tough but square. I never met him, but I'd like to. After all I've got a living to get. Here.'

He reached back across the table and dropped the crumpled paper. 'The name was – '

'Dolores Chiozza.'

Steve repeated it lingeringly. 'I like it. I like your singing too. I've heard a lot of it. You don't oversell a song, like most of these high-money torchers.' His eyes glistened.

The girl spread the paper on the table and read it slowly, without expression. Then she said quietly: 'Who tore it up?'

'Leopardi, I guess. The pieces were in his wastebasket last night. I put them together, after he was gone. The guy has guts – or else he gets these things so often they don't register any more.'

'Or else he thought it was a gag.' She looked across the table levelly, then folded the paper and handed it back.

'Maybe. But if he's the kind of guy I hear he is – one of them is going to be on the level and the guy behind it is going to do more than just shake him down.'

Dolores Chiozza said: 'He's the kind of guy you hear he is.'

'It wouldn't be hard for a woman to get to him then – would it – a woman with a gun?'

She went on staring at him. 'No. And everybody would give her a big hand, if you ask me. If I were you, I'd just forget the whole thing. If he wants protection – Walters can throw more around him than the police. If he doesn't – who cares? I don't. I'm damn sure I don't.'

'You're kind of tough yourself, Miss Chiozza – over some things.'

She said nothing. Her face was a little white and more than a little hard.

Steve finished his drink, pushed his chair back and reached for his hat. He stood up. 'Thank you very much for the drink, Miss Chiozza. Now that I've met you I'll look forward all the more to hearing you sing again.'

'You're damn formal all of a sudden,' she said.

He grinned. 'So long, Dolores.'

'So long, Steve. Good luck – in the sleuth racket. If I hear of anything – '

He turned and walked among the tables out of the bar lounge.

V

In the crisp fall evening the lights of Hollywood and Los Angeles winked at him. Searchlight beams probed the cloudless sky as if searching for bombing-planes.

Steve got his convertible out of the parking lot and drove it east along Sunset. At Sunset and Fairfax he bought an evening paper and pulled over to the curb to look through it. There was nothing in the paper about 118 Court Street.

He drove on and ate dinner at the little coffee shop beside the hotel and went to a movie. When he came out he bought a Home Edition of the *Tribune*, a morning sheet. They were in that – both of them.

Police thought Jake Stoyanoff might have strangled the girl, but she had not been attacked. She was described as a stenographer, unemployed at the moment. There was no picture of her. There was a picture of Stoyanoff that looked like a touched-up police photo. Police were looking for a man who had been talking to Stoyanoff just before he was shot. Several people said he was a tall man in a dark suit. That was all the description the police got – or gave out.

Steve grinned sourly, stopped at the coffee shop for a good-night cup of coffee and then went up to his room. It was a few minutes to eleven o'clock. As he unlocked his door the telephone started to ring.

He shut the door and stood in the darkness remembering where the phone was. Then he walked straight to it, catlike in the dark room, sat in an easy chair and reached the phone up from the lower shelf of a small table. He held the one-piece to his ear and said: 'Hello.'

'Is this Steve?' It was a rich, husky voice, low, vibrant. It held a note of strain.

'Yeah, this is Steve. I can hear you. I know who you are.'

There was a faint dry laugh. 'You'll make a detective after all. And it seems I'm to give you your first case. Will you come over to my place at once? It's Twenty-four-twelve Renfrew – North, there isn't any South – just half a block below Fountain. It's a sort of bungalow court. My house is the last in line, at the back.'

Steve said: 'Yes. Sure. What's the matter?'

There was a pause. A horn blared in the street outside the hotel. A wave of white light went across the ceiling from some car rounding the corner uphill. The low voice said very slowly: 'Leopardi. I can't get rid of him. He's – he's passed out in my bedroom.' Then a tinny laugh that didn't go with the voice at all.

Steve held the phone so tight his hand ached. His teeth clicked in the darkness. He said flatly, in a dull, brittle voice: 'Yeah. It'll cost you twenty bucks.'

'Of course. Hurry, please.'

He hung up, sat there in the dark room breathing hard. He pushed his hat back on his head, then yanked it forward again with a vicious jerk and laughed out loud. 'Hell,' he said. '*That* kind of a dame.'

2412 Renfrew was not strictly a bungalow court. It was a staggered row of six bungalows, all facing the same way, but so arranged that no two of their front entrances overlooked each other. There was a brick wall at the back and beyond the brick wall a church. There was a long smooth lawn, moon-silvered.

The door was up two steps, with lanterns on each side and an ironwork grill over the peep hole. This opened to his knock and a girl's face looked out, a small oval face with a Cupid's-bow mouth, arched and plucked eyebrows, wavy brown hair. The eyes were like two fresh and shiny chestnuts.

Steve dropped a cigarette and put his foot on it. 'Miss Chiozza. She's expecting me. Steve Grayce.'

'Miss Chiozza has retired, sir,' the girl said with a half-insolent twist to her lips.

'Break it up, kid. You heard me, I'm expected.'

The wicket slammed shut. He waited, scowling back along the narrow moonlit lawn towards the street. O.K. So it was like that – well, twenty bucks was worth a ride in the moonlight anyway.

The lock clicked and the door opened wide. Steve went past the maid into a warm cheerful room, old-fashioned with chintz. The lamps were neither old nor new and there were enough of them – in the right places. There was a hearth behind a paneled copper screen, a davenport close to it, a bar-top radio in the corner.

The maid said stiffly: 'I'm sorry, sir. Miss Chiozza forgot to tell me. Please to have a chair.' The voice was soft, and it might be cagey. The girl went off down the room – short skirts, sheer silk stockings, and four-inch spike heels.

Steve sat down and held his hat on his knee and scowled at the wall. A swing-door creaked shut. He got a cigarette out and rolled it between his fingers and then deliberately squeezed it to a shapeless flatness of white paper and ragged tobacco. He threw it away from him, at the fire screen.

Dolores Chiozza came towards him. She wore green velvet lounging pajamas with a long gold-fringed sash. She spun the end of the sash as if she might be going to throw a loop with it. She smiled a slight artificial smile. Her face had a clean scrubbed look and her eyelids were bluish and they twitched.

Steve stood up and watched the green morocco slippers peep out under the pajamas as she walked. When she was close to him he lifted his eyes to her face and said dully: 'Hello.'

She looked at him very steadily, then spoke in a high, carrying voice. 'I know it's late, but I knew you were used to being up all night. So I thought what we had to talk over – Won't you sit down?'

She turned her head very slightly, seemed to be listening for something.

Steve said: 'I never go to bed before two. Quite all right.'

She went over and pushed a bell beside the hearth. After a moment the maid came through the arch.

'Bring some ice cubes, Agatha. Then go along home. It's getting pretty late.'

'Yes'm.' The girl disappeared.

There was a silence then that almost howled till the tall girl took a cigarette absently out of a box, put it between her lips and Steve struck a match clumsily on his shoe. She pushed the end of the cigarette into the flame and her smoke-blue eyes were very steady on his black ones. She shook her head very slightly.

The maid came back with a copper ice-bucket. She pulled a low Indian-brass tray-table between them before the davenport, put the ice-bucket on it, then a siphon, glasses and spoons, and a triangular bottle that looked like good Scotch had come in it except that it was covered with silver filigree work and fitted with a stopper.

Dolores Chiozza said, 'Will you mix a drink?' in a formal voice.

He mixed two drinks, stirred them, handed her one. She sipped it, shook her head. 'Too light,' she said. He put more whiskey in it and handed it back. She said, 'Better,' and leaned back against the corner of the davenport.

The maid came into the room again. She had a small rakish red hat on her wavy brown hair and was wearing a gray coat trimmed with nice fur. She carried a black brocade bag that could have cleaned out a fair-sized icebox. She said: 'Good night, Miss Dolores.'

'Good-night, Agatha.'

The girl went out the front door, closed it softly. Her heels clicked down the walk. A car door opened and shut distantly and a motor started. Its sound soon dwindled away. It was a very quiet neighborhood.

Steve put his drink down on the brass tray and looked levelly at the tall girl, said harshly: 'That means she's out of the way?'

'Yes. She goes home in her own car. She drives me home

from the studio in mine – when I go to the studio, which I did tonight. I don't like to drive a car myself.'

'Well, what are we waiting for?'

The red-haired girl looked steadily at the paneled fire-screen and the unlit log fire behind it. A muscle twitched in her cheek.

After a moment she said: 'Funny that I called you instead of Walters. He'd have protected me better than you can. Only he wouldn't have believed me. I thought perhaps you would. I didn't invite Leopardi here. So far as I know – we two are the only people in the world who know he's here.'

Something in her voice jerked Steve upright.

She took a small crisp handkerchief from the breast pocket of the green velvet pajama-suit, dropped it on the floor, picked it up swiftly and pressed it against her mouth. Suddenly, without making a sound, she began to shake like a leaf.

Steve said swiftly: 'What the hell – I can handle that heel in my hip pocket. I did last night – and last night he had a gun and took a shot at me.'

Her head turned. Her eyes were very wide and staring. 'But it couldn't have been my gun,' she said in a dead voice.

'Huh? Of course not – what –?'

'It's my gun tonight,' she said and stared at him. 'You said a woman could get to him with a gun very easily.'

He just stared at her. His face was white now and he made a vague sound in his throat.

'He's not drunk, Steve,' she said gently. 'He's dead. In yellow pajamas – in my bed. With my gun in his hand. You didn't think he was just drunk – did you, Steve?'

He stood up in a swift lunge, then became absolutely motionless, staring down at her. He moved his tongue on his lips and after a long time he formed words with it. 'Let's go look at him,' he said in a hushed voice.

VI

The room was at the back of the house to the left. The girl took a key out of her pocket and unlocked the door. There was a low light on a table, and the Venetian blinds were drawn. Steve went in past her silently, on cat feet.

Leopardi lay squarely in the middle of the bed, a large smooth silent man, waxy and artificial in death. Even his mustache looked phony. His half-open eyes, sightless as marbles, looked as if they had never seen. He lay on his back, on the sheet, and the bedclothes were thrown over the foot of the bed.

The King wore yellow silk pajamas, the slip-on kind, with a turned collar. They were loose and thin. Over his breast they were dark with blood that had seeped into the silk as if into blotting-paper. There was a little blood on his bare brown neck.

Steve stared at him and said tonelessly: 'The King in Yellow. I read a book with that title once. He liked yellow, I guess. I packed some of his stuff last night. And he wasn't yellow either. Guys like him usually are – or are they?'

The girl went over to the corner and sat down in a slipper chair and looked at the floor. It was a nice room, as modernistic as the living-room was casual. It had a chenille rug, café-au-lait color, severely angled furniture in inlaid wood, and a trick dresser with a mirror for a top, a kneehole and drawers like a desk. It had a box mirror above and a semi-cylindrical frosted wall-light set above the mirror. In the corner there was a glass table with a crystal greyhound on top of it, and a lamp with the deepest drum shade Steve had ever seen.

He stopped looking at all this and looked at Leopardi again. He pulled the King's pajamas down gently and examined the wound. It was directly over the heart and the skin was scorched and mottled there. There was not so very much blood. He had died in a fraction of a second.

A small Mauser automatic lay cuddled in his right hand, on top of the bed's second pillow.

'That's artistic,' Steve said and pointed. 'Yeah, that's a nice touch. Typical contact wound, I guess. He even pulled his pajama shirt down. I've heard they do that. A Mauser Seven Sixty-three about. Sure it's your gun?'

'Yes.' She kept on looking at the floor. 'It was in a desk in the living-room – not loaded. But there were shells. I don't know why. Somebody gave it to me once. I didn't even know how to load it.'

Steve smiled. Her eyes lifted suddenly and she saw the smile and shuddered. 'I don't expect anybody to believe that,' she said. 'We may as well call the police, I suppose.'

Steve nodded absently, put a cigarette in his mouth and flipped it up and down with his lips that were still puffy from Leopardi's punch. He lit a match on his thumbnail, puffed a small plume of smoke and said quietly: 'No cops. Not yet. Just tell it.'

The red-haired girl said: 'I sing at KFQC, you know. Three nights a week – on a quarter-hour automobile program. This was one of the nights. Agatha and I got home – oh, close to half past ten. At the door I remembered there was no fizzwater in the house, so I sent her back to the liquor store three blocks away, and came in alone. There was a queer smell in the house. I don't know what it was. As if several men had been in here, somehow. When I came in the bedroom – he was exactly as he is now. I saw the gun and I went and looked and then I knew I was sunk. I didn't know what to do. Even if the police cleared me, everywhere I went from now on – '

Steve said sharply: 'He got in here – how?'

'I don't know.'

'Go on,' he said.

'I locked the door. Then I undressed – with that on my bed. I went into the bathroom to shower and collect my brains, if any. I locked the door when I left the room and took the key. Agatha was back then, but I don't think she saw me. Well, I took the shower and it braced me up a bit. Then I had a drink and then I came in here and called you.'

She stopped and moistened the end of a finger and smoothed the end of her left eyebrow with it. 'That's all, Steve – absolutely all.'

'Domestic help can be pretty nosy. This Agatha's nosier than most – or I miss my guess.' He walked over to the door and looked at the lock. 'I bet there are three or four keys in the house that knock this over.' He went to the windows and felt the catches, looked down at the screens through the glass. He said over his shoulder, casually: 'Was the King in love with you?'

Her voice was sharp, almost angry. 'He never was in love with any woman. A couple of years back in San Francisco, when I was with his band for a while, there was some slapsilly publicity about us. Nothing to it. It's been revived here in the hand-outs to the press, to build up his opening. I was telling him this afternoon I wouldn't stand for it, that I wouldn't be linked with him in anybody's mind. His private life was filthy. It reeked. Everybody in the business knows that. And it's not a business where daisies grow very often.'

Steve said: 'Yours was the only bedroom he couldn't make?'

The girl flushed to the roots of her dusky red hair.

'That sounds lousy,' he said. 'But I have to figure the angles. That's about true, isn't it?'

'Yes – I suppose so. I wouldn't say the only one.'

'Go on out in the other room and buy yourself a drink.'

She stood up and looked at him squarely across the bed. 'I didn't kill him, Steve. I didn't let him into this house tonight. I didn't know he was coming here, or had any reason to come here. Believe that or not. But something about this is wrong. Leopardi was the last man in the world to take his lovely life himself.'

Steve said: 'He didn't, angel. Go buy that drink. He was murdered. The whole thing is a frame – to get a cover-up from Jumbo Walters. Go on out.'

He stood silent, motionless, until sounds he heard from the living-room told him she was out there. Then he took out his handkerchief and loosened the gun from Leopardi's right hand and wiped it over carefully on the outside, broke out the magazine and wiped that off, spilled out all the shells and wiped every one, ejected the one in the breech and wiped that. He reloaded the gun and put it back in Leopardi's dead hand and closed his fingers around it and pushed his index finger against the trigger. Then he let the hand fall naturally back on the bed.

He pawed through the bedclothes and found an ejected shell and wiped that off, put it back where he had found it. He put the handkerchief to his nose, sniffed it wryly, went around the bed to a clothes closet and opened the door.

'Careless of your clothes, boy,' he said softly.

The rough cream-colored coat hung in there, on a hook, over dark gray slacks with a lizard-skin belt. A yellow satin shirt and a wine-colored tie, dangled alongside. A handkerchief to match the tie flowed loosely four inches from the breast pocket of the coat. On the floor lay a pair of gazelle-leather nutmeg-brown sports shoes, and socks without garters. And there were yellow satin shorts with heavy black initials on them lying close by.

Steve felt carefully in the gray slacks and got out a leather keyholder. He left the room, went along the cross-hall and into the kitchen. It had a solid door, a good spring lock with a key stuck in it. He took it out and tried keys from the bunch in the keyholder, found none that fitted, put the other key back and went into the living-room. He opened the front door, went outside and shut it again without looking at the girl huddled in a corner of the davenport. He tried keys in the lock, finally found the right one. He let himself back into the house, returned to the bedroom and put the keyholder in the pocket of the gray slacks again. Then he went back to the living-room.

The girl was still huddled motionless, staring at him.

He put his back to the mantel and puffed at a cigarette. 'Agatha with you all the time at the studio?'

She nodded. 'I suppose so. So he had a key. That was what you were doing, wasn't it?'

'Yes. Had Agatha long?'

'About a year.'

'She steal from you? Small stuff, I mean?'

Dolores Chiozza shrugged wearily. 'What does it matter? Most of them do. A little face cream or powder, a handkerchief, a pair of stockings once in a while. Yes, I think she stole from me. They look on that sort of thing as more or less legitimate.'

'Not the nice ones, angel.'

'Well – the hours were a little trying. I work at night, often get home very late. She's a dresser as well as a maid.'

'Anything else about her? She use cocaine or weed? Hit the bottle? Ever have laughing fits?'

'I don't think so. What has she got to do with it, Steve?'

'Lady, she sold somebody a key to your apartment. That's obvious. You didn't give him one, the landlord wouldn't give him one, but Agatha had one. Check?'

Her eyes had a stricken look. Her mouth trembled a little, not much. A drink was untasted at her elbow. Steve bent over and drank some of it.

She said slowly: 'We're wasting time, Steve. We have to call the police. There's nothing anybody can do. I'm done for as a nice person, even if not as a lady at large. They'll think it was a lovers' quarrel and I shot him and that's that. If I could convince them I didn't, then he shot himself in my bed, and I'm still ruined. So I might as well make up my mind to face the music.'

Steve said softly: 'Watch this. My mother used to do it.'

He put a finger to his mouth, bent down and touched her lips at the same spot with the same finger. He smiled, said: 'We'll go to Walters – or you will. He'll pick his cops and the ones he picks won't go screaming through the night with reporters sitting in their laps. They'll sneak in quiet, like process-servers. Walters can handle this. That was what was counted on. Me, I'm going to collect Agatha. Because I want a description of the guy she sold that key to – and I want it fast. And by the way, you owe me twenty bucks for coming over here. Don't let that slip your memory.'

The tall girl stood up, smiling. 'You're a kick, you are,' she said. 'What makes you so sure he was murdered?'

'He's not wearing his own pajamas. His have his initials on them. I packed his stuff last night – before I threw him out of the Carlton. Get dressed, angel – and get me Agatha's address.'

He went into the bedroom and pulled a sheet over Leopardi's body, held it a moment above the still waxen face before letting it fall.

'So long, guy,' he said gently. 'You were a louse – but you sure had music in you.'

It was a small frame house on Brighton Avenue near Jefferson, in a block of small frame houses, all old-fashioned, with front porches. This one had a narrow concrete walk which the moon made whiter than it was.

Steve mounted the steps and looked at the light-edged shade of the wide front window. He knocked. There were shuffling steps and a woman opened the door and looked at him through the hooked screen – a dumpy elderly woman with frizzled gray hair. Her body was shapeless in a wrapper and her feet slithered in loose slippers. A man with a polished bald head and milky eyes sat in a wicker chair beside a table. He held his hands in his lap and twisted the knuckles aimlessly. He didn't look towards the door.

Steve said: 'I'm from Miss Chiozza. Are you Agatha's mother?'

The woman said dully: 'I reckon. But she ain't home, mister.' The man in the chair got a handkerchief from somewhere and blew his nose. He snickered darkly.

Steve said: 'Miss Chiozza's not feeling so well tonight. She was hoping Agatha would come back and stay the night with her.'

The milky-eyed man snickered again, sharply. The woman said: 'We dunno where she is. She don't come home. Pa 'n me waits up for her to come home. She stays out till we're sick.'

The old man snapped in a reedy voice: 'She'll stay out till the cops get her one of these times.'

'Pa's half blind,' the woman said. 'Makes him kinda mean. Won't you step in?'

Steve shook his head and turned his hat around in his hands like a bashful cowpuncher in a horse opera. 'I've got to find her,' he said. 'Where would she go?'

'Out drinkin' liquor with cheap spenders,' Pa cackled. 'Panty-waists with silk handkerchiefs 'stead of neckties. If I had eyes, I'd strap her till she dropped.' He grabbed the arms of his chair and the muscles knotted on the backs of his hands. Then he began to cry. Tears welled from his milky eyes and started through the white stubble on his cheeks. The woman went across and took the handkerchief out of his fist and wiped his face with it. Then she blew her nose on it and came back to the door.

'Might be anywhere,' she said to Steve. 'This is a big town, mister. I dunno where at to say.'

Steve said dully: 'I'll call back. If she comes in, will you hang onto her? What's your phone number?'

'What's the phone number, Pa?' the woman called back over her shoulder.

'I ain't sayin',' Pa snorted.

The woman said: 'I remember now. South Two-four-five-four. Call any time. Pa 'n me ain't got nothing to do.'

Steve thanked her and went back down the white walk to the street and along the walk half a block to where he had left his car. He glanced idly across the way and started to get into his car, then stopped moving suddenly with his hand gripping the car door. He let go of that, took three steps sideways and stood looking across the street tight-mouthed.

All the houses in the block were much the same, but the one opposite had a FOR RENT placard stuck in the front window and a real-estate sign spiked into the small patch of front lawn. The house itself looked neglected, utterly empty, but in its little driveway stood a small neat black coupé.

Steve said under his breath: 'Hunch. Play it up, Stevie.'

He walked almost delicately across the wide dusty street, his hand touching the hard metal of the gun in his pocket, and came up behind the little car, stood and listened. He moved silently along its left side, glanced back across the street, then looked in the car's open left-front window.

The girl sat almost as if driving, except that her head was tipped a little too much into the corner. The little red hat was still on her head, the gray coat, trimmed with fur, still around her body. In the reflected moonlight her mouth was strained open. Her tongue stuck out. And her chestnut eyes stared at the roof of the car.

Steve didn't touch her. He didn't have to touch her or look any closer to know there would be heavy bruises on her neck.

'Tough on women, these guys,' he muttered.

The girl's big black brocade bag lay on the seat beside her, gaping open like her mouth – like Miss Marilyn Delorme's mouth, and Miss Marilyn Delorme's purple bag.

'Yeah – tough on women.'

He backed away till he stood under a small palm tree by the entrance to the driveway. The street was as empty and deserted as a closed theater. He crossed silently to his car, got into it and drove away.

Nothing to it. A girl coming home late at night, stuck up and strangled a few doors from her own home by some tough guy. Very simple. The first prowl car that cruised that block – if the boys were half awake – would take a look the minute they spotted the FOR RENT sign. Steve tramped hard on the throttle and went away from there.

At Washington and Figueroa he went into an all-night drug store and pulled shut the door of the phone-booth at the back. He dropped his nickel and dialed the number of police headquarters.

He asked for the desk and said: 'Write this down, will you, sergeant? Brighton Avenue, thirty-two-hundred block, west side, in driveway of empty house. Got that much?'

'Yeah. So what?'

'Car with dead woman in it,' Steve said, and hung up.

VII

Quillan, head day clerk and assistant manager of the Carlton Hotel, was on night duty, because Millar, the night auditor, was off for a week. It was half past one and things were dead and Quillan was bored. He had done everything there was to do long ago, because he had been a hotel man for twenty years and there was nothing to it.

The night porter had finished cleaning up and was in his room beside the elevator bank. One elevator was lighted and open, as usual. The main lobby had been tidied up and the lights had been properly dimmed. Everything was exactly as usual.

Quillan was a rather short, rather thickset man with clear bright toadlike eyes that seemed to hold a friendly expression without really having any expression at all. He had pale sandy hair and not much of it. His pale hands were clasped in front of him on the marble top of the desk. He was just the right height to put his weight on the desk without looking as if he were sprawling. He was looking at the wall across the entrance lobby, but he wasn't seeing it. He was half asleep, even though his eyes were wide open, and if the night porter struck a match behind his door, Quillan would know it and bang on his bell.

The brass-trimmed swing-doors at the street entrance pushed open and Steve Grayce came in, a summer-weight coat turned up around his neck, his hat yanked low and a cigarette wisping smoke at the corner of his mouth. He looked very casual, very alert, and very much at ease. He strolled over to the desk and rapped on it.

'Wake up!' he snorted.

Quillan moved his eyes an inch and said: 'All outside rooms with bath. But positively no parties on the eighth floor. Hiyah, Steve. So you finally got the axe. And for the wrong thing. That's life.'

Steve said: 'O.K. Have you got a new night man here?'

'Don't need one, Steve. Never did, in my opinion.'

'You'll need one as long as old hotel men like you register floozies on the same corridor with people like Leopardi.'

Quillan half closed his eyes and then opened them to where they had been before. He said indifferently: 'Not me, pal. But anybody can make a mistake. Millar's really an accountant – not a desk man.'

Steve leaned back and his face became very still. The smoke almost hung at the tip of his cigarette. His eyes were like black glass now. He smiled a little dishonestly.

'And why was Leopardi put in a four-dollar room on Eight instead of in a tower suite at eighteen per?'

Quillan smiled back at him. 'I didn't register Leopardi, old sock. There were reservations in. I suppose they were what he wanted. Some guys don't spend. Any other questions, Mr Grayce?'

'Yeah. Was Eight-fourteen empty last night?'

'It was on change, so it was empty. Something about the plumbing. Proceed.'

'Who marked it on change?'

Quillan's bright fathomless eyes turned and became curiously fixed. He didn't answer.

Steve said: 'Here's why. Leopardi was in Eight-fifteen and the two girls in Eight-eleven. Just Eight-thirteen between. A lad with a pass-key could have gone into Eight-thirteen and turned both the bolt locks on the communicating doors. Then, if the folks in the two other rooms had done the same thing on their side, they'd have a suite set up.'

'So what?' Quillan asked. 'We got chiseled out of four bucks, eh? Well, it happens, in better hotels than this.' His eyes looked sleepy now.

Steve said: 'Millar could have done that. But hell, it doesn't make sense. Millar's not that kind of a guy. Risk a job for a buck tip – phooey. Millar's no dollar pimp.'

Quillan said: 'All right, policeman. Tell me what's really on your mind.'

'One of the girls in Eight-eleven had a gun. Leopardi got a threat letter yesterday – I don't know where or how. It didn't faze him, though. He tore it up. That's how I know. I collected the pieces from his basket. I suppose Leopardi's boys all checked out of here.'

'Of course. They went to the Normandy.'

'Call the Normandy and ask to speak to Leopardi. If he's there, he'll still be at the bottle. Probably with a gang.'

'Why?' Quillan asked gently.

'Because you're a nice guy. If Leopardi answers – just hang up.' Steve paused and pinched his chin hard. 'If he went out, try to find out where.'

Quillan straightened, gave Steve another long quiet look and went behind the pebbled glass screen. Steve stood very still, listening, one hand clenched at his side, the other tapping noiselessly on the marble desk.

In about three minutes Quillan came back and leaned on the desk again and said: 'Not there. Party going on in his suite – they sold him a big one – and sounds loud. I talked to a guy who was fairly sober. He said Leopardi got a call around ten – some girl. He went out preening himself, as the fellow says. Hinting about a very juicy date. The guy was just lit enough to hand me all this.'

Steve said: 'You're a real pal. I hate not to tell you the rest. Well, I liked working here. Not much work at that.'

He started towards the entrance doors again. Quillan let him get his hand on the brass handle before he called out. Steve turned and came back slowly.

Quillan said: 'I heard Leopardi took a shot at you. I don't think it was noticed. It wasn't reported down here. And I don't think Peters fully realized that until he saw the mirror in Eight-fifteen. If you want to come back, Steve – '

Steve shook his head. 'Thanks for the thought.'

'And hearing about that shot,' Quillan added, 'made me remember something. Two years ago a girl shot herself in Eight-fifteen.'

Steve straightened his back so sharply that he almost jumped. 'What girl?' he almost yelled.

Quillan looked surprised. 'I don't know. I don't remember her real name. Some girl who had been kicked around all she could stand and wanted to die in a clean bed – alone.'

Steve reached across and took hold of Quillan's arm. 'The hotel files,' he rasped. 'The clippings, whatever there was in the papers will be in them. I want to see those clippings.'

Quillan stared at him for a long moment. Then he said: 'Whatever game you're playing, kid – you're playing it damn close to your vest. I will say that for you. And me bored stiff with a night to kill.'

He reached along the desk and thumped the call bell. The door of the night porter's room opened and the porter came across the entrance lobby. He nodded and smiled at Steve.

Quillan said: 'Take the board, Carl. I'll be in Mr Peters' office for a little while.'

He went to the safe and got keys out of it.

VIII

The cabin was high up on the side of the mountain, against a thick growth of digger pine, oak and incense cedar. It was solidly built, with a stone chimney, shingled all over and heavily braced against the slope of the hill. By daylight the roof was green and the sides dark reddish brown and the window frames and draw-curtains red. In the uncanny brightness of an all-night mid-October moon in the mountains, it stood out sharply in every detail, except color.

It was at the end of a road, a quarter of a mile from any other cabin. Steve rounded the bend towards it without lights, at five in the morning. He stopped his car at once, when he was sure it was the right cabin, got out and walked soundlessly along the side of the gravel road, on a carpet of wild iris.

On the road level there was a rough pine board garage, and from this a path went up to the cabin porch. The garage was unlocked. Steve swung the door open carefully, groped in past the dark bulk of a car and felt the top of the radiator. It was still warmish. He got a small flash out of his pocket and played it over the car. A gray sedan, dusty, the gas gauge low. He snapped the flash off, shut the garage door carefully and slipped into place the piece of wood that served for a hasp. Then he climbed the path to the house.

There was light behind the drawn red curtains. The porch was high and juniper logs were piled on it, with the bark still on them. The front door had a thumb latch and a rustic door-handle above.

He went up, neither too softly nor too noisily, lifted his hand, sighed deep in his throat, and knocked. His hand touched the butt of the gun in the inside pocket of his coat, once, then came away empty.

A chair creaked and steps padded across the floor and a voice called out softly: 'What is it?' Millar's voice.

Steve put his lips close to the wood and said: 'This is Steve, George. You up already?'

The key turned, and the door opened. George Millar, the dapper night auditor of the Carlton Hotel, didn't look dapper now. He was dressed in old trousers and a thick blue sweater with a roll collar. His feet were in ribbed wool socks and fleece-lined slippers. His clipped black mustache was a curved smudge across his pale face. Two electric bulbs burned in their sockets in a low beam across the room, below the slope of the high roof. A table lamp was lit and its shade was tilted to throw light on a big Morris chair with a leather seat and back-cushion. A fire burned lazily in a heap of soft ash on the big open hearth.

Millar said in his low, husky voice: 'Hell's sake, Steve. Glad to see you. How'd you find us anyway? Come on in, guy.'

Steve stepped through the door and Millar locked it. 'City habit,' he said grinning. 'Nobody locks anything in the mountains. Have a chair. Warm your toes. Cold out at this time of night.'

Steve said: 'Yeah. Plenty cold.'

He sat down in the Morris chair and put his hat and coat on the end of the solid wood table behind it. He leaned forward and held his hands out to the fire.

Millar said: 'How the hell did you find us, Steve? I didn't know – '

Steve didn't look at him. He said quietly: 'Not so easy at that. You told me last night your brother had a cabin up here – remember? So I had nothing to do, so I thought I'd drive up and bum some breakfast. The guy in the inn at Crestline didn't know who had cabins where. His trade is with people passing through. I rang up a garage man and he didn't know any Millar cabin. Then I saw a light come on down the street in a coal-and-wood yard and a little guy who is forest ranger and deputy sheriff and wood-and-gas dealer and half a dozen other things was getting his car out to go down to San Bernardino for some tank gas. A very smart little guy. The minute I said your brother had been a fighter he wised up. So here I am.'

Millar pawed at his mustache. Bedsprings creaked at the back of the cabin somewhere. 'Sure, he still goes under his fighting name – Gaff Talley. I'll get him up and we'll have some coffee. I guess you and me are both in the same boat. Used to working at night and can't sleep. I haven't been to bed at all.'

Steve looked at him slowly and looked away. A burly voice behind them said: 'Gaff is up. Who's your pal, George?'

Steve stood up casually and turned. He looked at the man's hands first. He couldn't help himself. They were large hands, well kept as to cleanliness, but coarse and ugly. One knuckle had been broken badly. He was a big man with reddish hair. He wore a sloppy bathrobe over outing-flannel pajamas. He had a leathery expressionless face, scarred over the cheekbones.

There were fine white scars over his eyebrows and at the corners of his mouth. His nose was spread and thick. His whole face looked as if it had caught a lot of gloves. His eyes alone looked vaguely like Millar's eyes.

Millar said: 'Steve Grayce. Night man at the hotel – until last night.' His grin was a little vague.

Gaff Talley came over and shook hands. 'Glad to meet you,' he said. 'I'll get some duds on and we'll scrape a breakfast off the shelves. I slept enough. George ain't slept any, the poor sap.'

He went back across the room towards the door through which he'd come. He stopped there and leaned on an old phonograph, put his big hand down behind a pile of records in paper envelopes. He stayed just like that, without moving.

Millar said: 'Any luck on a job, Steve? Or did you try yet?'

'Yeah. In a way. I guess I'm a sap, but I'm going to have a shot at the private agency racket. Not much in it unless I can land some publicity.' He shrugged. Then he said very quietly: 'King Leopardi's been bumped off.'

Millar's mouth snapped wide open. He stayed like that for almost a minute – perfectly still, with his mouth open. Gaff Talley leaned against the wall and stared without showing anything in his face. Millar finally said: 'Bumped off? Where? Don't tell me – '

'Not in the hotel, George. Too bad, wasn't it? In a girl's apartment. Nice girl too. She didn't entice him there. The old suicide gag – only it won't work. And the girl is my client.'

Millar didn't move. Neither did the big man. Steve leaned his shoulders against the stone mantel. He said softly: 'I went out to the Club Shalotte this afternoon to apologize to Leopardi. Silly idea, because I didn't owe him an apology. There was a girl there in the bar lounge with him. He took three socks at me and left. The girl didn't like that. We got rather clubby. Had a drink together. Then late tonight – last night – she called me up and said Leopardi was over at her place and he was drunk and she couldn't get rid of him. I went there. Only he wasn't drunk. He was dead, in her bed, in yellow pajamas.'

The big man lifted his left hand and roughed back his hair.

Millar leaned slowly against the edge of the table, as if he were afraid the edge might be sharp enough to cut him. His mouth twitched under the clipped black mustache.

He said huskily: 'That's lousy.'

The big man said: 'Well, for cryin' into a milk bottle.'

Steve said: 'Only they weren't Leopardi's pajamas. He had initials on them – big black initials. And his were satin, not silk. And although he had a gun in his hand – this girl's by the way – *he* didn't shoot himself in the heart. The cops will determine that. Maybe you birds never heard of the Lund test, with paraffin wax, to find out who did or didn't fire a gun recently. The kill ought to have been pulled in the hotel last night, in Room Eight-fifteen. I spoiled that by heaving him out on his neck before that black-haired girl in Eight-eleven could get to him. Didn't I, George?'

Millar said: 'I guess you did – if I know what you're talking about.'

Steve said slowly: 'I think you know what I'm talking about, George. It would have been a kind of poetic justice if King Leopardi had been knocked off in Room Eight-fifteen. Because that was the room where a girl shot herself two years ago. A girl who registered as Mary Smith – but whose usual name was Eve Talley. And whose real name was Eve Millar.'

The big man leaned heavily on the victrola and said thickly: 'Maybe I ain't woke up yet. That sounds like it might grow up to be a dirty crack. We had a sister named Eve that shot herself in the Carlton. So what?'

Steve smiled a little crookedly. He said: 'Listen, George. You told me Quillan registered those girls in Eight-eleven. *You* did. You told me Leopardi registered on Eight, instead of in a good suite, because he was tight. He wasn't tight. He just didn't care where he was put, as long as female company was handy. And you saw to that. You planned the whole thing, George. You even got Peters to write Leopardi at the Raleigh in Frisco and ask him to use the Carlton when he came down – because the same man owned it who owned the Club Shalotte. As if a guy like Jumbo Walters would care where a bandleader registered.'

Millar's face was dead white, expressionless. His voice

cracked. 'Steve – for God's sake, Steve, what are you talking about? How the hell could I – '

'Sorry, kid. I liked working with you. I liked you a lot. I guess I still like you. But I don't like people who strangle women – or people who smear women in order to cover up a revenge murder.'

His hand shot up – and stopped. The big man said: 'Take it easy – and look at this one.'

Gaff's hand had come up from behind the pile of records. A Colt .45 was in it. He said between his teeth: 'I always thought house dicks were just a bunch of cheap grafters. I guess I missed out on you. You got a few brains. Hell, I bet you even run out to One-eighteen Court Street. Right?'

Steve let his hand fall empty and looked straight at the big Colt. 'Right. I saw the girl – dead – with your fingers marked into her neck. They can measure those, fella. Killing Dolores Chiozza's maid the same way was a mistake. They'll match up the two sets of marks, find out that your black-haired gun girl was at the Carlton last night, and piece the whole story together. With the information they get at the hotel they can't miss. I give you two weeks, if you beat it quick. And I mean quick.'

Millar licked his dry lips and said softly: 'There's no hurry, Steve. No hurry at all. Our job is done. Maybe not the best way, maybe not the nicest way, but it wasn't a nice job. And Leopardi was the worst kind of a louse. We loved our sister, and he made a tramp out of her. She was a wide-eyed kid that fell for a flashy greaseball, and the greaseball went up in the world and threw her out on her ear for a red-headed torcher who was more his kind. He threw her out and broke her heart and she killed herself.'

Steve said harshly: 'Yeah – and what were you doing all that time – manicuring your nails?'

'We weren't around when it happened. It took us a little time to find out the why of it.'

Steve said: 'So that was worth killing four people for, was it? And as for Dolores Chiozza, she wouldn't have wiped her feet on Leopardi – then, or any time since. But you had to put her in the middle too, with your rotten little revenge murder.

You make me sick, George. Tell your big tough brother to get on with his murder party.'

The big man grinned and said: 'Nuff talk, George. See has he a gat – and don't get behind him or in front of him. This bean-shooter goes on through.'

Steve stared at the big man's .45. His face was hard as white bone. There was a thin cold sneer on his lips and his eyes were cold and dark.

Millar moved softly in his fleece-lined slippers. He came around the end of the table and went close to Steve's side and reached out a hand to tap his pockets. He stepped back and pointed: 'In there.'

Steve said softly: 'I must be nuts. I could have taken you then, George.'

Gaff Talley barked: 'Stand away from him.'

He walked solidly across the room and put the big Colt against Steve's stomach hard. He reached up with his left hand and worked the Detective Special from the inside breast pocket. His eyes were sharp on Steve's eyes. He held Steve's gun out behind him. 'Take this, George.'

Millar took the gun and went over beyond the big table again and stood at the far corner of it. Gaff Talley backed away from Steve.

'You're through, wise guy,' he said. 'You got to know that. There's only two ways outa these mountains and we gotta have time. And maybe you didn't tell nobody. See?'

Steve stood like a rock, his face white, a twisted half-smile working at the corners of his lips. He stared hard at the big man's gun and his stare was faintly puzzled.

Millar said: 'Does it have to be that way, Gaff?' His voice was a croak now, without tone, without its usual pleasant huskiness.

Steve turned his head a little and looked at Millar. 'Sure it has, George. You're just a couple of cheap hoodlums after all. A couple of nasty-minded sadists playing at being revengers of wronged girlhood. Hillbilly stuff. And right this minute you're practically cold meat – cold, rotten meat.'

Gaff Talley laughed and cocked the big revolver with his thumb. 'Say your prayers, guy,' he jeered.

Steve said grimly: 'What makes you think you're going to bump me off with that thing? No shells in it, strangler. Better try to take me the way you handle women – with your hands.'

The big man's eyes flicked down, clouded. Then he roared with laughter. 'Geez, the dust on that one must be a foot thick,' he chuckled. 'Watch.'

He pointed the big gun at the floor and squeezed the trigger. The firing-pin clicked dryly – on an empty chamber. The big man's face convulsed.

For a short moment nobody moved. Then Gaff turned slowly on the balls of his feet and looked at his brother. He said almost gently: 'You, George?'

Millar licked his lips and gulped. He had to move his mouth in and out before he could speak.

'Me, Gaff. I was standing by the window when Steve got out of his car down the road, I saw him go into the garage. I knew the car would still be warm. There's been enough killing, Gaff. Too much. So I took the shells out of your gun.'

Millar's thumb moved back the hammer on the Detective Special. Gaff's eyes bulged. He stared fascinated at the snubnosed gun. Then he lunged violently towards it, flailing with the empty Colt. Millar braced himself and stood very still and said dimly, like an old man: 'Good-bye, Gaff.'

The gun jumped three times in his small neat hand. Smoke curled lazily from its muzzle. A piece of burned log fell over in the fireplace.

Gaff Talley smiled queerly and stopped and stood perfectly still. The gun dropped at his feet. He put his big heavy hands against his stomach, said slowly, thickly: ''S all right, kid. 'S all right, I guess . . . I guess I . . .'

His voice trailed off and his legs began to twist under him. Steve took three long quick silent steps, and slammed Millar hard on the angle of the jaw. The big man was still falling – as slowly as a tree falls.

Millar spun across the room and crashed against the end wall and a blue-and-white plate fell off the plate-moulding and broke. The gun sailed from his fingers. Steve dived for it and came up with it. Millar crouched and watched his brother.

Gaff Talley bent his head to the floor and braced his hands

and then lay down quietly, on his stomach, like a man who was very tired. He made no sound of any kind.

Daylight showed at the windows, around the red glass-curtains. The piece of broken log smoked against the side of the hearth and the rest of the fire was a heap of soft gray ash with a glow at its heart.

Steve said dully: 'You saved my life, George – or at least you saved a lot of shooting. I took the chance because what I wanted was evidence. Step over there to the desk and write it all out and sign it.'

Millar said: 'Is he dead?'

'He's dead, George. You killed him. Write that too.'

Millar said quietly: 'It's funny. I wanted to finish Leopardi myself, with my own hands, when he was at the top, when he had the farthest to fall. Just finish him and then take what came. But Gaff was the guy who wanted it done cute. Gaff, the tough mug who never had any education and never dodged a punch in his life, wanted to do it smart and figure angles. Well, maybe that's why he owned property, like that apartment house on Court Street that Jake Stoyanoff managed for him. I don't know how he got to Dolores Chiozza's maid. It doesn't matter much, does it?'

Steve said: 'Go and write it. You were the one called Leopardi up and pretended to be the girl, huh?'

Millar said: 'Yes. I'll write it all down, Steve. I'll sign it and then you'll let me go – just for an hour. Won't you, Steve? Just an hour's start. That's not much to ask of an old friend, is it, Steve?'

Millar smiled. It was a small, frail, ghostly smile. Steve bent beside the big sprawled man and felt his neck artery. He looked up, said: 'Quite dead . . . Yes, you get an hour's start, George – if you write it all out.'

Millar walked softly over to a tall oak highboy desk, studded with tarnished brass nails. He opened the flap and sat down and reached for a pen. He unscrewed the top from a bottle of ink and began to write in his neat, clear accountant's handwriting.

Steve Grayce sat down in front of the fire and lit a cigarette and stared at the ashes. He held the gun with his left hand on his knee. Outside the cabin, birds began to sing. Inside there was no sound but the scratching pen.

IX

The sun was well up when Steve left the cabin, locked it up, walked down the steep path and along the narrow gravel road to his car. The garage was empty now. The gray sedan was gone. Smoke from another cabin floated lazily above the pines and oaks half a mile away. He started his car, drove it around a bend, past two old box-cars that had been converted into cabins, then on to a main road with a stripe down the middle and so up the hill to Crestline.

He parked on the main street before the Rim-of-the-World Inn, had a cup of coffee at the counter, then shut himself in a phone-booth at the back of the empty lounge. He had the long distance operator get Jumbo Walters' number in Los Angeles, then called the owner of the Club Shalotte.

A voice said silkily: 'This is Mr Walters' residence.'

'Steve Grayce. Put him on, if you please.'

'One moment, please.' A click, another voice, not so smooth and much harder. 'Yeah?'

'Steve Grayce. I want to speak to Mr Walters.'

'Sorry. I don't seem to know you. It's a little early, amigo. What's your business?'

'Did he go to Miss Chiozza's place?'

'Oh.' A pause. 'The shamus. I get it. Hold the line, pal.'

Another voice now – lazy, with the faintest color of Irish in it. 'You can talk, son. This is Walters.'

'I'm Steve Grayce. I'm the man – '

'I know all about that, son. The lady is O.K., by the way. I think she's asleep upstairs. Go on.'

'I'm at Crestline – top of the Arrowhead grade. Two men murdered Leopardi. One was George Millar, night auditor at the Carlton Hotel. The other his brother, an ex-fighter named Gaff Talley. Talley's dead – shot by his brother. Millar got away – but he left me a full confession signed, detailed, complete.'

Walters said slowly: 'You're a fast worker, son – unless you're just plain crazy. Better come in here fast. Why did they do it?'

'They had a sister.'

Walters repeated quietly: 'They had a sister . . . What about this fellow that got away? We don't want some hick sheriff or publicity-hungry county attorney to get ideas – '

Steve broke in quietly: 'I don't think you'll have to worry about that, Mr Walters. I think I know where he's gone.'

He ate breakfast at the inn, not because he was hungry, but because he was weak. He got into his car again and started down the long smooth grade from Crestline to San Bernardino, a broad paved boulevard skirting the edge of a sheer drop into the deep valley. There were places where the road went close to the edge, white guard-fences alongside.

Two miles below Crestline was the place. The road made a sharp turn around a shoulder of the mountain. Cars were parked on the gravel off the pavement – several private cars, an official car, and a wrecking-car. The white fence was broken through and men stood around the broken place looking down.

Eight hundred feet below, what was left of a gray sedan lay silent and crumpled in the morning sunshine.

THE ABSENCE OF MR GLASS

G. K. Chesterton

THE consulting-rooms of Dr Orion Hood, the eminent criminologist and specialist in certain moral disorders, lay along the sea-front at Scarborough, in a series of very large and well-lighted french windows, which showed the North Sea like one endless outer wall of blue-green marble. In such a place the sea had something of the monotony of a blue-green dado: for the chambers themselves were ruled throughout by a terrible tidiness not unlike the terrible tidiness of the sea. It must not be supposed that Dr Hood's apartments excluded luxury, or even poetry. These things were there, in their place; but one felt that they were never allowed out of their place. Luxury was there: there stood upon a special table eight or ten boxes of the best cigars; but they were built upon a plan so that the strongest were always nearest the wall and the mildest nearest the window. A tantalus containing three kinds of spirit, all of a liqueur excellence, stood always on this table of luxury; but the fanciful have asserted that the whisky, brandy, and rum seemed always to stand at the same level. Poetry was there: the left-hand corner of the room was lined with as complete a set of English classics as the right hand could show of English and foreign physiologists. But if one took a volume of Chaucer or Shelley from that rank, its absence irritated the mind like a gap in a man's front teeth. One could not say the books were never read; probably they were, but there was a sense of their being chained to their places, like the Bibles in the old churches. Dr Hood treated his private book-shelf as if it were a public library. And if this strict scientific intangibility steeped even the shelves laden with lyrics and ballads and the tables laden with drink and tobacco, it goes without saying that yet more of such heathen holiness protected the other shelves that held the specialist's library, and the other tables that sustained the frail and even fairylike instruments of chemistry or mechanics.

Dr Hood paced the length of his string of apartments, bounded – as the boys' geographies say – on the east by the North Sea and on the west by the serried ranks of his sociological and criminologist library. He was clad in an artist's velvet, but with none of an artist's negligence; his hair was heavily shot with grey, but growing thick and healthy; his face was lean, but sanguine and expectant. Everything about him and his room indicated something at once rigid and restless, like that great northern sea by which (on pure principles of hygiene) he had built his home.

Fate, being in a funny mood, pushed the door open and introduced into those long, strict, sea-flanked apartments one who was perhaps the most startling opposite of them and their master. In answer to a curt but civil summons, the door opened inwards and there shambled into the room a shapeless little figure, which seemed to find its own hat and umbrella as unmanageable as a mass of luggage. The umbrella was a black and prosaic bundle long past repair; the hat was a broad-curved black hat, clerical but not common in England; the man was the very embodiment of all that is homely and helpless.

The doctor regarded the new-comer with a restrained astonishment, not unlike that he would have shown if some huge but obviously harmless sea-beast had crawled into his room. The new-comer regarded the doctor with that beaming but breathless geniality which characterizes a corpulent charwoman who has just managed to stuff herself into an omnibus. It is a rich confusion of social self-congratulation and bodily disarray. His hat tumbled to the carpet, his heavy umbrella slipped between his knees with a thud; he reached after the one and ducked after the other, but with an unimpaired smile on his round face spoke simultaneously as follows:

'My name is Brown. Pray excuse me. I've come about that

business of the MacNabs. I have heard you often help people out of such troubles. Pray excuse me if I am wrong.'

By this time he had sprawlingly recovered the hat, and made an odd little bobbing bow over it, as if setting everything quite right.

'I hardly understand you,' replied the scientist, with a cold intensity of manner. 'I fear you have mistaken the chambers. I am Dr Hood, and my work is almost entirely literary and educational. It is true that I have sometimes been consulted by the police in cases of peculiar difficulty and importance, but – '

'Oh, this is of the greatest importance,' broke in the little man called Brown. 'Why, her mother won't let them get engaged.' And he leaned back in his chair in radiant rationality.

The brows of Dr Hood were drawn down darkly, but the eyes under them were bright with something that might be anger or might be amusement. 'And still,' he said, 'I do not quite understand.'

'You see, they want to get married,' said the man with the clerical hat. 'Maggie MacNab and young Todhunter want to get *married*. Now, what can be more important than that?'

The great Orion Hood's scientific triumphs had deprived him of many things – some said of his health, others of his God; but they had not wholly despoiled him of his sense of the absurd. At the last plea of the ingenuous priest a chuckle broke out of him from inside, and he threw himself into an arm-chair in an ironical attitude of the consulting physician.

'Mr Brown,' he said gravely, 'it is quite fourteen and a half years since I was personally asked to test a personal problem: then it was the case of an attempt to poison the French President at a Lord Mayor's Banquet. It is now, I understand, a question of whether some friend of yours called Maggie is a suitable fiancée for some friend of hers called Todhunter. Well, Mr Brown, I am a sportsman. I will take it on. I will give the MacNab family my best advice, as good as I gave the French Republic and the King of England – no, better: fourteen years better. I have nothing else to do this afternoon. Tell me your story.'

The little clergyman called Brown thanked him with unquestionable warmth, but still with a queer kind of simplicity. It was rather as if he were thanking a stranger in a smoking-room for some trouble in passing the matches, than as if he were (as he was) practically thanking the Curator of Kew Gardens for coming with him into a field to find a four-leaved clover. With scarcely a semi-colon after his hearty thanks, the little man began his recital:

'I told you my name was Brown; well, that's the fact, and I'm the priest of the little Catholic Church I dare say you've seen beyond those straggly streets, where the town ends towards the north. In the last and straggliest of those streets which runs along the sea like a sea-wall there is a very honest but rather sharp-tempered member of my flock, a widow called MacNab. She has one daughter, and she lets lodgings, and between her and the daughter, and between her and the lodgers – well, I dare say there is a great deal to be said on both sides. At present she has only one lodger, the young man called Todhunter; but he has given more trouble than all the rest, for he wants to marry the young woman of the house.'

'And the young woman of the house,' asked Dr Hood, with huge and silent amusement, 'what does she want?'

'Why, she wants to marry him,' cried Father Brown, sitting up eagerly. 'That is just the awful complication.'

'It is indeed a hideous enigma,' said Dr Hood.

'This young James Todhunter,' continued the cleric, 'is a very decent man so far as I know; but then nobody knows very much. He is a bright, brownish little fellow, agile like a monkey, clean-shaven like an actor, and obliging like a born courtier. He seems to have quite a pocketful of money, but nobody knows what his trade is. Mrs MacNab, therefore (being of a pessimistic turn), is quite sure it is something dreadful, and probably connected with dynamite. The dynamite must be of a shy and noiseless sort, for the poor fellow only shuts himself up for several hours of the day and studies something behind a locked door. He declares his privacy is temporary and justified, and promises to explain before the wedding. That is all that anyone knows for certain, but Mrs MacNab will tell you a great deal more than even she is certain of. You know how the tales grow like grass on such a patch of ignorance as that. There are tales of two voices heard talking in the room; though, when the door is opened, Todhunter is always found alone. There are tales of a mysterious tall man in a silk hat, who once came out of the sea-mists and apparently out of the sea, stepping softly across the sandy fields and through the small back garden at twilight, till he was heard talking to the lodger at his open window. The colloquy seemed to end in a quarrel. Todhunter dashed down his window with violence, and the man in the high hat melted into the sea-fog again. This story is told by the family with the fiercest mystification; but I really think Mrs MacNab prefers her own original tale: that the Other Man (or whatever it is) crawls out every night from the big box in the corner, which is kept locked all day. You see, therefore, how this sealed door of Todhunter's is treated as the gate of all the fancies and monstrosities of the "Thousand and One Nights". And yet there is the little fellow in his respectable black jacket, as punctual and innocent as a parlour clock. He pays his rent to the tick; he is practically a teetotaller; he is tirelessly kind with the younger children, and can keep them amused for a day on end; and, last and most urgent of all, he has made himself equally popular with the eldest daughter, who is ready to go to church with him tomorrow.'

A man warmly concerned with any large theories has always a relish for applying them to any triviality. The great specialist having condescended to the priest's simplicity, condescended expansively. He settled himself with comfort in his arm-chair and began to talk in the tone of a somewhat absent-minded lecturer:

'Even in a minute instance, it is best to look first to the main tendencies of Nature. A particular flower may not be dead in early winter, but the flowers are dying; a particular pebble may never be wetted with the tide, but the tide is coming in. To the scientific eye all human history is a series of collective movements, destructions or migrations, like the massacre of flies in winter or the return of birds in spring. Now the root fact in all history is Race. Race produces religion; Race produces legal and ethical wars. There is no stronger case than that of the wild, unworldly and perishing stock which we commonly call the Celts, of whom your friends the MacNabs are specimens. Small, swarthy, and of this dreamy and drifting blood, they accept easily the superstitious explanation of any incidents, just as they still accept (you will excuse me for saying) that superstitious explanation of all incidents which you and your Church represent. It is not remarkable that such people, with the sea moaning behind them and the Church (excuse me again) droning in front of them, should put fantastic features into what are probably plain events. You, with your small parochial responsibilities, see only this particular Mrs MacNab, terrified with this particular tale of two voices and a tall man out of the sea. But the man with the scientific imagination sees, as it were, the whole clans of MacNab scattered over the whole world, in its ultimate average as uniform as a tribe of birds. He sees thousands of Mrs MacNabs, in thousands of houses, dropping their little drop of morbidity in the tea-cups of their friends; he sees – '

Before the scientist could conclude his sentence, another and more impatient summons sounded from without; someone with swishing skirts was marshalled hurriedly down the corridor, and the door opened on a young girl, decently dressed but disordered and red-hot with haste. She had sea-blown blonde hair, and would have been entirely beautiful if her cheek-bones had not been, in the Scotch manner, a little high in relief as well as in colour. Her apology was almost as abrupt as a command.

'I'm sorry to interrupt you, sir,' she said, 'but I had to follow Father Brown at once; it's nothing less than life or death.'

Father Brown began to get to his feet in some disorder. 'Why, what has happened, Maggie?' he said.

'James has been murdered, for all I can make out,' answered the girl, still breathing hard from her rush. 'That man Glass has been with him again; I heard them talking through the door quite plain. Two separate voices: for James speaks low, with a burr, and the other voice was high and quavery.'

'That man Glass?' repeated the priest in some perplexity.

'I know his name is Glass,' answered the girl, in great impatience. 'I heard it through the door. They were quarrelling – about money, I think – for I heard James say again and again, "That's right, Mr Glass," or "No, Mr Glass," and then, "Two or three, Mr Glass." But we're talking too much; you must come at once, and there may be time yet.'

'But time for what?' asked Dr Hood, who had been studying the young lady with marked interest. 'What is there about Mr Glass and his money troubles that should impel such urgency?'

'I tried to break down the door and couldn't,' answered the girl shortly. 'Then I ran to the back-yard, and managed to climb on to the window-sill that looks into the room. It was all dim, and seemed to be empty, but I swear I saw James lying huddled up in a corner, as if he were drugged or strangled.'

'This is very serious,' said Father Brown, gathering his errant hat and umbrella and standing up; 'in point of fact I was just putting your case before this gentleman, and his view – '

'Has been largely altered,' said the scientist gravely. 'I do not think this young lady is so Celtic as I had supposed. As I have nothing else to do, I will put on my hat and stroll down town with you.'

In a few minutes all three were approaching the dreary tail of the MacNabs' street: the girl with the stern and breathless stride of the mountaineer, the criminologist with a lounging grace (which was not without a certain leopard-like swiftness), and the priest at an energetic trot entirely devoid of distinction. The aspect of this edge of the town was not entirely without justification for the doctor's hints about desolate moods and environments. The scattered houses stood farther and farther apart in a broken string along the seashore; the afternoon was closing with a premature and partly lurid twilight; the sea was of an inky purple and murmuring ominously. In the scrappy back garden of the MacNabs which ran down towards the sand, two black, barren-looking trees stood up like demon hands held up in astonishment, and as Mrs MacNab ran down the street to meet them with lean hands similarly spread, and her fierce face in shadow, she was a little like a demon herself. The doctor and the priest made scant reply to her shrill reiterations of her daughter's story, with more disturbing details of her own, to the divided vows of vengeance against Mr Glass for murdering, and against Mr Todhunter for being murdered, or against the latter for having dared to want to marry her daughter, and for not having lived to do it. They passed through the narrow passage in the front of the house until they came to the lodger's door at the back, and there Dr Hood, with the trick of an old detective, put his shoulder sharply to the panel and burst in the door.

It opened on a scene of silent catastrophe. No one seeing it, even for a flash, could doubt that the room had been the theatre of some thrilling collision between two, or perhaps more, persons. Playing-cards lay littered across the table or fluttered about the floor as if a game had been interrupted. Two wine glasses stood ready for wine on a side-table, but a third lay smashed in a star of crystal upon the carpet. A few feet from it lay what looked like a long knife or short sword, straight, but with an ornamental and pictured handle; its dull blade just caught a grey glint from the dreary window behind, which showed the black trees against the leaden level of the sea. Towards the opposite corner of the room was rolled a gentleman's silk top hat, as if it had just been knocked off his head; so much so, indeed, that one almost looked to see it still rolling. And in the corner behind it, thrown like a sack of potatoes, but corded like a railway trunk, lay Mr James Todhunter, with a scarf across his mouth, and six or seven ropes knotted round his elbows and ankles. His brown eyes were alive and shifted alertly.

Dr Orion Hood paused for one instant on the doormat and drank in the whole scene of voiceless violence. Then he stepped swiftly across the carpet, picked up the tall silk hat, and gravely put it upon the head of the yet pinioned Todhunter. It was so much too large for him that it almost slipped down on to his shoulders.

'Mr Glass's hat,' said the doctor, returning with it and peering into the inside with a pocket lens. 'How to explain the absence of Mr Glass and the presence of Mr Glass's hat? For Mr Glass is not a careless man with his clothes. That hat is of a stylish shape and systematically brushed and burnished, though not very new. An old dandy, I should think.'

'But, good heavens!' called out Miss MacNab, 'aren't you going to untie the man first?'

'I say "old" with intention, though not with certainty,' continued the expositor; 'my reason for it might seem a little far-fetched. The hair of human beings falls out in very varying degrees, but almost always falls out slightly, and with the lens I should see the tiny hairs in a hat recently worn. It has none, which leads me to guess that Mr Glass is bald. Now when this is taken with the high-pitched and querulous voice which Miss NacNab described so vividly (patience, my dear lady, patience), when we take the hairless head together with the tone common in senile anger, I should think we may deduce some advance in years. Nevertheless, he was probably vigorous, and he was almost certainly tall. I might rely in some degree on the story of his previous appearance at the window, as a tall man in a silk hat, but I think I have more exact indication. This wine glass has been smashed all over the place, but one of its splinters lies on the high bracket beside the mantelpiece. No such fragment could have fallen there if the vessel had been smashed in the hand of a comparatively short man like Mr Todhunter.'

'By the way,' said Father Brown, 'might it not be as well to untie Mr Todhunter?'

'Our lesson from the drinking-vessels does not end here,' proceeded the specialist. 'I may say at once that it is possible that the man Glass was bald or nervous through dissipation rather than age. Mr Todhunter, as has been remarked, is a quiet thrifty gentleman, essentially an abstainer. These cards and wine-cups are no part of his normal habit; they have been produced for a particular companion. But, as it happens, we may go farther. Mr Todhunter may or may not possess this wine-service, but there is no appearance of his possessing any wine. What, then, were these vessels to contain? I would at once suggest some brandy or whisky, perhaps of a luxurious sort, from a flask in the pocket of Mr Glass. We have thus something like a picture of the man, or at least of the type: tall, elderly, fashionable, but somewhat frayed, certainly fond of play and strong waters, perhaps rather too fond of them. Mr Glass is a gentleman not unknown on the fringes of society.'

'Look here,' cried the young woman, 'if you don't let me pass to untie him I'll run outside and scream for the police.'

'I should not advise *you*, Miss MacNab,' said Dr Hood gravely, 'to be in any hurry to fetch the police. Father Brown,

I seriously ask you to compose your flock, for their sakes, not for mine. Well, we have seen something of the figure and quality of Mr Glass; what are the chief facts known of Mr Todhunter? They are substantially three: that he is economical, that he is more or less wealthy, and that he has a secret. Now, surely it is obvious that there are the three chief marks of the kind of man who is blackmailed. And surely it is equally obvious that the faded finery, the profligate habits, and the shrill irritation of Mr Glass are the unmistakable marks of the kind of man who blackmails him. We have the two typical figures of a tragedy of hush money: on the one hand, the respectable man with a mystery; on the other, the West-end vulture with a scent for a mystery. These two men have met here today and have quarrelled, using blows and a bare weapon.'

'Are you going to take those ropes off?' asked the girl stubbornly.

Dr Hood replaced the silk hat carefully on the side table, and went across to the captive. He studied him intently, even moving him a little and half-turning him round by the shoulders, but he only answered:

'No; I think these ropes will do very well till your friends the police bring the handcuffs.'

Father Brown, who had been looking dully at the carpet, lifted his round face and said: 'What do you mean?'

The man of science had picked up the peculiar dagger-sword from the carpet and was examining it intently as he answered:

'Because you find Mr Todhunter tied up,' he said, 'you all jump to the conclusion that Mr Glass had tied him up; and then, I suppose, escaped. There are four objections to this: First, why should a gentleman so dressy as our friend Glass leave his hat behind him, if he left of his own free will? Second,' he continued, moving towards the window, 'this is the only exit, and it is locked on the inside. Third, this blade here has a tiny touch of blood at the point, but there is no wound on Mr Todhunter. Mr Glass took that wound away with him, dead or alive. Add to all this primary probability. It is much more likely that the blackmailed person would try to kill his incubus, rather than that the blackmailer would try to kill the goose that lays his golden egg. There, I think, we have a pretty complete story.'

'But the ropes?' inquired the priest, whose eyes had remained open with a rather vacant admiration.

'Ah, the ropes,' said the expert with a singular intonation. 'Miss MacNab very much wanted to know why I did not set Mr Todhunter free from his ropes. Well, I will tell her. I did not do it because Mr Todhunter can set himself free from them at any minute he chooses.'

'What?' cried the audience on quite different notes of astonishment.

'I have looked at all the knots on Mr Todhunter,' reiterated Hood quietly. 'I happen to know something about knots; they are quite a branch of criminal science. Every one of those knots he has made himself and could loosen himself; not one of them would have been made by an enemy really trying to pinion him. The whole of this affair of the ropes is a clever fake, to make us think him the victim of the struggle instead of the wretched Glass, whose corpse may be hidden in the garden or stuffed up the chimney.'

There was a rather depressed silence; the room was darkening, the sea-blighted boughs of the garden trees looked leaner and blacker than ever, yet they seemed to have come nearer to the window. One could almost fancy they were sea-monsters like krakens or cuttlefish, writhing polypi who had crawled up from the sea to see the end of this tragedy, even as *he*, the villain and victim of it, the terrible man in the tall hat, had once crawled up from the sea. For the whole air was dense with the morbidity of blackmail, which is the most morbid of human things, because it is a crime concealing a crime; a black plaster on a blacker wound.

The face of the little Catholic priest, which was commonly complacent and even comic, had suddenly become knotted with a curious frown. It was not the blank curiosity which comes when a man has the beginnings of an idea. 'Say it again, please,'

'My good sir,' cried the mild little man, with his first movement akin to impatience, 'if you will walk down the street to the nearest hatter's shop, you will see that there is, in common speech, a difference between a man's hat and the hats that are his.'

'But a hatter,' protested Hood, 'can get money out of his stock of new hats. What could Todhunter get out of this one old hat?'

'Rabbits,' replied Father Brown promptly.

'*What?*' cried Dr Hood.

'Rabbits, ribbons, sweetmeats, goldfish, rolls of coloured paper,' said the reverend gentleman with rapidity. 'Didn't you see it all when you found out the faked ropes? It's just the same with the sword. Mr Todhunter hasn't got a scratch on him, as you say; but he's got a scratch in him, if you follow me.'

'Do you mean inside Mr Todhunter's clothes?' inquired Mrs MacNab sternly.

'I do not mean inside Mr Todhunter's clothes,' said Father Brown. 'I mean inside Mr Todhunter.'

'Well, what in the name of Bedlam *do* you mean?'

'Mr Todhunter,' explained Father Brown placidly, 'is learning to be a professional conjurer, as well as juggler, ventriloquist, and expert in the rope trick. The conjuring explains the hat. It is without traces of hair, not because it is worn by the prematurely bald Mr Glass, but because it has never been worn by anybody. The juggling explains the three glasses, which Todhunter was teaching himself to throw up and catch in rotation. But, being only at the stage of practice, he smashed one glass against the ceiling. And the juggling also explains the sword, which it was Mr Todhunter's professional pride and duty to swallow. But, again, being at the stage of practice, he very slightly grazed the inside of his throat with the weapon. Hence he has a wound inside him, which I am sure (from the expression on his face) is not a serious one. He was also practising the trick of a release from ropes, like the Davenport Brothers, and he was just about to free himself when we all burst into the room. The cards, of course, are for card tricks, and they are scattered on the floor because he had just been practising one of those dodges of sending them flying through the air. He merely kept his trade secret, because he had to keep his tricks secret, like any other conjurer. But the mere fact of an idler in a top hat having once looked in at his back window, and been driven away by him with great indignation, was enough to set us all on a wrong track of romance, and make us imagine his whole life overshadowed by the silk-hatted spectre of Mr Glass.'

'But what about the two voices?' asked Maggie, staring.

'Have you never heard a ventriloquist?' asked Father Brown. 'Don't you know they speak first in their natural voice, and then answer themselves in just that shrill, squeaky, unnatural voice that you heard?'

There was a long silence, and Dr Hood regarded the little man who had spoken with a dark and attentive smile. 'You are certainly a very ingenious person,' he said; 'it could not have been done better in a book. But there is just one part of Mr Glass you have not succeeded in explaining away, and that is his name. Mrs MacNab distinctly heard him so addressed by Mr Todhunter.'

The Rev. Mr Brown broke into a rather childish giggle. 'Well, that,' he said, 'that's the silliest part of the whole silly story. When our juggling friend here threw up the three glasses in turn, he counted them aloud as he caught them, and also commented aloud when he failed to catch them. What he really said was: "One, two and three – missed a glass; one, two – missed a glass." And so on.'

There was a second of stillness in the room, and then everyone with one accord burst out laughing. As they did so the figure in the corner complacently uncoiled all the ropes and let them fall with a flourish. Then, advancing into the middle of room with a bow, he produced from his pocket a big bill printed in blue and red, which announced that ZALADIN, the World's Greatest Conjurer, Contortionist, Ventriloquist and Human Kangaroo would be ready with an entirely new series of Tricks at the Empire Pavilion, Scarborough, on Monday next at eight o'clock precisely.

THE HEROINE

Patricia Highsmith

THE girl was so sure she would get the job, she had unabashedly come out to Westchester with her suitcase. She sat in a comfortable chair in the living-room of the Christiansens' house, looking in her navy-blue coat and beret even younger than twenty-one, and replied earnestly to their questions.

'Have you worked as a governess before?' Mr Christiansen asked. He sat beside his wife on the sofa, his elbows on the knees of his grey flannel trousers, and his hands clasped. 'Any references, I mean?'

'I was a maid in Mrs Dwight Howell's house in New York for the last seven months.' Lucille looked at him with suddenly wide grey eyes. 'I could get a reference from there if you like . . . But when I saw your advertisement this morning, I didn't want to wait. I've always wanted a place where there were children.'

Mrs Christiansen smiled, but mainly to herself, at the girl's enthusiasm. She took a silver box from the coffee table, stood up and offered it to the girl. 'Will you have one?'

'No, thank you. I don't smoke.'

'Well,' Mrs Christiansen said, lighting her own cigarette, 'we might call them, of course, but my husband and I set more store by appearances than references . . . What do you say, Ronald? You told me you wanted someone who really liked children.'

And fifteen minutes later, Lucille Smith was standing in her room in the servant's quarters back of the house, buttoning the belt of her new white uniform. She touched her mouth lightly with lipstick. 'You're starting all over again, Lucille,' she told herself in the mirror. 'You're going to have a happy, useful life from now on, and forget everything that was before.'

But there went her eyes too wide again, as if to deny her words. Her eyes looked much like her mother's when they opened like that, and her mother was part of what she must forget. She must overcome that habit of stretching her eyes. It made her look surprised and uncertain, too, which was not at all the way to look around children. Her hand trembled as she set the lipstick down. She recomposed her face in the mirror, smoothed the starched front of her uniform. There were only a few things like the eyes to remember, a few silly habits, really, like burning little bits of paper in ash trays, forgetting time sometimes – little things that many people did, but that she must remember not to do. With practice the remembering would come automatically. Because she was just like other people (had the psychiatrist not told her so?), and other people never thought of them at all.

She crossed the room, sank on to the windowseat under the blue curtains, and looked out on the garden and lawn that lay between the servants' house and the big house. The yard was longer than it was wide, with a round fountain in the centre and two flagstone walks lying like a crooked cross in the grass. There were benches here and there, against a tree, under an arbour, that seemed to be made of white lace. A beautiful yard!

And the house was the house of her dreams! A white, two-storey house with dark-red shutters, with oaken doors and brass knockers and latches that opened with a press of the thumb . . . and broad lawns and poplar trees so dense and high one could not see through, so that one did not have to admit or believe that there was another house somewhere beyond . . . The rain-streaked Howell house in New York, granite pillared and heavily ornamented, had looked, Lucille thought, like a stale wedding cake in a row of other stale wedding cakes . . .

She rose suddenly from her seat. The Christiansen house was blooming, friendly, and alive! There were children in it.

Thank God for the children! But she had not even met them yet.

She hurried downstairs, crossed the yard on the path that ran from the door, lingered a few seconds to watch the plump faun blowing water from his reeds into the rock pond . . . What was it the Christiansens had agreed to pay her? She did not remember and she did not care. She would have worked for nothing just to live in such a place.

Mrs Christiansen took her upstairs to the nursery. She opened the door of a room whose walls were decorated with bright peasant designs, dancing couples and dancing animals, and twisting trees in blossom. There were twin beds of buff-coloured oak, and the floor was yellow linoleum, spotlessly clean.

The two children lay on the floor in one corner, amid scattered crayons and picture books.

'Children this is your new nurse,' their mother said. 'Her name is Lucille.'

The little boy stood up and said, 'How do you do,' as he solemnly held out a crayon-stained hand.

Lucille took it, and with a slow nod of her head repeated his greeting.

'And Heloise,' Mrs Christiansen said, leading the second child, who was smaller, toward Lucille.

Heloise stared up at the figure in white and said, 'How do you do.'

'Nicky is nine and Heloise six,' Mrs Christiansen told her.

'Yes,' Lucille said. She noticed that both children had a touch of red in their blond hair, like their father. Both wore blue overalls without shirts, and their backs and shoulders were sun-brown beneath the straps. Lucille could not take her eyes from them. They were the perfect children of her perfect house. They looked up at her frankly, with no mistrust, no hostility. Only love, and some childlike curiosity.

'. . . and most people do prefer living where there's more country,' Mrs Christiansen was saying.

'Oh, yes . . . yes, ma'am. It's ever so much nicer here than in the city.'

Mrs Christiansen was smoothing the little girl's hair with a tenderness that fascinated Lucille. 'It's just about time for their lunch,' she said. 'You'll have your meals up here, Lucille. And would you like tea or coffee or milk?'

'I'd like coffee, please.'

'All right, Lisabeth will be up with the lunch in a few minutes.' She paused at the door. 'You aren't nervous about anything, are you, Lucille?' she asked in a low voice.

'Oh, no ma'am.'

'Well, you mustn't be.' She seemed about to say something else, but she only smiled and went out.

Lucille stared after her, wondering what that something else might have been.

'You're a lot prettier than Catherine,' Nicky told her.

She turned around. 'Who's Catherine?' Lucille seated herself on a hassock, and as she gave all her attention to the two children who still gazed at her, she felt her shoulders relax their tension.

'Catherine was our nurse before. She went back to Scotland . . . I'm glad you're here. We didn't like Catherine.'

Heloise stood with her hands behind her back, swaying from side to side as she regarded Lucille. 'No,' she said, 'We didn't like Catherine.'

Nicky stared at his sister. 'You shouldn't say that. That's what I said!'

Lucille laughed and hugged her knees. Then Nicky and Heloise laughed, too.

A coloured maid entered with a steaming tray and set it on the blond wood table in the centre of the room. She was slender and of indefinite age. 'I'm Lisabeth Jenkins, miss,' she said shyly as she laid some paper napkins at three places.

'My name's Lucille Smith,' the girl said.

'Well, I'll just leave you to do the rest, miss. If you need anything else, just holler.' She went out, her hips small and hard-looking under the blue uniform.

The three sat down to the table, and Lucille lifted the cover from the large dish, exposing three parsley-garnished omelettes, bright yellow in the bar of sunlight that crossed the table. But first there was tomato soup for her to ladle out, and triangles of buttered toast to pass. Her coffee was in a silver pot, and the children had two large glasses of milk. The table was low for Lucille, but she did not mind. It was so wonderful merely to be sitting here with these children, with the sun warm and cheerful on the yellow linoleum floor, on the table, on Heloise's ruddy face opposite her. How pleasant not to be in the Howell house! She had always been clumsy there. But here it would not matter if she dropped a pewter cover or let a gravy spoon fall in someone's lap. The children would only laugh.

Lucille sipped her coffee.

'Aren't you going to eat?' Heloise asked, with her mouth already full.

The cup slipped in Lucille's fingers, and she spilled half her coffee on the cloth. No, it was not cloth, thank goodness, but oilcloth. She could get it up with a paper towel, and Lisabeth would never know.

'Piggy!' laughed Heloise.

'Heloise!' Nicky admonished, and went to fetch some paper towels from the bathroom.

They mopped up together.

'Dad always gives us a little bit of his coffee,' Nicky remarked as he took his place again.

Lucille had been wondering whether the children would mention the accident to their mother. She sensed that Nicky was offering her a bribe. 'Does he?' she asked.

'He pours a little in our milk,' Nicky went on, 'just so you can see the colour.'

'Like this?' And Lucille poured a bit from the graceful silver spout into each glass.

The children gasped with pleasure. 'Yes!'

'Mother doesn't like us to have coffee,' Nicky explained, 'But when she's not looking, Dad let's us have a little like you did. Dad says his day wouldn't be any good without his coffee, and I'm the same way . . . Gosh, Catherine wouldn't give us any coffee like that, would she, Heloise?'

'Not her!' Heloise took a long, delicious draught from her glass which she held with both hands.

Lucille felt a glow rise from deep inside her until it settled in her face and burned there. The children liked her, there was no doubt of that. She remembered how often she had gone to the public parks in the city, during the three years she had worked as maid in various houses (to be a maid was all she was fit for, she used to think), merely to sit on a bench and watch the children play. But the children there had usually been dirty or foul-mouthed, and she herself had always been an outsider. Once she had seen a mother slap her own child across the face. She remembered how she had fled in pain and horror . . .

'Why do you have such big eyes?' Heloise demanded.

Lucille started. 'My mother had big eyes, too,' she said deliberately, like a confession.

'Oh,' Heloise replied, satisfied.

Lucille cut slowly into the omelette she did not want. Her mother had been dead three weeks now. Only three weeks and it seemed much, much longer. That was because she was forgetting, she thought, forgetting all the hopeless hope of the last three years, that her mother might recover in the sanatorium. But recover to what? The illness was something separate, something which had killed her. It had been senseless to hope for a complete sanity which she knew her mother had never had. Even the doctors had told her that. And they had told her other things, too, about herself. Good, encouraging things they were, that she was as normal as her father had been. Looking at Heloise's friendly little face across from her, Lucille felt the comforting glow return. Yes, in this perfect house, closed from all the world, she could forget and start anew.

'Are we ready for some Jello?' she asked.

Nicky pointed to her plate. 'You're not finished eating.'

'I wasn't very hungry.' Lucille divided the extra dessert between them.

'We could go out to the sandbox now,' Nicky suggested. 'We always go just in the mornings, but I want you to see our castle.'

The sandbox was in the back of the house in a corner made by a projecting ell. Lucille seated herself on the wooden rim of the box while the children began piling and patting like gnomes.

'I must be the captured princess!' Heloise shouted.

'Yes, and I'll rescue her, Lucille. You'll see!'

The castle of moist sand rose rapidly. There were turrets with tin flags sticking from their tops, a moat, and a drawbridge made of the lid of a cigar box covered with sand. Lucille watched, fascinated. She remembered vividly the story of Brian de Bois-Guilbert and Rebecca. She had read *Ivanhoe* through at one long sitting, oblivious of time and place just as she was now.

When the castle was done, Nicky put half a dozen marbles inside it just behind the drawbridge. 'These are good soldiers imprisoned,' he told her. He held another cigar box lid in front of them until he had packed up a barrier of sand. Then he lifted the lid and the sand door stood like a porte-cochère.

Meanwhile Heloise gathered ammunition of small pebbles from the ground next to the house. 'We break the door down and the good soldiers come down the hill across the bridge. Then I'm saved!'

'Don't tell her! She'll see!'

Seriously Nicky thumped the pebbles from the rim of the sandbox opposite the castle door, while Heloise behind the castle thrust a hand forth to repair the destruction as much as she could between shots, for besides being the captured princess she was the defending army.

Suddenly Nicky stopped and looked at Lucille. 'Dad knows how to shoot with a stick. He puts the rock on one end and hits the other. That's a balliska.'

'Ballista,' Lucille said.

'Golly, how did *you* know?'

'I read about it in a book – about castles.'

'Golly!' Nicky went back to his thumping, embarrassed that he had pronounced the word wrong. 'We got to get the good soldiers out fast. They're captured, see? Then when they're released that means we can all fight together and *take the castle!*'

'And save the princess!' Heloise put in.

As she watched, Lucille found herself wishing for some real catastrophe, something dangerous and terrible to befall Heloise, so that she might throw herself between her and the attacker, and prove her great courage and devotion . . . She would be seriously wounded herself, perhaps with a bullet or a knife, but she would beat off the assailant. Then the Christiansens would love her and keep her with them always. If some madman were to come upon them suddenly now, someone with a loose mouth and bloodshot eyes, she would not be afraid for an instant.

She watched the sand wall crumble and the first good soldier marble struggled free and came wobbling down the hill. Nicky and Heloise whooped with joy. The wall gave way completely, and two, three, four soldiers followed the first, their stripes turning gaily over the sand. Lucille leaned forward. Now she understood! She was like the good soldiers imprisoned in the castle. The castle was the Howell house in the city, and Nicky and Heloise had set her free. She was free to do good deeds. And now if only something would happen . . .

'O-o-ow!'

It was Heloise. Nicky had mashed one of her fingers against the edge of the box as they struggled to get the same marble.

Lucille seized the child's hand, her heart thumping at the sight of the blood that rose from many little points in the scraped flesh. 'Heloise, does it hurt very much?'

'Oh, she wasn't supposed to touch the marbles in the first place!' Disgruntled, Nicky sat in the sand.

Lucille held her handkerchief over the finger and half carried her into the house, frantic lest Lisabeth or Mrs Christiansen see them. She took Heloise into the bathroom that adjoined the nursery, and in the medicine cabinet found mercurochrome and gauze. Gently she washed the finger. It was only a small scrape, and Heloise stopped her tears when she saw how slight it was.

'See, it's just a little scratch!' Lucille said, but that was only to calm the child. To her it was not a little scratch. It was a terrible thing to happen the first afternoon she was in charge, a catastrophe she had failed to prevent. She wished over and over that the hurt might be on her own hand, twice as severe.

Heloise smiled as she let the bandage be tied. 'Don't punish Nicky,' she said. 'He didn't mean to do it. He just plays rough.'

But Lucille had no idea of punishing Nicky. She wanted

only to punish herself, to seize a stick and thrust it into her own palm.

'Why do you make your teeth like that?'

'I – I thought it might be hurting you.'

'It doesn't hurt any more.' And Heloise went skipping out of the bathroom. She leaped on to her bed and lay on the tan cover that fitted the corners and came all the way to the floor. Her bandaged finger showed startlingly white against the brown of her arm. 'We have to take a nap now,' she told Lucille, and closed her eyes. 'Good-bye.'

'Good-bye,' Lucille answered, and tried to smile.

She went down to get Nicky and when they came up the stairs Mrs Christiansen was at the nursery door.

Lucille blanched. 'I don't think it's bad, ma'am. It – It's a scratch from the sandbox.'

'Heloise's finger? Oh, no, don't worry, my dear. They're always getting little scratches. It does them good. Makes them more careful.'

Mrs Christiansen went in and sat on the edge of Nicky's bed. 'Nicky, dear, you must learn to be more gentle. Just see how you frightened Lucille!' She laughed and ruffled his hair.

Lucille watched from the doorway. Again she felt herself an outsider, but this time because of her incompetence. Yet how different this was from the scenes she had watched in the parks!

Mrs Christiansen patted Lucille's shoulder as she went out. 'They'll forget all about it by nightfall.'

'Nightfall,' Lucille whispered as she went back into the nursery. 'What a beautiful word!'

While the children slept, Lucille looked through an illustrated book of *Pinocchio*. She was avid for stories, any kind of stories, but most of all adventure stories and fairy tales. And at her elbow on the children's shelf there were scores of them. It would take her months to read them all. It did noc matter that they were for children. In fact, she found that kind more to her liking, because such stories were illustrated with pictures of animals dressed up, and tables and houses and all sorts of things come to life.

Now she turned the pages of *Pinocchio* with a sense of contentment and happiness so strong that it intruded upon the story she was reading. The doctor at the sanatorium had encouraged her reading, she remembered, and had told her to go to movies, too. 'Be with normal people and forget all about your mother's difficulties . . .' (Difficulties, he had called it then, but all other times he had said strain. Strain it was, like a thread, running through the generations. She had thought, through her.) Lucille could still see the psychiatrist's face, his head turned a little to one side, his glasses in his hand as he spoke, just as she had thought a psychiatrist should look. 'Just because your mother had a strain, there's no reason why you should not be as normal as your father was. I have every reason to believe you are. You are an intelligent girl, Lucille . . . Get yourself a job out of the city . . . relax . . . enjoy life . . . I want you to forget even the house your family lived in . . . After a year in the country . . .'

That, too, was three weeks ago just after her mother had died in the ward. And what the doctor had said was true. In this house where there were peace and love, beauty and children, she could feel the moils of the city sloughing off her like a snake's outworn skin. Already, in this one half day! In a week she would forget for ever her mother's face.

With a little gasp of joy that was almost ecstasy she turned to the bookshelf and chose at random six or seven tall, slender, brightly coloured books. One she laid open, face down, in her lap. Another she opened and leaned against her breast. Still holding the rest in one hand, she pressed her face into *Pinocchio*'s pages, her eyes half closed. Slowly she rocked back and forth in the chair, conscious of nothing but her own happiness and gratitude. The chimes downstairs struck three times, but she did not hear them.

'What are you doing?' Nicky asked, his voice politely curious.

Lucille brought the book down from her face. When the meaning of his question struck her, she flushed and smiled like a happy but guilty child. 'Reading!' she laughed.

Nicky laughed, too. 'You read awful close.'

'Ya-yuss,' said Heloise, who had also sat up.

Nicky came over and examined the books in her lap. 'We

get up at three o'clock. Would you read to us now? Catherine always read to us until dinner.'

'Shall I read to you out of *Pinocchio?*' Lucille suggested, happy that she might possibly share with them the happiness she had gained from the first pages of its story. She sat down on the floor so they could see the pictures as she read.

Nicky and Heloise pushed their eager faces over the pictures, and sometimes Lucille could hardly see to read. She did not realize that she read with a tense interest that communicated itself to the two children, and that this was why they enjoyed it so much. For two hours she read, and the time slipped by almost like so many minutes.

Just after five Lisabeth brought in the tray with their dinner, and when the meal was over Nicky and Heloise demanded more reading until their bedtime at seven. Lucille gladly began another book, but when Lisabeth returned to remove the tray, she told Lucille that it was time for the children's bath, and that Mrs Christiansen would be up to say good night in a little while.

Mrs Christiansen was up at seven, but the two children by that time were in their robes, freshly bathed, and deep in another story with Lucille on the floor.

'You know,' Nicky said to his mother, 'we've read all these books before with Catherine, but when Lucille reads them they seem like *new* books!'

Lucille flushed with pleasure. When the children were in bed, she went downstairs with Mrs Christiansen.

'Is everything fine, Lucille? . . . I thought there might be something you'd like to ask me about the running of things.'

'No, ma'am, except . . . might I come up once in the night to see how the children are doing?'

'Oh, I wouldn't want you to break your sleep, Lucille. That's very thoughtful, but it's really unnecessary.'

Lucille was silent.

'And I'm afraid the evenings are going to seem long to you. If you'd ever like to go to a picture in town, Alfred, that's the chauffeur, he'll be glad to take you in the car.'

'Thank you, ma'am.'

'Then good night, Lucille.'

'Good night, ma'am.'

She went out the back way, across the garden where the fountain was still playing. And when she put her hand on the knob of her door, she wished that it were the nursery door, that it were eight o'clock in the morning and time to begin another day.

Still she was tired, pleasantly tired. How very pleasant it was, she thought, as she turned out the light, to feel properly tired in the evening (although it was only nine o'clock) instead of bursting with energy, instead of being unable to sleep for thinking of her mother or worrying about herself . . . She remembered one day not so long ago when for fifteen minutes she had been unable to think of her name. She had run in panic to the doctor . . .

That was past! She might even ask Alfred to buy her a pack of cigarettes in town – a luxury she had denied herself for months.

She took a last look at the house from her window. The curtains in the nursery billowed out now and then and were swept back again. The wind spoke in the nodding tops of the poplars like friendly voices, like the high-pitched, ever rippling voices of children . . .

The second day was like the first, except that there was no mishap, no scraped hand – and the third and the fourth. Regular and identical like the row of Nicky's lead soldiers on the playtable in the nursery. The only thing that changed was Lucille's love for the family and the children – a blind and passionate devotion which seemed to redouble each morning. She noticed and loved many things: the way Heloise drank her milk in little gulps at the back of her throat, how the blond down on their backs swirled up to meet the hair on the napes of their necks, and when she bathed them the painful vulnerability of their bodies.

Saturday evening she found an envelope addressed to herself in the mailbox at the door of the servants' house. Inside was a blank sheet of paper and inside that a couple of new twenty-dollar bills. Lucille held one of them by its crisp edges. Its value meant nothing to her. To use it she would have to go to stores where other people were. What use had she for money if she were never to leave the Christiansen home? It would simply pile up, forty dollars each week. In a year's time she would have two thousand and eighty dollars, and in two years' time twice that. Eventually she might have as much as the Christiansens themselves and that would not be right.

Would they think it very strange if she asked to work for nothing? Or for ten dollars perhaps?

She had to speak to Mrs Christiansen, and she went to her the next morning. It was an inopportune time. Mrs Christiansen was making up a menu for a dinner.

'Yes?' Mrs Christiansen said in her pleasant voice.

Lucille watched the yellow pencil in her hand moving swiftly over the paper. 'It's too much for me, ma'am.'

The pencil stopped. Mrs Christiansen's lips parted slightly in surprise. 'You *are* such a funny girl, Lucille!'

How do you mean – funny?' Lucille asked curiously.

'Well, first you want to be practically day and night with the children. You never even want your afternoon off. You're always talking about doing something "important" for us, though what that could be I can't imagine . . . And now your salary's too much! We've never had a girl like you, Lucille. I can assure you, you're different!' She laughed, and the laugh was full of ease and relaxation that contrasted with the tension of the girl who stood before her.

Lucille was rapt by the conversation. 'How do you mean different, ma'am?'

'Why, I've just told you, my dear. And I refuse to lower your salary because that would be sheer exploitation. In fact, if you ever change your mind and want a raise – '

'Oh, no ma'am . . . but I just wish there was something more I could do for you . . . all of you . . .'

'Lucille! You're working for us, aren't you? Taking care of our children. What could be more important than that?'

'But I mean something bigger – I mean more – '

'Nonsense, Lucille,' Mrs Christiansen interrupted. 'Just because the people you were with before were not so – friendly as we are doesn't mean you have to work your fingers to the bone for us.' She waited for the girl to make some move to go, but she still stood by the desk, her face puzzled. 'Mr Christiansen and I are very well pleased with you, Lucille.'

'Thank you, ma'am.'

She went back to the nursery where the children were playing. She had not made Mrs Christiansen understand. If she could just go back and explain what she felt, tell her about her mother and her fear of herself for so many months, how she had never dared take a drink or even a cigarette . . . and how just being with the family in this beautiful house had made her well again . . . telling her all that might relieve her. She turned toward the door, but the thought of disturbing her or boring her with the story, a servant girl's story, made her stop. So during the rest of the day she carried her unexpressed gratitude like a great weight in her breast.

That night she sat in her room with the light on until after twelve o'clock. She had her cigarettes now, and she allowed herself three in the evening, but even those were sufficient to set her blood tingling, to relax her mind, to make her dream heroic dreams. And when the three cigarettes were smoked, and she would have liked another, she rose very light in the head and put the cigarette pack in her top drawer to close away temptation. Just as she slid the drawer she noticed on her handkerchief box the two twenty-dollar bills the Christiansens had given her. She took them now, and sat down again in her chair.

From the book of matches she took a match, struck it, and leaned it, burning end down, against the side of her ashtray. Slowly she struck matches one after another and laid them strategically to make a tiny, flickering, well-controlled fire. When the matches were gone, she tore the pasteboard cover into little bits and dropped them in slowly. Finally she took the twenty-dollar bills and with some effort tore bits from them of the same size. These, too, she meted to the fire.

Mrs Christiansen did not understand, but if she saw *this*, she might. Still *this* was not enough. Mere faithful service was not enough either. Anyone would give that, for money. She was different. Had not Mrs Christiansen herself told her that? Then she remembered what else she had said: 'Mr Christiansen and I are very well pleased with you, Lucille.'

The memory of those words brought her up from her chair with an enchanted smile upon her lips. She felt wonderfully strong and secure in her own strength of mind and her position in the household. *Mr Christiansen and I are very well pleased with you, Lucille.* There was really only one thing lacking in her happiness. She had to prove herself in crisis.

If only a plague like those she had read of in the Bible . . . 'And it came to pass that there was a great plague over all the land.' That was how the Bible would say it. She imagined waters lapping higher against the big house, until they swept almost into the nursery. She would rescue the children and swim with them to safety, wherever that might be.

She moved restlessly about the room.

Or if there came an earthquake . . . She would rush in among falling walls and drag the children out. Perhaps she would go back for some trifle, like Nicky's lead soldiers or Heloise's paint set, and be crushed to death. Then the Christiansens would know her devotion.

Or if there might be a fire. Anyone might have a fire. Fires were common things and needed no wrathful visitations from the upper world. There might be a terrible fire just with the gasoline in the garage and a match.

She went downstairs, through the inside door that opened to the garage. The tank was three feet high and entirely full, so that unless she had been inspired with the necessity and importance of her deed, she would not have been able to lift the thing over the threshold of the garage and of the servants' house, too. She rolled the tank across the yard in the same manner as she had seen men roll beer barrels and ashcans. It made no noise on the grass and only a brief bump and rumble over one of the flagstone paths, lost in the night.

No lights shone at any of the windows, but if they had, Lucille would not have been deterred. She would not have been deterred had Mr Christiansen himself been standing there by the fountain, for probably she would not have seen him. And if she had, was she not about to do a noble thing? No, she would have seen only the house and the children's faces in the room upstairs.

She unscrewed the cap and poured some gasoline on a corner

of the house, rolled the tank farther, poured more against the white shingles, and so on until she reached the far corner. Then she struck her match and walked back the way she had come, touching off the wet places. Without a backward glance she went to stand at the door of the servants' house and watch.

The flames were first pale and eager, then they became yellow with touches of red. As Lucille watched, all the tension that was left in her, in body or mind, flowed evenly upward and was lifted from her for ever, leaving her muscles and brain free for the voluntary tension of an athlete before a starting gun. She would let the flames leap tall, even to the nursery window, before she rushed in, so that the danger might be at its highest. A smile like that of a saint settled on her mouth, and anyone seeing her there in the doorway, her face glowing in the lambent light, would certainly have thought her a beautiful young woman.

She had lit the fire at five places, and these now crept up the house like the fingers of a hand, warm and flickering, gentle and caressing. Lucille smiled and held herself in check. Then suddenly the gasoline tank, having grown too warm, exploded with a sound like a cannon and lighted the entire scene for an instant.

As though this had been the signal for which she waited, Lucille went confidently forward.

HUNTED DOWN

Charles Dickens

I

MOST of us see some romances in life. In my capacity as Chief Manager of a Life Assurance Office, I think I have within the last thirty years seen more romances than the generality of men, however unpromising the opportunity may, at first sight, seem.

As I have retired, and live at my ease, I possess the means that I used to want, of considering what I have seen, at leisure. My experiences have a more remarkable aspect, so reviewed, than they had when they were in progress. I have come home from the Play now, and can recall the scenes of the Drama upon which the curtain has fallen, free from the glare, bewilderment, and bustle of the Theatre.

Let me recall one of these Romances of the real world.

There is nothing truer than physiognomy, taken in connection with manner. The art of reading that book of which Eternal Wisdom obliges every human creature to present his or her own page with the individual character written on it, is a difficult one, perhaps, and is little studied. It may require some natural aptitude, and it must require (for everything does) some patience and some pains. That these are not usually given to it, – that numbers of people accept a few stock commonplace expressions of the face as the whole list of characteristics, and neither seek nor know the refinements that are the truest, – that You, for instance, give a great deal of time and attention to the reading of music, Greek, Latin, French, Italian, Hebrew, if you please, and do not qualify yourself to read the face of the master or mistress looking over your shoulder teaching it to you, – I assume to be five hundred times more probable than improbable. Perhaps a little self-sufficiency may be at the bottom of this; facial expression requires no study from you, you think; it comes by nature to you to know enough about it, and you are not to be taken in.

I confess, for my part, that I *have* been taken in, over and over again. I have been taken in by acquaintances, and I have been taken in (of course) by friends; far oftener by friends than by any other class of persons. How came I to be so deceived? Had I quite misread their faces?

No. Believe me, my first impression of those people, founded on face and manner alone, was invariably true. My mistake was in suffering them to come nearer to me and explain themselves away.

II

The partition which separated my own office from our general outer office in the City was of thick plate-glass. I could see through it what passed in the outer office, without hearing a word. I had it put up in place of a wall that had been there for years, – ever since the house was built. It is no matter whether I did or did not make the change in order that I might derive my first impression of strangers, who came to us on business, from their faces alone, without being influenced by anything they said. Enough to mention that I turned my glass partition to that account, and that a Life Assurance Office is at all times exposed to be practised upon by the most crafty and cruel of the human race.

It was through my glass partition that I first saw the gentleman whose story I am going to tell.

He had come in without my observing it, and had put his hat and umbrella on the broad counter, and was bending over it to take some papers from one of the clerks. He was about forty or so, dark, exceedingly well dressed in black, – being in mourning, – and the hand he extended with a polite air, had a particularly well-fitting black-kid glove upon it. His hair, which was elaborately brushed and oiled, was parted straight up the middle; and he presented this parting to the clerk, exactly (to my thinking) as if he had said, in so many words: 'You must take me, if you please, my friend, just as I show myself. Come straight up here, follow the gravel path, keep off the grass, I allow no trespassing.'

I conceived a very great aversion to that man the moment I thus saw him.

He had asked for some of our printed forms, and the clerk was giving them to him and explaining them. An obliged and agreeable smile was on his face, and his eyes met those of the clerk with a sprightly look. (I have known a vast quantity of nonsense talked about bad men not looking you in the face. Don't trust that conventional idea. Dishonesty will stare honesty out of countenance, any day in the week, if there is anything to be got by it.)

I saw, in the corner of his eyelash, that he became aware of my looking at him. Immediately he turned the parting in his hair toward the glass partition, as if he said to me with a sweet smile, 'Straight up here, if you please. Off the grass!'

In a few moments he had put on his hat and taken up his umbrella, and was gone.

I beckoned the clerk into my room, and asked, 'Who was that?'

He had the gentleman's card in his hand. 'Mr Julius Slinkton, Middle Temple.'

'A barrister, Mr Adams?'

'I think not, sir.'

'I should have thought him a clergyman, but for his having no Reverend here,' said I.

'Probably, from his appearance,' Mr Adams replied, 'he is reading for orders.'

I should mention that he wore a dainty white cravat, and dainty linen altogether.

'What did he want, Mr Adams?'

'Merely a form of proposal, sir, and form of reference.'

'Recommended here? Did he say?'

'Yes, he said he was recommended here by a friend of yours.

He noticed you, but said that as he had not the pleasure of your personal acquaintance he would not trouble you.'

'Did he know my name?'

'O yes, sir! He said, "There *is* Mr Sampson, I see!" '

'A well-spoken gentleman, apparently?'

'Remarkably so, sir.'

'Insinuating manners, apparently?'

'Very much so, indeed, sir.'

'Hah!' said I. 'I want nothing at present, Mr Adams.'

Within a fortnight of that day I went to dine with a friend of mine, a merchant, a man of taste, who buys pictures and books, and the first man I saw among the company was Mr Julius Slinkton. There he was, standing before the fire, with good large eyes and an open expression of face; but still (I thought) requiring everybody to come at him by the prepared way he offered, and by no other.

I noticed him ask my friend to introduce him to Mr Sampson, and my friend did so. Mr Slinkton was very happy to see me. Not too happy; there was no over-doing of the matter; happy in a thoroughly well-bred, perfectly unmeaning way.

'I thought you had met,' our host observed.

'No,' said Mr Slinkton. 'I did look in at Mr Sampson's office, on your recommendation; but I really did not feel justified in troubling Mr Sampson himself, on a point in the everyday routine of an ordinary clerk.'

I said I should have been glad to show him any attention on our friend's introduction.

'I am sure of that,' said he, 'and am much obliged. At another time, perhaps, I may be less delicate. Only, however, if I have real business; for I know, Mr Sampson, how precious business time is, and what a vast number of impertinent people there are in the world.'

I acknowledged his consideration with a slight bow. 'You were thinking,' said I, 'of effecting a policy on your life?'

'O dear no! I am afraid I am not so prudent as you pay me the compliment of supposing me to be, Mr Sampson. I merely inquired for a friend. But you know what friends are in such matters. Nothing may ever come of it. I have the greatest reluctance to trouble men of business with inquiries for friends, knowing the probabilities to be a thousand to one that the friends will never follow them up. People are so fickle, so selfish, so inconsiderate. Don't you, in your business, find them so every day, Mr Sampson?'

I was going to give a qualified answer; but he turned his smooth, white parting on me with its 'Straight up here, if you please!' and I answered 'Yes.'

'I hear, Mr Sampson,' he resumed presently, for our friend had a new cook, and dinner was not so punctual as usual, 'that your profession has recently suffered a great loss.'

'In money?' said I.

He laughed at my ready association of loss with money, and replied, 'No, in talent and vigour.'

Not at once following out his allusion, I considered for a moment. '*Has* it sustained a loss of that kind?' said I. 'I was not aware of it.'

'Understand me, Mr Sampson. I don't imagine that you have retired. It is not so bad as that. But Mr Meltham–'

'O, to be sure!' said I. 'Yes! Mr Meltham, the young actuary of the "Inestimable".'

'Just so,' he returned in a consoling way.

'He is a great loss. He was at once the most profound, the most original, and the most energetic man I have ever known connected with Life Assurance.'

I spoke strongly; for I had a high esteem and admiration for Meltham; and my gentleman had indefinitely conveyed to me some suspicion that he wanted to sneer at him. He recalled me to my guard by presenting that trim pathway up his head, with its infernal 'Not on the grass, if you please – the gravel.'

'You knew him, Mr Slinkton.'

'Only by reputation. To have known him as an acquaintance or as a friend, is an honour I should have sought if he had remained in society, though I might never have had the good fortune to attain it, being a man of far inferior mark. He was scarcely above thirty, I suppose?'

'About thirty.'

'Ah!' he sighed in his former consoling way. 'What creatures we are! To break up, Mr Sampson, and become incapable of business at that time of life! – Any reason assigned for the melancholy fact?'

('Humph!' thought I, as I looked at him. 'But I WON'T go up the track, and I WILL go on the grass.')

'What reason have you heard assigned, Mr Slinkton?' I asked, point-blank.

'Most likely a false one. You know what Rumour is, Mr Sampson. I never repeat what I hear; it is the only way of paring the nails and shaving the head of Rumour. But when *you* ask me what reason I have heard assigned for Mr Meltham's passing away from among men, it is another thing. I am not gratifying idle gossip then. I was told, Mr Sampson, that Mr Meltham had relinquished all his avocations and all his prospects, because he was, in fact, broken-hearted. A disappointed attachment I heard, – though it hardly seems probable, in the case of a man so distinguished and so attractive.'

'Attractions and distinctions are no armour against death,' said I.

'O, she died? Pray pardon me. I did not hear that. That, indeed, makes it very, very sad. Poor Mr Meltham! She died? Ah, dear me! Lamentable, lamentable!'

I still thought his pity was not quite genuine, and I still suspected an unaccountable sneer under all this, until he said, as we were parted, like the other knots of talkers, by the announcement of dinner:

'Mr Sampson, you are surprised to see me so moved on behalf of a man whom I have never known. I am not so disinterested as you may suppose. I have suffered, and recently too, from death myself. I have lost one of two charming nieces, who were my constant companions. She died young – barely three-and-twenty; and even her remaining sister is far from strong. The world is a grave!'

He said this with deep feeling, and I felt reproached for the coldness of my manner. Coldness and distrust had been engendered in me, I knew, by my bad experiences; they were not natural to me; and I often thought how much I had lost in life, losing trustfulness, and how little I had gained, gaining hard caution. This state of mind being habitual to me, I troubled myself more about this conversation than I might have troubled myself about a greater matter. I listened to his talk at dinner, and observed how readily other men responded to it, and with what a graceful instinct he adapted his subjects to the knowledge and habits of those he talked with. As, in talking with me, he had easily started the subject I might be supposed to understand best, and to be the most interested in, so, in talking with others, he guided himself by the same rule. The company was of a varied character; but he was not at fault, that I could discover, with any member of it. He knew just as much of each man's pursuit as made him agreeable to that man in reference to it, and just as little as made it natural in him to seek modestly for information when the theme was broached.

As he talked and talked – but really not too much, for the rest of us seemed to force it upon him – I became quite angry with myself. I took his face to pieces in my mind, like a watch, and examined it in detail. I could not say much against any of his features separately; I could say even less against them when they were put together. 'Then is it not monstrous,' I asked myself, 'that because a man happens to part his hair straight up the middle of his head, I should permit myself to suspect, and even to detest him?'

(I may stop to remark that this was no proof of my sense. An observer of men who finds himself steadily repelled by some apparently trifling thing in a stranger is right to give it great weight. It may be the clue to the whole mystery. A hair or two will show where a lion is hidden. A very little key will open a very heavy door.)

I took my part in the conversation with him after a time, and we got on remarkably well. In the drawing-room I asked the host how long he had known Mr Slinkton. He answered, not many months; he had met him at the house of a celebrated painter then present, who had known him well when he was travelling with his nieces in Italy for their health. His plans in life being broken by the death of one of them, he was reading with the intention of going back to college as a matter of form, taking his degree, and going into orders. I could not but argue with myself that here was the true explanation of his interest in poor Meltham, and that I had been almost brutal in my distrust on that simple head.

III

On the very next day but one I was sitting behind my glass partition, as before, when he came into the outer office, as before. The moment I saw him again without hearing him, I hated him worse than ever.

It was only for a moment that I had this opportunity; for he waved his tight-fitting black glove the instant I looked at him, and came straight in.

'Mr Sampson, good-day! I presume, you see, upon your kind permission to intrude upon you. I don't keep my word in being justified by business, for my business here – if I may so abuse the word – is of the slightest nature.'

I asked, was it anything I could assist him in?

'I thank you, no. I merely called to inquire outside whether my dilatory friend had been so false to himself as to be practical and sensible. But, of course, he has done nothing. I gave him your papers with my own hand, and he was hot upon the intention, but of course he has done nothing. Apart from the general human disinclination to do anything that ought to be done, I dare say there is a specialty about assuring one's life. You find it like will-making. People are so superstitious, and take it for granted they will die soon afterwards.'

'Up here, if you please; straight up here, Mr Sampson. Neither to the right nor to the left.' I almost fancied I could hear him breathe the words as he sat smiling at me, with that intolerable parting exactly opposite the bridge of my nose.

'There is such a feeling sometimes, no doubt,' I replied; 'but I don't think it obtains to any great extent.'

'Well,' said he, with a shrug and a smile, 'I wish some good angel would influence my friend in the right direction. I rashly promised his mother and sister in Norfolk to see it done, and he promised them that he would do it. But I suppose he never will.'

He spoke for a minute or two on indifferent topics, and went away.

I had scarcely unlocked the drawers of my writing-table next morning, when he reappeared. I noticed that he came straight to the door in the glass partition, and did not pause a single moment outside.

'Can you spare me two minutes, my dear Mr Sampson?'

'By all means.'

'Much obliged,' laying his hat and umbrella on the table; 'I came early, not to interrupt you. The fact is, I am taken by surprise in reference to this proposal my friend has made.'

'Has he made one?' said I.

'Ye-es,' he answered, deliberately looking at me; and then a bright idea seemed to strike him – 'or he only tells me he has. Perhaps that may be a new way of evading the matter. By Jupiter, I never thought of that!'

Mr Adams was opening the morning's letters in the outer office. 'What is the name, Mr Slinkton?' I asked.

'Beckwith.'

I looked out at the door and requested Mr Adams, if there were a proposal in that name, to bring it in. He had already laid it out of his hand on the counter. It was easily selected from the rest, and he gave it me. Alfred Beckwith. Proposal to effect a policy with us for two thousand pounds. Dated yesterday.

'From the Middle Temple, I see, Mr Slinkton.'

'Yes. He lives on the same staircase with me; his door is opposite. I never thought he would make me his reference though.'

'It seems natural enough that he should.'

'Quite so, Mr Sampson; but I never thought of it. Let me see.' He took the printed paper from his pocket. 'How am I to answer all these questions?'

'According to the truth, of course,' said I.

'O, of course!' he answered, looking up from the paper with a smile; 'I meant they were so many. But you do right to be particular. It stands to reason that you must be particular. Will you allow me to use your pen and ink?'

'Certainly.'

'And your desk?'

'Certainly.'

He had been hovering about between his hat and his umbrella for a place to write on. He now sat down in my chair, at my blotting-paper and inkstand, with the long walk up his head in accurate perspective before me, as I stood with my back to the fire.

Before answering each question he ran over it aloud, and discussed it. How long had he known Mr Alfred Beckwith? That he had to calculate by years upon his fingers. What were his habits? No difficulty about them; temperate in the last degree, and took a little too much exercise, if anything. All the answers were satisfactory. When he had written them all, he looked them over, and finally signed them in a very pretty hand. He supposed he had now done with the business. I told him he was not likely to be troubled any farther. Should he leave the papers there? If he pleased. Much obliged. Good-morning.

I had had one other visitor before him; not at the office, but at my own house. That visitor had come to my bedside when it was not yet daylight, and had been seen by no one else but by my faithful confidential servant.

A second reference paper (for we required always two) was sent down into Norfolk, and was duly received back by post. This, likewise, was satisfactorily answered in every respect. Our forms were all complied with; we accepted the proposal, and the premium for one year was paid.

IV

For six or seven months I saw no more of Mr Slinkton. He called once at my house, but I was not at home; and he once asked me to dine with him in the Temple, but I was engaged. His friend's assurance was effected in March. Late in September or early in October I was down at Scarborough for a breath of sea-air, where I met him on the beach. It was a hot evening; he came toward me with his hat in his hand; and there was the walk I had felt so strongly disinclined to take in perfect order again, exactly in front of the bridge of my nose.

He was not alone, but had a young lady on his arm.

She was dressed in mourning, and I looked at her with great interest. She had the appearance of being extremely delicate, and her face was remarkably pale and melancholy; but she was very pretty. He introduced her as his niece, Miss Niner.

'Are you strolling, Mr Sampson? Is it possible you can be idle?'

It *was* possible, and I *was* strolling.

'Shall we stroll together?'

'With pleasure.'

The young lady walked between us, and we walked on the cool sea sand, in the direction of Filey.

'There have been wheels here,' said Mr Slinkton. 'And now, I look again, the wheels of a hand-carriage! Margaret, my love, your shadow without doubt!'

'Miss Niner's shadow?' I repeated, looking down at it on the sand.

'Not that one,' Mr Slinkton returned, laughing. 'Margaret, my dear, tell Mr Sampson.'

'Indeed,' said the young lady, turning to me, 'there is nothing to tell – except that I constantly see the same invalid old gentleman at all times, wherever I go. I have mentioned it to my uncle, and he calls the gentleman my shadow.'

'Does he live in Scarborough?' I asked.

'He is staying here.'

'Do you live in Scarborough?'

'No, I am staying here. My uncle has placed me with a family here, for my health.'

'And your shadow?' said I, smiling.

'My shadow,' she answered, smiling too, 'is – like myself – not very robust, I fear; for I lose my shadow sometimes, as my shadow loses me at other times. We both seem liable to confinement to the house. I have not seen my shadow for days and days; but it does oddly happen, occasionally, that wherever I go, for many days together, this gentleman goes. We have come together in the most unfrequented nooks on this shore.'

'Is this he?' said I, pointing before us.

The wheels had swept down to the water's edge, and described a great loop on the sand in turning. Bringing the loop back towards us, and spinning it out as it came, was a hand-carriage, drawn by a man.

'Yes,' said Miss Niner, 'this really is my shadow, uncle.'

As the carriage approached us and we approached the carriage, I saw within it an old man, whose head was sunk on his breast, and who was enveloped in a variety of wrappers. He was drawn by a very quiet but very keen-looking man, with iron-grey hair, who was slightly lame. They had passed us, when the carriage stopped, and the old gentleman within, putting out his arm, called to me by name. I went back, and was absent from Mr Slinkton and his niece for about five minutes.

When I rejoined them, Mr Slinkton was the first to speak. Indeed, he said to me in a raised voice before I came up with him:

'It is well you have not been longer, or my niece might have died of curiosity to know who her shadow is, Mr Sampson.'

'An old East India Director,' said I. 'An intimate friend of our friend's, at whose house I first had the pleasure of meeting you. A certain Major Banks. You have heard of him?'

'Never.'

'Very rich, Miss Niner; but very old, and very crippled. An amiable man, sensible – much interested in you. He has just been expatiating on the affection that he has observed to exist between you and your uncle.'

Mr Slinkton was holding his hat again, and he passed his hand up the straight walk, as if he himself went up it serenely, after me.

'Mr Sampson,' he said, tenderly pressing his niece's arm in his, 'our affection was always a strong one, for we have had but few near ties. We have still fewer now. We have associations to bring us together, that are not of his world, Margaret.'

'Dear uncle!' murmured the young lady, and turned her face aside to hide her tears.

'My niece and I have such remembrances and regrets in common, Mr Sampson,' he feelingly pursued, 'that it would be strange indeed if the relations between us were cold or indifferent. If I remember a conversation we once had together, you will understand the reference I make. Cheer up, dear Margaret. Don't droop, don't droop. My Margaret! I cannot bear to see you droop!'

The poor young lady was very much affected, but controlled

herself. His feelings, too, were very acute. In a word, he found himself under such great need of a restorative, that he presently went away, to take a bath of sea-water, leaving the young lady and me sitting by a point of rock, and probably presuming – but that you will say was a pardonable indulgence in a luxury – that she would praise him with all her heart.

She did, poor thing! With all her confiding heart, she praised him to me, for his care of her dead sister, and for his untiring devotion in her last illness. The sister had wasted away very slowly, and wild and terrible fantasies had come over her toward the end, but he had never been impatient with her, or at a loss; had always been gentle, watchful, and self-possessed. The sister had known him, as she had known him, to be the best of men, the kindest of men, and yet a man of such admirable strength of character, as to be a very tower for the support of their weak natures while their poor lives endured.

'I shall leave him, Mr Sampson, very soon,' said the young lady; 'I know my life is drawing to an end; and when I am gone, I hope he will marry and be happy. I am sure he has lived single so long, only for my sake, and for my poor, poor sister's.'

The little hand-carriage had made another great loop on the damp sand, and was coming back again, gradually spinning out a slim figure of eight, half a mile long.

'Young lady,' said I, looking around, laying my hand upon her arm, and speaking in a low voice, 'time presses. You hear the gentle murmur of that sea?'

She looked at me with the utmost wonder and alarm, saying, 'Yes.'

'And you know what a voice is in it when the storm comes?'

'Yes.'

'You see how quiet and peaceful it lies before us, and you know what an awful sight of power without pity it might be, this very night!'

'Yes!'

'But if you had never heard or seen it, or heard of it in its cruelty, could you believe that it beats every inanimate thing in its way to pieces, without mercy, and destroys life without remorse?'

'You terrify me, sir, by these questions!'

'To save you, young lady, to save you! For God's sake, collect your strength and collect your firmness! If you were here alone, and hemmed in by the rising tide on the flow to fifty feet above your head, you could not be in greater danger than the danger you are now to be saved from.'

The figure on the sand was spun out, and straggled off into a crooked little jerk that ended at the cliff very near us.

'As I am, before Heaven and the Judge of all mankind, your friend, and your dead sister's friend, I solemnly entreat you, Miss Niner, without one moment's loss of time, to come to this gentleman with me!'

If the little carriage had been less near to us, I doubt if I could have got her away; but it was so near that we were there before she had recovered the hurry of being urged from the rock. I did not remain there with her two minutes. Certainly within five, I had the inexpressible satisfaction of seeing her – from the point we had sat on, and to which I had returned – half supported and half carried up some rude steps notched in the cliff, by the figure of an active man. With that figure beside her, I knew she was safe anywhere.

I sat alone on the rock, awaiting Mr Slinkton's return. The twilight was deepening and the shadows were heavy, when he came round the point, with his hat hanging at his button-hole, smoothing his wet hair with one of his hands, and picking out the old path with the other and a pocket-comb.

'My niece not here, Mr Sampson?' he said, looking about.

'Miss Niner seemed to feel a chill in the air after the sun was down, and has gone home.'

He looked surprised, as though she were not accustomed to do anything without him; even to orginate so slight a proceeding.

'I persuaded Miss Niner,' I explained.

'Ah!' said he. 'She is easily persuaded – for her good. Thank you, Mr Sampson; she is better within doors. The bathing-place was farther than I thought, to say the truth.'

'Miss Niner is very delicate,' I observed.

He shook his head and drew a deep sigh. 'Very, very, very. You may recollect my saying so. The time that has since intervened has not strengthened her. The gloomy shadow that fell upon her sister so early in life seems, in my anxious eyes, to gather over her, ever darker, ever darker. Dear Margaret, dear Margaret! But we must hope.'

The hand-carriage was spinning away before us at a most indecorous pace for an invalid vehicle, and was making most irregular curves upon the sand. Mr Slinkton, noticing it after he had put his handkerchief to his eyes, said:

'If I may judge from appearances, your friend will be upset, Mr Sampson.'

'It looks probable, certainly,' said I.

'The servant must be drunk.'

'The servants of old gentlemen will get drunk sometimes,' said I.

'The major draws very light, Mr Sampson.'

'The major does draw light,' said I.

By this time the carriage, much to my relief, was lost in the darkness. We walked on for a little, side by side over the sand, in silence. After a short while he said, in a voice still affected by the emotion that his niece's state of health had awakened in him,

'Do you stay here long, Mr Sampson?'

'Why, no. I am going away to-night.'

'So soon? But business always holds you in request. Men like Mr Sampson are too important to others, to be spared to their own need of relaxation and enjoyment.'

'I don't know about that,' said I. 'However, I am going back.'

'To London?'

'To London.'

'I shall be there too, soon after you.'

I knew that as well as he did. But I did not tell him so. Any more than I told him what defensive weapon my right hand rested on in my pocket, as I walked by his side. Any more than I told him why I did not walk on the sea side of him with the night closing in.

We left the beach, and our ways diverged. We exchanged good-night, and had parted indeed, when he said, returning,

'Mr Sampson, *may* I ask? Poor Meltham, whom we spoke of, – dead yet?'

'Not when I last heard of him; but too broken a man to live long, and hopelessly lost to his old calling.'

'Dear, dear, dear!' said he, with great feeling. 'Sad, sad, sad! The world is a grave!' And so went his way.

It was not his fault if the world were not a grave; but I did not call that observation after him, any more than I had mentioned those other things just now enumerated. He went his way, and I went mine with all expedition. This happened, as I have said, either at the end of September or beginning of October. The next time I saw him, and the last time, was late in November.

V

I had a very particular engagement to breakfast in the Temple. It was a bitter north-easterly morning, and the sleet and slush lay inches deep in the streets. I could get no conveyance, and was soon wet to the knees; but I should have been true to that appointment, though I had to wade to it up to my neck in the same impediments.

The appointment took me to some chambers in the Temple. They were at the top of a lonely corner house overlooking the river. The name, MR ALFRED BECKWITH, was painted on the outer door. On the door opposite, on the same landing, the name MR JULIUS SLINKTON. The doors of both sets of chambers stood open, so that anything said aloud in one set could be heard in the other.

I had never been in those chambers before. They were dismal, close, unwholesome, and oppressive; the furniture, originally good, and not yet old, was faded and dirty, – the rooms were in great disorder; there was a strong prevailing smell of opium, brandy, and tobacco; the grate and fire-irons were splashed all over with unsightly blotches of rust; and on a sofa by the fire, in the room where breakfast had been prepared, lay the host, Mr Beckwith, a man with all the appearances of the worst kind of drunkard, very far advanced upon his shameful way to death.

'Slinkton is not come yet,' said this creature, staggering up when I went in; 'I'll call him. – Halloa! Julius Cæsar! Come and drink!' As he hoarsely roared this out, he beat the poker and tongs together in a mad way, as if that were his usual manner of summoning his associate.

The voice of Mr Slinkton was heard through the clatter from the opposite side of the staircase, and he came in. He had not expected the pleasure of meeting me. I have seen several artful men brought to a stand, but I never saw a man so aghast as he was when his eyes rested on mine.

'Julius Cæsar,' cried Beckwith, staggering between us, 'Mist' Sampson! Mist' Sampson, Julius Cæsar! Julius, Mist' Sampson, is the friend of my soul. Julius keeps me plied with liquor, morning, noon, and night. Julius is a real benefactor. Julius threw the tea and coffee out of window when I used to have any. Julius empties all the water-jugs of their contents, and fills 'em with spirits. Julius winds me up and keeps me going. – Boil the brandy, Julius!'

There was a rusty and furred saucepan in the ashes, – the ashes looked like the accumulation of weeks, – and Beckwith, rolling and staggering between us as if he were going to plunge headlong into the fire, got the saucepan out, and tried to force it into Slinkton's hand.

'Boil the brandy, Julius Cæsar! Come! Do your usual office. Boil the brandy!'

He became so fierce in his gesticulations with the saucepan, that I expected to see him lay open Slinkton's head with it. I therefore put out my hand to check him. He reeled back to the sofa, and sat there panting, shaking, and red-eyed, in his rags of dressing-gown, looking at us both. I noticed then that there was nothing to drink on the table but brandy, and nothing to eat but salted herrings, and a hot, sickly, highly-peppered stew.

'At all events, Mr Sampson,' said Slinkton, offering me the smooth gravel path for the last time, 'I thank you for interfering between me and this unfortunate man's violence. However you came here, Mr Sampson, or with whatever motive you came here, at least I thank you for that.'

'Boil the brandy,' muttered Beckwith.

Without gratifying his desire to know how I came there, I said, quietly, 'How is your niece, Mr Slinkton?'

He looked hard at me, and I looked hard at him.

'I am sorry to say, Mr Sampson, that my niece has proved treacherous and ungrateful to her best friend. She left me without a word of notice or explanation. She was misled, no doubt, by some designing rascal. Perhaps you may have heard of it.'

'I did hear that she was misled by a designing rascal. In fact, I have proof of it.'

'Are you sure of that?' said he.

'Quite.'

'Boil the brandy,' muttered Beckwith. 'Company to breakfast, Julius Cæsar. Do your usual office, – provide the usual breakfast, dinner, tea, and supper. Boil the brandy!'

The eyes of Slinkton looked from him to me, and he said, after a moment's consideration,

'Mr Sampson, you are a man of the world, and so am I. I will be plain with you.'

'O no, you won't,' said I, shaking my head.

'I tell you, sir, I will be plain with you.'

'And I tell you you will not,' said I. 'I know all about you. *You* plain with any one? Nonsense, nonsense!'

'I plainly tell you, Mr Sampson,' he went on, with a manner almost composed, 'that I understand your object. You want to save your funds, and escape from your liabilities; these are old tricks of trade with you Office-gentlemen. But you will not do it, sir; you will not succeed. You have not an easy adversary to play against, when you play against me. We shall have to inquire, in due time, when and how Mr Beckwith fell into his present habits. With that remark, sir, I put this poor creature, and his incoherent wanderings of speech, aside, and wish you a good morning and a better case next time.'

While he was saying this, Beckwith had filled a half-pint glass with brandy. At this moment, he threw the brandy at his face, and threw the glass after it. Slinkton put his hands up, half blinded with the spirit, and cut with the glass across the forehead. At the sound of the breakage, a fourth person came into the room, closed the door, and stood at it; he was a very quiet but very keen-looking man, with iron-grey hair, and slightly lame.

Slinkton pulled out his handkerchief, assuaged the pain in his smarting eyes, and dabbled the blood on his forehead. He was a long time about it, and I saw that in the doing of it, a tremendous change came over him, occasioned by the change in Beckwith, – who ceased to pant and tremble, sat upright, and never took his eyes off him. I never in my life saw a face in which abhorrence and determination were so forcibly painted as in Beckwith's then.

'Look at me, you villain,' said Beckwith, 'and see me as I really am. I took these rooms, to make them a trap for you. I came into them as a drunkard, to bait the trap for you. You fell into the trap, and you will never leave it alive. On the morning when you last went to Mr Sampson's office, I had seen him first. Your plot has been known to both of us, all along, and you have been counter-plotted all along. What? Having been cajoled into putting that prize of two thousand pounds in your power, I was to be done to death with brandy, and, brandy not proving quick enough, with something quicker? Have I never seen you, when you thought my senses gone, pouring from your little bottle into my glass? Why, you Murderer and Forger, alone here with you in the dead of night, as I have so often been, I have had my hand upon the trigger of a pistol, twenty times, to blow your brains out!'

This sudden starting up of the thing that he had supposed to be his imbecile victim into a determined man, with a settled resolution to hunt him down and be the death of him, mercilessly expressed from head to foot, was, in the first shock, too much for him. Without any figure of speech, he staggered under it. But there is no greater mistake than to suppose that a man who is a calculating criminal, is in any phase of his guilt, otherwise than true to himself, and perfectly consistent with his whole character. Such a man commits murder, and murder is the natural culmination of his course; such a man has to outface murder, and will do it with hardihood and effrontery. It is a sort of fashion to express surprise that any notorious criminal, having such crime upon his conscience, can so brave it out. Do you think that if he had it on his conscience at all, or had a conscience to have it upon, he would ever have committed the crime?

Perfectly consistent with himself, as I believe all such monsters to be, this Slinkton recovered himself, and showed a defiance that was sufficiently cold and quiet. He was white, he was haggard, he was changed; but only as a sharper who had played for a great stake and had been outwitted and had lost the game.

'Listen to me, you villain,' said Beckwith, 'and let every word you hear me say be a stab in your wicked heart. When I took these rooms, to throw myself in your way and lead you on to the scheme that I knew my appearance and supposed character and habits would suggest to such a devil, how did I know that? Because you were no stranger to me. I knew you well. And I knew you to be the cruel wretch who, for so much money, had killed one innocent girl while she trusted him implicitly, and who was by inches killing another.'

Slinkton took out a snuff-box, took a pinch of snuff, and laughed.

'But see here,' said Beckwith, never looking away, never raising his voice, never relaxing his face, never unclenching his hand. 'See what a dull wolf you have been, after all! The infatuated drunkard who never drank a fiftieth part of the liquor you plied him with, but poured it away, here, there, everywhere – almost before your eyes; who bought over the fellow you set to watch him and to ply him, by outbidding you in his bribe, before he had been at his work three days – with whom you have observed no caution, yet who was so bent on ridding the earth of you as a wild beast, that he would have defeated you if you had been ever so prudent – that drunkard whom you have, many a time, left on the floor of this room, and who has even let you go out of it, alive and undeceived, when you have turned him over with your foot – has, almost as often, on the same night, within an hour, within a few minutes, watched you awake, had his hand at your pillow when you were asleep, turned over your papers, taken samples from your bottles and packets of powder, changed their contents, rifled every secret of your life!'

He had had another pinch of snuff in his hand, but had gradually let it drop from between his fingers to the floor; where he now smoothed it out with his foot, looking down at it the while.

'That drunkard,' said Beckwith, 'who had free access to your rooms at all times, that he might drink the strong drinks that you left in his way and be the sooner ended, holding no more terms with you than he would hold with a tiger, has had his master-key for all your locks, his test for all your poisons, his clue to your cipher-writing. He can tell you, as well as you can tell him, how long it took to complete that deed, what doses there were, what intervals, what signs of gradual decay upon mind and body; what distempered fancies were produced, what observable changes, what physical pain. He can tell you, as well as you can tell him, that all this was recorded day by day, as a lesson of experience for future service. He can tell you, better than you can tell him, where that journal is at this moment.

Slinkton stopped the action of his foot, and looked at Beckwith.

'No,' said the latter, as if answering a question from him. 'Not in the drawer of the writing-desk that opens with a spring; it is not there, and it never will be there again.'

'Then you are a thief!' said Slinkton.

Without any change whatever in the inflexible purpose, which it was quite terrific even to me to contemplate, and from the power of which I had always felt convinced it was impossible for this wretch to escape, Beckwith returned,

'And I am your niece's shadow, too.'

With an imprecation Slinkton put his hand to his head, tore out some hair, and flung it to the ground. It was the end of the smooth walk; he destroyed it in the action, and it will soon be seen that his use for it was past.

Beckwith went on: 'Whenever you left here, I left here. Although I understood that you found it necessary to pause in the completion of that purpose, to avert suspicion, still I watched you close, with the poor confiding girl. When I had the diary, and could read it word by word, – it was only about the night before your last visit to Scarborough, – you remember the night? you slept with a small flat vial tied to your wrist, – I sent to Mr Sampson, who was kept out of view. This is Mr Sampson's trusty servant standing by the door. We three saved your niece among us.'

Slinkton looked at us all, took an uncertain step or two from the place where he had stood, returned to it, and glanced about him in a very curious way, – as one of the meaner reptiles might, looking for a hole to hide in. I noticed at the same time, that a singular change took place in the figure of the man, – as if it collapsed within his clothes, and they consequently became ill-shapen and ill-fitting.

'You shall know,' said Beckwith, 'for I hope the knowledge will be bitter and terrible to you, why you have been pursued by one man, and why, when the whole interest that Mr Sampson represents would have expended any money in hunting you down, you have been tracked to death at a single individual's charge. I hear you have had the name of Meltham on your lips sometimes?'

I saw, in addition to those other changes, a sudden stoppage come upon his breathing.

'When you sent the sweet girl whom you murdered (you know with what artfully made-out surroundings and probabilities you sent her) to Meltham's office, before taking her abroad to originate the transaction that doomed her to the grave, it fell to Meltham's lot to see her and to speak with her. It did not fall to his lot to save her, though I know he would freely give his own life to have done it. He admired her; – I would say he loved her deeply, if I thought it possible that you could understand the word. When she was sacrificed, he was thoroughly assured of your guilt. Having lost her, he had but one object left in life, and that was to avenge her and destroy you.'

I saw the villain's nostrils rise and fall convulsively; but I saw no moving at his mouth.

'That man Meltham,' Beckwith steadily pursued, 'was as absolutely certain that you could never elude him in this world, if he devoted himself to your destruction with his utmost fidelity and earnestness, and if he divided the sacred duty with no other duty in life, as he was certain that in achieving it he would be a poor instrument in the hands of Providence, and would do well before Heaven in striking you out from among living men. I am that man, and I thank God that I have done my work!'

If Slinkton had been running for his life from swift-footed savages, a dozen miles, he could not have shown more emphatic signs of being oppressed at heart and labouring for breath, than he showed now, when he looked at the pursuer who had so relentlessly hunted him down.

'You never saw me under my right name before; you see me under my right name now. You shall see me once again in the body, when you are tried for your life. You shall see me once again in the spirit, when the cord is round your neck, and the crowd are crying against you!'

When Meltham had spoken these last words, the miscreant suddenly turned away his face, and seemed to strike his mouth with his open hand. At the same instant, the room was filled with a new and powerful odour, and, almost at the same instant, he broke into a crooked run, leap, start, – I have no name for the spasm, – and fell, with a dull weight that shook the heavy old doors and windows in their frames.

That was the fitting end of him.

When we saw that he was dead, we drew away from the room, and Meltham, giving me his hand, said, with a weary air,

'I have no more work on earth, my friend. But I shall see her again elsewhere.'

It was in vain that I tried to rally him. He might have saved her, he said; he had not saved her, and he reproached himself; he had lost her, and he was broken-hearted.

'The purpose that sustained me is over, Sampson, and there is nothing now to hold me to life. I am not fit for life; I am weak and spiritless; I have no hope and no object; my day is done.'

In truth, I could hardly have believed that the broken man who then spoke to me was the man who had so strongly and so differently impressed me when his purpose was before him.

I used such entreaties with him, as I could; but he still said, and always said, in a patient, undemonstrative way, – nothing could avail him, – he was broken-hearted.

He died early in the next spring. He was buried by the side of the poor young lady for whom he had cherished those tender and unhappy regrets; and he left all he had to her sister. She lived to be a happy wife and mother; she married my sister's son, who succeeded poor Meltham; she is living now, and her children ride about the garden on my walking-stick when I go to see her.

RUMPOLE AND THE TAP END

John Mortimer

THERE are many reasons why I could never become one of Her Majesty's judges. I am unable to look at my customer in the dock without feeling 'There but for the Grace of God goes Horace Rumpole.' I should find it almost impossible to order any fellow citizen to be locked up in a Victorian slum with a couple of psychopaths and three chamber-pots, and I cannot imagine a worse way of passing your life than having to actually listen to the speeches of the learned friends. It also has to be admitted that no sane Lord Chancellor would ever dream of the appointment of Mr Justice Rumpole. There is another danger inherent in the judicial office: a judge, any judge, is always liable to say, in a moment of boredom or impatience, something downright silly. He is then denounced in the public prints, his resignation is called for, he is stigmatized as malicious or at least mad and his Bench becomes a bed of nails and his ermine a hair-shirt. There is, perhaps, no judge more likely to open his mouth and put his foot in it than that, on the whole well meaning, old darling, Mr Justice Featherstone, once Guthrie Featherstone, Q.C., M.P., a Member of Parliament so uninterested in politics that he joined the Social Democrats and who, during many eventful years of my life, was Head of our Chambers in Equity Court. Now, as a judge, Guthrie Featherstone had swum somewhat out of our ken; but he hadn't lost his old talent for giving voice to the odd uncalled-for and disastrous phrase. He, I'm sure, will never forget the furore that arose when, in passing sentence in a case of attempted murder in which I was engaged for the Defence, his Lordship made an unwise reference to the 'tap end' of a matrimonial bath-tub. At least the account which follows may serve as a terrible warning to anyone contemplating a career as a judge.

I have spoken elsewhere, and on frequent occasions, of my patrons the Timsons, that extended family of South London villains for whom, over the years, I have acted as Attorney-General. Some of you may remember Tony Timson, a fairly mild-mannered receiver of stolen video-recorders, hi-fi sets and microwave ovens, married to that April Timson who once so offended her husband's male chauvinist prejudices by driving a getaway car at a somewhat unsuccessful bank robbery. Tony and April lived in a semi on a large housing estate with their offspring, Vincent Timson, now aged eight, who I hoped would grow up in the family business and thus ensure a steady flow of briefs for Rumpole's future. Their house was brightly, not to say garishly, furnished with mock tiger-skin rugs, Italian-tile-style linoleum and wallpaper which simulated oak panelling. (I knew this from a large number of police photographs in various cases.) It was also equipped with almost every labour-saving device which ever dropped off the back of a lorry. On the day when my story starts this desirable home was rent with screams from the bathroom and a stream of soapy water flowing out from under the door. In the screaming, the word 'murderer' was often repeated at a volume which was not only audible to young Vincent, busy pushing a blue-flashing toy police car round the hallway, but to the occupants of the adjoining house and those of the neighbours who were hanging out their washing. Someone, it was not clear who it was at the time, telephoned the local cop shop for assistance.

In a surprisingly short while a real, flashing police car arrived and the front door was flung open by a wet and desperate April Timson, her leopard-skin-style towelling bath-robe clutched about her. As Detective Inspector Brush, an officer who had fought a running battle with the Timson family for years, came up the path to meet her she sobbed out, at the top of her voice, a considerable voice for so petite a redhead, 'Thank God, you've come! He was only trying to bloody murder me.' Tony

Timson emerged from the bathroom a few seconds later, water dripping from his ear-lobe-length hair and his gaucho moustache. In spite of the word RAMBO emblazoned across his bathrobe, he was by no means a man of formidable physique. Looking down the stairs, he saw his wife in hysterics and his domestic hearth invaded by the Old Bill. No sooner had he reached the hallway than he was arrested and charged with attempted murder of his wife, the particulars being, that, while sharing a bath with her preparatory to going to a neighbour's party, he had tried to cause her death by drowning.

In course of time I was happy to accept a brief for the defence of Tony Timson and we had a conference in Brixton prison where the alleged wife-drowner was being held in custody. I was attended, on that occasion, by Mr Bernard, the Timsons' regular solicitor, and that up-and-coming young radical barrister, Mizz Liz Probert, who had been briefed to take a note and generally assist me in the *cause célèbre*.

'Attempted murderer, Tony Timson?' I opened the proceedings on a somewhat incredulous note. 'Isn't that rather out of your league?'

'April told me,' he began his explanation, 'she was planning on wearing her skin-tight leatherette trousers with the revealing halter-neck satin top. That's what she was planning on wearing, Mr Rumpole!'

'A somewhat tasteless outfit, and not entirely *haute couture*,' I admitted. 'But it hardly entitles you to drown your wife, Tony.'

'We was both invited to a party round her friend Chrissie's. And that was the outfit she was keen on wearing . . .'

'She says you pulled her legs and so she became submerged.' Bernard, like a good solicitor, was reading the evidence.

' "The Brides in the Bath"!' My mind went at once to one of the classic murders of all times. 'The very method! And you hit on it with no legal training. How did you come to be in the same bath, anyway?'

'We always shared, since we was courting.' Tony looked surprised that I had asked. 'Don't all married couples?'

'Speaking for myself and She Who Must Be Obeyed the answer is, thankfully, no. I can't speak for Mr Bernard.'

'Out of the question.' Bernard shook his head sadly. 'My wife has a hip.'

'Sorry, Mr Bernard. I'm really sorry.' Tony Timson was clearly an attempted murderer with a soft heart.

'Quite all right, Mr Timson,' Bernard assured him. 'We're down for a replacement.'

'April likes me to sit up by the taps.' Tony gave us further particulars of the Timson bathing habits. 'So I can rinse off her hair after a shampoo. Anyway, she finds her end that much more comfortable.'

'She makes you sit at the tap end, Tony?' I began to feel for the fellow.

'Oh, I never made no objection,' my client assured me. 'Although you can get your back a bit scalded. And those old taps does dig into you sometimes.'

'So were you on friendly terms when you both entered the water?' My instructing solicitor was quick on the deductions.

'She was all right then. We was both, well, affectionate. Looking forward to the party, like.'

'She didn't object to what you planned on wearing?' I wanted to cover all the possibilities.

'My non-structured silk-style suiting from Toy Boy Limited!' Tony protested. 'How could she object to that, Mr Rumpole? No. She washed her hair as per usual. And I rinsed it off for her. Then she told me who was going to be at the party, like.'

'Mr Peter Molloy,' Bernard reminded me. 'It's in the brief, Mr Rumpole.' Now I make it a rule to postpone reading my brief until the last possible moment so that it's fresh in my mind when I go into Court, so I said, somewhat testily, 'Of course I know that, but I thought I'd like to get the story from the client. Peanuts Molloy! Mizz Probert, we have a defence. Tony Timson's wife was taking him to a party attended by Peanuts Molloy.'

The full implications of this piece of evidence won't be apparent to those who haven't made a close study of my previous handling of the Timson affairs. Suffice it to say the

Molloys are to the Timsons as the Montagues were to the Capulets or the Guelphs to the Ghibellines, and their feud goes back to the days when the whole of South London was laid down to pasture, and they were quarrelling about stolen sheep. The latest outbreak of hostilities occurred when certain Molloys, robbing a couple of elderly Timsons as *they* were robbing a bank, almost succeeded in getting Tony's relatives convicted for an offence they had not committed. Peter, better known as 'Peanuts', Molloy was the young hopeful of the clan Molloy and it was small wonder that Tony Timson took great exception to his wife putting on her leatherette trousers for the purpose of meeting the family enemy.

Liz Probert, however, a white-wig at the Bar who knew nothing of such old legal traditions as the Molloy–Timson hostility, said, 'Why should Mrs Timson's meeting Molloy make it all right to drown her?' I have to remind you that Miss Liz was a pillar of the North Islington women's movement.

'It wasn't just that she was meeting him, Mr Rumpole,' Tony explained. 'It was the words she used.'

'What did she say?'

'I'd rather not tell you if you don't mind. It was humiliating to my pride.'

'Oh, for heaven's sake, Tony. Let's hear the worst.' I had never known a Timson behave so coyly.

'She made a comparison like, between me and Peanuts.'

'What comparison?'

Tony looked at Liz and his voice sank to a whisper. 'Ladies present,' he said.

'Tony,' I had to tell him, 'Miss Liz Probert has not only practised in the criminal courts, but in the family division. She is active on behalf of gay and lesbian rights in her native Islington. She marches, quite often, in aid of abortion on demand. She is a regular reader of the woman's page of the *Guardian*. You and I, Tony, need have no secrets from Miss Probert. Now, what was this comparison your wife made between you and Peanuts Molloy?'

'On the topic of virility. I'm sorry, Miss.'

'That's quite all right.' Liz Probert was unshocked and unamused.

'What we need, I don't know if you would agree, Mr Rumpole,' Mr Bernard suggested, 'is a predominance of *men* on the Jury.'

'Underendowed males would condone the attempted murder of a woman, you mean?' The Probert hackles were up.

'Please, Mizz Probert.' I tried to call the meeting to order. 'Let us face this problem in a spirit of detachment. What we need is a sympathetic judge who doesn't want to waste his time on a long case. Have we got a fixed date for this, Mr Bernard?'

'We have, sir. Before the Red Judge.' Mr Bernard meant that Tony Timson was to be tried before the High Court judge visiting the Old Bailey.

'They're pulling out all the stops.' I was impressed.

'It *is* attempted murder, Mr Rumpole. So we're fixed before Mr Justice Featherstone.'

'Guthrie Featherstone.' I thought about it. 'Our one-time Head of Chambers. Now, I just wonder . . .'

We were in luck. Sir Guthrie Featherstone was in no mood to try a long case, so he summoned me and Counsel for the Prosecution to his room before the start of the proceedings. He sat robed but with his wig on the desk in front of him, a tall, elegant figure who almost always wore the slightly hunted expression of a man who's not entirely sure what he's up to – an unfortunate state of mind for a fellow who has to spend his waking hours coming to firm and just decisions. For all his indecision, however, he knew for certain that he didn't want to spend the whole day trying a ticklish attempted murder.

'Is this a long case?' the Judge asked. 'I am bidden to take tea in the neighbourhood of Victoria. Can you fellows guess where?'

'Sorry, Judge. I give up.' Charles Hearthstoke, our serious-minded young prosecutor, seemed in no mood for party games.

'The station buffet?' I hazarded a guess.

'The station buffet!' Guthrie enjoyed the joke. 'Isn't that you all over, Horace? You will have your joke. Not far off, though.' The joke was over and he went on impressively. 'Buck House. Her Majesty has invited me – no, correction – "commanded" me to a Royal Garden Party.'

'God Save The Queen!' I murmured loyally.

'Not only Her Majesty,' Guthrie told us, 'more seriously one's lady wife, would be extremely put out if one didn't parade in grey top-hat order!'

'He's blaming it on his wife!' Liz Probert, who had followed me into the presence, said in a penetrating aside.

'So naturally one would have to be free by lunch-time. Hearthstoke, is this a long case from the prosecution point of view?' the Judge asked.

'It is an extremely serious case, Judge.' Our prosecutor spoke like a man of twice his years. 'Attempted murder. We've put it down for a week.' I have always thought young Charlie Hearthstoke a mega-sized pill ever since he joined our Chambers for a blessedly brief period and tried to get everything run by a computer.

'I'm astonished,' I gave Guthrie a little comfort, 'that my learned friend Mr Hearthrug should think it could possibly last so long.'

'Hearth*stoke*,' young Charlie corrected me.

'Have it your own way. With a bit of common sense we could finish this in half an hour.'

'Thereby saving public time and money.' Hope sprang eternal in the Judge's breast.

'Exactly!' I cheered him up. 'As you know, it is an article of my religion never to plead guilty. But, bearing in mind all the facts in this case, I'm prepared to advise Timson to put his hands up to common assault. He'll agree to be bound over to keep the peace.'

'Common assault?' Hearthstoke was furious. 'Binding over? Hold on a minute. He tried to drown her!'

'Judge.' I put the record straight. 'He was seated at the tap end of the bath. His wife, lying back comfortably in the depths, passed an extremely wounding remark about my client's virility.'

It was then I saw Mr Justice Featherstone looking at me,

apparently shaken to the core. 'The *tap end*,' he gasped. 'Did you say he was seated at the *tap end*, Horace?'

'I'm afraid so, Judge.' I confirmed the information sorrowfully.

'This troubles me.' Indeed the Judge looked extremely troubled. 'How does it come about that he was seated at the tap end?'

'His wife insisted on it.' I had to tell him the full horror of the situation.

'This woman insisted that her husband sat with his back squashed up against the taps?' The Judge's voice rose in incredulous outrage.

'She made him sit in that position so he could rinse off her hair.'

'At the *tap end*?' Guthrie still couldn't quite believe it.

'Exactly so.'

'You're sure?'

'There can be no doubt about it.'

'Hearthrug . . . I mean, *stoke*. Is this one of the facts agreed by the Prosecution?'

'I can't see that it makes the slightest difference.' The Prosecution was not pleased with the course its case was taking.

'You can't see! Horace, was this conduct in any way typical of this woman's attitude to her husband?'

'I regret to say, entirely typical.'

'Rumpole . . .' Liz Probert, appalled by the chauvinist chatter around her, seemed about to burst, and I calmed her with a quiet 'Shut up, Mizz.'

'So you are telling me that this husband deeply resented the position in which he found himself.' Guthrie was spelling out the implications exactly as I had hoped he would.

'What married man wouldn't, Judge?' I asked mournfully.

'And his natural resentment led to a purely domestic dispute?'

'Such as might occur, Judge, in the best bathrooms.'

'And you are content to be bound over to keep the peace?' His Lordship looked at me with awful solemnity.

'Reluctantly, Judge,' I said after a suitable pause for contemplation, 'I would agree to that restriction on my client's liberty.'

'Liberty to drown his wife!' Mizz Probert had to be 'shushed' again.

'Hearth*stoke*.' The Judge spoke with great authority. 'My compliments to those instructing you and in my opinion it would be a gross waste of public funds to continue with this charge of attempted murder. We should be finished by half past eleven.' He looked at his watch with the deep satisfaction of a man who was sure that he would be among those present at the Royal Garden Party, after the ritual visit to Moss Bros to hire the grey topper and all the trimmings. As we left the sanctum, I stood aside to let Mizz Probert out of the door. 'Oh, no, Rumpole, you're a man,' she whispered with her fury barely contained. 'Men always go first, don't they?'

So we all went into Court to polish off *R.* v *Timson* and to make sure that Her Majesty had the pleasure of Guthrie's presence over the tea and strawberries. I made a token speech in mitigation, something of a formality as I knew that I was pushing at an open door. Whilst I was speaking, I was aware of the fact that the Judge wasn't giving me his full attention. That was reserved for a new young shorthand writer, later to become known to me as a Miss (not, I'm sure in her case, a Mizz) Lorraine Frinton. Lorraine was what I believe used to be known as a 'bit of an eyeful', being young, doe-eyed and clearly surrounded by her own special fragrance. When I sat down, Guthrie thanked me absent-mindedly and reluctantly gave up the careful perusal of Miss Frinton's beauty. He then proceeded to pass sentence on Tony Timson in a number of peculiarly ill-chosen words.

'Timson,' his Lordship began harmlessly enough. 'I have heard about you and your wife's habit of taking a bath together. It is not for this Court to say that communal bathing, in time of peace when it is not in the national interest to save water, is appropriate conduct in married life. *Chacun à son goût*, as a wise Frenchman once said.' Miss Frinton, the shorthand writer, looked hopelessly confused by the words of the wise Frenchman. 'What throws a flood of light on this case,' the

Judge went on, 'is that you, Timson, habitually sat at the tap end of the bath. It seems you had a great deal to put up with. And your wife, she, it appears from the evidence, washed her hair in the more placid waters of the other end. I accept that this was a purely domestic dispute. For the common assault to which you have pleaded guilty you will be bound over to keep the peace . . .' And the Judge added the terrible words, '. . . in the sum of fifty pounds.'

So Tony Timson was at liberty, the case was over and a furious Mizz Liz Probert banged out of Court before Guthrie was half way out of the door. Catching up with her, I rebuked my learned Junior. 'It's not in the best traditions of the Bar to slam out before the Judge in any circumstances. When we've just had a famous victory it's quite ridiculous.'

'A famous victory.' She laughed in a cynical fashion. 'For men!'

'Man, woman or child, it doesn't matter who the client is. We did our best and won.'

'Because he was a man! Why shouldn't he sit at the tap end? I've got to do something about it!' She moved away purposefully. I called after her. 'Mizz Probert! Where're you going?'

'To my branch of the women's movement. The protest's got to be organized on a national level. I'm sorry, Rumpole. The time for talking's over.'

And she was gone. I had no idea, then, of the full extent of the tide which was about to overwhelm poor old Guthrie Featherstone, but I had a shrewd suspicion that his Lordship was in serious trouble.

The Featherstones' two children were away at university, and Guthrie and Marigold occupied a flat which Lady Featherstone found handy for Harrods, her favourite shopping centre, and a country cottage near Newbury. Marigold Featherstone was a handsome woman who greatly enjoyed life as a judge's wife and was full of that strength of character and quickness of decision his Lordship so conspicuously lacked. They went to the Garden Party together with three or four hundred other pillars of the establishment: admirals, captains of industry, hospital matrons and drivers of the Royal Train. Picture them, if you will, safely back home with Marigold kicking off her shoes on the sofa and Guthrie going out to the hall to fetch that afternoon's copy of the *Evening Sentinel*, which had just been delivered. You must, of course, understand that I was not present at the scene or other similar scenes which are necessary to this narrative. I can only do my best to reconstruct it from what I know of subsequent events and what the participants told me afterwards. Any gaps I have been able to fill in are thanks to the talent for fiction which I have acquired during a long career acting for the Defence in criminal cases.

'There might just be a picture of us arriving at the Palace.' Guthrie brought back the *Sentinel* and then stood in horror, rooted to the spot by what he saw on the front page.

'Well, then. Bring it in here.' Marigold, no doubt, called from her reclining position.

'Oh, there's absolutely nothing to read in it. The usual nonsense. Nothing of the slightest interest. Well, I think I'll go and have a bath and get changed.' And he attempted to sidle out of the room, holding the newspaper close to his body in a manner which made the contents invisible to his wife.

'Why're you trying to hide that *Evening Sentinel*, Guthrie?'

'Hide it? Of course I'm not trying to hide it. I just thought I'd take it to read in the bath.'

'And make it all soggy? Let me have it, Guthrie.'

'I told you . . .'

'Guthrie. I want to see what's in the paper.' Marigold spoke in an authoritative manner and her husband had no alternative but to hand it over, murmuring the while, 'It's completely inaccurate, of course.'

And so Lady Featherstone came to read, under a large photograph of his Lordship in a full-bottomed wig, the story which was being enjoyed by every member of the legal profession in the Greater London area. CARRY ON DROWNING screamed the banner headline. TAP END JUDGE'S AMAZING DECISION. And then came the full denunciation:

Wives who share baths with their husbands will have to be careful where they sit in the future. Because 29-year-old April Timson of Bexley Heath made her husband Tony sit at the tap end the Judge dismissed a charge of attempted murder against him. 'It seems you had a good deal to put up with,' 55-year-old Mr Justice Featherstone told Timson, a 36-year-old window cleaner. 'This is male chauvinism gone mad,' said a spokesperson of the Islington Women's Organization. 'There will be protests up and down the country and questions asked in Parliament. No woman can sit safely in her bath while this Judge continues on the bench.'

'It's a travesty of what I said, Marigold. You know exactly what these Court reporters are. Head over heels in Guinness after lunch.' Guthrie no doubt told his wife.

'This must have been in the morning. We went to the Palace after lunch.'

'Well, anyway. It's a travesty.'

'What do you mean, Guthrie? Didn't you say all that about the tap end?'

'Well, I may just have mentioned the tap end. Casually. In passing. Horace told me it was part of the evidence.'

'Horace?'

'Rumpole.'

'I suppose he was defending.'

'Well, yes . . .'

'You're clay in the hands of that little fellow, Guthrie. You're a Red Judge and he's only a Junior, but he can twist you round his little finger,' I rather hope she told him.

'You think Horace Rumpole led me up the garden?'

'Of course he did! He got his chap off and he encouraged you to say something monumentally stupid about tap ends. Not, I suppose, that you needed much encouragement.'

'This gives an entirely false impression. I'll put it right, Marigold. I promise you. I'll see it's put right.'

'I think you'd better, Guthrie.' The Judge's wife, I knew, was not a woman to mince her words. 'And for heaven's sake try not to put your foot in it again.'

So Guthrie went off to soothe his troubles up to the neck in bath water and Marigold lay brooding on the sofa until, so she told Hilda later, she was telephoned by the Tom Creevey Diary Column on the *Sentinel* with an inquiry as to which end of the bath she occupied when she and her husband were at their ablutions. Famous couples all over London, she was assured, were being asked the same question. Marigold put down the instrument without supplying any information, merely murmuring to herself, 'Guthrie! What have you done to us now?'

Marigold Featherstone wasn't the only wife appalled by the Judge's indiscretions. As I let myself in to our mansion flat in the Gloucester Road, Hilda, as was her wont, called to me from the living-room, 'Who's that?'

'I am thy father's spirit,' I told her in sepulchral tones.

> 'Doomed for a certain term to walk the night,
> And for the day confined to fast in fires,
> Till the foul crimes done in my days of nature
> Are burnt and purged away.'

'I suppose you think it's perfectly all right.' She was, I noticed, reading the *Evening Sentinel*.

'What's perfectly all right?'

'Drowning wives!' She said in the unfriendliest of tones. 'Like puppies. I suppose you think that's all perfectly understandable. Well, Rumpole, all I can say is, you'd better not try anything like that with me!'

'Hilda! It's never crossed my mind. Anyway, Tony Timson didn't drown her. He didn't come anywhere near drowning her. It was just a matrimonial tiff in the bathroom.'

'Why should *she* have to sit at the tap end?'

'Why indeed?' I made for the sideboard and a new bottle of Pommeroy's plonk. 'If she had, and if she'd tried to drown him because of it, I'd have defended her with equal skill and success. There you are, you see. Absolutely no prejudice when it comes to accepting a brief.'

'You think men and women are entirely equal?'

'Everyone is equal in the dock.'

'And in the home?'

'Well, yes, Hilda. Of course. Naturally. Although I suppose some are born to command.' I smiled at her in what I hoped was a soothing manner, well designed to unruffle her feathers, and took my glass of claret to my habitual seat by the gas fire.

'Trust me, Hilda,' I told her. 'I shall always be a staunch defender of Women's Rights.'

'I'm glad to hear that.'

'I'm glad you're glad.'

'That means you can do the weekly shop for us at Safeways.'

'Well, I'd really love that, Hilda,' I said eagerly. 'I should regard that as the most tremendous fun. Unfortunately I have to earn the boring stuff that pays for our weekly shop. I have to be at the service of my masters.'

'Husbands who try to drown their wives?' she asked unpleasantly.

'And vice versa.'

'They have late-night shopping on Thursdays, Rumpole. It won't cut into your work-time at all. Only into your drinking time in Pommeroy's Wine Bar. Besides which I shall be far too busy for shopping from now on.'

'Why, Hilda? What on earth are you planning to do?' I asked innocently. And when the answer came I knew the sexual revolution had hit Froxbury Mansions at last.

'Someone has to stand up for Women's Rights,' Hilda told me, 'against the likes of you and Guthrie Featherstone. I shall read for the Bar.'

Such was the impact of the decision in *R.* v. *Timson* on life in the Rumpole home. When Tony Timson was sprung from custody he was not taken lovingly back into the bosom of his family. April took her baths alone and frequently left the house tricked out in her skin-tight, wet-look trousers and the exotic halter-neck. When Tony made so bold as to ask where she was going, she told him to mind his own business. Vincent, the young hopeful, also treated his father with scant respect and, when asked where he was off to on his frequent departures from the front door, also told his father to mind his own business.

When she was off on the spree, April Timson, it later transpired, called round to an off licence in neighbouring Morrison Avenue. There she met the notorious Peanuts Molloy, also dressed in alluring leather, who was stocking up from Ruby, the large black lady who ran the 'offey', with raspberry crush.

Champanella, crème de cacao and three-star cognac as his contribution to some party or other. He and April would embrace openly and then go off partying together. On occasion Peanuts would ask her how 'that wally of a husband' was getting on, and express his outrage at the lightness of the sentence inflicted on him. 'Someone ought to give that Tony of yours a bit of justice,' was what he was heard to say.

Peanuts Molloy wasn't alone in feeling that being bound over in the sum of fifty pounds wasn't an adequate punishment for the attempted drowning of a wife. This view was held by most of the newspapers, a large section of the public, and all the members of the North Islington Women's Movement (Chair, Mizz Liz Probert). When Guthrie arrived for business at the Judge's entrance of the Old Bailey, he was met by a vociferous posse of women, bearing banners with the following legend: WOMEN OF ENGLAND, KEEP YOUR HEADS ABOVE WATER. GET JUSTICE FEATHERSTONE SACKED. As the friendly police officers kept these angry ladies at bay, Guthrie took what comfort he might from the thought that a High Court judge can only be dismissed by a Bill passed through both Houses of Parliament.

Something, he decided, would have to be done to answer his many critics. So Guthrie called Miss Lorraine Frinton, the doe-eyed shorthand writer, into his room and did his best to correct the record of his ill-considered judgment. Miss Frinton, breathtakingly decorative as ever, sat with her long legs neatly crossed in the Judge's armchair and tried to grasp his intentions with regard to her shorthand note. I reconstruct this conversation thanks to Miss Frinton's later recollection. She was, she admits, very nervous at the time because she thought that the Judge had sent for her because she had, in some way, failed in her duties. 'I've been living in dread of someone pulling me up about my shorthand,' she confessed. 'It's not my strongest suit, quite honestly.'

'Don't worry, Miss Frinton,' Guthrie did his best to reassure her. 'You're in no sort of trouble at all. But you are a shorthand writer, of course you are, and if we could just get to the point when I passed sentence. Could you read it out?'

The beautiful Lorraine looked despairingly at her notebook

and spelled out, with great difficulty, 'Mr Hearthstoke has quite wisely . . .'

'A bit further on.'

'Jackie a saw goo . . . a wise Frenchman . . .' Miss Frinton was decoding.

'*Chacun à son goût!*'

'I'm sorry, my Lord. I didn't quite get the name.'

'*Ça ne fait rien.*'

'How are you spelling that?' She was now lost.

'Never mind.' The Judge was at his most patient. 'A little further on, Miss Frinton. Lorraine. I'm sure you and I can come to an agreement. About a full stop.'

After much hard work, his Lordship had his way with Miss Frinton's shorthand note, and Counsel and solicitors engaged in the case were assembled in Court to hear, in the presence of the gentlemen of the Press, his latest version of his unfortunate judgment.

'I have had my attention drawn to the report of the case in *The Times*,' he started with some confidence, 'in which I am quoted as saying to Timson, "It seems you had a great deal to put up with. And your wife, she, it appears from the evidence, washed her hair in the more placid waters" etc. It's the full stop that has been misplaced. I have checked this carefully with the learned shorthand writer and she agrees with me. I see her nodding her head.' He looked down at Lorraine who nodded energetically, and the Judge smiled at her. 'Very well, yes. The sentence in my judgment in fact read "It seems you had a great deal to put up with, and your wife." Full stop! What I intended to convey, and I should like the Press to take note of this, was that both Mr and Mrs Timson had a good deal to put up with. At different ends of the bath, of course. Six of one and half a dozen of the other. I hope that's clear?' It was, as I whispered to Mizz Probert sitting beside me, as clear as mud.

The Judge continued. 'I certainly never said that I regarded being seated at the tap end as legal provocation to attempted murder. I would have said it was one of the facts that the Jury might have taken into consideration. It might have thrown some light on this wife's attitude to her husband.'

'What's he trying to do?' *sotto voce* Hearthstoke asked me.

'Trying to get himself out of hot water,' I suggested.

'But the attempted murder charge was dropped,' Guthrie went on.

'He twisted my arm to drop it,' Hearthstoke was muttering.

'And the entire tap end question was really academic,' Guthrie told us, 'as Timson pleaded guilty to common assault. Do you agree, Mr Rumpole?'

'Certainly, my Lord.' I rose in my most servile manner. 'You gave him a very stiff binding over.'

'Have you anything to add, Mr Hearthstoke?'

'No, my Lord.' Hearthstoke couldn't very well say anything else, but when the Judge had left us he warned me that Tony Timson had better watch his step in future as Detective Inspector Brush was quite ready to throw the book at him.

Guthrie Featherstone left Court well pleased with himself and instructed his aged and extremely disloyal clerk, Wilfred, to send a bunch of flowers, or, even better, a handsome pot plant to Miss Lorraine Frinton in recognition of her loyal services. So Wilfred told me he went off to telephone Interflora and Guthrie passed his day happily trying a perfectly straightforward robbery. On rising he retired to his room for a cup of weak Lapsang and a glance at the *Evening Sentinel*. This glance was enough to show him that he had achieved very little more, by his statement in open Court, than inserting his foot into the mud to an even greater depth.

BATHTUB JUDGE SAYS IT AGAIN screamed the headline. *Putting her husband at the tap end may be a factor to excuse the attempted murder of a wife.* 'Did I say that?' the appalled Guthrie asked old Wilfred who was busy pouring out the tea.

'To the best of my recollection, my Lord. Yes.'

There was no comfort for Guthrie when the telephone rang. It was old Keith from the Chancellor's office saying that the Lord Chancellor, as Head of the Judiciary, would like to see Mr Justice Featherstone at the earliest available opportunity.

'A Bill through the Houses of Parliament.' A stricken Guthrie put down the telephone. 'Would they do it to me, Wilfred?' he asked, but answer came there none.

'You do look, my clerk, in a moved sort, as if you were

dismayed.' In fact, Henry, when I encountered him in the clerk's room, seemed distinctly rattled. 'Too right, sir. I am dismayed. I've just had Mrs Rumpole on the telephone.'

'Ah. She Who Must wanted to speak to me?'

'No, Mr Rumpole. She wanted to speak to me. She said I'd be clerking for her in the fullness of time.'

'Henry,' I tried to reassure the man, 'there's no immediate cause for concern.'

'She said as she was reading for the Bar, Mr Rumpole, to make sure women get a bit of justice in the future.'

'Your missus coming into Chambers, Rumpole?' Uncle Tom, our oldest and quite briefless inhabitant, was pursuing his usual hobby of making approach shots to the waste-paper basket with an old putter.

'Don't worry, Uncle Tom.' I sounded as confident as I could. 'Not in the foreseeable future.'

'My motto as a barrister's clerk, sir, is anything for a quiet life,' Henry outlined his philosophy. 'I have to say that my definition of a quiet life does not include clerking for Mrs Hilda Rumpole.'

'Old Sneaky MacFarlane in Crown Office Row had a missus who came into his Chambers.' Uncle Tom was off down Memory Lane. 'She didn't come in to practice, you understand. She came in to watch Sneaky. She used to sit in the corner of his room and knit during all his conferences. It seems she was dead scared he was going to get off with one of his female divorce petitioners.'

'Mrs Rumpole, Henry, has only just written off for a legal course in the Open University. She can't yet tell provocation from self defence or define manslaughter.' I went off to collect things from my tray and Uncle Tom missed a putt and went on with his story. 'And you know what? In the end Mrs MacFarlane went off with a co-respondent she'd met at one of these conferences. Some awful fellow, apparently, in black and white shoes! Left poor old Sneaky high and dry. So, you see, it doesn't do to have wives in Chambers.

'Oh, I meant to ask you, Henry. Have you seen my Ackerman on *The Causes of Death?*' One of my best-loved books had gone missing.

'I think Mr Ballard's borrowed it, sir.' And then Henry asked, still anxious, 'How long do they take then, those courses at the Open University?'

'Years, Henry,' I told him. 'It's unlikely to finish during our lifetime.'

When I went up to Ballard's room to look for my beloved Ackerman, the door had been left a little open. Standing in the corridor I could hear the voices of those arch-conspirators, Claude Erskine-Brown and Soapy Sam Ballard, Q.C. I have to confess that I lingered to catch a little of the dialogue.

'Keith from the Lord Chancellor's office sounded *you* out about Guthrie Featherstone?' Erskine-Brown was asking.

'As the fellow who took over his Chambers. He thought I might have a view.'

'And have you? A view, I mean.'

'I told Keith that Guthrie was a perfectly charming chap, of course.' Soapy Sam was about to damn Guthrie with the faintest of praise.

'Oh, perfectly charming. No doubt about that,' Claude agreed.

'But as a judge, perhaps, he lacks judgment.'

'Which is a pretty important quality in a judge,' Claude thought.

'Exactly. And perhaps there is some lack of . . .'

'Gravitas?'

'The very word I used, Claude.'

'There was a bit of lack of gravitas in Chambers, too,' Claude remembered, 'when Guthrie took a shine to a temporary typist . . .'

'So the upshot of my talk with Keith was . . .

'What was the upshot?'

'I think we may be seeing a vacancy on the High Court Bench.' Ballard passed on the sad news with great satisfaction. 'And old Keith was kind enough to drop a rather interesting hint.'

'Tell me, Sam?'

'He said they might be looking for a replacement from the same stable.'

'Meaning these Chambers in Equity Court?'

'How could it mean anything else?'

'Sam, if you go on the Bench, we should need another silk in Chambers!' Claude was no doubt licking his lips as he considered the possibilities.

'I don't see how they could refuse you.' These two were clearly hand in glove.

'There's no doubt Guthrie'll have to go.' Claude pronounced the death sentence on our absent friend.

'He comes out with such injudicious remarks.' Soapy Sam put in another drop of poison. 'He was just like that at Marlborough.'

'Did you tell old Keith that?' Claude asked and then sat open-mouthed as I burst from my hiding-place with 'I bet you did!'

'Rumpole!' Ballard also looked put out. 'What on earth have you been doing?'

'I've been listening to the Grand Conspiracy.'

'You must admit, Featherstone J. has made the most tremendous boo-boo.' Claude smiled as though he had never made a boo-boo in his life.

'In the official view,' Soapy Sam told me, 'he's been remarkably stupid.'

'He wasn't stupid.' I briefed myself for Guthrie's defence. 'As a matter of fact he understood the case extremely well. He came to a wise decision. He might have phrased his judgment more elegantly, if he hadn't been to Marlborough. And let me tell you something, Ballard. My wife, Hilda, is about to start a law course at the Open University. She is a woman, as I know to my cost, of grit and determination. I expect to see her Lord Chief Justice of England before you get your bottom within a mile of the High Court Bench!'

'Of course you're entitled to your opinion.' Ballard looked tolerant. 'And you got your fellow off. All I know for certain is that the Lord Chancellor has summoned Guthrie Featherstone to appear before him.'

The Lord Chancellor of England was a small, fat, untidy man with steel-rimmed spectacles which gave him the schoolboy look which led to his nickname 'The Owl of the Remove'. He was given to fits of teasing when he would laugh aloud at his own jokes and unpredictable bouts of biting sarcasm during which he would stare at his victims with cold hostility. He had been, for many years, the Captain of the House of Lords croquet team, a game in which his ruthless cunning found full scope. He received Guthrie in his large, comfortably furnished room overlooking the Thames at Westminster, where his long wig was waiting on its stand and his gold-embroidered purse and gown were ready for his procession to the woolsack. Two years after this confrontation, I found myself standing with Guthrie at a Christmas party given in our Chambers to members past and present, and he was so far gone in *Brut* (not to say Brutal) Pommeroy's *Méthode Champenoise* as to give me the bare bones of this historic encounter. I have fleshed them out from my knowledge of both characters and their peculiar habits of speech.

'Judgeitis, Featherstone,' I hear the Lord Chancellor saying. 'It goes with piles as one of the occupational hazards of the judicial profession. Its symptoms are pomposity and self-regard. It shows itself by unnecessary interruptions during the proceedings or giving utterance to private thoughts far, far better left unspoken.'

'I did correct the press report, Lord Chancellor, with reference to the shorthand writer.' Guthrie tried to sound convincing.

'Oh, I read that.' The Chancellor was unimpressed. 'Far better to have left the thing alone. Never give the newspapers a second chance. That's my advice to you.'

'What's the cure for judgeitis?' Guthrie asked anxiously.

'Banishment to a golf club where the sufferer may bore the other members to death with recollections of his old triumphs on the Western Circuit.'

'You mean, A Bill through two Houses of Parliament?' The Judge stared into the future, dismayed.

'Oh, that's quite unnecessary!' The Chancellor laughed mirthlessly. 'I just get a Judge in this room and say, "Look here, old fellow. You've got it badly. Judgeitis. The Press is after your blood and quite frankly you're a profound embarrassment to us all. Go out to Esher, old boy," I say, "and improve your handicap. I'll give it out that you're retiring early for reasons of health." And then I'll make a speech defending the independence of the Judiciary against scurrilous and unjustified attacks by the Press.'

Guthrie thought about this for what seemed a silent eternity and then said, 'I'm not awfully keen on golf.'

'Why not take up croquet?' The Chancellor seemed anxious to be helpful. 'It's a top-hole retirement game. The women of England are against you. I hear they've been demonstrating outside the Old Bailey.'

'They were only a few extremists.'

'Featherstone, all women are extremists. You must know that, as a married man.'

'I suppose you're right, Lord Chancellor.' Guthrie now felt his position to be hopeless. 'Retirement! I don't know how Marigold's going to take it.'

The Lord Chancellor still looked like a hanging judge, but he stood up and said in businesslike tones, 'Perhaps it can be postponed in your case. I've talked it over with old Keith.'

'Your right-hand man?' Guthrie felt a faint hope rising.

'Exactly.' The Lord Chancellor seemed to be smiling at some private joke. 'You may have an opportunity some time in the future, in the not-too-distant future, let us hope, to make your peace with the women of England. You may be able to put right what they regard as an injustice to one of their number.'

'You mean, Lord Chancellor, my retirement is off?' Guthrie could scarcely believe it.

'Perhaps adjourned. *Sine die*.'

'Indefinitely?'

'Oh, I'm so glad you keep up with your Latin.' The Chancellor patted Guthrie on the shoulder. It was an order to dismiss. 'So many fellows don't.'

So Guthrie had a reprieve and, in the life of Tony Timson also, dramatic events were taking place. April's friend Chrissie was once married to Shaun Molloy, a well-known safe breaker, but their divorce seemed to have severed her connections with the Molloy clan and Tony Timson had agreed to receive and visit her. It was Chrissie who lived on their estate and had given the party before which April and Tony had struggled in the bath together; but it was at Chrissie's house, it seemed, that Peanuts Molloy was to be a visitor. So Tony's friendly feelings had somewhat abated, and when Chrissie rang the chimes on his front door one afternoon when April was out, he received her with a brusque 'What you want?'

'I thought you ought to know, Tony. It's not right.'

'What's not right?'

'Your April and Peanuts. It's not right.'

'You're one to talk, aren't you, Chrissie? April was going round yours to meet Peanuts at a party.'

'He just keeps on coming to mine. I don't invite him. Got no time for Peanuts, quite honestly. But him and your April. They're going out on dates. It's not right. I thought you ought to know.'

'What you mean, dates?' As I have said, Tony's life had not been a bed of roses since his return home, but now he was more than usually troubled.

'He takes her out partying. They're meeting tonight round the offey in Morrison Avenue. Nine thirty time, she told me. Just thought you might like to know, that's all,' the kindly Chrissie added.

So it happened that at nine thirty that night, when Ruby was presiding over an empty off licence in Morrison Avenue, Tony Timson entered it and stood apparently surveying the tempting bottles on display but really waiting to confront the errant April and Peanuts Molloy. He heard a door bang in some private area behind Ruby's counter and then the strip lights stopped humming and the off licence was plunged into darkness. It was not a silent darkness, however; it was filled with the sound of footsteps scuffling and heavy blows.

Not long afterwards a police car with a wailing siren was screaming towards Morrison Avenue; it was wonderful with what rapidity the Old Bill was summoned whenever Tony Timson was in trouble. When Detective Inspector Brush and his sergeant got into the off licence, their torches illuminated a scene of violence. Two bodies were on the floor. Ruby was lying by the counter, unconscious, and Tony was lying beside some shelves, nearer to the door, with a wound in his forehead. The Sergeant's torch beam showed a heavy cosh lying by his right hand and pound notes scattered around him. 'Can't you leave the women alone, boy?' the Detective Inspector said as Tony Timson slowly opened his eyes.

So another Timson brief came to Rumpole, and Mr Justice Featherstone got a chance to redeem himself in the eyes of the Lord Chancellor and the women of Islington.

Like two knights of old approaching each other for combat, briefs at the ready, helmeted with wigs and armoured with gowns, the young black-haired Sir Hearthrug and the cunning old Sir Horace, with his faithful page Mizz Liz in attendance, met outside Number One Court at the Old Bailey and threw down their challenges.

'Nemesis,' said Hearthrug.

'What's that meant to mean?' I asked him.

'Timson's for it now.'

'Let's hope justice will be done,' I said piously.

'Guthrie's not going to make the same mistake twice.'

'Mr Justice Featherstone's a wise and upright judge,' I told him, 'even if his foot does get into his mouth occasionally.'

'He's a judge with the Lord Chancellor's beady eye upon him, Rumpole.'

'I wasn't aware that this case was going to be decided by the Lord Chancellor.'

'By him and the women of England.' Hearthstoke smiled at Mizz Probert in what I hoped she found a revolting manner. 'Ask your learned Junior.'

'Save your breath for Court, Hearthrug. You may need it.' So we moved on, but as we went my learned Junior disappointed me by saying, 'I don't think Tony Timson should get away with it again.' 'Happily, that's not for you to decide,' I told her. 'We can leave that to the good sense of the Jury.'

However, the Jury, when we saw them assembled, were not a particularly cheering lot. For a start, the women outnumbered the men by eight to four and the women in question looked large and severe. I was at once reminded of the mothers' meetings that once gathered round the guillotine and I seemed to hear, as Hearthstoke opened the prosecution case, the ghostly click of knitting needles.

His opening speech was delivered with a good deal of ferocity and he paused now and again to flash a white-toothed smile at Miss Lorraine Frinton, who sat once more, looking puzzled, in front of her shorthand notebook.

'Members of the Jury,' Hearthrug intoned with great solemnity. 'Even in these days, when we are constantly sickened by crimes of violence, this is a particularly horrible and distressing event. An attack with this dangerous weapon' – here he picked up the cosh, Exhibit One, and waved it at the Jury – 'upon a weak and defenceless woman.'

'Did you say a *woman*, Mr Hearthstoke?' Up spoke the anxious figure of the Red Judge upon the Bench. I cannot believe that pure chance had selected Guthrie Featherstone to preside over Tony Timson's second trial.

Our Judge clearly meant to redeem himself and appear, from the outset, as the dedicated protector of that sex which is sometimes called the weaker by those who have not the good fortune to be married to She Who Must Be Obeyed.

'I'm afraid so, my Lord,' Hearthstoke said, more in anger than in sorrow.

'This man Timson attacked a *woman*!' Guthrie gave the Jury the benefit of his full outrage. I had to put some sort of a stop to this so I rose to say, 'That, my Lord, is something the Jury has to decide.'

'Mr Rumpole,' Guthrie told me, 'I am fully aware of that. All I can say about this case is that should the Jury convict, I take an extremely serious view of any sort of attack on a woman.'

'If they were bathing it wouldn't matter,' I muttered to Liz as I subsided.

'I didn't hear that, Mr Rumpole.'

'Not a laughing matter, my Lord,' I corrected myself rapidly.

'Certainly not. Please proceed, Mr Hearth*stoke*.' And here his Lordship whispered to his clerk, Wilfred, 'I'm not having old Rumpole twist me round his little finger in *this* case.'

'Very wise, if I may say so, my Lord,' Wilfred whispered back as he sat beside the Judge, sharpening his pencils.

'Members of the Jury,' an encouraged Hearthstoke proceeded. 'Mrs Ruby Churchill, the innocent victim, works in an off licence near the man Timson's home. Later we shall look at a plan of the premises. The Prosecution does not allege that Timson carried out this robbery alone. He no doubt had an accomplice who entered by an open window at the back of the shop and turned out the lights. Then, we say, under cover of darkness, Timson coshed the unfortunate Mrs Churchill, whose evidence you will hear. The accomplice escaped with most of the money from the till. Timson, happily for justice, slipped and struck his head on the corner of the shelves. He was found in a half-stunned condition, with the cosh and some of the money. When arrested by Detective Inspector Brush he said, "You got me this time, then". You may think that a clear admission of guilt.' And now Hearthstoke was into his peroration. 'Too long, Members of the Jury,' he said, 'have women suffered in our Courts. Too long have men seemed licensed to attack them. Your verdict in this case will be awaited eagerly and hopefully by the women of England.'

I looked at Mizz Liz Probert and I was grieved to note that she was receiving this hypocritical balderdash with starry-eyed attention. During the mercifully short period when the egregious Hearthrug had been a member of our Chambers in Equity Court, I remembered, Mizz Liz had developed an inexplicably soft spot for the fellow. I was pained to see that the spot remained as soft as ever.

Even as we sat in Number One Court, the Islington women were on duty in the street outside bearing placards with the legend JUSTICE FOR WOMEN. Claude Erskine-Brown and Soapy Sam Ballard passed these demonstrators and smiled with some satisfaction. 'Guthrie's in the soup again, Ballard,' Claude told his new friend. 'They're taking to the streets!'

Ruby Churchill, large, motherly, and clearly anxious to tell the truth, was the sort of witness it's almost impossible to cross-examine effectively. When she had told her story to Hearthstoke, I rose and felt the silent hostility of both Judge and Jury.

'Before you saw him in your shop on the night of this attack,' I asked her, 'did you know my client, Mr Timson?'

'I knew him. He lives round the corner.'

'And you knew his wife, April Timson?'

'I know her. Yes.'

'She's been in your shop?'

'Oh, yes, sir.'

'With her husband?'

'Sometimes with him. Sometimes without.'

'Sometimes without? How interesting.'

'Mr Rumpole. Have you many more questions for this unfortunate lady?' Guthrie seemed to have been converted to the view that female witnesses shouldn't be subjected to cross-examination.

'Just a few, my Lord.'

'Please. Mrs Churchill,' his Lordship gushed at Ruby. 'Do take a seat. Make yourself comfortable. I'm sure we all admire the plucky way in which you are giving your evidence. *As a woman.*'

'And as a woman,' I made bold to ask, after Ruby had been offered all the comforts of the witness-box, 'did you know that Tony Timson had been accused of trying to drown his wife in the bath? And that he was tried and bound over?'

'My Lord. How can that possibly be relevant?' Hearthrug arose, considerably narked.

'I was about to ask the same question.' Guthrie sided with the Prosecution. 'I have no idea what Mr Rumpole is driving at!'

'Oh, I thought your Lordship might remember the case,' I said casually. 'There was some newspaper comment about it at the time.'

'Was there really?' Guthrie affected ignorance. 'Of course, in a busy life one can't hope to read every little paragraph about one's cases that finds its way into the newspapers.'

'This found its way slap across the front page, my Lord.'

'Did it really? Do you remember that, Mr Hearthstoke?'

'I think I remember some rather ill-informed comment, my Lord.' Hearthstoke was not above buttering up the Bench.

'Ill-informed. Yes. No doubt it was. One has so many cases before one . . .' As Guthrie tried to forget the past, I hastily drew the witness back into the proceedings. 'Perhaps your memory is better than his Lordship's?' I suggested to Ruby. 'You remember the case, don't you, Mrs Churchill?'

'Oh, yes. I remember it.' Ruby had no doubt.

'Mr Hearthstoke. Are you objecting to this?' Guthrie was looking puzzled.

'If Mr Rumpole wishes to place his client's previous convictions before the Jury, my Lord, why should I object?' Hearthstoke looked at me complacently, as though I were playing into his hands, and Guthrie whispered to Wilfred, 'Bright chap, this prosecutor.'

'And can you remember what you thought about it at the time?' I went on plugging away at Ruby.

'I thought Mr Timson had got away with murder!'

The Jury looked severely at Tony, and Guthrie appeared to think I had kicked a sensational own goal. 'I suppose that was hardly the answer you wanted, Mr Rumpole,' he said.

'On the contrary, my Lord. It was exactly the answer I wanted! And having got away with it then, did it occur to you that someone . . . some avenging angel, perhaps, might wish to frame Tony Timson on this occasion?'

'My Lord. That is pure speculation!' Hearthstoke arose, furious, and I agreed with him. 'Of course it is. But it's a speculation I wish to put in the mind of the Jury at the earliest possible opportunity.' So I sat down, conscious that I had at least chipped away at the Jury's certainty. They knew that I should return to the possibility of Tony having been framed and were prepared to look at the evidence with more caution.

That morning two events of great pith and moment occurred in the case of the Queen against Tony Timson. April went shopping in Morrison Avenue and saw something which considerably changed her attitude. Peanuts Molloy and her friend Chrissie were coming out of the off licence with a plastic bag full of assorted bottles. As Peanuts held his car door open for Chrissie they engaged in a passionate and public embrace, unaware that they were doing so in the full view of Mrs April Timson, who uttered the single word 'Bastard!' in the hearing of the young hopeful Vincent who, being on his school holidays, was accompanying his mother. The other important matter was that Guthrie, apparently in a generous mood as he saw a chance of re-establishing his judicial reputation, sent a note to me and Hearthstoke asking if we would be so kind as to join him, and the other judges sitting at the Old Bailey, for luncheon.

Guthrie's invitation came as Hearthstoke was examining Miss Sweating, the schoolmistress-like scientific officer, who was giving evidence as to the bloodstains found about the off licence on the night of the crime. As this evidence was of some importance I should record that blood of Tony Timson's group was traced on the floor and on the corner of the shelf by which he had fallen. Blood of the same group as that which flowed in Mrs Ruby Churchill's veins was to be found on the floor where she lay and on the cosh by Tony's hand. Talk of blood groups, as you will know, acts on me like the smell of grease-paint to an old actor, or the cry of hounds to John Peel. I was pawing the ground and snuffling a little at the nostrils as I rose to cross-examine.

'Miss Sweating,' I began. 'You say there was blood of Timson's group on the corner of the shelf?'

'There was. Yes.'

'And from that you assumed that he had hit his head against the shelf?'

'That seemed the natural assumption. He had been stunned by hitting his head.'

'Or by someone else hitting his head?'

'But the Detective Inspector told me . . .' the witness began, but I interrupted her with 'Listen to me and don't bother about what the Detective Inspector told you!'

'Mr Rumpole!' That grave protector of the female sex on the Bench looked pained. 'Is that the tone to adopt? The witness is a woman!'

'The witness is a scientific officer, my Lord,' I pointed out, 'who pretends to know something about bloodstains. Looking at the photograph of the stains on the corner of the shelf, Miss Sweating, might not they be splashes of blood which fell when the accused was struck in that part of the room?'

Miss Sweating examined the photograph in question through her formidable horn-rims and we were granted two minutes' silence which I broke into at last with 'Would you favour us with an answer, Miss Sweating? Or do you want to exercise a woman's privilege and not make up your mind?'

'Mr Rumpole!' The newly converted feminist judge was outraged. But the witness admitted, 'I suppose they might have got there like that. Yes.'

'They are consistent with his having been struck by an assailant. Perhaps with another weapon similar to this cosh?'

'Yes,' Miss Sweating agreed, reluctantly.

'Thank you. "Trip no further, pretty sweeting" . . .' I whispered as I sat down, thereby shocking the shockable Mizz Probert.

'Miss Sweating' – Guthrie tried to undo my good work – 'you have also said that the bloodstains on the shelf are consistent with Timson having slipped when he was running out of the shop and striking his head against it?'

'Oh, yes,' Miss Sweating agreed eagerly. 'They are consistent with that, my Lord.'

'Very well.' His Lordship smiled ingratiatingly at the women of the Jury. 'Perhaps the ladies of the Jury would like to take a little light luncheon now?' And he added, more brusquely, 'The gentlemen too, of course. Back at five past two, Members of the Jury.'

When we got out of Court, I saw my learned friend Charles Hearthstoke standing in the corridor in close conversation with the beautiful shorthand writer. He was, I noticed, holding her lightly and unobtrusively by the hand. Mizz Probert, who also noticed this, walked away in considerable disgust.

A large variety of judges sit at the Old Bailey. These include the Old Bailey regulars, permanent fixtures such as the Mad Bull Bullingham and the sepulchral Graves, judges of the lower echelon who wear black gowns. They also include a judge called the Common Sergeant, who is neither common nor a sergeant, and the Recorder who wears red and is the senior Old Bailey judge – a man who has to face, apart from the usual diet of murder, robbery and rape, a daunting number of City dinners. These are joined by the two visiting High Court judges, the Red Judges of the Queen's Bench, of whom Guthrie was one, unless and until the Lord Chancellor decided to put him permanently out to grass. All these judicial figures trough together at a single long table in a back room of the Bailey. They do it, and the sight comes as something of a shock to the occasional visitor, wearing their wigs. The sight of Judge Bullingham's angry and purple face ingesting stew and surmounted with horse-hair is only for the strongest stomachs. They are joined by various City aldermen and officials wearing lace jabots and tailed coats and other guests from the Bar or from the world of business.

Before the serious business of luncheon begins, the company is served sherry, also taken whilst wearing wigs, and I was ensconced in a corner where I could overhear a somewhat strange preliminary conversation between our judge and Counsel for the Prosecution.

'Ah, Hearth*stoke*,' Guthrie greeted him. 'I thought I'd invite both Counsel to break bread with me. Just want to make sure neither of you had anything to object to about the trial.'

'Of course not, Judge!' Hearthstoke was smiling. 'It's been a very pleasant morning. Made even more pleasant by the appearance of the shorthand writer.'

'The . . . ? Oh, yes! Pretty girl, is she? I hadn't noticed,' Guthrie fibbed.

'Hadn't you? Lorraine said you'd been extraordinarily kind to her. She so much appreciated the beautiful pot plant you sent her.'

'Pot plant?' Guthrie looked distinctly guilty, but Hearthstoke pressed on with 'Something rather gorgeous she told me. With pink blooms. Didn't she help you straighten out the shorthand note in the last Timson case?'

'She corrected her mistake,' Guthrie said carefully.

'*Her* mistake, was it?' Hearthstoke was looking at the Judge. 'She said it'd been yours.'

'Perhaps we should all sit down now.' Guthrie was keen to end this embarrassing scene. 'Oh and, Hearthstoke, no need to mention that business of the pot plant around the Bailey. Otherwise they'll all be wanting one.' He gave a singularly unconvincing laugh. 'I can't give pink blooms to everyone, including Rumpole!'

'Of course, Judge.' Hearthstoke was understanding. 'No need to mention it at all *now*.'

'*Now?*'

'Now,' the Prosecutor said firmly, 'justice is going to be done to Timson. At last.'

Guthrie seemed thankful to move away and find his place at the table, until he discovered that I had been put next to him. He made the best of it, pushed one of the decanters in my direction and hoped I was quite satisfied with the fairness of the proceedings.

'Are *you* content with the fairness of the proceedings?' I asked him.

'Yes, of course. I'm the Judge, aren't I?'

'Are you sure?'

'What on earth's that meant to mean?'

'Haven't you asked yourself why you, a High Court judge, a Red Judge, have been given a paltry little robbery with violence?' I refreshed myself with a generous gulp of the City of London's claret.

'I suppose it's the luck of the draw.'

'Luck of the draw, my eye! I detect the subtle hand of old Keith from the Lord Chancellor's office.'

'Keith?' His Lordship looked around him nervously.

'Oh, yes. "Give Guthrie *Timson*," he said. "Give him a chance to redeem himself by potting the fellow and sending him down for ten years. The women of England will give three hearty cheers and Featherstone will be the Lord Chancellor's blue-eyed boy again." Don't fall for it! You can be better than that, if you put your mind to it. Sum up according to the evidence and the hell with the Lord Chancellor's office!'

'Horace! I don't think I've heard anything you've been saying.'

'It's up to you, old darling. Are you a man or a rubber stamp for the Civil Service?'

Guthrie looked round desperately for a new subject of conversation and his eye fell on our prosecutor who was being conspicuously bored by an elderly alderman. 'That young Hearthstoke seems a pretty able sort of fellow,' he said.

'Totally ruthless,' I told him. 'He'd stop at nothing to win a case.'

'Nothing?'

'Absolutely nothing.'

Guthrie took the decanter and started to pour wine into his own glass. His hand was trembling slightly and he was staring at Hearthstoke in a haunted way.

'Horace,' he started confidentially, 'you've been practising at the Old Bailey for a considerable number of years.'

'Almost since the dawn of time.'

'And you can see nothing wrong with a judge, impressed by the hard work of a court official, say a shorthand writer, for instance, sending that official some little token of gratitude?'

'What sort of token are you speaking of, Judge?'

'Something like' – he gulped down wine – 'a pot plant.'

'A plant?'

'In a pot. With pink blossoms.'

'Pink blossoms, eh?' I thought it over. 'That sounds quite appropriate.'

'You can see nothing in any way improper in such a gift, Horace?' The Judge was deeply grateful.

'Nothing improper at all. A "Busy Lizzie"?'

'I think her name's Lorraine.'

'Nothing wrong with that.'

'You reassure me, Horace. You comfort me very much.' He took another swig of the claret and looked fearfully at Hearthstoke. Poor old Guthrie Featherstone, he spent most of his judicial life painfully perched between the horns of various dilemmas.

'In the car after we arrested him, driving away from the off licence, Tony Timson said, "You got me this time, then," ' This was the evidence of that hammer of the Timsons, Detective Inspector Brush. When he had given it, Hearthstoke looked hard at the Jury to emphasize the point, thanked the officer profusely and I rose to cross-examine.

'Detective Inspector. Do you know a near neighbour of the Timsons named Peter, better known as "Peanuts", Molloy?'

'Mr Peter Molloy is known to the police, yes,' the Inspector answered cautiously.

'He and his brother Greg are leading lights of the Molloy firm? Fairly violent criminals?'

'Yes, my Lord,' Brush told the Judge.

'Have you known both Peanuts and his brother to use coshes like this one in the course of crime?'

'Well. Yes, possibly . . .'

'My Lord, I really must object!' Hearthstoke was on his feet and Guthrie said, 'Mr Rumpole. Your client's own character . . .

'He is a petty thief, my Lord.' I was quick to put Tony's character before the Jury. 'Tape-recorders and freezer-packs. No violence in his record, is there, Inspector?'

'Not up to now, my Lord,' Brush agreed reluctantly.

'Very well, Did you think he had been guilty of that attempted murder charge, after he and his wife quarrelled in the bathroom?'

'I thought so, yes.'

'You were called to the scene very quickly when the quarrel began.

'A neighbour called us.'

'Was that neighbour a member of the Molloy family?

'Mr Rumpole, I prefer not to answer that question.'

'I won't press it.' I left the Jury to speculate. 'But you think he got off lightly at his first trial?' I was reading the note Tony Timson had scribbled in the dock while listening to the evidence as D. I. Brush answered, 'I thought so, yes.'

'What he actually said in the car was "I suppose you think you got me this time, then?" '

'No.' Brush looked at his notebook. 'He just said, "You got me this time, then." '

'You left out the words "I suppose you think" because you don't want him to get off lightly this time?'

'Now would I do a thing like that, sir?' Brush gave us his most honestly pained expression.

'That, Inspector Brush, is a matter for this Jury to decide.'

And the Jury looked, by now, as though they were prepared to consider all the possibilities.

Lord Justice MacWhitty's wife, it seems, met Marigold Featherstone in Harrods, and told her she was sorry that Guthrie had such a terrible attitude to women. There was one old judge, apparently, who made his wife walk behind him when he went on circuit, carrying the luggage, and Lady MacWhitty said she felt that poor Marigold was married to just such a tyrant. When we finally discussed the whole history of the Tony Timson case at the Chambers party, Guthrie told me that Marigold had said that she was sick and tired of women coming up to her and feeling sorry for her in Harrods.

'You see,' Guthrie had said to his wife, 'if Timson gets off, the Lord Chancellor and all the women of England will be down on me like a ton of bricks. But the evidence isn't entirely satisfactory. It's just possible he's innocent. It's hard to tell where a fellow's duty lies.'

'Your duty, Guthrie, lies in keeping your nose clean!' Marigold had no doubt about it.

'My nose?'

'Clean. For the sake of your family. And if this Timson has to go inside for a few years, well, I've no doubt he richly deserves it.'

'Nothing but decisions!'

'I really don't know what else you expected when you became a judge.' Marigold poured herself a drink. Seeking some comfort after a hard day, the Judge went off to soak in a hot bath. In doing so, I believe Lady Featherstone made it clear to him, he was entirely on his own.

Things were no easier in the Rumpole household. I was awakened at some unearthly hour by the wireless booming in the living-room and I climbed out of bed to see Hilda, clad in a dressing-gown and hairnet, listening to the device with her pencil and notebook poised whilst it greeted her brightly with 'Good morning, students. This is first-year Criminal Law on the Open University. I am Richard Snellgrove, law teacher at Hollowfield Polytechnic, to help you on this issue . . . Can a wife give evidence against her husband?'

'Good God!' I asked her, 'what time does the Open University open?'

'For many years a wife could not give evidence against her husband,' Snellgrove told us. 'See *R.* v. *Boucher* 1952. Now, since the Police and Criminal Evidence Act 1984, a wife can be called to give such evidence.'

'You see, Rumpole.' Hilda took a note. 'You'd better watch out!' I found and lit the first small cigar of the day and coughed gratefully. Snellgrove continued to teach me law. 'But she can't be compelled to. She has been a competent witness for the defence of her husband since the Criminal Evidence Act 1898. But a judgment in the House of Lords suggests she's not compellable..'

'What's that mean, Rumpole?' She asked me.

'Well, we could ask April Timson to give evidence for Tony. But we couldn't make her,' I began to explain, and then, perhaps because I was in a state of shock from being awoken so early, I had an idea of more than usual brilliance. 'April Timson!' I told Hilda, 'she won't know she's not compellable. I don't suppose she tunes into the "Open at Dawn University". Now I wonder . . .'

'What, Rumpole. What do you wonder?'

'Quarter to six.' I looked at the clock on the mantelpiece. 'High time to wake up Bernard.' I went to the phone and started to dial my instructing solicitor's number.

'You see how useful I'll be to you' – Hilda looked extremely pleased with herself – 'when I come to work in your Chambers.'

'Oh, Bernard,' I said to the telephone, 'wake you up, did I? Well, it's time to get moving. The Open University's been open for hours. Look, an idea has just crossed my mind . . .'

'It crossed *my* mind, Rumpole,' Hilda corrected me. 'And I was kind enough to hand it on to you.'

When Mr Bernard called on April Timson an hour later, there was no need for him to go into the nice legal question of whether she was a compellable witness or not. Since she had seen Peanuts and her friend Chrissie come out of the 'offey' she was, she made it clear, ready and willing to come to Court and tell her whole story.

'Mrs April Timson,' I asked Tony's wife when, to the surprise of most people in Court including my client, she entered the witness-box, as a witness for the defence, 'some while ago you had a quarrel with your husband in a bathtub. What was that quarrel about?'

'Peanuts Molloy.'

'About a man called Peter "Peanuts" Molloy. What did you tell your husband about Peanuts?'

'About him as a man, like . . . ?'

'Did you compare the virility of these two gentlemen?'

'Yes, I did.' April was able to cope with this part of the evidence without embarrassment.

'And who got the better of the comparison?'

'Peanuts.' Tony, lowering his head, got his first look of sympathy from the Jury.

'Was there a scuffle in your bath then?'

'Yes.'

'Mrs April Timson, did your husband ever try to drown you?'

'No. He never.' Her answer caused a buzz in Court. Guthrie stared at her, incredulous.

'Why did you suggest he did?' I asked.

'My Lord. I object. What possible relevance?' Hearthrug tried to interrupt but I and everyone else ignored him.

'Why did you suggest he tried to murder you?' I repeated.

'I was angry with him, I reckon,' April told us calmly, and the Prosecutor lost heart and subsided. The Judge, however, pursued the matter with a pained expression. 'Do I understand,' he asked, 'you made an entirely false accusation against your husband?'

'Yes.' April didn't seem to think it an unusual thing to do.

'Don't you realize, madam,' the Judge said, 'the suffering that accusation has brought to innocent people?'

'Such as you, old cock,' I muttered to Mizz Liz.

'What was that, Rumpole?' the Judge asked me. 'Such as the man in the dock, my Lord,' I repeated.

'And other innocent, innocent people.' His Lordship shook his head sadly and made a note.

'After your husband's trial did you continue to see Mr Peanuts Molloy?' I went on with my questions to the uncompellable witness.

'We went out together. Yes.'

'Where did you meet?'

'We met round the offey in Morrison Avenue. Then we went out in his car.

'Did you meet him at the off licence on the night this robbery took place?'

'I never.' April was sure of it.

'Your husband says that your neighbour Chrissie came round and told him that you and Peanuts Molloy were going to meet at the off licence at nine thirty that evening. So he went up there to put a stop to your affair.'

'Well, Chrissie was well in with Peanuts by then, wasn't she?' April smiled cynically. 'I reckon he sent her to tell Tony that.'

'Why do you reckon he sent her?'

Hearthstoke rose again, determined. 'My Lord, I must object,' he said. 'What this witness "reckons" is entirely inadmissible.' When he had finished, I asked the Judge if I might have a word with my learned friend in order to save time. I then moved along our row and whispered to him vehemently, 'One more peep out of you, Hearthrug, and I lay a formal complaint on your conduct!'

'What conduct?' he whispered back.

'Trying to blackmail a learned judge on the matter of a pot plant sent to a shorthand writer.' I looked across at Lorraine. 'Not in the best traditions of the Bar, that!' I left him thinking hard and went back to my place. After due consideration he said, 'My Lord. On second thoughts, I withdraw my objection.'

Hearthstroke resumed his seat. I smiled at him cheerfully and continued with April's evidence. 'So why do you think

Peanuts wanted to get your husband up to the off licence that evening?'

'Pretty obvious, innit?'

'Explain it to us.'

'So he could put him in the frame. Make it look like Tony done Ruby up, like.'

'So he could put him in the frame. An innocent man!' I looked at the Jury. 'Had Peanuts said anything to make you think he might do such a thing?'

'After the first trial.'

'After Mr Timson was bound over?'

'Yes. Peanuts said he reckoned Tony needed a bit of justice, like. He said he was going to see he got put inside. 'Course, Peanuts didn't mind making a bit hisself, out of robbing the offey.'

One more thing, Mrs Timson. Have you ever seen a weapon like that before?'

I held up the cosh. The Usher came and took it to the witness.

'I saw that one. I think I did.'

'Where?'

'In Peanuts' car. That's where he kept it.'

'Did your husband ever own anything like that?'

'What, Tony?' April weighed the cosh in her hand and clearly found the idea ridiculous. 'Not him. He wouldn't have known what to do with it.'

When the evidence was complete and we had made our speeches, Guthrie had to sum up the case of *R.* v. *Timson* to the Jury. As he turned his chair towards them, and they prepared to give him their full attention, a distinguished visitor slipped unobtrusively into the back of the Court. He was none other than old Keith from the Lord Chancellor's office. The Judge must have seen him, but he made no apology for his previous lenient treatment of Tony Timson.

'Members of the Jury,' he began. 'You have heard of the false accusation of attempted murder that Mrs Timson made against an innocent man. Can you imagine, Members of the

Jury, what misery that poor man has been made to suffer? Devoted to ladies as he may be, he has been called a heartless "male chauvinist". Gentle and harmless by nature, he has been thought to connive at crimes of violence. Perhaps it was even suggested that he was the sort of fellow who would make his wife carry heavy luggage! He may well have been shunned in the streets, hooted at from the pavements, and the wife he truly loves has perhaps been unwilling to enter a warm, domestic bath with him. And then, consider,' Guthrie went on, 'if the unhappy Timson may not have also been falsely accused in relation to the robbery with violence of his local "offey". Justice must be done, Members of the Jury. We must do justice even if it means we do nothing else for the rest of our lives but compete in croquet competitions.' The Judge was looking straight at Keith from the Lord Chancellor's office as he said this. I relaxed, lay back and closed my eyes. I knew, after all his troubles, how his Lordship would feel about a man falsely accused, and I had no further worries about the fate of Tony Timson.

When I got home, Hilda was reading the result of the trial in the *Evening Sentinel*. 'I suppose you're cock-a-hoop, Rumpole,' she said.

'Hearthrug routed!' I told her. 'The women of England back on our side and old Keith from the Lord Chancellor's office looking extremely foolish. And a miraculous change came over Guthrie.'

'What?'

'He suddenly found courage. It's something you can't do without, not if you concern yourself with justice.'

'That April Timson!' Hilda looked down at her evening paper. 'Making it all up about being drowned in the bathwater.'

'When lovely woman stoops to folly' – I went to the sideboard and poured a celebratory glass of Château Thames Embankment – 'And finds too late that men betray,/What charm can soothe her melancholy . . .'

'I'm not going to the Bar to protect people like her, Rumpole.' Hilda announced her decision. 'She's put me to a great deal of trouble. Getting up at a quarter to six every morning for the Open University.'

' "What art can wash her guilt away?" *What* did you say, Hilda?'

'I'm not going to all that trouble, learning Real Property and Company Law and eating dinners and buying a wig, not for the likes of April Timson.'

'Oh, Hilda! Everyone in Chambers will be extremely disappointed.'

'Well, I'm sorry.' She had clearly made up her mind. 'They'll just have to do without me. I've really got better things to do, Rumpole, than come home cock-a-hoop just because April Timson changes her mind and decides to tell the truth.'

'Of course you have, Hilda.' I drank gratefully. 'What sort of better things?'

'Keeping you in order for one, Rumpole. Seeing you wash up properly.' And then she spoke with considerable feeling. 'It's disgusting!'

'The washing up?'

"No. People having baths together.'

'Married people?' I reminded her.

'I don't see that makes it any better. Don't you ever ask me to do that, Rumpole.'

'Never, Hilda. I promise faithfully.' To hear, of course, was to obey.

That night's *Sentinel* contained a leading article which appeared under the encouraging headline BATHTUB JUDGE PROVED RIGHT. *Mrs April Timson*, it read, *has admitted that her husband never tried to drown her and the Jury have acquitted Tony Timson on a second trumped-up charge. It took a Judge of Mr Justice Featherstone's perception and experience to see through this woman's inventions and exaggerations and to uphold the law without fear or favour. Now and again the British legal system produces a Judge of exceptional wisdom and integrity who refuses to yield to pressure groups and does justice though the heavens fall. Such a one is Sir Guthrie Featherstone.*

Sir Guthrie told me later that he read those comforting

words whilst lying in a warm bath in his flat near Harrods. I have no doubt at all that Lady Featherstone was with him on that occasion, seated at the tap end.

THE WOMAN IN THE BIG HAT

Baroness Orczy

I

LADY Molly always had the idea that if the finger of Fate had pointed to Mathis' in Regent Street, rather than to Lyons', as the most advisable place for us to have a cup of tea that afternoon, Mr Culledon would be alive at the present moment.

My dear lady is quite sure – and needless to say that I share her belief in herself – that she would have anticipated the murderer's intentions, and thus prevented one of the most cruel and callous of crimes which were ever perpetrated in the heart of London.

She and I had been to a matinée of 'Trilby', and were having tea at Lyons', which is exactly opposite Mathis' Vienna café in Regent Street. From where we sat we commanded a view of the street and of the café, which had been very crowded during the last hour.

We had lingered over our toasted muffin until past six, when our attention was drawn to the unusual commotion which had arisen both outside and in the brilliantly lighted place over the road.

We saw two men run out of the doorway, and return a minute or two later in company with a policeman. You know what is the inevitable result of such a proceeding in London. Within three minutes a crowd had collected outside Mathis'.

Two or three more constables had already assembled, and had some difficulty in keeping the entrance clear of intruders.

But already my dear lady, keen as a pointer on the scent, had hastily paid her bill, and, without waiting to see if I followed her or not, had quickly crossed the road, and the next moment her graceful form was lost in the crowd.

I went after her, impelled by curiosity, and presently caught sight of her in close conversation with one of our own men. I have always thought that Lady Molly must have eyes at the back of her head, otherwise how could she have known that I stood behind her now? Anyway, she beckoned to me, and together we entered Mathis', much to the astonishment and anger of the less fortunate crowd.

The usually gay little place was indeed sadly transformed. In one corner the waitresses, in dainty caps and aprons, had put their heads together, and were eagerly whispering to one another whilst casting furtive looks at the small group assembled in front of one of those pretty alcoves, which as you know, line the walls all round the big tearooms at Mathis'.

Here two of our men were busy with pencil and notebook, whilst one fair-haired waitress, dissolved in tears, was apparently giving them a great deal of irrelevant and confused information.

Chief Inspector Saunders had, I understood, been already sent for; the constables, confronted with this extraordinary tragedy, were casting anxious glances towards the main entrance, whilst putting the conventional questions to the young waitress.

And in the alcove itself, raised from the floor of the room by a couple of carpeted steps, the cause of all this commotion, all this anxiety, and all these tears, sat huddled up on a chair, with arms lying straight across the marble-topped table, on which the usual paraphernalia of afternoon tea still lay scattered about. The upper part of the body, limp, backboneless, and awry, half propped up against the wall, half falling back upon the outstretched arms, told quite plainly its weird tale of death.

Before my dear lady and I had time to ask any questions, Saunders arrived in a taxicab. He was accompanied by the medical officer, Dr Townson, who at once busied himself with the dead man, whilst Saunders went up quickly to Lady Molly.

'The chief suggested sending for you,' he said quickly; 'he was phoning you when I left. There's a woman in this case, and we shall rely on you a good deal.'

'What has happened?' asked my dear lady, whose fine eyes were glowing with excitement at the mere suggestion of work.

'I have only a few stray particulars,' replied Saunders, 'but the chief witness is that yellow-haired girl over there. We'll find out what we can from her directly Dr Townson has given us his opinion.'

The medical officer, who had been kneeling beside the dead man, now rose and turned to Saunders. His face was very grave.

'The whole matter is simple enough, so far as I am concerned,' he said. 'The man has been killed by a terrific dose of morphia – administered, no doubt, in this cup of chocolate,' he added, pointing to a cup in which there still lingered the cold dregs of the thick beverage.

'But when did this occur?' asked Saunders, turning to the waitress.

'I can't say,' she replied, speaking with obvious nervousness. 'The gentleman came in very early with a lady, somewhere about four. They made straight for this alcove. The place was just beginning to fill, and the music had begun.'

'And where is the lady now?'

'She went off almost directly. She had ordered tea for herself and a cup of chocolate for the gentleman, also muffins and cakes. About five minutes afterwards, as I went past their table, I heard her say to him, "I am afraid I must go now, or Jay's will be closed, but I'll be back in less than half an hour. You'll wait for me, won't you?" '

'Did the gentleman seem all right then?'

'Oh, yes,' said the waitress. 'He had just begun to sip his chocolate, and merely said "S'long" as she gathered up her gloves and muff and then went out of the shop.'

'And she has not returned since?'

'No.'

'When did you first notice there was anything wrong with this gentleman?' asked Lady Molly.

'Well,' said the girl with some hesitation, 'I looked at him once or twice as I went up and down, for he certainly seemed to have fallen all of a heap. Of course, I thought that he had gone to sleep, and I spoke to the manageress about him, but she thought that I ought to leave him alone for a bit. Then we got very busy, and I paid no more attention to him, until about six o'clock, when most afternoon tea customers had gone, and we were beginning to get the tables ready for dinners. Then I certainly did think there was something wrong with the man. I called to the manageress, and we sent for the police.'

'And the lady who was with him at first, what was she like? Would you know her again?' queried Saunders.

'I don't know,' replied the girl; 'you see, I have to attend to such crowds of people of an afternoon, I can't notice each one. And she had on one of those enormous mushroom hats; no one could have seen her face – not more than her chin – unless they looked right under the hat.'

'Would you know the hat again?; asked Lady Molly.

'Yes – I think I should,' said the waitress. 'It was black velvet and had a lot of plumes. It was enormous,' she added, with a sigh of admiration and of longing for the monumental headgear.

During the girl's narrative one of the constables had searched the dead man's pockets. Among other items, he had found several letters addressed to Mark Culledon, Esq., some with an address in Lombard Street, others with one in Fitzjohn's Avenue, Hampstead. The initials M. C., which appeared both in the hat and on the silver mount of a lettercase belonging to the unfortunate gentleman, proved his identity beyond a doubt.

A house in Fitzjohn's Avenue does not, somehow, suggest a bachelor establishment. Even whilst Saunders and the other men were looking through the belongings of the deceased, Lady Molly had already thought of his family – children, perhaps a wife, a mother – who could tell?

What awful news to bring to an unsuspecting happy family, who might even now be expecting the return of father, husband, or son, at the very moment when he lay murdered in a public place, the victim of some hideous plot or feminine revenge!

As our amiable friends in Paris would say, it jumped to the eyes that there was a woman in the case – a woman who had worn a gargantuan hat for the obvious purpose of remaining unidentifiable when the question of the unfortunate victim's companion that afternoon came up for solution. And all these facts to put before an expectant wife or an anxious mother!

As, no doubt, you have already foreseen, Lady Molly took the difficult task on her own kind shoulders. She and I drove together to Lorbury House, Fitzjohn's Avenue, and on asking of the manservant who opened the door if his mistress were at home, we were told that Lady Irene Culledon was in the drawing-room.

Mine is not a story of sentiment, so I am not going to dwell on that interview, which was one of the most painful moments I recollect having lived through.

Lady Irene was young – not five-and-twenty, I should say – petite and frail-looking, but with a quiet dignity of manner which was most impressive. She was Irish, as you know, the daughter of the Earl of Athyville, and, it seems, had married Mr Mark Culledon in the teeth of strenuous opposition on the part of her family, which was as penniless as it was aristocratic, whilst Mr Culledon had great prospects and a splendid business, but possessed neither ancestors nor high connections. She had only been married six months, poor little soul, and from all accounts must have idolized her husband.

Lady Molly broke the news to her with infinite tact, but there it was! It was a terrific blow – wasn't it? – to deal to a young wife – now a widow; and there was so little that a stranger could say in these circumstances. Even my dear Lady's gentle voice, her persuasive eloquence, her kindly words, sounded empty and conventional in the face of such appalling grief.

II

Of course, everyone expected that the inquest would reveal something of the murdered man's inner life – would, in fact, allow the over-eager public to get a peep into Mr Mark Culledon's secret orchard, wherein walked a lady who wore abnormally large velvet hats, and who nourished in her heart one of those terrible grudges against a man which can only find satisfaction in crime.

Equally, of course, the inquest revealed nothing that the public did not already know. The young widow was extremely reticent on the subject of her late husband's life, and the servants had all been fresh arrivals when the young couple, just home from their honeymoon, organized their new household at Lorbury House.

There was an old aunt of the deceased – a Mrs Steinberg – who lived with the Culledons, but who at the present moment was very ill. Someone in the house – one of the younger servants, probably – very foolishly had told her every detail of the awful tragedy. With positively amazing strength, the invalid thereupon insisted on making a sworn statement, which she desired should be placed before the coroner's jury. She wished to bear solemn testimony to the integrity of her late nephew, Mark Culledon, in case the personality of the mysterious woman in the big hat suggested to evilly disposed minds any thoughts of scandal.

'Mark Culledon was the one nephew whom I loved,' she stated with solemn emphasis. 'I have shown my love for him by bequeathing to him the large fortune which I inherited from the late Mr Steinberg. Mark was the soul of honour, or I should have cut him out of my will as I did my other nephews and nieces. I was brought up in a Scotch home, and I hate all this modern fastness and smartness, which are only other words for what I call profligacy.'

Needless to say, the old lady's statement, solemn though it was, was of no use whatever for the elucidation of the mystery which surrounded the death of Mr Mark Culledon. But as Mrs Steinberg had talked of 'other nephews', whom she had cut out of her will in favour of the murdered man, the police directed inquiries in those various quarters.

Mr Mark Culledon certainly had several brothers and sisters, also cousins, who at different times – usually for some peccadillo or other – seemed to have incurred the wrath of the strait-laced old lady. But there did not appear to have been any ill-feeling in the family owing to this. Mrs Steinberg was sole mistress of her fortune. She might just as well have bequeathed it *in toto* to some hospital as to one particular nephew whom she favoured, and the various relations were glad, on the whole, that the money was going to remain in the family rather than be cast abroad.

The mystery surrounding the woman in the big hat deepened as the days went by. As you know, the longer the period of time which elapses between a crime and the identification of the criminal, the greater chance the latter has of remaining at large.

In spite of strenuous efforts and close questionings of everyone of the employees at Mathis', no one could give a very accurate description of the lady who had tea with the deceased on that fateful afternoon.

The first glimmer of light on the mysterious occurrence was thrown, about three weeks later, by a young woman named Katherine Harris, who had been parlourmaid at Lorbury House when first Mr and Lady Irene Culledon returned from their honeymoon.

I must tell you that Mrs Steinberg had died a few days after the inquest. The excitement had been too much for her enfeebled heart. Just before her death she had deposited £250 with her banker, which sum was to be paid over to any person giving information which would lead to the apprehension and conviction of the murderer of Mr Mark Culledon.

This offer had stimulated everyone's zeal, and, I presume, had aroused Katherine Harris to a realization of what had all the while been her obvious duty.

Lady Molly saw her in the chief's private office, and had much ado to disentangle the threads of the girl's confused narrative. But the main point of Harris's story was that a foreign lady had once called at Lorbury House, about a week after the master and mistress had returned from their honeymoon. Lady Irene was out at the time, and Mr Culledon saw the lady in his smoking-room.

'She was a very handsome lady,' explained Harris, 'and was beautifully dressed.'

'Did she wear a large hat?' asked the chief.

'I don't remember if it was particularly large,' replied the girl.

'But you remember what the lady was like?' suggested Lady Molly.

'Yes, pretty well. She was very, very tall, and very good-looking.'

'Would you know her again if you saw her?' rejoined my dear lady.

'Oh, yes; I think so,' was Katherine Harris's reply.

Unfortunately, beyond this assurance the girl could say nothing very definite. The foreign lady seems to have been closeted with Mr Culledon for about an hour, at the end of which time Lady Irene came home.

The butler being out that afternoon it was Harris who let her mistress in, and as the latter asked no questions, the girl did not volunteer the information that her master had a visitor. She went back to the servants' hall, but five minutes later the smoking-room bell rang, and she had to run up again. The foreign lady was then in the hall alone, and obviously waiting to be shown out. This Harris did, after which Mr Culledon came out of his room, and, in the girl's own graphic words, 'he went on dreadful'.

'I didn't know I 'ad done anything so very wrong,' she explained, 'but the master seemed quite furious, and said I wasn't a proper parlour-maid, or I'd have known that visitors must not be shown in straight away like that. I ought to have said that I didn't know if Mr Culledon was in; that I would go and see. Oh, he did go on at me!' continued Katherine Harris, volubly. 'And I suppose he complained to the mistress, for she gave me notice the next day.'

'And you have never seen the foreign lady since?' concluded Lady Molly.

'No; she never come while I was there.'

'By the way, how did you know she was foreign? Did she speak like a foreigner?'

'Oh, no,' replied the girl. 'She did not say much – only asked for Mr Culledon – but she looked French like.'

This unanswerable bit of logic concluded Katherine's statement. She was very anxious to know whether, if the foreign lady was hanged for murder, she herself would get the £250.

On Molly's assurance that she certainly would, she departed in apparent content.

III

'Well we are no nearer than we were before,' said the chief, with an impatient sigh, when the door had closed behind Katherine Harris.

'Don't you think so?' rejoined Lady Molly, blandly.

'Do you consider that what we have heard just now has helped us to discover who was the woman in the big hat?' retorted the chief, somewhat testily.

'Perhaps not,' replied my dear lady, with her sweet smile; 'but it may help us to discover who murdered Mr Culledon.'

With which enigmatical statement she effectually silenced the chief, and finally walked out of his office, followed by her faithful Mary.

Following Katherine Harris's indications, a description of the lady who was wanted in connection with the murder of Mr Culledon was very widely circulated, and within two days of the interview with the ex-parlour-maid another very momentous one took place in the same office.

Lady Molly was at work with the chief over some reports, whilst I was taking shorthand notes at a side desk, when a card was brought in by one of the men, and the next moment, without waiting either for permission to enter or to be more formally announced, a magnificent apparition literally sailed into the dust-covered little back office, filling it with an atmosphere of Parma violets and Russian leather.

I don't think that I had ever seen a more beautiful woman in my life. Tall, with a splendid figure and perfect carriage, she vaguely reminded me of the portraits one sees of the late Empress of Austria. This lady was, moreover, dressed to perfection, and wore a large hat adorned with a quantity of plumes.

The chief had instinctively risen to greet her, whilst Lady Molly, still and placid was eyeing her with a quizzical smile.

'You know who I am, sir,' began the visitor as soon as she had sunk gracefully into a chair; 'my name is on that card. My appearance, I understand, tallies exactly with that of a woman who is supposed to have murdered Mark Culledon.'

She said this so calmly, with such perfect self-possession, that I literally gasped. The chief, too, seemed to have been metaphorically lifted off his feet. He tried to mutter a reply.

'Oh, don't trouble yourself, sir!' she interrupted him, with a smile. 'My landlady, my servant, my friends have all read the description of the woman who murdered Mr Culledon. For the past twenty-four hours I have been watched by your police, therefore I come to you of my own accord, before they came to arrest me in my flat. I am not too soon, am I?' she asked, with that same cool indifference which was so startling, considering the subject of her conversation.

She spoke English with a scarcely perceptible foreign accent, but I quite understood what Katherine Harris had meant when she said that the lady looked 'French like'. She certainly did not look English, and when I caught sight of her name on the card, which the chief had handed to Lady Molly, I put her down at once as Viennese. Miss Elizabeth Lowenthal had all the charm, the grace, the elegance, which one associates with Austrian women more than with those of any other nation.

No wonder the chief found it difficult to tell her that, as a matter of fact, the police were about to apply for a warrant that very morning for her arrest on a charge of wilful murder.

'I know – I know' she said, seeming to divine his thoughts; 'but let me tell you at once, sir, that I did not murder Mark Culledon. He treated me shamefully, and I would willingly have made a scandal just to spite him; he had become so respectable and strait-laced. But between scandal and murder there is a wide gulf. Don't you think so, madam?' she added, turning for the first time towards Lady Molly.

'Undoubtedly,' replied my dear lady, with the same quizzical smile.

'A wide gulf which, no doubt, Miss Elizabeth Lowenthal will best be able to demonstrate to the magistrate tomorrow,' rejoined the chief, with official sternness of manner.

I thought that, for the space of a few seconds, the lady lost her self-assurance at this obvious suggestion – the bloom on her cheeks seemed to vanish, and two hard lines appeared between her fine eyes. But, frightened or not, she quickly recovered herself, and said quietly:

'Now, my dear sir, let us understand one another. I came here for that express purpose. I take it that you don't want your police to look ridiculous any more than I want a scandal. I don't want detectives to hang about round my flat, questioning my neighbours and my servants. They would soon find out that I did not murder Mark Culledon, of course; but the atmosphere of the police would hang round me, and I – I prefer Parma violets,' she added, raising a daintily perfumed handkerchief to her nose.

'Then you have come to make a statement?' asked the chief.

'Yes,' she replied; 'I'll tell you all I know. Mr Culledon was engaged to marry me; then he met the daughter of an earl, and thought he would like her better as a wife than a simple Miss Lowenthal. I suppose I should be considered an undesirable match for a young man who has a highly respectable and snobbish aunt, who would leave him all her money only on the condition that he made a suitable marriage. I have a voice, and I came over to England two years ago to study English, so that I might sing in oratorio at the Albert Hall. I met Mark on the Calais-Dover boat, when he was returning from a holiday abroad. He fell in love with me, and presently he asked me to be his wife. After some demur, I accepted him; we became engaged, but he told me that our engagement must remain a secret, for he had an old aunt from whom he had great expectations, and who might not approve of his marrying a foreign girl, who was without connections and a professional singer. From that moment I mistrusted him, nor was I very astonished when gradually his affection for me seemed to cool. Soon after he informed me quite callously that he had changed his mind, and was going to marry some swell English lady. I didn't care much, but I wanted to punish him by making a scandal, you understand. I went to his house just to worry him, and finally I decided to bring an action for breach of promise against him. It would have upset him, I know; no doubt his aunt would have cut him out of her will. That is all I wanted, but I did not care enough about him to murder him.'

Somehow her tale carried conviction. We were all of us obviously impressed. The chief alone looked visibly disturbed, and I could read what was going on in his mind.

'As you say, Miss Lowenthal,' he rejoined, 'the police would have found all this out within the next few hours. Once your connection with the murdered man was known to us, the record of your past and his becomes an easy one to peruse. No doubt, too,' he added insinuatingly, 'our men would soon have been placed in possession of the one undisputable proof of your complete innocence with regard to that fateful afternoon spent at Mathis' café.'

'What is that?' she queried blandly.

'An alibi.'

'You mean, where I was during the time that Mark was being murdered in a tea shop?'

'Yes,' said the chief.

'I was out for a walk,' she replied quietly.

'Shopping perhaps?'

'No.'

'You met someone who would remember the circumstances – or your servants could say at what time you came in?'

'No,' she repeated dryly; 'I met no one, for I took a brisk walk on Primrose Hill. My two servants could only say that I went out at three o'clock that afternoon and returned after five.'

There was silence in the little office for a moment or two. I could hear the scraping of the pen with which the chief was idly scribbling geometrical figures on his blotting pad.

Lady Molly was quite still. Her large, luminous eyes were fixed on the beautiful woman who had just told us her strange story, with its unaccountable sequel, its mystery which had deepened with the last phrase which she had uttered. Miss

Lowenthal, I felt sure, was conscious of her peril. I am not sufficiently a psychologist to know whether it wás guilt or merely fear which was distorting the handsome features now, hardening the face and causing the lips to tremble.

Lady Molly scribbled a few words on a scrap of paper, which she then passed over to the chief. Miss Lowenthal was making visible efforts to steady her nerves.

'That is all I have to tell you,' she said, in a voice which sounded dry and harsh. 'I think I will go home now.'

But she did not rise from her chair, and seemed to hesitate as if fearful lest permission to go were not granted her.

To her obvious astonishment – and, I must add, to my own – the chief immediately rose and said, quite urbanely:

'I thank you very much for the helpful information which you have given me. Of course, we may rely on your presence in town for the next few days, may we not?'

She seemed greatly relieved, and all at once resumed her former charm of manner and elegance of attitude. The beautiful face was lit up by a smile.

The chief was bowing to her in quite a foreign fashion, and in spite of her visible reassurance she eyed him very intently. Then she went up to Lady Molly and held out her hand.

My dear lady took it without an instant's hesitation. I, who knew that it was the few words hastily scribbled by Lady Molly which had dictated the chief's conduct with regard to Miss Lowenthal, was left wondering whether the woman I loved best in all the world had been shaking hands with a murderess.

IV

No doubt you will remember the sensation which was caused by the arrest of Miss Lowenthal, on a charge of having murdered Mr Mark Culledon, by administering morphia to him in a cup of chocolate at Mathis' café in Regent Street.

The beauty of the accused, her undeniable charm of manner, the hitherto blameless character of her life, all tended to make the public take violent sides either for or against her, and the usual budget of amateur correspondence, suggestions, recriminations and advice poured into the chief's office in titanic proportions.

I must say that, personally, all my sympathies went out to Miss Lowenthal. As I have said before, I am no psychologist, but I had seen her in the original interview at the office, and I could not get rid of an absolutely unreasoning certitude that the beautiful Viennese singer was innocent.

The magistrate's court was packed, as you may well imagine, on that first day of the inquiry; and, of course, sympathy with the accused went up to fever pitch when she staggered into the dock, beautiful still, despite the ravages caused by horror, anxiety, fear, in face of the deadly peril in which she stood.

The magistrate was most kind to her; her solicitor was unimpeachably assiduous; even our fellows, who had to give evidence against her, did no more than their duty, and were as lenient in their statements as possible.

Miss Lowenthal had been arrested in her flat by Danvers, accompanied by two constables. She had loudly protested her innocence all along, and did so still, pleading 'Not guilty' in a firm voice.

The great points in favour of the arrest were, firstly, the undoubted motive of disappointment and revenge against a faithless sweetheart, then the total inability to prove any kind of alibi, which, under the circumstances, certainly added to the appearance of guilt.

The question of where the fatal drug was obtained was more difficult to prove. It was stated that Mr Mark Culledon was director of several important companies, one of which carried on business as wholesale druggists.

Therefore it was argued that the accused, at different times and under some pretext or other, had obtained drugs from Mr Culledon himself. She had admitted to having visited the deceased at his office in the City, both before and after his marriage.

Miss Lowenthal listened to all this evidence against her with a hard, set face, as she did also to Katherine Harris's statement about her calling on Mr Culledon at Lorbury House, but she brightened up visibly when the various attendants at Mathis' café were placed in the box.

A very large hat belonging to the accused was shown to the witnesses, but, though the police upheld the theory that this was the headgear worn by the mysterious lady at the café on that fatal afternoon, the waitresses made distinctly contradictory statements with regard to it.

Whilst one girl swore that she recognized the very hat, another was equally positive that it was distinctly smaller than the one she recollected, and when the hat was placed on the head of Miss Lowenthal, three out of the four witnesses positively refused to identify her.

Most of these young women declared that though the accused, when wearing the big hat, looked as if she might have been the lady in question, yet there was a certain something about her which was different.

With that vagueness which is a usual and highly irritating characteristic of their class, the girls finally parried every question by refusing to swear positively either for or against the identity of Miss Lowenthal.

'There's something that's different about her somehow,' one of the waitresses asserted positively.

'What is it that's different?' asked the solicitor for the accused, pressing his point.

'I can't say,' was the perpetual, maddening reply.

Of course the poor young widow had to be dragged into the case, and here, I think, opinions and even expressions of sympathy were quite unanimous.

The whole tragedy had been inexpressibly painful to her, of course, and now it must have seemed doubly so. The scandal which had accumulated round her late husband's name must have added the poignancy of shame to that of grief. Mark Culledon had behaved as callously to the girl whom clearly he had married from interested, family motives, as he had to the one whom he had heartlessly cast aside.

Lady Irene, however, was most moderate in her statements. There was no doubt that she had known of her husband's previous entanglement with Miss Lowenthal, but apparently had not thought fit to make him accountable for the past. She did not know that Miss Lowenthal had threatened a breach of promise action against her husband.

Throughout her evidence, she spoke with absolute calm and dignity, and looked indeed a strange contrast, in her closely fitting tailor-made costume of black serge and tiny black toque, to the more brilliant woman who stood in the dock.

The two great points in favour of the accused were, firstly, the vagueness of the witnesses who were called to identify her, and, secondly, the fact that she had undoubtedly begun proceedings for breach of promise against the deceased. Judging by the latter's letters to her, she would have had a splendid case against him, which fact naturally dealt a severe blow to the theory as to motive for the murder.

On the whole, the magistrate felt that there was not a sufficiency of evidence against the accused to warrant his committing her for trial; he therefore discharged her, and amid loud applause from the public, Miss Lowenthal left the court a free woman.

Now, I know that the public did loudly, and, to my mind, very justly, blame the police for that arrest, which was denounced as being as cruel as it was unjustifiable. I felt as strongly as anybody on the subject, for I knew that the prosecution had been instituted in defiance of Lady Molly's express advice, and in distinct contradiction to the evidence which she had collected. When, therefore, the chief again asked my dear lady to renew her efforts in that mysterious case, it was small wonder that her enthusiasm did not respond to his anxiety. That she would do her duty was beyond a doubt, but she had very naturally lost her more fervent interest in the case.

The mysterious woman in the big hat was still the chief subject of leading articles in the papers, coupled with that of the ineptitude of the police who could not discover her. There were caricatures and picture post-cards in all the shop windows of a gigantic hat covering the whole figure of its wearer, only the feet and a very long and pointed chin protruding from beneath the enormous brim. Below was the device, 'Who is she? Ask the police?'

One day – it was the second since the discharge of Miss Lowenthal – my dear lady came into my room beaming. It was the first time I had seen her smile for more than a week, and already I had guessed what it was that had cheered her.

'Good news, Mary,' she said gaily. 'At last I've got the chief to let me have a free hand. Oh, dear! what a lot of argument it takes to extricate that man from the tangled meshes of red tape!'

'What are you going to do? I asked.

'Prove that my theory is right as to who murdered Mark Culledon,' she replied seriously; 'and as a preliminary we'll go and ask his servants at Lorbury House a few questions.'

It was then three o'clock in the afternoon. At Lady Molly's bidding, I dressed somewhat smartly, and together we went off in a taxi to Fitzjohn's Avenue.

Lady Molly had written a few words on one of her cards, urgently requesting an interview with Lady Irene Culledon. This she handed over to the man-servant who opened the door at Lorbury House. A few moments later we were sitting in the cosy boudoir. The young widow, high-bred and dignified in her tight-fitting black gown, sat opposite to us, her white hands folded demurely before her, her small head, with its very close coiffure, bent in closest attention towards Lady Molly.

'I most sincerely hope, Lady Irene,' began my dear lady, in her most gentle and persuasive voice, 'that you will look with all possible indulgence on my growing desire – shared, I may say, by all my superiors at Scotland Yard – to elucidate the mystery which still surrounds your late husband's death.'

Lady Molly paused, as if waiting for encouragement to proceed. The subject must have been extremely painful to the young widow; nevertheless she responded quite gently:

'I can understand that the police wish to do their duty in the matter; as for me, I have done all, I think, that could be expected of me. I am not made of iron, and after that day in the police court–'

She checked herself, as if afraid of having betrayed more emotion than was consistent with good breeding, and concluded more calmly:

'I cannot do any more.'

'I fully appreciate your feelings in the matter,' said Lady

Molly, 'but you would not mind helping me – would you – in a passive way, if you could, by some simple means, further the cause of justice?'

'What is it you want me to do?' asked Lady Irene.

'Only to allow me to ring for two of your maids and to ask them a few questions. I promise you that they shall not be of such a nature as to cause you the slightest pain.'

For a moment I thought that the young widow hesitated, then, without a word, she rose and rang the bell.

'Which of my servants did you wish to see?' she asked, turning to my dear lady as soon as the butler entered in answer to the bell.

'Your own maid and your parlour-maid, if I may,' replied Lady Molly.

Lady Irene gave the necessary orders, and we all sat expectant and silent until, a minute or two later, two girls entered the room. One wore a cap and apron, the other, in neat black dress and dainty lace collar, was obviously the lady's maid.

'This lady,' said their mistress, addressing the two girls, 'wishes to ask you a few questions. She is a representative of the police, so you had better do your best to satisfy her with your answers.'

'Oh!' rejoined Lady Molly pleasantly – choosing not to notice the tone of acerbity with which the young widow had spoken, nor the unmistakable barrier of hostility and reserve which her words had immediately raised between the young servants and the 'representative of the police' – 'what I am going to ask these two young ladies is neither very difficult nor very unpleasant. I merely want their kind help in a little comedy which will have to be played this evening, in order to test the accuracy of certain statements made by one of the waitresses at Mathis' tea shop with regard to the terrible tragedy which has darkened this house. You will do that much, will you not?' she added, speaking directly to the maids.

No one can be so winning or so persuasive as my dear lady. In a moment I saw the girls' hostility melting before the sunshine of Lady Molly's smile.

'We'll do what we can, ma'am,' said the maid.

'That's a brave, good girl!' replied my lady. 'You must

know that the chief waitress at Mathis' has, this very morning, identified the woman in the big hat who, we all believe, murdered your late master. Yes!' she continued, in response to a gasp of astonishment which seemed to go round the room like a wave, 'the girl seems quite positive, both as regards the hat and the woman who wore it. But, of course, one cannot allow a human life to be sworn away without bringing every possible proof to bear on such a statement, and I am sure that everyone in this house will understand that we don't want to introduce strangers more than we can help into this sad affair, which already has been bruited abroad too much.'

She paused a moment; then, as neither Lady Irene nor the maids made any comment, she continued:

'My superiors at Scotland yard think it their duty to try and confuse the witness as much as possible in her act of identification. They desire that a certain number of ladies wearing abnormally large hats should parade before the waitress. Among them will be, of course, the one whom the girl has already identified as being the mysterious person who had tea with Mr Culledon at Mathis' that afternoon.

'My superiors can then satisfy themselves whether the waitress is or is not so sure of her statement that she invariably picks out again and again one particular individual amongst a number of others or not.'

'Surely,' interrupted Lady Irene, dryly, 'you and your superiors do not expect my servants to help in such a farce?'

'We don't look upon such a proceeding as a farce, Lady Irene,' rejoined Lady Molly, gently. 'It is often resorted to in the interests of an accused person, and we certainly would ask the co-operation of your household.'

'I don't see what they can do.'

But the two girls did not seem unwilling. The idea appealed to them, I felt sure, it suggested an exciting episode, and gave promise of variety in their monotonous lives.

'I am sure both these young ladies possess fine big hats,' continued Lady Molly with an encouraging smile.

'I should not allow them to wear ridiculous headgear,' retorted Lady Irene, sternly.

'I have the one your ladyship wouldn't wear and threw

away,' interposed the young parlour-maid. 'I put it together again with the scraps I found in the dusthole.'

There was just one instant of absolute silence, one of those magnetic moments when Fate seems to have dropped the spool on which she was spinning the threads of a life, and is just stooping in order to pick it up.

Lady Irene raised a black-bordered handkerchief to her lips, then said quietly:

'I don't know what you mean, Mary. I never wear big hats.'

'No, my lady,' here interposed the lady's maid; 'but Mary means the one you ordered at Sanchia's and only wore the once – the day you went to that concert.'

'Which day was that?'; asked Lady Molly, blandly.

'Oh! I couldn't forget that day,' ejaculated the maid; 'her ladyship came home from the concert – I had undressed her, and she told me that she would never wear her big hat again – it was too heavy. That same day Mr Culledon was murdered.'

'That hat would answer our purpose very well,' said Lady Molly, quite calmly. 'Perhaps Mary will go and fetch it, and you had better go and help her put it on.'

The two girls went out of the room without another word, and there were we three women left facing one another, with that awful secret, only half-revealed, hovering in the air like an intangible spectre.

'What are you going to do, Lady Irene?' asked Lady Molly, after a moment's pause, during which I literally could hear my own heart beating, whilst I watched the rigid figure of the widow in deep black crepe, her face set and white, her eyes fixed steadily on Lady Molly.

'You can't prove it!' she said defiantly.

'I think we can,' rejoined Lady Molly, simply; 'at any rate, I mean to try. I have two of the waitresses from Mathis' outside in a cab, and I have already spoken to the attendant who served you at Sanchia's, an obscure milliner in a back street near Portland Road. We know that you were at great pains there to order a hat of certain dimensions and to your own minute description; it was a copy of one you had once seen Miss Lowenthal wear when you met her at your late husband's office. We can prove that meeting, too. Then we have your maid's testimony that you wore that same hat once, and once only, the day, presumably, that you went out to a concert – a statement which you will find it difficult to substantiate – and also the day on which your husband was murdered.'

'Bah! the public will laugh at you!' retorted Lady Irene, still defiantly. 'You would not dare to formulate so monstrous a charge!'

'It will not seem monstrous when justice has weighed in the balance the facts which we can prove. Let me tell you a few of these, the result of careful investigation. There is the fact that you knew of Mr Culledon's entanglement with Miss Elizabeth Lowenthal, and did your best to keep it from old Mrs Steinberg's knowledge, realizing that any scandal round her favourite nephew would result in the old lady cutting him – and therefore you – out of her will. You dismissed a parlourmaid for the sole reason that she had been present when Miss Lowenthal was shown into Mr Culledon's study. There is the fact that Mrs Steinberg had so worded her will that, in the event of her nephew dying before her, her fortune would devolve on you; the fact that, with Miss Lowenthal's action for breach of promise against your husband, your last hope of keeping the scandal from the old lady's ears had effectually vanished. You saw the fortune eluding your grasp; you feared Mrs Steinberg would alter her will. Had you found the means, and had you dared, would you not rather have killed the old lady? But discovery would have been certain. The other crime was bolder and surer. You have inherited the old lady's millions, for she never knew of her nephew's earlier peccadilloes.

'All this we can state and prove, and the history of the hat, bought and worn one day only, that same memorable day, and then thrown away.'

A loud laugh interrupted her – a laugh that froze my very marrow.

'There is one fact you have forgotten, my lady of Scotland Yard,' came in sharp, strident accents from the black-robed figure, which seemed to have become strangely spectral in the fast gathering gloom which had been enveloping the luxurious little boudoir. 'Don't omit to mention the fact that the accused took the law into her own hands.'

And before my dear lady and I could rush to prevent her, Lady Irene Culledon had conveyed something – we dared not think what – to her mouth.

'Find Danvers quickly, Mary!' said Lady Molly, calmly. 'You'll find him outside. Bring a doctor back with you.'

Even as she spoke Lady Irene, with a cry of agony, fell senseless in my dear lady's arms.

The doctor, I may tell you, came too late. The unfortunate woman evidently had a good knowledge of poisons. She had been determined not to fail; in case of discovery, she was ready and able to mete out justice to herself.

I don't think the public ever knew the real truth about the woman in the big hat. Interest in her went the way of all things. Yet my dear lady had been right from beginning to end. With unerring precision she had placed her dainty finger on the real motive and the real perpetrator of the crime – the ambitious woman who had married solely for money, and meant to have that money even at the cost of one of the most dastardly murders that have ever darkened the criminal annals of this country.

I asked Lady Molly what it was that first made her think of Lady Irene as the possible murderess. No one else for a moment had thought her guilty.

'The big hat,' replied my dear lady with a smile. 'Had the mysterious woman at Mathis' been tall, the waitresses would not, one and all, have been struck by the abnormal size of the hat. The wearer must have been petite, hence the reason that under a wide brim only the chin would be visible. I at once sought for a small woman. Our fellows did not think of that, because they are men.'

You see how simple it all was!

INSPECTOR GHOTE AND THE MIRACLE BABY

H. R. F. Keating

WHAT has Santa Claus got in store for me, Inspector Ghote said to himself, bleakly echoing the current cheerful Bombay newspaper advertisements, as he waited to enter the office of Deputy Superintendent Naik that morning of December 25th.

Whatever the DSP had lined up for him, Ghote knew it was going to be nasty. Ever since he had recently declined to turn up for 'voluntary' hockey, DSP Naik had viewed him with sad-eyed disapproval. But what exact form would his displeasure take?

Almost certainly it would have something to do with the big Navy Week parade that afternoon, the chief preoccupation at the moment of most of the ever-excitable and drama-loving Bombayites. Probably he would be ordered out into the crowds watching the Fire Power demonstration in the bay, ordered to come back with a beltful of pickpocketing arrests.

'Come,' the DSP's voice barked out.

Ghote went in and stood squaring his bony shoulders in front of the papers-strewn desk.

'Ah, Ghote, yes. Tulsi Pipe Road for you. Up at the north end. Going to be big trouble there. Rioting. Intercommunity outrages even.'

Ghote's heart sank even deeper than he had expected. Tulsi Pipe Road was a two-kilometres-long thoroughfare that shot straight up from the racecourse into the heart of a densely crowded mill district where badly paid Hindus, Muslims in hundreds and Goans by the thousand, all lived in prickling closeness, either in great areas of tumbledown hutments or in high tottering chawls, floor upon floor of massed humanity. Trouble between the religious communities there meant hell, no less.

'Yes, DSP?' he said, striving not to sound appalled.

'We are having a virgin birth business, Inspector.'

'Virgin birth, DSP sahib?'

'Come, man, you must have come across such cases.'

'I am sorry, DSP' Ghote said, feeling obliged to be true to hard-won scientific principles. 'I am unable to believe in virgin birth.'

The DSP's round face suffused with instant wrath.

'Of course I am not asking you to believe in virgin birth, man! It is not you who are to believe: it is all those Christians in the Goan community who are believing it about a baby born two days ago. It is the time of year, of course. These affairs are always coming at Christmas. I have dealt with half a dozen in my day.'

'Yes, DSP,' Ghote said, contriving to hit on the right note of awe.

'Yes. And there is only one way to deal with it. Get hold of the girl and find out the name of the man. Do that pretty damn quick and the whole affair drops away to nothing, like monsoon water down a drain.'

'Yes, DSP.'

'Well, what are you waiting for man? Hop it!'

'Name and address of the girl in question, DSP sahib.'

The DSP's face darkened once more. He padded furiously over the jumble of papers on his desk top. And at last he found the chit he wanted.

'There you are, man. And also you will find there the name of the Head Constable who first reported the matter. See him straightaway. You have got a good man there, active, quick on his feet, sharp. If he could not make that girl talk, you will be having a first-class damn job, Inspector.'

Ghote located Head Constable Mudholkar one hour later at the local chowkey where he was stationed. The Head Constable confirmed at once the blossoming dislike for a sharp bully that Ghote had been harbouring ever since DSP Naik had praised the fellow. And, what was worse, the chap turned out to be very like the DSP in looks as well. He had the same round type of face, the same puffy-looking lips, even a similar soft blur of moustache. But the Head Constable's appearance was nevertheless a travesty of the DSP's. His face was, simply, slewed.

To Ghote's prejudiced eyes, at the first moment of their encounter, the man's features seemed grotesquely distorted, as if in some distant time some god had taken one of the Head Constable's ancestors and had wrenched his whole head sideways between two omnipotent god-hands.

But, as the fellow supplied him with the details of the affair, Ghote forced himself to regard him with an open mind, and he then had to admit that the facial twist which had seemed so pronounced was in fact no more than a drooping corner of the mouth and of one ear being oddly longer than the other.

Ghote had to admit, too, that the chap was efficient. He had all the circumstances of the affair at his fingertips. The girl, named D'Mello, now in a hospital for her own safety, had been rigorously questioned both before and after the birth, but she had steadfastly denied that she had ever been with any man. She was indeed not the sort, the sole daughter of a Goan railway waiter on the Madras Express, a quiet girl, well brought up though her parents were poor enough; she attended Mass regularly with her mother, and the whole family kept themselves to themselves.

'But with those Christians you can never tell,' Head Constable Mudholkar concluded.

Ghote felt inwardly inclined to agree. Fervid religion had always made him shrink inwardly, whether it was a Hindu holy man spending twenty years silent and standing upright or whether it was the Catholics, always caressing lifeless statues in their churches till glass protection had to be installed, and even then they still stroked the thick panes. Either manifestation rendered him uneasy.

That was the real reason, he now acknowledged to himself, why he did not want to go and see Miss D'Mello in the hospital where she would be surrounded by nuns amid all the trappings of an alien religion, surrounded with all the panoply of a newly found goddess.

Yet go and see the girl he must.

But first he permitted himself to do every other thing that might possibly be necessary to the case. He visited Mrs D'Mello, and by dint of patient wheedling, and a little forced toughness, confirmed from her the names of the only two men that Head Constable Mudholkar – who certainly proved to know inside-out the particular chawl where the D'Mellos lived – had suggested as possible fathers. They were both young men – a Goan, Charlie Lobo, and a Sikh, Kuldip Singh.

The Lobo family lived one floor below the D'Mellos. But that one flight of dirt-spattered stairs, bringing them just that much nearer the courtyard tap that served the whole crazily leaning chawl, represented a whole layer higher in social status. And Mrs Lobo, a huge, tightly fat woman in a brightly flowered western-style dress, had decided views about the unexpected fame that had come to the people upstairs.

'Has my Charlie been going with that girl?' she repeated after Ghote had managed to put the question, suitably wrapped up, to the boy. 'No, he has not. Charlie, tell the man you hate and despise trash like that.'

'Oh, Mum,' said Charlie, a teenage wisp of a figure suffocating in a necktie beside his balloon-hard mother.

'Tell the man, Charlie.'

And obediently Charlie muttered something that satisfied his passion-filled parent. Ghote put a few more questions for form's sake, but he realized that only by getting hold of the boy on his own was he going to get any worthwhile answers. Yet it turned out that he did not have to employ any cunning. Charlie proved to have a strain of sharp slyness of his own, and hardly had Ghote climbed the stairs to the floor above the D'Mellos where Kuldip Singh lived when he heard a whispered call from the shadow-filled darkness below.

'Mum's got her head over the stove,' Charlie said. 'She don't know I slipped out.'

'There is something you have to tell me?' Ghote said, acting the indulgent uncle. 'You are in trouble – that's it, isn't it?'

'My only trouble is Mum,' the boy replied. 'Listen, mister,

I had to tell you. I love Miss D'Mello – yes, I love her. She's the most wonderful girl ever was.'

'And you want to marry her, and because you went too far before – '

'No, no, no. She's far and away too good for me. Mister, I've never even said "Good morning" to her in the two years we've lived here. But I love her, mister, and I'm not going to have Mum make me say different.'

Watching him slip cunningly back home, Ghote made his mental notes and then turned to tackle Kuldip Singh, his last comparatively easy task before the looming interview at the nun-ridden hospital he knew he must have.

Kuldip Singh, as Ghote had heard from Head Constable Mudholkar, was different from his neighbours. He lived in this teeming area from choice not necessity. Officially a student, he spent all his time in a series of antisocial activities – protesting, writing manifestos, drinking. He seemed an ideal candidate for the unknown and elusive father.

Ghote's suspicions were at once heightened when the young Sikh opened his door. The boy, though old enough to have a beard, lacked this status symbol. Equally he had discarded the obligatory turban of his religion. But all the Sikh bounce was there, as Ghote discovered when he identified himself.

'Policewallah, is it? Then I want nothing at all to do with you. Me and the police are enemies, bhai. Natural enemies.'

'Irrespective of such considerations,' Ghote said stiffly, 'it is my duty to put to you certain questions concerning one Miss D'Mello.'

The young Sikh burst into a roar of laughter.

'The miracle girl, is it?' he said. 'Plenty of trouble for policemen there, I promise you. Top-level rioting coming from that business. The fellow who fathered that baby did us a lot of good.'

Ghote plugged away a good while longer – the hospital nuns awaited – but for all his efforts he learned no more than he had in that first brief exchange. And in the end he still had to go and meet his doom.

Just what he had expected at the hospital he never quite formulated to himself. What he did find was certainly almost the exact opposite of his fears. A calm reigned. White-habited nuns, mostly Indian but with a few Europeans, flitted silently to and fro or talked quietly to the patients whom Ghote glimpsed lying on beds in long wards. Above them swung frail but bright paper chains in honour of the feast day, and these were all the excitement there was.

The small separate ward in which Miss D'Mello lay in a broad bed all alone was no different. Except that the girl was isolated, she seemed to be treated in just the same way as the other new mothers in the big maternity ward that Ghote had been led through on his way in. In the face of such matter-of-factness he felt hollowly cheated.

Suddenly, too, to his own utter surprise he found, looking down at the big calm-after-storm eyes of the Goan girl, that he wanted the story she was about to tell him to be true. Part of him knew that, if it were so, or if it was widely believed to be so, appalling disorders could result from the feverish religious excitement that was bound to mount day by day. But another part of him now simply wanted a miracle to have happened.

He began, quietly and almost diffidently, to put his questions. Miss D'Mello would hardly answer at all, but such syllables as she did whisper were of blank inability to name anyone as the father of her child. After a while Ghote brought himself, with a distinct effort of will, to change his tactics. He banged out the hard line. Miss D'Mello went quietly and totally mute.

Then Ghote slipped in, with adroit suddenness, the name of Charlie Lobo. He got only a small puzzled frown.

Then, in an effort to make sure that her silence was not a silence of fear, he presented, with equal suddenness, the name of Kuldip Singh. If the care-for-nothing young Sikh had forced this timid creature, this might be the way to get an admission. But instead there came something approaching a laugh.

'That Kuldip is a funny fellow,' the girl said, with an out-of-place and unexpected offhandedness.

Ghote almost gave up. But at that moment a nun nurse appeared carrying in her arms a small, long, white-wrapped, minutely crying bundle – the baby.

While she handed the hungry scrap to its mother Ghote stood and watched. Perhaps holding the child she would -?

He looked down at the scene on the broad bed, awaiting his moment again. The girl fiercely held the tiny agitated thing to her breast and in a moment or two quiet came, the tiny head applied to the life-giving nipple. How human the child looked already, Ghote thought. How much a man at two days old. The round skull, almost bald, as it might become again toward the end of its span. The frown on the forehead that would last a lifetime, the tiny, perfectly formed, plainly asymmetrical ears –

And then Ghote knew that there had not been any miracle. It was as he had surmised, but with different circumstances. Miss D'Mello was indeed too frightened to talk. No wonder, when the local bully, Head Constable Mudholkar with his slewed head and its one ear so characteristically longer than the other, was the man who had forced himself on her.

A deep smothering of disappointment floated down on Ghote. So it had been nothing miraculous after all. Just a sad case, to be cleared up painfully. He stared down at the bed.

The tiny boy suckled energetically. And with a topsy-turvy welling up of rose-pink pleasure, Ghote saw that there had after all been a miracle. The daily, hourly, every-minute miracle of a new life, of a new flicker of hope in the tired world.

THE EVIDENCE OF THE ALTAR-BOY

Georges Simenon

A fine cold rain was falling. The night was very dark; only at the far end of the street, near the barracks from which, at half past five, there had come the sound of bugle calls and the noise of horses being taken to be watered, was there a faint light shining in someone's window – an early riser, or an invalid who had lain awake all night.

The rest of the street was asleep. It was a broad, quiet, newish street, with almost identical one- or two-stored houses such as are to be seen in the suburbs of most big provincial towns.

The whole district was new, devoid of mystery, inhabited by quite unassuming people, clerks and commercial travellers, retired men and peaceful widows.

Maigret, with his overcoat collar turned up, was huddling in the angle of a carriage gateway, that of the boys' school; he was waiting, watch in hand, and smoking his pipe.

At a quarter to six exactly, bells rang out from the parish church behind him, and he knew that, as the boy had said, it was the 'first stroke' for six o'clock Mass.

The sound of the bells was still vibrating in the damp air when he heard, or rather guessed at, the shrill clamour of an alarm clock. This lasted only a few seconds. The boy must already have stretched a hand out of his warm bed and groped in the darkness for the safety-catch that would silence the clock. A few minutes later, the attic window on the second floor lit up.

It all happened exactly as the boy had said. He must have risen noiselessly, before anyone else, in the sleeping house. Now he must be picking up his clothes, his socks, washing his face and hands and combing his hair. As for his shoes, he had declared:

'I carry them downstairs and put them on when I get to the last step, so as not to wake up my parents.'

This had happened every day, winter and summer, for nearly two years, ever since Justin had first begun to serve at Mass at the hospital.

He had asserted, furthermore: 'The hospital clock always strikes three or four minutes later than the parish church clock.'

And this had proved to be the case. The inspectors of the Flying Squad to which Maigret had been seconded for the past few months had shrugged their shoulders over these tiresome details about first bells and second bells.

Was it because Maigret had been an altar-boy himself for a long time that he had not dismissed the story with a smile?

The bells of the parish church rang first, at a quarter to six. Then Justin's alarm clock went off, in the attic where the boy slept. Then a few moments later came the shriller, more silvery sound of the hospital chapel bells, like those of a convent.

He still had his watch in his hand. The boy took barely more than four minutes to dress. Then the light went out. He must be groping his way down the stairs, anxious not to waken his parents, then sitting down on the bottom step to put on his shoes, and taking down his coat and cap from the bamboo coat-rack on the right in the passage.

The door opened. The boy closed it again without making a sound, looked up and down the street anxiously and then saw the Superintendent's burly figure coming up to him.

'I was afraid you might not be there.'

And he started walking fast. He was a thin, fair-haired little twelve-year-old with an obstinate look about him.

'You want me to do just what I usually do, don't you? I always walk fast, for one thing because I've worked out to the minute how long it takes, and for another, because in winter, when it's dark, I'm frightened. In a month it'll be getting light by this time in the morning.'

He took the first turning on the right into another quiet, somewhat shorter street, which led on to an open square planted with elms and crossed diagonally by tramlines.

And Maigret noted tiny details that reminded him of his own childhood. He noticed, for one thing, that the boy did not walk closely to the houses, probably because he was afraid of seeing someone suddenly emerge from a dark doorway. Then, that when he crossed the square he avoided the trees in the same way, because a man might have been hiding behind them.

He was a brave boy, really, since for two whole winters, in all weathers, sometimes in thick fog or in the almost total darkness of a moonless night, he had made the same journey every morning all alone.

'When we get to the middle of the Rue Sainte-Catherine you'll hear the second bell for Mass from the parish church . . .'

'At what time does the first tram pass?'

'At six o'clock. I've only seen it two or three times, when I was late . . . once because my alarm clock hadn't rung, another time because I'd fallen asleep again. That's why I jump out of bed as soon as it rings.'

A pale little face in the rainy night, with eyes that still retained something of the fixed stare of a sleepwalker, and a thoughtful expression with just a slight tinge of anxiety.

'I shan't go on serving at Mass. It's because you insisted that I've come today . . .'

They turned left down the Rue Sainte-Catherine, where, as in all the streets in this district, there was a lamp every fifty metres, each of them shedding a pool of light; and the child unconsciously quickened his pace each time he left the reassuring zone of brightness.

The noises from the barracks could still be heard in the distance. A few windows lit up. Footsteps sounded in a side street; probably a workman going to his job.

'When you got to the corner of the street, did you see nothing?'

This was the trickiest point, for the Rue Sainte-Catherine was very straight and empty, with its rectilinear pavements and its street lamps at regular intervals, leaving so little shadow between them that one could not have failed to see a couple of men quarrelling even at a hundred metres' distance.

'Perhaps I wasn't looking in front of me . . . I was talking to myself, I remember . . . I often do talk to myself in a whisper, when I'm going along there in the morning . . . I wanted to ask mother something when I got home and I was repeating to myself what I was going to say to her . . .'

'What did you want to say to her?'

'I've wanted a bike for ever such a long time . . . I've already saved up three hundred francs out of my church money.'

Was it just an impression? It seemed to Maigret that the boy was keeping further away from the houses. He even stepped off the pavement, and returned to it a little further on.

'It was here . . . Look . . . There's the second bell ringing for Mass at the parish church.'

And Maigret endeavoured, in all seriousness, to enter into the world which was the child's world every morning.

'I must have looked up suddenly . . . You know, like when you're running without looking where you're going and find yourself in front of a wall . . . It was just here.'

He pointed to the line on the pavement dividing the darkness from the lamplight, where the drizzle formed a luminous haze.

'First I saw that there was a man lying down and he looked so big that I could have sworn he took up the whole width of the pavement.'

That was impossible, for the pavement was at least two and a half metres across.

'I don't know what I did exactly . . . I must have jumped aside . . . I didn't run away immediately, for I saw the knife stuck in his chest, with a big handle made of brown horn. I noticed it because my uncle Henri has a knife just like it and he told me it was made out of a stag's horn. I'm certain the man was dead . . .'

'Why?'

'I don't know . . . He looked like a corpse.'

'Were his eyes shut?'

'I didn't notice his eyes . . . I don't know . . . But I had the feeling he was dead . . . It all happened very quickly, as I told you yesterday in your office . . . They made me repeat the same thing so many times yesterday that I'm all muddled . . . Specially when I feel people don't believe me . . .'

'And the other man?'

'When I looked up I saw that there was somebody a little further on, five metres away maybe, a man with very pale eyes who looked at me for a moment and then started running. It was the murderer . . .'

'How do you know that?'

'Because he ran off as fast as he could.'

'In which direction?'

'Right over there . . .'

'Towards the barracks?'

'Yes . . .'

It was a fact that Justin had been interrogated at least ten times the previous day. Before Maigret appeared in the office the detectives had even made a sort of game of it. His story had never varied in a single detail.

'And what did you do?'

'I started running too . . . It's hard to explain . . . I think it was when I saw the man running away that I got frightened . . . And then I ran as hard as I could . . .'

'In the opposite direction?'

'Yes.'

'Did you not think of calling for help?'

'No . . . I was too frightened . . . I was specially afraid my legs might give way, for I could scarcely feel them . . . I turned right-about as far as the Place du Congrès . . . I took the other street, that leads to the hospital too after making a bend.'

'Let's go on.'

More bells, the shrill-toned bells of the chapel. After walking some fifty metres they reached a crossroads, on the left of which were the walls of the barracks, pierced with loopholes, and on the right a huge gateway dimly lit and surmounted by a clock-face of greenish glass.

It was three minutes to six.

'I'm a minute late . . . Yesterday I was on time in spite of it all, because I ran . . .'

There was a heavy knocker on the solid oak door; the child

lifted it, and the noise reverberated through the porch. A porter in slippers opened the door, let Justin go in but barred the way to Maigret, looking at him suspiciously.

'What is it?'

'Police.'

'Let's see your card.'

Hospital smells were perceptible as soon as they entered the porch. They went on through a second door into a huge courtyard surrounded by various hospital buildings. In the distance could be glimpsed the white head-dresses of nuns on their way to the chapel.

'Why didn't you say anything to the porter yesterday?'

'I don't know . . . I was in a hurry to get there . . .'

Maigret could understand that. The haven was not the official entrance with its crabbed, mistrustful porter, nor the unwelcoming courtyard through which stretchers were being carried in silence; it was the warm vestry near the chapel, where a nun was lighting candles on the altar.

'Are you coming in with me?'

'Yes.'

Justin looked vexed, or rather shocked, probably at the thought that this policeman, who might be an unbeliever, was going to enter into his hallowed world. And this, too, explained to Maigret why every morning the child had the courage to get up so early and overcome his fears.

The chapel had a warm and intimate atmosphere. Patients in the blue-grey hospital uniform, some with bandaged heads, some with crutches or with their arms in slings, were already sitting in the pews of the nave. Up in the gallery the nuns formed a flock of identical figures, and all their white cornets bowed simultaneously in pious worship.

'Follow me.'

They went up a few steps, passing close to the altar where candles were already burning. To the right was a vestry panelled in dark wood, where a tall gaunt priest was putting on his vestments, while a surplice edged with fine lace lay ready for the altar-boy. A nun was busy filling the holy vessels.

It was here that, on the previous day, Justin had come to a

halt at last, panting and weak-kneed. It was here that he had shouted: 'A man's been killed in the Rue Sainte-Catherine!'

A small clock set in the wainscot pointed to six o'clock exactly. Bells were ringing again, sounding fainter here than outside. Justin told the nun who was helping him on with his surplice: 'This is the Police Superintendent . . .'

And Maigret stood waiting while the child went in, ahead of the chaplain, the skirts of his red cassock flapping as he hurried towards the altar steps.

The vestry nun had said: 'Justin is a good little boy, who's very devout and who's never lied to us . . . Occasionally he's failed to come and serve at Mass . . . He might have pretended he'd been ill . . . Well, he never did; he always admitted frankly that he'd not had the courage to get up because it was too cold, or because he'd had a nightmare during the night and was feeling too tired . . .'

And the chaplain, after saying Mass, had gazed at the Superintendent with the clear eyes of a saint in a stained glass window: 'Why should the child have invented such a tale?'

Maigret knew, now, what had gone on in the hospital chapel on the previous morning. Justin, his teeth chattering, at the end of his tether, had been in a state of hysterics. The service could not be delayed; the vestry nun had informed the Sister Superior and had herself served at Mass in the place of the child, who was meanwhile being attended to in the vestry.

Ten minutes later, the Sister Superior had thought of informing the police. She had gone out through the chapel, and everyone had realized that something was happening.

At the local police station the sergeant on duty had failed to understand.

'What's that? . . . The Sister Superior? . . . Superior to what?'

And she had told him, in the hushed tone they use in convents, that there had been a crime in the Rue Sainte-Catherine; and the police had found nothing, no victim, and, needless to say, no murderer . . .

Justin had gone to school at half past eight, just as usual, as though nothing had happened; and it was in his classroom that

Inspector Besson, a strapping little fellow who looked like a boxer and who liked to act tough, had picked him up at 9.30 as soon as the Flying Squad had got the report.

Poor kid! For two whole hours, in a dreary office that reeked of tobacco fumes and the smoke from a stove that wouldn't draw, he had been interrogated not as a witness but as a suspect.

Three inspectors in turn, Besson, Thiberge and Vallin, had tried to catch him out, to make him contradict himself.

To make matters worse his mother had come too. She sat in the waiting-room, weeping and snivelling and telling everybody: 'We're decent people and we've never had anything to do with the police.'

Maigret, who had worked late the previous evening on a case of drug-smuggling, had not reached his office until eleven o'clock.

'What's happening?' he had asked when he saw the child standing there, dry-eyed but as stiffly defiant as a little fighting-cock.

'A kid who's been having us on . . . He claims to have seen a dead body in the street and a murderer who ran away when he got near. But a tram passed along the same street four minutes later and the driver saw nothing . . . It's a quiet street, and nobody heard anything . . . And finally when the police were called, a quarter of an hour later, by some nun or other, there was absolutely nothing to be seen on the pavement, not the slightest trace of a bloodstain . . .'

'Come along into my office, boy.'

And Maigret was the first of them, that day, not to address Justin by the familiar *tu*, the first to treat him not as a fanciful or malicious urchin but as a small man.

He had listened to the boy's story simply and quietly, without interrupting or taking any notes.

'Shall you go on serving at Mass in the hospital?'

'No. I don't want to go back. I'm too frightened.'

And yet it meant a great sacrifice for him. Not only was he a devout child, deeply responsive to the poetry of that early Mass in the warm and somewhat mysterious atmosphere of the chapel; but in addition, he was paid for his services – not much, but enough to enable him to get together a little nest-egg. And he so badly wanted a bicycle which his parents could not afford to buy for him!

'I should like you to go just once more, tomorrow morning.'

'I shan't dare.'

'I'll go along with you . . . I'll wait for you in front of your home. You must behave exactly as you always do.'

This was what had been happening, and Maigret, at seven in the morning, was now standing alone outside the door of the hospital, in a district which, on the previous day, he had known only from having been through it by car or in a tram.

An icy drizzle was still falling from the sky which was now paler, and it clung to the Superintendent's shoulders; he sneezed twice. A few pedestrians hurried past, their coat collars turned up and their hands in their pockets; butchers and grocers had begun taking down the shutters of their shops.

It was the quietest, most ordinary district imaginable. At a pinch one might picture a quarrel between two men, two drunks for instance, at five minutes to six on the pavement of the Rue Sainte-Catherine. One might even conceive of an assault by some ruffian on an early passer-by.

But the sequel was puzzling. According to the boy, the murderer had run off when he came near, and it was then five minutes to six. At six o'clock, however, the first tram had passed, and the driver had declared that he had seen nothing.

He might, of course, have been inattentive, or looking in the other direction. But at five minutes past six two policemen on their beat had walked along that very pavement. And they had seen nothing!

At seven or eight minutes past six a cavalry officer who lived three houses away from the spot indicated by Justin had left home, as he did every morning, to go to the barracks.

And he had seen nothing either!

Finally, at twenty-past six, the police cyclists dispatched from the local station had found no trace of the victim.

Had someone come in the meantime to remove the body in a car or van? Maigret had deliberately and calmly sought to consider every hypothesis, and this one had proved as unreliable as all the rest. At no. 42 in the same street, there was a sick woman whose husband had sat up with her all night. He had asserted categorically:

'We hear all the noises outside. I notice them all the more because my wife is in great pain, and the least noise makes her wince. The tram woke her when she'd only just dropped off . . . I can give you my word no car came past before seven o'clock. The dustcart was the earliest.'

'And you heard nothing else?'

'Somebody running, at one point . . .'

'Before the tram?'

'Yes, because my wife was asleep . . . I was making myself some coffee on the gas-ring.'

'One person running?'

'More like two.'

'You don't know in which direction?'

'The blind was down . . . As it creaks when you lift it I didn't try to look out.'

This was the only piece of evidence in Justin's favour. There was a bridge two hundred metres further on. And the policeman on duty there had seen no car pass.

Could one assume that barely a few minutes after he'd run away the murderer had come back, picked up his victim's body and carried it off somewhere or other, without attracting attention?

Worse still, there was one piece of evidence which made people shrug their shoulders when they talked about the boy's story. The place he had indicated was just opposite no. 61. Inspector Thiberge had called at this house the day before, and Maigret, who left nothing to chance, now visited it himself.

It was a new house of pinkish brick; three steps led up to a shiny pitchpine door with a letter-box of gleaming brass.

Although it was only 7.30 in the morning, the Superintendent had been given to understand that he might call at that early hour.

A gaunt old woman with a moustache peered through a spyhole and argued before letting him into the hall, where there was a pleasant smell of fresh coffee.

'I'll go and see if the Judge will see you.'

For the house belonged to a retired magistrate, who was

reputed to have private means and who lived there alone with a housekeeper.

Some whispering went on in the front room, which should by rights have been a drawing-room. Then the old woman returned and said sourly:

'Come in . . . Wipe your feet, please . . . You're not in a stable.'

The room was no drawing-room; it bore no resemblance to what one usually thinks of as such. It was very large, and it was part bedroom, part study, part library and part junk-room, being cluttered with the most unexpected objects.

'Have you come to look for the corpse?' said a sneering voice that made the Superintendent jump.

Since there was a bed, he had naturally looked towards it, but it was empty. The voice came from the chimney corner, where a lean old man was huddled in the depths of an armchair, with a plaid over his legs.

'Take off your overcoat, for I adore heat and you'll not be able to stand it here.'

It was quite true. The old man, holding a pair of tongs, was doing his best to encourage the biggest possible blaze from a log fire.

'I have thought that the police had made some progress since my time and had learnt to mistrust evidence given by children. Children and girls are the most unreliable of witnesses, and when I was on the Bench . . .'

He was wearing a thick dressing-gown, and in spite of the heat of the room, he had a scarf as broad as a shawl round his neck.

'So the crime is supposed to have been committed in front of my house? And if I'm not mistaken, you are the famous Superintendent Maigret, whom they have graciously sent to our town to reorganize our Flying Squad?'

His voice grated. It was that of a spiteful, aggressive, savagely sarcastic old man.

'Well, my dear Superintendent, unless you're going to accuse me of being in league with the murderer, I am sorry to tell you, as I told your young inspector yesterday, that you're on the wrong track.

'You've probably heard that old people need very little sleep. Moreover there are people who, all their life long, sleep very little. Erasmus was one such, for instance, as was also a gentleman known as Voltaire . . .'

He glanced smugly at the bookshelves where volumes were piled ceiling-high.

'This has been the case with many other people whom you're not likely to know either . . . It's the case with me, and I pride myself on not having slept more than three hours a night during the last fifteen years . . . Since for the past ten my legs have refused to carry me, and since furthermore I've no desire to visit any of the places to which they might take me, I spend my days and nights in this room which, as you can see for yourself, gives directly on to the street.

'By four in the morning I am sitting in this armchair, with all my wits about me, believe me . . . I could show you the book in which I was deep yesterday morning, only it was by a Greek philosopher and I can't imagine you'd be interested.

'The fact remains that if an incident of the sort described by your over-imaginative young friend had taken place under my window, I can promise you I should have noticed it . . . My legs are weak, as I've said, but my hearing is still good.

'Moreover, I have retained enough natural curiosity to take an interest in all that happens in the street, and if it amuses you I could tell you at what time every housewife in the neighbourhood goes past my window to do her shopping.'

He was looking at Maigret with a smile of triumph.

'So you usually hear young Justin passing in front of the house?' the Superintendent asked in the meekest and gentlest of tones.

'Naturally.'

'You both hear him and see him?'

'I don't follow.'

'For most of the year, for almost two-thirds of the year, it's broad daylight at six in the morning . . . Now the child served at six o'clock Mass both summer and winter.'

'I used to see him go past.'

'Considering that this happened every day with as much

regularity as the passing of the first tram, you must have been attentively aware of it . . .'

'What do you mean?'

'I mean that, for instance, when a factory siren sounds every day at the same time in a certain district, when somebody passes your window with clockwork regularity, you naturally say to yourself: Hullo, it must be such and such a time.

'And if one day the siren doesn't sound, you think: Why, it's Sunday. And if the person doesn't come past you wonder: What can have happened to him? Perhaps he's ill?'

The judge was looking at Maigret with sharp, sly little eyes. He seemed to resent being taught a lesson.

'I know all that . . .' he grumbled, cracking his bony finger-joints. 'I was a magistrate before you were a policeman.'

'When the altar-boy went past . . .'

'I used to hear him, if that's what you're trying to make me admit.'

'And if he didn't go past?'

'I might have happened to notice it. But I might have happened not to notice it. As in the case of the factory siren you mentioned. One isn't struck every Sunday by the silence of the siren . . .'

'What about yesterday?'

Could Maigret be mistaken? He had the impression that the old magistrate was scowling, that there was something sullen and savagely secretive about his expression. Old people sometimes sulk, like children; they often display the same puerile stubbornness.

'Yesterday?'

'Yes . . .'

Why did he repeat the question, unless to give himself time to make a decision?

'I noticed nothing.'

'Not that he had passed?'

'No . . .'

'Nor that he hadn't passed?'

'No . . .'

One or the other answer was untrue, Maigret was convinced. He was anxious to continue the test, and he went on with his questions:

'Nobody ran past your windows?'

'No.'

This time the *no* was spoken frankly and the old man must have been telling the truth.

'You heard no unusual sound?'

'No' again, uttered with the same downrightness and almost with a note of triumph.

'No sound of trampling, of groaning, no sound of a body falling?'

'Nothing at all.'

'I'm much obliged to you.'

'Don't mention it.'

'Seeing that you've been a magistrate I need not of course ask you if you are willing to repeat your statement under oath?'

'Whenever you like.'

And the old man said that with a kind of delighted impatience.

'I apologize for disturbing you, Judge.'

'I wish you all success in your inquiry, Superintendent.'

The old housekeeper must have been hiding behind the door, for she was waiting on the threshold to show out the Superintendent and shut the front door behind him.

Maigret experienced a curious sensation as he re-emerged into everyday life in that quiet suburban street where housewives were beginning their shopping and children were on their way to school.

It seemed to him that he had been hoaxed, and yet he could have sworn that the judge had not withheld the truth except on one point. He had the impression, furthermore, that at a certain moment he had been about to discover something very odd, very elusive, very unexpected; that he would only have had to make a tiny effort but that he had been unable to do so.

Once again he pictured the boy, he pictured the old man; he tried to find a link between them.

Slowly he filled his pipe, standing on the kerb. Then, since he had had no breakfast, not even a cup of coffee on rising, and since his wet overcoat was clinging to his shoulders, he went to wait at the corner of the Place du Congrès for the tram that would take him home.

II

Out of the heaving mass of sheets and blankets an arm emerged, and a red face glistening with sweat appeared on the pillow; finally a sulky voice growled: 'Pass me the thermometer.'

And Madame Maigret, who was sewing by the window – she had drawn aside the net curtain so as to see in the gathering dusk – rose with a sigh and switched on the electric light.

'I thought you were asleep. It's not half an hour since you last took your temperature.'

Resignedly, for she knew from long marital experience that it was useless to cross the big fellow, she shook the thermometer to bring down the mercury and slipped the tip of it between his lips.

He asked, meanwhile: 'Has anybody come?'

'You'd know if they had, since you've not been asleep.'

He must have dozed off though, if only for a few minutes. But he was continually being roused from his torpor by that blasted jingle from down below.

They were not in their own home. Since his mission in this provincial town was to last for six months at least, and since Madame Maigret could not bear the thought of letting her husband eat in restaurants for so long a period, she had followed him, and they had rented a furnished flat in the upper part of the town.

It was too bright, with flowery wallpaper, gimcrack furniture and a bed that groaned under the Superintendent's weight. They had, at any rate, chosen a quiet street, where, as the landlady Madame Danse had told them, not a soul passed.

What she had failed to add was that, the ground floor of the house being occupied by a dairy, the whole place was pervaded by a sickly smell of cheese. Another fact which she had not revealed but which Maigret had just discovered for himself, since this was the first time he had stayed in bed in the daytime, was that the door of the dairy was equipped not with a bell but with a strange contraption of metal tubes which, whenever a customer came in, clashed together with a prolonged jingling sound.

'How high?'

'38.5 . . .'

'A little while ago it was 38.8.'

'And by tonight it'll be over 39.'

He was furious. He was always bad tempered when he was ill, and he glowered resentfully at Madame Maigret, who obstinately refused to go out when he was longing to fill himself a pipe.

It was still pouring with rain, the same fine rain that clung to the windows and fell in mournful silence, giving one the impression of living in an aquarium. A crude glare shone down from the electric light bulb which swung, unshaded, at the end of its cord. And one could imagine an endless succession of streets equally deserted, windows lighting up one after the other, people caged in their rooms, moving about like fishes in a bowl.

'You must have another cup of tisane.'

It was probably the tenth since twelve o'clock, and then all that lukewarm water had to be sweated away into his sheets, which ended up as damp as compresses.

He must have caught flu or tonsillitis while waiting for the boy in the cold early morning rain outside the school, or else afterwards while he was roaming the streets. By ten o'clock, when he was back in his room in the Flying Squad's offices, and while he was poking the stove with what had become almost a ritual gesture, he had been seized with the shivers. Then he had felt too hot. His eyelids were smarting and when he looked at himself in the bit of mirror in the cloakroom, he had seen round staring eyes that were glistening with fever.

Moreover his pipe no longer tasted the same, and that was a sure sign.

'Look here, Besson: if by any chance I shouldn't come back this afternoon, will you carry on investigating the altar-boy problem?'

And Besson, who always thought himself cleverer than anybody else: 'Do you really think, Chief, that there *is* such a problem, and that a good spanking wouldn't put an end to it?'

'All the same, you must get one of your colleagues, Vallin for instance, to keep an eye on the Rue Sainte-Catherine.'

'In case the corpse comes back to lie down in front of the judge's house?'

Maigret was too dazed by his incipient fever to follow Besson on to that ground. He had just gone on deliberately giving instructions.

'Draw up a list of all the residents in the street. It won't be a big job, because it's a short street.'

'Shall I question the kid again?'

'No . . .'

And since then he had felt too hot; he was conscious of drops of sweat beading on his skin, he had a sour taste in his mouth, he kept hoping to sink into oblivion but was constantly disturbed by the ridiculous jingle of the brass tubes from the dairy.

He loathed being ill because it was humiliating and also because Madame Maigret kept a fierce watch to prevent him from smoking his pipe. If only she'd had to go out and buy something at the pharmacist's! But she was always careful to take a well-stocked medicine chest about with her.

He loathed being ill, and yet there were moments when he almost enjoyed it, moments when, closing his eyes, he felt ageless because he experienced once again the sensations of his childhood.

Then he remembered the boy Justin, whose pale face already showed such strength of character. All that morning's scenes recurred to his mind, not with the precision of everyday reality nor with the sharp outline of things seen, but with the peculiar intensity of things felt.

For instance he could have described almost in detail the attic room that he had never seen, the iron bedstead, the alarm clock on the bedside table, the boy stretching out his arm, dressing silently, the same gestures invariably repeated . . .

Invariably the same gestures! It seemed to him an important and obvious truth. When you've been serving at Mass for two years at a regular time, your gestures become almost completely automatic . . . The first bell at a quarter to six . . . The alarm clock . . . the shriller sound of the chapel bells . . . Then the child would put on his shoes at the foot of the stairs, open the front door and meet the cold breath of early morning.

'You know, Madame Maigret, he's never read any detective stories.' For as long back as they could remember, possibly because it had begun as a joke, they had called one another Maigret and Madame Maigret, and they had almost forgotten that they had Christian names like other people . . .

'He doesn't read the papers either . . .'

'You'd better try to sleep.'

He closed his eyes, after a longing glance at his pipe, which lay on the black marble mantelpiece.

'I questioned his mother at great length; she's a decent woman, but she's mightily in awe of the police . . .'

'Go to sleep!'

He kept silence for a while. His breathing became deeper; it sounded as if he was really dozing off.

'She declares he's never seen a dead body . . . It's the sort of thing you try to keep from children.'

'Why is it important?'

'He told me the body was so big that it seemed to take up the whole pavement . . . Now that's the impression that a dead body lying on the ground makes on one . . . A dead person always looks bigger than a living one . . . D'you understand?'

'I can't think why you're worrying, since Besson's looking after the case.'

'Besson doesn't believe in it.'

'In what?'

'In the dead body.'

'Shall I put out the light?'

In spite of his protests, she climbed on to a chair and fastened a band of waxed paper round the bulb so as to dim its light.

'Now try to get an hour's sleep, then I'll make you another cup of tisane. You haven't been sweating enough . . .'

'Don't you think if I were to have just a tiny puff at my pipe . . .'

'Are you mad?'

She went into the kitchen to keep an eye on the vegetable broth, and he heard her tiptoeing back and forth. He kept picturing the same section of the Rue Sainte-Catherine, with street lamps every fifty metres.

'The judge declares he heard nothing . . .'

'What are you saying?'

'I bet they hate one another . . .'

And her voice reached him from the far end of the kitchen:

'Who are you talking about? You see I'm busy . . .'

'The judge and the altar-boy. They've never spoken to one another, but I'll take my oath they hate each other. You know, very old people, particularly old people who live by themselves, end up by becoming like children . . . Justin went past every morning, and every morning the old judge was behind his window . . . He looks like an owl.'

'I don't know what you're trying to say . . .'

She stood framed in the doorway, a steaming ladle in her hand.

'Try to follow me. The judge declares that he heard nothing, and it's too serious a matter for me to suspect him of lying.'

'You see! Try to stop thinking about it.'

'Only he dared not assert that he had or had not heard Justin go past yesterday morning.'

'Perhaps he went back to sleep.'

'No . . . He daren't tell a lie, and so he's deliberately vague. And the husband at no. 42 who was sitting up with his sick wife heard somebody running in the street.'

He kept reverting to that. His thoughts, sharpened by fever, went round in a circle.

'What would have become of the corpse?' objected Madame Maigret with her womanly common sense. 'Don't think any more about it! Besson knows his job, you've often said so yourself . . .'

He slumped back under the blankets, discouraged, and tried hard to go to sleep, but was inevitably haunted before long by the image of the altar-boy's face, and his pallid legs above black socks.

'There's something wrong . . .'

'What did you say? Something wrong? Are you feeling worse? Shall I ring the doctor?'

Not that. He started again from scratch, obstinately; he went back to the threshold of the boys' school and crossed the Place du Congrès.

'And this is where there's something amiss.'

For one thing, because the judge had heard nothing. Unless one was going to accuse him of perjury it was hard to believe that a fight could have gone on under his window, just a few metres away, that a man had started running off towards the barracks while the boy had rushed off in the opposite direction.

'Listen, Madame Maigret . . .'

'What is it now?'

'Suppose they had both started running in the same direction?'

With a sigh, Madame Maigret picked up her needlework and listened, dutifully, to her husband's monologue interspersed with wheezy gasps.

'For one thing, it's more logical . . .'

'What's more logical?'

'That they should both have run in the same direction . . . Only in that case it wouldn't have been towards the barracks.'

'Could the boy have been running after the murderer?'

'No. The murderer would have run after the boy . . .'

'What for, since he didn't kill him?'

'To make him hold his tongue, for instance.'

'He didn't succeed, since the child spoke . . .'

'Or to prevent him from telling something, from giving some particular detail . . . Look here, Madame Maigret.'

'What is it you want?'

'I know you'll start by saying no, but it's absolutely necessary . . . Pass me my pipe and my tobacco . . . Just a few puffs . . . I've got the feeling that I'm going to understand the whole thing, that in a few minutes – if I don't lose the thread.'

She went to fetch his pipe from the mantelpiece and handed it to him resignedly, sighing: 'I knew you'd think of some good excuse . . . In any case tonight I'm going to make you a poultice whether you like it or not.'

Luckily there was no telephone in the flat and one had to go down into the shop to ring up from behind the counter.

'Will you go downstairs, Madame Maigret, and call Besson for me? It's seven o'clock. He may still be at the office. Otherwise call the *Café du Centre*, where he'll be playing billiards with Thiberge.'

'Shall I ask him to come here?'

'To bring me as soon as possible a list, not of all the residents in the street but of the tenants of the houses on the left side of it, between the Place du Congrès and the Judge's house.'

'Do try to keep covered up . . .'

Barely had she set foot on the staircase when he thrust both legs out of bed and rushed, barefooted, to fetch his tobacco pouch and fill himself a fresh pipe; then he lay back innocently between the sheets.

Through the flimsy floorboards he could hear a hum of voices and Madame Maigret's, speaking on the telephone. He smoked his pipe in greedy little puffs, although his throat was very sore. He could see raindrops slowly sliding down the dark panes, and this again reminded him of his childhood, of childish illnesses when his mother used to bring him caramel custard in bed.

Madame Maigret returned, panting a little, glanced round the room as if to take note of anything unusual, but did not think of the pipe.

'He'll be here in about an hour.'

'I'm going to ask you one more favour, Madame Maigret . . . Will you put on your coat . . .'

She cast a suspicious glance at him.

'Will you go to young Justin's home and ask his parents to let you bring him to me . . . Be very kind to him . . . If I were to send a policeman he'd undoubtedly take fright, and he's liable enough to be prickly as it is . . . Just tell him I'd like a few minutes' chat with him.'

'And suppose his mother wants to come with him?'

'Work out your own plan, but I don't want the mother.'

Left to himself, he sank back into the hot, humid depths of the bed, the tip of his pipe emerging from the sheets and emitting a slight cloud of smoke. He closed his eyes, and he could keep picturing the corner of the Rue Sainte-Catherine; he was no longer Superintendent Maigret, he had become the altar-boy who hurried along, covering the same ground every morning at the same time and talking to himself to keep up his courage.

As he turned into the Rue Sainte-Catherine: 'Maman, I wish you'd buy me a bike . . .'

For the kid had been rehearsing the scene he would play for his mother when he got back from the hospital. It would have to be more complicated; he must have thought up subtler approaches.

'You know, maman, if I had a bike, I could . . .' Or else, 'I've saved three hundred francs already . . . If you'd lend me the rest, which I promise to pay back with what I earn from the chapel, I could . . .'

The corner of the Rue Sainte-Catherine . . . a few seconds before the bells of the parish church rang out for the second time. And there were only a hundred and fifty metres of dark empty street to go through before reaching the safe haven of the hospital . . . A few jumps between the pools of brightness shed by the street lamps . . .

Later the child was to declare: 'I looked up and I saw . . .'

That was the whole problem. The judge lived practically in the middle of the street, half way between the Place du Congrès and the corner of the barracks, and he had seen nothing and heard nothing.

The husband of the sick woman, the man from no. 42, lived closer to the Place du Congrès, on the right side of the street, and he had heard the sound of running footsteps.

Yet, five minutes later, there had been no dead or injured body on the pavement. And no car or van had passed. The policeman on duty on the bridge, the others on the beat at various spots in the neighbourhood, had seen nothing unusual such as, for instance, a man carrying another man on his back.

Maigret's temperature was certainly going up but he no longer thought of consulting the thermometer. Things were find as they were; words evoked images, and images assumed unexpected sharpness.

It was just like when he was a sick child and his mother,

bending over him, seemed to have grown so big that she took up the whole house.

There was that body lying across the pavement, looking so long because it was a dead body, with a brown-handled knife sticking out of its chest.

And a few metres away a man, a pale-eyed man who had begun running . . . Running towards the barracks, whereas Justin ran for all he was worth in the opposite direction.

'That's it!'

That's what? Maigret had made the remark out loud, as though it contained the solution of the problem, as though it had actually been the solution of the problem, and he smiled contentedly as he drew on his pipe with ecstatic little puffs.

Drunks are like that. Things suddenly appear to them self-evidently true, which they are nevertheless incapable of explaining, and which dissolve into vagueness as soon as they are examined coolly.

Something was untrue, that was it! And Maigret, in his feverish imagining, felt sure that he had put his finger on the weak point in the story.

Justin had not made it up . . . His terror, his panic on arriving at the hospital had been genuine. Neither had he made up the picture of the long body sprawling across the pavement. Moreover there was at least one person in the street who had heard running footsteps.

What had the judge with the sneering smile remarked? 'You haven't yet learned to mistrust the evidence of children?' . . . or something of the sort.

However the judge was wrong. Children are incapable of inventing because one cannot construct truths out of nothing. One needs materials. Children transpose maybe, they don't invent.

And that was that! At each stage, Maigret repeated that self-congratulatory *voilà*!

There had been a body on the pavement . . . And no doubt there had been a man close by. Had he had pale eyes? Quite possibly. And somebody had run.

And the old judge, Maigret could have sworn, was not the sort of man to tell a deliberate lie.

He felt hot. He was bathed in sweat, but none the less he left his bed to go and fill one last pipe before Madame Maigret's return. While he was up, he took the opportunity to open the cupboard and drink a big mouthful of rum from the bottle. What did it matter if his temperature was up that night? Everything would be finished by then!

And it would be quite an achievement; a difficult case solved from a sick-bed! Madame Maigret was not likely to appreciate that, however.

The judge had not lied, and yet he must have tried to play a trick on the boy whom he hated as two children of the same age can hate one another.

Customers seemed to be getting fewer down below, for the ridiculous chimes over the door sounded less frequently. Probably the dairyman and his wife, with their daughter whose cheeks were as pink as ham, were dining together in the room at the back of the shop.

There were steps on the pavement; there were steps on the stair. Small feet were stumbling. Madame Maigret opened the door and ushered in young Justin, whose navy-blue duffel coat was glistening with rain. He smelt like a wet dog.

'Here, my boy, let me take off your coat.'

'I can take it off myself.'

Another mistrustful glance from Madame Maigret. Obviously she could not believe he was still smoking the same pipe. Who knows, perhaps she even suspected the shot of rum?

'Sit down, Justin,' said the Superintendent, pointing to a chair.

'Thanks, I'm not tired.'

'I asked you to come so that we could have a friendly chat together for a few minutes. What were you busy with?'

'My arithmetic homework.'

'Because in spite of all you've been through you've gone back to school?'

'Why shouldn't I have gone?'

The boy was proud. He was on his high horse again. Did Maigret seem to him bigger and longer than usual, now that he was lying down?

'Madame Maigret, be an angel and go and look after the vegetable broth in the kitchen, and close the door.'

When that was done he gave the boy a knowing wink.

'Pass me my tobacco pouch, which is on the mantelpiece . . . And the pipe, which must be in my overcoat pocket . . . Yes, the one that's hanging behind the door . . . Thanks, my boy . . . Were you frightened when my wife came to fetch you?'

'No.' He said that with some pride.

'Were you annoyed?'

'Because everyone keeps saying that I've made it up.'

'And you haven't, have you?'

'There was a dead man on the pavement and another who . . .'

'Hush!'

'What?'

'Not so quick . . . Sit down . . .'

'I'm not tired.'

'So you've said, but I get tired of seeing you standing up . . .' He sat down on the very edge of the chair, and his feet didn't touch the ground; his legs were dangling, his bare knobbly knees protruding between the short pants and the socks.

'What sort of trick did you play on the judge?'

A swift, instinctive reaction: 'I never did anything to him.'

'You know what judge I mean?'

'The one who's always peering out of his window and who looks like an owl?'

'Just how I'd describe him . . . What happened between you?'

'In winter I didn't see him because his curtains were drawn when I went past.'

'But in summer?'

'I put out my tongue at him.'

'Why?'

'Because he kept looking at me as if he was making fun of me; he sniggered to himself as he looked at me.'

'Did you often put out your tongue at him?'

'Every time I saw him . . .'

'And what did he do?'

'He laughed in a spiteful sort of way . . . I thought it was because I served at Mass and he's an unbeliever . . .'

'Has he told a lie, then?'

'What did he say?'

'That nothing happened yesterday morning in front of his house, because he would have noticed.'

The boy stared intently at Maigret, then lowered his head.

'He was lying, wasn't he?'

'There was a body on the pavement with a knife stuck in its chest.'

'I know . . .'

'How do you know?'

'I know because it's the truth . . .' repeated Maigret gently. 'Pass me the matches . . . I've let my pipe go out.'

'Are you too hot?'

'It's nothing . . . just the flu . . .'

'Did you catch it this morning?'

'Maybe . . . Sit down.'

He listened attentively and then called: 'Madame Maigret! Will you run downstairs? I think I heard Besson arriving and I don't want him to come up before I'm ready . . . Will you keep him company downstairs? My friend Justin will call you . . .'

Once more, he said to his young companion: 'Sit down . . . It's true, too, that you both ran . . .'

'I told you it was true . . .'

'And I believe you . . . Go and make sure there's nobody behind the door and that it's properly shut.'

The child obeyed without understanding, impressed by the importance that his actions had suddenly acquired.

'Listen, Justin, you're a brave little chap.'

'Why do you say that?'

'It was true about the corpse. It was true about the man running.'

The child raised his head once again, and Maigret saw his lip quivering.

'And the judge, who didn't lie; because a judge would not dare to lie, didn't tell the whole truth . . .'

The room smelt of flu and rum and tobacco. A whiff of vegetable broth came in under the kitchen door, and raindrops were still falling like silver tears on the black window pane beyond which lay the empty street. Were the two now facing one another still a man and a small boy? Or two men, or two small boys?

Maigret's head felt heavy; his eyes were glistening. His pipe had a curious medical flavour that was not unpleasant, and he remembered the smells of the hospital, its chapel and its vestry.

'The judge didn't tell the whole truth because he wanted to rile you. And you didn't tell the whole truth either . . . Now I forbid you to cry. We don't want everyone to know what we've been saying to each other . . . You understand, Justin?'

The boy nodded.

'If what you described hadn't happened at all, the man in no. 42 wouldn't have heard running footsteps.'

'I didn't make it up.'

'Of course not! But if it had happened just as you said, the judge would not have been able to say that he had heard nothing . . . And if the murderer had run away towards the barracks, the old man would not have sworn that nobody had run past his house.'

The child sat motionless, staring down at the tips of his dangling feet.

'The judge was being honest, on the whole, in not daring to assert that you had gone past his house yesterday morning. But he might perhaps have asserted that you had not gone past. That's the truth, since you ran off in the opposite direction . . . He was telling the truth, too, when he declared that no man had run past on the pavement under his window . . . For the man did not go in that direction.'

'How do you know?'

He had stiffened, and was staring wide-eyed at Maigret as he must have stared on the previous night at the murderer or his victim.

'Because the man inevitably rushed off in the same direction as yourself, which explains why the husband in no. 42 heard him go past . . . Because, knowing that you had seen him, that you had seen the body, that you could get him caught, he ran *after* you . . .'

'If you tell my mother, I . . .'

'Hush! . . . I don't wish to tell your mother or anyone else anything at all . . . You see, Justin my boy, I'm going to talk to you like a man . . . A murderer clever and cool enough to make a corpse disappear without trace in a few minutes would not have been foolish enough to let you escape after seeing what you had seen.'

'I don't know . . .'

'But I do . . . It's my job to know . . . The most difficult thing is not to kill a man, it's to make the body disappear afterwards, and this one disappeared magnificently . . . It disappeared, even though you had seen it and seen the murderer . . . In other words, the murderer's a really smart guy . . . And a really smart guy, with his life at stake, would never have let you get away like that.'

'I didn't know . . .'

'What didn't you know?'

'I didn't know it mattered so much . . .'

'It doesn't matter at all now, since everything has been put right.'

'Have you arrested him?'

There was immense hope in the tone in which these words were uttered.

'He'll be arrested before long . . . Sit still; stop swinging your legs . . .'

'I won't move.'

'For one thing, if it had all happened in front of the judge's house, that's to say in the middle of the street, you'd have been aware of it from further off, and you'd have had time to run away . . . That was the only mistake the murderer made, for all his cleverness . . .'

'How did you guess?'

'I didn't guess. But I was once an altar-boy myself, and I served at six o'clock Mass like you . . . You wouldn't have gone a hundred metres along the street without looking in front of you . . . So the corpse must have been closer, much closer, just round the corner of the street.'

'Five houses past the corner.'

'You were thinking of something else, of your bike, and you may have gone twenty metres without seeing anything.'

'How can you possibly know?'

'And when you saw, you ran towards the Place du Congrès to get to the hospital by the other street. The man ran after you . . .'

'I thought I should die of fright.'

'Did he grab you by the shoulder?'

'He grabbed my shoulders with both hands. I thought he was going to strangle me . . .'

'He asked you to say . . .'

The child was crying, quietly. He was pale and the tears were rolling slowly down his cheeks.

'If you tell my mother she'll blame me all my life long. She's always nagging at me.'

'He ordered you to say that it had happened further on . . .'

'Yes.'

'In front of the judge's house?'

'It was me that thought of the judge's house, because of putting out my tongue at him . . . The man only said the other end of the street, and that he'd run off towards the barracks.'

'And so we very nearly had a perfect crime, because nobody believed you, since there was no murderer and no body, no traces of any sort, and it all seemed impossible . . .'

'But what about you?'

'I don't count. It just so happens that I was once an altar-boy, and that today I'm in bed with flu . . . What did he promise you?'

'He told me that if I didn't say what he wanted me to, he would always be after me, wherever I went, in spite of the police, and that he would wring my neck like a chicken's.'

'And then?'

'He asked me what I wanted to have . . .'

'And you said a bike . . . ?'

'How do you know?'

'I've told you, I was once an altar-boy too.'

'And you wanted a bike?'

'That, and a great many other things that I've never had . . . Why did you say he had pale eyes?'

'I don't know. I didn't see his eyes. He was wearing thick glasses. But I didn't want him to be caught . . .'

'Because of the bike?'

'Maybe . . . You're going to tell my mother, aren't you?'

'Not your mother nor anyone else . . . Aren't we pals now? . . . Look, you hand me my tobacco pouch and don't tell Madame Maigret that I've smoked three pipes since we've been here together . . . You see, grown-ups don't always tell the whole truth either . . . Which door was it in front of, Justin?'

'The yellow house next door to the delicatessen.'

'Go and fetch my wife.'

'Where is she?'

'Downstairs . . . She's with Inspector Besson, the one who was so beastly to you.'

'And who's going to arrest me?'

'Open the wardrobe . . .'

'Right . . .'

'There's a pair of trousers hanging there . . .'

'What am I to do with it?'

'In the left hand pocket you'll find a wallet.'

'Here it is.'

'In the wallet there are some visiting-cards.'

'Do you want them?'

'Hand me one . . . And also the pen that's on the table . . .'

With which, Maigret wrote on one of the cards that bore his name: *Supply bearer with one bicycle.*

III

'Come in, Besson.'

Madame Maigret glanced up at the dense cloud of smoke that hung round the lamp in its waxed-paper shade; then she hurried into the kitchen, because she could smell something burning there.

As for Besson, taking the chair just vacated by the boy, for whom he had only a disdainful glance, he announced:

'I've got the list you asked me to draw up. I must tell you right away . . .'

'That it's useless . . . Who lives in no. 14?'

'One moment . . .' He consulted his notes. 'Let's see . . . no. 14 . . . There's only a single tenant there.'

'I suspected as much.'

'Oh?' An uneasy glance at the boy. 'It's a foreigner, name of Frankelstein, a dealer in jewellery.'

Maigret had slipped back among his pillows; he muttered, with an air of indifference: 'A fence.'

'What did you say, Chief?'

'A fence . . . Possibly the boss of a gang.'

'I don't understand.'

'That doesn't matter . . . Be a good fellow, Besson, pass me the bottle of rum that's in the cupboard. Quickly, before Madame Maigret comes back . . . I bet my temperature's soaring and I'll need to have my sheets changed a couple of times tonight . . . Frankelstein . . . Get a search warrant from the examining magistrate . . . No . . . At this time of night, it'll take too long, for he's sure to be out playing bridge somewhere . . . Have you had dinner? . . . Me, I'm waiting for my vegetable broth . . . There are some blank warrants in my desk – left-hand drawer. Fill one in. Search the house. You're sure to find the body, even if it means knocking down a cellar wall.'

Poor Besson stared at his Chief in some anxiety, then glanced at the boy, who was sitting waiting quietly in a corner.

'Act quickly, old man . . . If he knows that the kid's been here tonight, you won't find him in his lair . . . He's a tough guy, as you'll find out.'

He was indeed. When the police rang at his door, he tried to escape through backyards and over walls; it took them all night to catch him, which they finally did among the rooftops. Meanwhile other policemen searched the house for hours before discovering the corpse, decomposing in a bath of quicklime.

It had obviously been a settling of accounts. A disgruntled

and frustrated member of the gang had called on the boss in the small hours; Frankelstein had done him in on the doorstep, unaware that an altar-boy was at that very instant coming round the street corner.

'What does it say?' Maigret no longer had the heart to look at the thermometer himself.

'39.3 . . .'

'Aren't you cheating?'

He knew that she was cheating, that his temperature was higher than that, but he didn't care; it was good, it was delicious to sink into unconsciousness, to let himself glide at a dizzy speed into a misty, yet terribly real world where an altar-boy bearing a strong resemblance to Maigret as he had once been was tearing wildly down the street, sure that he was either going to be strangled or to win a shiny new bicycle.

'What are you talking about?' asked Madame Maigret, whose plump fingers held a scalding hot poultice which she was proposing to apply to her husband's throat.

He was muttering nonsense like a feverish child, talking about the first bell and the second bell.

'I'm going to be late . . .'

'Late for what?'

'For Mass . . . Sister . . . Sister . . .'

He meant the vestry-nun, the sacristine, but he could not find the word.

He fell asleep at last, with a huge compress round his neck, dreaming of Mass in his own village and of Marie Titin's inn, past which he used to run because he was afraid.

Afraid of what? . . .

'I got him, all the same . . .'

'Who?'

'The judge.'

'What judge?'

It was too complicated to explain. The judge reminded him of somebody in his village at whom he used to put out his tongue. The blacksmith? No . . . It was the baker's wife's stepfather . . . It didn't matter. Somebody he disliked. And it was the judge who had misled him the whole way through, in order to be revenged on the altar-boy and to annoy people . . . He had said he had heard no footsteps *in front of his house* . . .

But he had not said that he had heard two people running off in the opposite direction . . .

Old people become childish. And they quarrel with children. Like children.

Maigret was satisfied, in spite of everything. He had cheated by three whole pipes, even four . . . He had a good taste of tobacco in his mouth and he could let himself drift away . . .

And tomorrow, since he had flu, Madame Maigret would make him some caramel custard.

A VERY COMMONPLACE MURDER

P. D. James

'WE close at twelve on Saturday,' said the blonde in the estate office. 'So if you keep the key after then, please drop it back through the letter box. It's the only key we have, and there may be other people wanting to view on Monday. Sign here, please, sir.'

The 'sir' was grudging, an afterthought. Her tone was reproving. She didn't really think he would buy the flat, this seedy old man with his air of spurious gentility, with his harsh voice. In her job you soon got a nose for the genuine inquirer. Ernest Gabriel. An odd name, half-common, half-fancy.

But he took the key politely enough and thanked her for her trouble. No trouble, she thought. God knew there were few enough people interested in that sordid little dump, not at the price they were asking. He could keep the key a week, for all she cared.

She was right. Gabriel hadn't come to buy, only to view. It was the first time he had been back since it all happened sixteen years ago. He came neither as a pilgrim nor a penitent. He had returned under some compulsion which he hadn't even bothered to analyse. He had been on his way to visit his only living relative, an elderly aunt, who had recently been admitted to a geriatric ward. He hadn't even realized the bus would pass the flat.

But suddenly they were lurching through Camden Town, and the road became familiar, like a photograph springing into focus; and with a *frisson* of surprise he recognized the double-fronted shop and the flat above. There was an estate agent's notice in the window. Almost without thinking, he had got off at the next stop, gone back to verify the name, and walked the half-mile to the office. It had seemed as natural and inevitable as his daily bus journey to work.

Twenty minutes later he fitted the key into the lock of the front door and passed into the stuffy emptiness of the flat. The grimy walls still held the smell of cooking. There was a spatter of envelopes on the worn linoleum, dirtied and trampled by the feet of previous viewers. The light bulb swung naked in the hall, and the door into the sitting room stood open. To his right was the staircase, to his left the kitchen.

Gabriel paused for a moment, then went into the kitchen. From the windows, half-curtained with grubby gingham, he looked upward to the great black building at the rear of the flat, eyeless except for the one small square of window high on the fifth floor. It was from this window, sixteen years ago, that he had watched Denis Speller and Eileen Morrisey play out their commonplace little tragedy to its end.

He had no right to be watching them, no right to be in the building at all after six o'clock. That had been the nub of his awful dilemma. It had happened by chance. Mr Maurice Bootman had instructed him, as the firm's filing clerk, to go through the papers in the late Mr Bootman's upstairs den in case there were any which should be in the files. They weren't confidential or important papers – those had been dealt with by the family and the firm's solicitors months before. They were just a miscellaneous, yellowing collection of out-of-date memoranda, old accounts, receipts, and fading press clippings which had been bundled together into old Mr Bootman's desk. He had been a great hoarder of trivia.

But at the back of the left-hand bottom drawer Gabriel had found a key. It was by chance that he tried it in the lock of the corner cupboard. It fitted. And in the cupboard Gabriel found the late Mr Bootman's small but choice collection of pornography.

He knew that he had to read the books; not just to snatch surreptitious minutes with one ear listening for a footstep on the stairs or the whine of the approaching elevator, and fearful always that his absence from his filing room would be noticed. No, he had to read them in privacy and in peace. So he devised his plan.

It wasn't difficult. As a trusted member of the staff, he had one of the Yale keys to the side door at which goods were delivered. It was locked on the inside at night by the porter before he went off duty. It wasn't difficult for Gabriel, always among the last to leave, to find the opportunity of shooting back the bolts before leaving with the porter by the main door. He dared risk it only once a week, and the day he chose was Friday.

He would hurry home, eat his solitary meal beside the gas fire in his bed-sitting-room, then make his way back to the building and let himself in by the side door. All that was necessary was to make sure he was waiting for the office to open on Monday morning so that, among the first in, he could lock the side door before the porter made his ritual visit to unlock it for the day's deliveries.

These Friday nights became a desperate but shameful joy to Gabriel. Their pattern was always the same. He would sit crouched in old Mr Bootman's low leather chair in front of the fireplace, his shoulders hunched over the book in his lap, his eyes following the pool of light from his torch as it moved over each page. He never dared to switch on the room light, and even on the coldest night he never lit the gas fire. He was fearful that its hiss might mask the sound of approaching feet, that its glow might shine through the thick curtains at the window, or that, somehow, the smell of gas would linger in the room next Monday morning to betray him. He was morbidly afraid of discovery, yet even this fear added to the excitement of his secret pleasure.

It was on the third Friday in January that he first saw them. It was a mild evening, but heavy and starless. An early rain had slimed the pavements and bled the scribbled headlines from the newspaper placards. Gabriel wiped his feet carefully before climbing to the fifth floor. The claustrophobic room smelled sour and dusty, the air struck colder than the night outside. He wondered whether he dared open the window and let in some of the sweetness of the rain-cleansed sky.

It was then that he saw the woman. Below him were the back entrances of the two shops, each with a flat above. One flat had boarded windows, but the other looked lived in. It was approached by a flight of iron steps leading to an asphalt yard. He saw the woman in the glow of a street lamp as she paused at the foot of the steps, fumbling in her handbag. Then, as if gaining resolution, she came swiftly up the steps and almost ran across the asphalt to the flat door.

He watched as she pressed herself into the shadow of the doorway, then swiftly turned the key in the lock and slid out of his sight. He had time only to notice that she was wearing a pale mackintosh buttoned high under a mane of fairish hair and that she carried a string bag of what looked like groceries. It seemed an oddly furtive and solitary homecoming.

Gabriel waited. Almost immediately he saw the light go on in the room to the left of the door. Perhaps she was in the kitchen. He could see her faint shadow passing to and fro, bending and then lengthening. He guessed that she was unpacking the groceries. Then the light in the room went out.

For a few moments the flat was in darkness. Then the light in the upstairs window went on, brighter this time, so that he could see the woman more plainly. She could not know how plainly. The curtains were drawn, but they were thin. Perhaps the owners, confident that they were not overlooked, had grown careless. Although the woman's silhouette was only a faint blur, Gabriel could see that she was carrying a tray. Perhaps she was intending to eat her supper in bed. She was undressing now.

He could see her lifting the garments over her head and twisting down to release stockings and take off her shoes. Suddenly she came very close to the window, and he saw the outline of her body plainly. She seemed to be watching and listening. Gabriel found that he was holding his breath. Then she moved away, and the light dimmed. He guessed that she had switched off the central bulb and was using the bedside lamp. The room was now lit with a softer, pinkish glow within which the woman moved, insubstantial as a dream.

Gabriel stood with his face pressed against the cold window, still watching. Shortly after eight o'clock the boy arrived.

Gabriel always thought of him as 'the boy'. Even from that distance his youth, his vulnerability, were apparent. He approached the flat with more confidence than the woman, but still swiftly, pausing at the top of the steps as if to assess the width of the rain-washed yard.

She must have been waiting for his knock. She let him in at once, the door barely opening. Gabriel knew that she had come naked to let him in. And then there were two shadows in the upstairs room, shadows that met and parted and came together again before they moved, joined, to the bed and out of Gabriel's sight.

The next Friday he watched to see if they would come again. They did, and at the same times, the woman first, at twenty minutes past seven, the boy forty minutes later. Again Gabriel stood, rigidly intent at his watching post, as the light in the upstairs window sprang on and then was lowered. The two naked figures, seen dimly behind the curtains, moved to and fro, joined and parted, fused and swayed together in a ritualistic parody of a dance.

This Friday Gabriel waited until they left. The boy came out first, sidling quickly from the half-open door and almost leaping down the steps, as if in exultant joy. The woman followed five minutes later, locking the door behind her and darting across the asphalt, her head bent.

After that he watched for them every Friday. They held a fascination for him even greater than Mr Bootman's books. Their routine hardly varied. Sometimes the boy arrived a little late, and Gabriel would see the woman watching motionless for him behind the bedroom curtains. He too would stand with held breath, sharing her agony of impatience, willing the boy to come. Usually the boy carried a bottle under his arm, but one week it was in a wine basket, and he bore it with great care. Perhaps it was an anniversary, a special evening for them. Always the woman had the bag of groceries. Always they ate together in the bedroom.

Friday after Friday Gabriel stood in the darkness, his eyes fixed on that upstairs window, straining to decipher the outlines of their naked bodies, picturing what they were doing to each other.

They had been meeting for seven weeks when it happened. Gabriel was late at the building that night. His usual bus did not run, and the first to arrive was full. By the time he reached his watching post, there was already a light in the bedroom. He pressed his face to the window, his hot breath smearing the pane. Hastily rubbing it clear with the cuff of his coat, he looked again. For a moment he thought that there were two figures in the bedroom. But that must surely be a freak of the light. The boy wasn't due for thirty minutes yet. But the woman, as always, was on time.

Twenty minutes later he went into the bathroom on the floor below. He had become much more confident during the last few weeks and now moved about the building, silently, and using only his torch for light, but with almost as much assurance as during the day. He spent nearly ten minutes in the bathroom. His watch showed that it was just after eight by the time he was back at the window, and, at first, he thought that he had missed the boy. But no, the slight figure was even now running up the steps and across the asphalt to the shelter of the doorway.

Gabriel watched as he knocked and waited for the door to open. But it didn't open. She didn't come. There was a light in the bedroom, but no shadow moved on the curtains. The boy knocked again. Gabriel could just detect the quivering of his knuckles against the door. Again he waited. Then the boy drew back and looked up at the lighted window. Perhaps he was risking a low-pitched call. Gabriel could hear nothing, but he could sense the tension in that waiting figure.

Again the boy knocked. Again there was no response. Gabriel watched and suffered with him until, at twenty past eight, the boy finally gave up and turned away. Then Gabriel too stretched his cramped limbs and made his way into the night. The wind was rising, and a young moon reeled through the torn clouds. It was getting colder. He wore no coat and missed its comfort. Hunching his shoulders against the bite of the wind, he knew that this was the last Friday he would come late to the building. For him, as for that desolate boy, it was the end of a chapter.

He first read about the murder in his morning paper on his

way to work the following Monday. He recognized the picture of the flat at once, although it looked oddly unfamiliar with the bunch of plainclothes detectives conferring at the door and the stolid uniformed policeman at the top of the steps.

The story so far was slight. A Mrs Eileen Morrisey, aged thirty-four, had been found stabbed to death in a flat in Camden Town late on Sunday night. The discovery was made by the tenants, Mr and Mrs Kealy, who had returned late on Sunday from a visit to Mr Kealy's parents. The dead woman, who was the mother of twin daughters aged twelve, was a friend of Mrs Kealy. Detective Chief-Inspector William Holbrook was in charge of the investigation. It was understood that the dead woman had been sexually assaulted.

Gabriel folded his paper with the same precise care as he did on any ordinary day. Of course, he would have to tell the police what he had seen. He couldn't let an innocent man suffer, no matter what the inconvenience to himself. The knowledge of his intention, of his public-spirited devotion to justice, was warmly satisfying. For the rest of the day he crept around his filing cabinets with the secret complacency of a man dedicated to sacrifice.

But somehow his first plan of calling at a police station on his way home from work came to nothing. There was no point in acting hastily. If the boy were arrested, he would speak. But it would be ridiculous to prejudice his reputation and endanger his job before he even knew whether the boy was a suspect. The police might never learn of the boy's existence. To speak up now might only focus suspicion on the innocent. A prudent man would wait. Gabriel decided to be prudent.

The boy was arrested three days later. Again Gabriel read about it in his morning paper. There was no picture this time, and few details. The news had to compete with a society elopement and a major air crash and did not make the first page. The inch of newsprint stated briefly: 'Denis John Speller, a butcher's assistant, aged nineteen, who gave an address at Muswell Hill, was today charged with the murder of Mrs Eileen Morrisey, the mother of twelve-year-old twins, who was stabbed to death last Friday in a flat in Camden Town.'

So the police now knew more precisely the time of death. Perhaps it was time for him to see them. But how could he be sure that this Denis Speller was the young lover he had been watching these past Friday nights? A woman like that – well, she might have had any number of men. No photograph of the accused would be published in any paper until after the trial. But more information would come out at the preliminary hearing. He would wait for that. After all, the accused might not even be committed for trial.

Besides, he had himself to consider. There had been time to think of his own position. If young Speller's life were in danger, then, of course, Gabriel would tell what he had seen. But it would mean the end of his job with Bootman's. Worse, he would never get another. Mr Maurice Bootman would see to that. He, Gabriel, would be branded as a dirty-minded, sneaking little voyeur, a Peeping Tom who was willing to jeopardize his livelihood for an hour or two with a naughty book and a chance to pry into other people's happiness. Mr Maurice would be too angry at the publicity to forgive the man who had caused it.

And the rest of the firm would laugh. It would be the best joke in years, funny and pathetic and futile. The pedantic, respectable, censorious Ernest Gabriel found out at last! And they wouldn't even give him credit for speaking up. It simply wouldn't occur to them that he could have kept silent.

If only he could think of a good reason for being in the building that night. But there was none. He could hardly say that he had stayed behind to work late, when he had taken such care to leave with the porter. And it wouldn't do to say that he had returned later to catch up with his filing. His filing was always up-to-date, as he was fond of pointing out. His very efficiency was against him.

Besides, he was a poor liar. The police wouldn't accept his story without probing. After they had spent so much time on the case, they would hardly welcome his tardy revelation of new evidence. He pictured the circle of grim, accusing faces, the official civility barely concealing their dislike and contempt. There was no sense in inviting such an ordeal before he was sure of the facts.

But after the preliminary hearing, at which Denis Speller was sent up for trial, the same arguments seemed equally valid. By now he knew that Speller was the lover he had seen. There had never really been much room for doubt. By now, too, the outlines of the case for the Crown were apparent. The Prosecution would seek to prove that this was a crime of passion, that the boy, tormented by her threat to leave him, had killed in jealousy or revenge. The accused would deny that he had entered the flat that night, would state again and again that he had knocked and gone away. Only Gabriel could support his story. But it would still be premature to speak.

He decided to attend the trial. In that way he would hear the strength of the Crown's case. If it appeared likely that the verdict would be 'Not Guilty', he could remain silent. And if things went badly, there was an excitement, a fearful fascination, in the thought of rising to his feet in the silence of that crowded court and speaking out his evidence before all the world. The questioning, the criticism, the notoriety would have come later. But he would have had his moment of glory.

He was surprised and a little disappointed by the court. He had expected a more imposing, more dramatic setting for justice than this modern, clean-smelling, businesslike room. Everything was quiet and orderly. There was no crowd at the door jostling for seats. It wasn't even a popular trial.

Sliding into his seat at the back of the court, Gabriel looked round, at first apprehensively and then with more confidence. But he needn't have worried. There was no one there he knew. It was really a very dull collection of people, hardly worthy, he thought, of the drama that was to be played out before them. Some of them looked as if they might have worked with Speller or lived in the same street. All looked ill-at-ease, with the slightly furtive air of people who find themselves in unusual or intimidating surroundings. There was a thin woman in black crying softly into a handkerchief. No one took any notice of her; no one comforted her.

From time to time one of the doors at the back of the court would open silently, and a newcomer would sidle almost furtively into his seat. When this happened, the row of faces would turn momentarily to him without interest, without recognition, before turning their eyes again to the slight figure in the dock.

Gabriel stared too. At first he dared to cast only fleeting glances, averting his eyes suddenly, as if each glance were a desperate risk. It was unthinkable that the prisoner's eyes should meet his, should somehow know that here was the man who could save him and should signal a desperate appeal. But when he had risked two or three glances, he realized that there was nothing to fear. That solitary figure was seeing no one, caring about no one except himself. He was only a bewildered and terrified boy, his eyes turned inward to some private hell. He looked like a trapped animal, beyond hope and beyond fight.

The judge was rotund, red-faced, his chins sunk into the bands at his neck. He had small hands, which he rested on the desk before him except when he was making notes. Then counsel would stop talking for a moment before continuing more slowly, as if anxious not to hurry his Lordship, watching him like a worried father explaining with slow deliberation to a not very bright child.

But Gabriel knew where lay the power. The judge's chubby hands, folded on the desk like a parody of a child in prayer, held a man's life in their grasp. There was only one person in the court with more power than that scarlet-sashed figure high under the carved coat-of-arms. And that was he, Gabriel. The realization came to him in a spurt of exultation, at once intoxicating and satisfying. He hugged his knowledge to himself gloatingly. This was a new sensation, terrifyingly sweet.

He looked round at the solemn watching faces and wondered how they would change if he got suddenly to his feet and called out what he knew. He would say it firmly, confidently. They wouldn't be able to frighten him. He would say, 'My Lord. The accused is innocent. He did knock and go away. I, Gabriel, saw him.'

And then what would happen? It was impossible to guess. Would the judge stop the trial so that they could all adjourn to his chambers and hear his evidence in private? Or would Gabriel be called now to take his stand in the witness box? One thing was certain – there would be no fuss, no hysteria.

But suppose the judge merely ordered him out of the court. Suppose he was too surprised to take in what Gabriel had said. Gabriel could picture him leaning forward irritably, hand to his ear, while the police at the back of the court came silently forward to drag out the offender. Surely in this calm, aseptic atmosphere, where justice itself seemed an academic ritual, the voice of truth would be merely a vulgar intrusion. No one would believe him. No one would listen. They had set this elaborate scene to play out their drama to the end. They wouldn't thank him for spoiling it now. The time to speak had passed.

Even if they did believe him, he wouldn't get any credit now for coming forward. He would be blamed for leaving it so late, for letting an innocent man get so close to the gallows. If Speller were innocent, of course. And who could tell that? They would say that he might have knocked and gone away, only to return later and gain access to kill. He, Gabriel, hadn't waited at the window to see. So his sacrifice would have been for nothing.

And he could hear those taunting office voices: 'Trust old Gabriel to leave it to the last minute. Bloody coward. Read any naughty books lately, Archangel?' He would be sacked from Bootman's without even the consolation of standing well in the public eye.

Oh, he would make the headlines, all right. He could imagine them: *Outburst in Old Bailey. Man Upholds Accused's Alibi.* Only it wasn't an alibi. What did it really prove? He would be regarded as a public nuisance, the pathetic little voyeur who was too much of a coward to go to the police earlier. And Denis Speller would still hang.

Once the moment of temptation had passed and he knew with absolute certainty that he wasn't going to speak, Gabriel began almost to enjoy himself. After all, it wasn't every day that one could watch British justice at work. He listened, noted, appreciated. It was a formidable case which the Prosecution unfolded. Gabriel approved of the prosecuting counsel. With his high forehead, beaked nose, and bony, intelligent face, he looked so much more distinguished than the judge. This was how a famous lawyer should look. He made his case without passion, almost without interest. But that, Gabriel knew, was how the law worked. It wasn't the duty of prosecuting counsel to work for a conviction. His job was to state with fairness and accuracy the case for the Crown.

He called his witnesses. Mrs Brenda Kealy, the wife of the tenant of the flat. A blonde, smartly dressed, common little slut if ever Gabriel saw one. Oh, he knew her type, all right. He could guess what his mother would have said about her. Anyone could see what she was interested in. And by the look of her, she was getting it regularly, too. Dressed up for a wedding. A tart if ever he saw one.

Snivelling into her handkerchief and answering counsel's questions in a voice so low that the judge had to ask her to speak up. Yes, she had agreed to lend Eileen the flat on Friday nights. She and her husband went every Friday to visit his parents at Southend. They always left as soon as he shut the shop. No, her husband didn't know of the arrangement. She had given Mrs Morrisey the spare key without consulting him. There wasn't any other spare key that she knew of. Why had she done it? She was sorry for Eileen. Eileen had pressed her. She didn't think the Morriseys had much of a life together.

Here the judge interposed gently that the witness should confine herself to answering counsel's questions. She turned to him. 'I was only trying to help Eileen, my Lord.'

Then there was the letter. It was passed to the snivelling woman in the box, and she confirmed that it had been written to her by Mrs Morrisey. Slowly it was collected by the clerk and borne majestically across to counsel, who proceeded to read it aloud:

> Dear Brenda,
>
> We shall be at the flat on Friday after all. I thought I'd better let you know in case you and Ted changed your plans. But it will definitely be for the last time. George is getting suspicious, and I must think of the children. I always knew it would have to end. Thank you for being such a pal.
>
> Eileen

The measured, upper-class voice ceased. Looking across at the jury, counsel laid the letter slowly down. The judge bent his head and made another notation. There was a moment of silence in the court. Then the witness was dismissed.

And so it went on. There was the paper-seller at the end of Moulton Street who remembered Speller buying an *Evening Standard* just before eight o'clock. The accused was carrying a bottle under his arm and seemed very cheerful. He had no doubt his customer was the accused.

There was the publican's wife from the Rising Sun at the junction of Moulton Mews and High Street who testified that she served the prisoner with a whisky shortly before half-past eight. He hadn't stayed long. Just long enough to drink it down. He had seemed very upset. Yes, she was quite sure it was the accused. There was a motley collection of customers to confirm her evidence. Gabriel wondered why the prosecution had bothered to call them, until he realized that Speller had denied visiting the Rising Sun, had denied that he had needed a drink.

There was George Edward Morrisey, described as an estate agent's clerk, thin-faced, tight-lipped, standing rigidly in his best blue serge suit. He testified that his marriage had been happy, that he had known nothing, suspected nothing. His wife had told him that she spent Friday evenings learning to make pottery at LCC evening classes. The court tittered. The judge frowned.

In reply to counsel's questions, Morrisey said that he had stayed at home to look after the children. They were still a little young to be left alone at night. Yes, he had been at home the night his wife was killed. Her death was a great grief to him. Her liaison with the accused had come as a terrible shock. He spoke the word 'liaison' with an angry contempt, as if it were bitter on his tongue. Never once did he look at the prisoner.

There was the medical evidence – sordid, specific, but mercifully clinical and brief. The deceased had been raped, then stabbed three times through the jugular vein. There was the evidence of the accused's employer, who contributed a vague and imperfectly substantiated story about a missing meat-skewer. There was the prisoner's landlady, who testified that he had arrived home on the night of the murder in a distressed state and that he had not got up to go to work next morning. Some of the threads were thin. Some, like the evidence of the butcher, obviously bore little weight even in the eyes of the Prosecution. But together they were weaving a rope strong enough to hang a man.

The defending counsel did his best, but he had the desperate air of a man who knows that he is foredoomed to lose. He called witnesses to testify that Speller was a gentle, kindly boy, a generous friend, a good son and brother. The jury believed them. They also believed that he had killed his mistress. He called the accused. Speller was a poor witness, unconvincing, inarticulate. It would have helped, thought Gabriel, if the boy had shown some sign of pity for the dead woman. But he was too absorbed in his own danger to spare a thought for anyone else. Perfect fear casteth out love, thought Gabriel. The aphorism pleased him.

The judge summed up with scrupulous impartiality, treating the jury to an exposition on the nature and value of circumstantial evidence and an interpretation of the expression 'reasonable doubt'. The jury listened with respectful attention. It was impossible to guess what went on behind those twelve pairs of watchful, anonymous eyes. But they weren't out long.

Within forty minutes of the court rising, they were back, the prisoner reappeared in the dock, the judge asked the formal question. The foreman gave the expected answer, loud and clear. 'Guilty, my Lord.' No one seemed surprised.

The judge explained to the prisoner that he had been found guilty of the horrible and merciless killing of the woman who had loved him. The prisoner, his face taut and ashen, stared wild-eyed at the judge, as if only half hearing. The sentence was pronounced, sounding doubly horrible spoken in those soft judicial tones.

Gabriel looked with interest for the black cap and saw with surprise and some disappointment that it was merely a square of some black material perched incongruously atop the judge's wig. The jury was thanked. The judge collected his notes like a businessman clearing his desk at the end of a busy day. The court rose. The prisoner was taken below. It was over.

The trial caused little comment at the office. No one knew

that Gabriel had attended. His day's leave 'for personal reasons' was accepted with as little interest as any previous absence. He was too solitary, too unpopular, to be included in office gossip. In his dusty and ill-lit office, insulated by tiers of filing cabinets, he was the object of vague dislike or, at best, of a pitying tolerance. The filing room had never been a centre for cosy office chat. But he did hear the opinion of one member of the firm.

On the day after the trial, Mr Bootman, newspaper in hand, came into the general office while Gabriel was distributing the morning mail. 'I see they've disposed of our little local trouble,' Mr Bootman said. 'Apparently the fellow is to hang. A good thing too. It seems to have been the usual sordid story of illicit passion and general stupidity. A very commonplace murder.'

No one replied. The office staff stood silent, then stirred into life. Perhaps they felt that there was nothing more to be said.

It was shortly after the trial that Gabriel began to dream. The dream, which occurred about three times a week, was always the same. He was struggling across a desert under a blood-red sun, trying to reach a distant fort. He could sometimes see the fort clearly, although it never got any closer. There was an inner courtyard crowded with people, a silent black-clad multitude whose faces were all turned toward a central platform. On the platform was a gallows. It was a curiously elegant gallows, with two sturdy posts at either side and a delicately curved crosspiece from which the noose dangled.

The people, like the gallows, were not of this age. It was a Victorian crowd, the women in shawls and bonnets, the men in top-hats or narrow-brimmed bowlers. He could see his mother there, her thin face peaked under the widow's veil. Suddenly she began to cry, and as she cried, her face changed and became the face of the weeping woman at the trial. Gabriel longed desperately to reach her, to comfort her. But with every step he sank deeper into the sand.

There were people on the platform now. One, he knew, must be the prison governor, top-hatted, frock-coated, bewhiskered, and grave. His clothes were those of a Victorian gentleman, but his face, under that luxuriant beard, was the face of Mr Bootman. Beside him stood the chaplain, in gown and bands, and, on either side, were two warders, their dark jackets buttoned high to their necks.

Under the noose stood the prisoner. He was wearing breeches and an open-necked shirt, and his neck was as white and delicate as a woman's. It might have been that other neck, so slender it looked. The prisoner was gazing across the desert towards Gabriel, not with desperate appeal but with great sadness in his eyes. And, this time, Gabriel knew that he had to save him, had to get there in time.

But the sand dragged at his aching ankles, and although he called that he was coming, coming, the wind, like a furnace blast, tore the words from his parched throat. His back, bent almost double, was blistered by the sun. He wasn't wearing a coat. Somehow, irrationally, he was worried that his coat was missing, that something had happened to it that he ought to remember.

As he lurched forward, floundering through the gritty morass, he could see the fort shimmering in the heat haze. Then it began to recede, getting fainter and farther, until at last it was only a blur among the distant sandhills. He heard a high, despairing scream from the courtyard – then awoke to know that it was his voice and that the damp heat on his brow was sweat, not blood.

In the comparative sanity of the morning, he analysed the dream and realized that the scene was one pictured in a Victorian newssheet which he had once seen in the window of an antiquarian bookshop. As he remembered, it showed the execution of William Corder for the murder of Maria Marten in the red barn. The remembrance comforted him. At least he was still in touch with the tangible and sane world.

But the strain was obviously getting him down. It was time to put his mind to his problem. He had always had a good mind, too good for his job. That, of course, was why the other staff resented him. Now was the time to use it. What, exactly, was he worrying about? A woman had been murdered. Whose fault had it been? Weren't there a number of people who shared the responsibility?

That blonde tart, for one, who had lent them the flat. The husband, who had been so easily fooled. The boy, who had enticed her away from her duty to husband and children. The victim herself – particularly the victim. The wages of sin are death. Well, she had taken her wages now. One man hadn't been enough for her.

Gabriel pictured again that dim shadow against the bedroom curtains, the raised arms as she drew Speller's head down to her breast. Filthy. Disgusting. Dirty. The adjectives smeared his mind. Well, she and her lover had taken their fun. It was right that both of them should pay for it. He, Ernest Gabriel, wasn't concerned. It had only been by the merest chance that he had seen them from that upper window, only by chance that he had seen Speller knock and go away again.

Justice was being served. He had sensed its majesty, the beauty of its essential rightness, at Speller's trial. And he, Gabriel, was a part of it. If he spoke now, an adulterer might even go free. His duty was clear. The temptation to speak had gone for ever.

It was in this mood that he stood with the small silent crowd outside the prison on the morning of Speller's execution. At the first stroke of eight, he, like the other men present, took off his hat. Staring up at the sky high above the prison walls, he felt again the warm exultation of his authority and power. It was on his behalf, it was at his, Gabriel's, bidding that the nameless hangman inside was exercising his dreadful craft . . .

But that was sixteen years ago. Four months after the trial the firm, expanding and conscious of the need for a better address, had moved from Camden Town to north London. Gabriel had moved with it. He was one of the few people on the staff who remembered the old building. Clerks came and went so quickly nowadays; there was no sense of loyalty to the job.

When Gabriel retired at the end of the year, only Mr Bootman and the porter would remain from the old Camden Town days. Sixteen years. Sixteen years of the same job, the same bed-sitting-room, the same half-tolerant dislike on the part of the staff. But he had had his moment of power. He recalled it now, looking round the small sordid sitting room with its peeling wallpaper, its stained boards. It had looked different sixteen years ago.

He remembered where the sofa had stood, the very spot where she had died. He remembered other things – the pounding of his heart as he made his way across the asphalt; the quick knock; the sidling through the half-opened door before she could realize it wasn't her lover; the naked body cowering back into the sitting room; the taut white throat; the thrust with his filing bodkin that was as smooth as puncturing soft rubber. The steel had gone in so easily, so sweetly.

And there was something else which he had done to her. But that was something it was better not to remember. And afterwards he had taken the bodkin back to the office, holding it under the tap in the bathroom until no spot of blood could have remained. Then he had replaced it in his desk drawer with half-a-dozen identical others. There had been nothing to distinguish it any more, even to his eyes.

It had all been so easy. The only blood had been a gush on his right cuff as he withdrew the bodkin. And he had burned the coat in the office furnace. He still recalled the blast on his face as he thrust it in, and the spilled cinders like sand under his feet.

There had been nothing left to him but the key of the flat. He had seen it on the sitting-room table and had taken it away with him. He drew it now from his pocket and compared it with the key from the estate agent, laying them side by side on his outstretched palm. Yes, they were identical. They had had another one cut, but no one had bothered to change the lock.

He stared at the key, trying to recall the excitement of those weeks when he had been both judge and executioner. But he could feel nothing. It was all so long ago. He had been fifty then; now he was sixty-six. It was too old for feeling. And then he recalled the words of Mr Bootman. It was, after all, a very commonplace murder.